CONNECTING

ABOUT THE AUTHORS

Roy M. Berko

Roy Berko is the associate director of the Speech Communication Association. He was formerly the coordinator of professional development at Lorain County Community College, as well as an administrator and professor. He has also taught at The University of Maryland, Towson State University, The Pennsylvania State University, and Cleveland State University.

Dr. Berko holds advanced degrees from the University of Michigan and The Pennsylvania State University and a B.A. from Kent State University. He is the author of 17 communication and education textbooks and the recipient of numerous teaching awards. He was selected as Outstanding Community College Teacher by the Speech Communication Association and named a Teacher on Teaching by that organization. He was designated a Master Teacher by the National Institute for Teaching and Learning and was given the Teacher Recognition Award several times by the Consortium for Higher Education.

Dr. Berko also has a private counseling practice and does consulting for educational institutions, businesses, and governmental agencies. He has served as a television communication and psychology expert, and he has been an entertainment critic for public radio.

Lawrence B. Rosenfeld

Lawrence B. Rosenfeld is a professor of speech communication at the University of North Carolina at Chapel Hill. He received a Ph.D. from The Pennsylvania State University, an M.A. from The University of Iowa, and a B.A. from Hunter College of the City University of New York.

Dr. Rosenfeld's recent honors include receiving the Robert J. Kibler Memorial Award for Life Time Achievement from the Speech Communication Association, serving as the editor of *Communication Education* and *The Western Journal of Speech Communication,* and being recognized as the fourteenth most actively published author in the field of communication. He has authored or coauthored over sixty articles for national and international journals in communication, education, social work, sports psychology and psychology; and he has presented over sixty papers and programs at professional meetings in communication, education, social work, and psychology.

Dr. Rosenfeld is the author or coauthor of eleven books on small group, interpersonal, and nonverbal communication, and two books on conducting research in communication.

Larry A. Samovar

Larry A. Samovar is a professor of speech communication at San Diego State University. He is known as one of the nation's leading intercultural communication researchers and writers, and has authored eleven books on that topic as well as materials dealing with business communication, organizational communication, interviewing, and communicating on television.

Dr. Samovar holds a Ph.D. and an M.A. from Purdue University where he also taught, and a B.A. from California State University at Los Angeles. He is active in the International Communication Association, the Speech Communication Association, the Western States Communication Association, the International Society for General Semantics, the World Communication Association, the Society for Intercultural Education, Training and Research, and Pi Kappa Delta (Forensics Honorary). He has presented numerous professional papers and has served on many panels and discussions.

CONNECTING

A CULTURE-SENSITIVE APPROACH TO INTERPERSONAL COMMUNICATION COMPETENCY

Roy M. Berko
Speech Communication Association—National Office

Lawrence B. Rosenfeld
University of North Carolina at Chapel Hill

Larry A. Samovar
San Diego State University

Harcourt Brace College Publishers
Fort Worth   Philadelphia   San Diego   New York   Orlando   Austin   San Antonio
Toronto   Montreal   London   Sydney   Tokyo

Publisher	Ted Buchholz
Acquisitions Editors	Janet Wilhite/Barbara Rosenberg
Developmental Editor	Laurie Runion
Senior Project Editor	Katherine Vardy Lincoln
Senior Production Manager	Kathleen Ferguson
Art Directors	Priscilla Mingus/Beverly Baker
Photo/Permissions Editor	Steven Lunetta
Compositor	The Clarinda Company

Cover Illustration by Tim Grajek

Library of Congress Cataloging-in-Publication Number: 92-75743

ISBN: 0-15-500237-6

Photo Credits in the back of the book.

Requests for editorial correspondence: Harcourt Brace College Publishers, 301 Commerce Street, Suite 3700, Fort Worth, Texas 76102.

Address for Orders: Harcourt Brace & Company, 6277 Sea Harbor Drive, Orlando, FL 32887 /Tel: 1-800-782-4479, or 1-800-443-0001 (in Florida)

Printed in the United States of America
3 4 5 6 7 8 9 0 1 016 9 8 7 6 5 4 3 2 1

PREFACE

To be a competent interpersonal communicator requires an understanding of communication in general, of *interpersonal communication* in particular, and of the behaviors that assist people in attaining their communicative goals. Competent interpersonal communication requires self-understanding, recognition that the setting of an encounter exerts its own special influence, and a realization that each person's background is necessarily reflected in her or his communication.

Instructors who decide to write a textbook do so because they believe they can add to their field by providing new insights; by sharing a new slant on information published in journals and research-oriented books; and by presenting ideas in ways that make them more understandable, interesting, and useful. These are the reasons we wrote **Connecting: A Culture-Sensitivie Approach to Interpersonal Communication Competency.** We believe that our unique backgrounds, professional expertise, and writing experience allows us to bring new dimensions to the examination of interpersonal communication.

Connecting guides the reader through materials intended to provide an understanding of the field—its research and theories—and to develop personal understanding and competency. Each chapter begins by identifying the competencies that students should expect to gain from the chapter. These competencies are then developed by reading the text material and doing the Knowledge Checkups and Skill Developments throughout the chapter. Each chapter concludes with a Competency Checkup which summarizes the chapter material and encourages the students to put the skills and knowledge to use.

The Knowledge Checkups and Skill Developments constitute a variety of exercises. Each activity is designed to help students better understand the material they have read and, ultimately, themselves. To obtain the maximum benefit from these exercises, it is recommended that students complete all of the activities. And if not, that they at least peruse all the activities in order to understand the textual material that refers to them.

Because the way people communicate reflects the culture in which they were raised, **Connecting** pays careful attention to the role of culture in interpersonal communication. Examples from a variety of cultures, as well as indications of how different cultures communicate in unique ways, illustrate the concepts presented.

While the way we communicate expresses individual cultural uniqueness, it also bridges the gap between individuals. That bridge unites us in the common struggle for individual and social meaning—the struggle to work, live, and play together, while retaining our individual identity.

We hope that as you read **Connecting** and do the activities, you will gain a new understanding of yourself, of the process of interpersonal communication, and of the differences in the cultures of the people with whom you communicate.

For instructors who adopt this book, there are several ancillary materials available. An instructor's manual, developed by Joan E. Aitken, University of Missouri—Kansas City, contains multiple choice, true/false, and essay test questions; a series of activities first published in the Speech Communication Association's *The Speech Communication Teacher;* and additional teaching and learning tools. Also available are a computerized version of the instructor's manual, and a test bank, including a set of overhead transparencies to accompany the visuals found in the textbook. To obtain copies of any of these ancillaries, contact your local Harcourt Brace sales representative.

Connecting is the result of a team effort beyond that provided by the three authors. We want to thank those reviewers who provided us with critiques and suggestions: Joan E. Aitken, University of Missouri—Kansas City; Vincent Bloom, California State University—Fresno; Brant R. Burleson, Purdue University; Jamie Comstock, University of West Florida; Charity Granata, Fresno City College; Richard Halley, Weber State University; Thomas E. Jewell, University of New Mexico; Marylin Kelly, McLennan Community College; Shirlee A. Levin, Charles County Community College; Preston Ni, Foothill College; Alexis Olds, California Polytechnic State University; Terry Perkins, Eastern Illinois University; Susan Richardson, Prince George's Community College; and Edwina Stoll, DeAnza College.

We also want to thank Janet Wilhite, who initiated the project that resulted in this book, Laurie Runion, Katherine Vardy Lincoln, Steven Lunetta, Sheila Shutter, and the rest of the staff at Harcourt Brace College Publishers who guided this book to its publication.

Finally, and most importantly, we thank our students and colleagues who provided us with the stimulation to develop this book and helped us to test the usefulness of the ideas and activities we present.

Roy M. Berko
Lawrence B. Rosenfeld
Larry A. Samovar

BRIEF CONTENTS

CONTENTS

CHAPTER 2

Conceiving the Self 32

Chapter 3

The Self and Others 66

Chapter 4

Nonverbal Communication 96

Chapter 6

Listening 176

Chapter 7

Stress and Communication Anxiety 210

Chapter 8

Dimensions of Interpersonal Relationships 242

Chapter 9

Beginning, Maintaining, and Ending Interpersonal Relationships 270

Chapter 10

Interpersonal Relationships in the Family 304

Chapter 11

Managing Relational Discord 334

Chapter 12

Creativity, Power, and Interpersonal Satisfaction 382

CHAPTER 1

Foundations for Communication Competency

COMMUNICATION COMPETENCIES

This chapter defines what *communication* and *interpersonal communication* are and explains the characteristics of competent communication. It also provides the background you need to understand and apply the material presented in the rest of the book. Subsequent chapters focus on both presenting principles of effective communication and developing your communication competencies. Specifically, the objective of this chapter is for you to learn to:

- Define the characteristics of communication and interpersonal communication.
- Appreciate the role of culture in interpersonal communication.
- Understand the components of interpersonal communication competency.
- Understand the functions of competent interpersonal communication.
- Define the qualities of a competent interpersonal communicator.

KEY WORDS

The key words in this chapters are:

communication
sender
message
receiver
context
purpose
linear process
feedback
adapt
interactive process
transactive process
proactive process
culture
ethnocentrism
interpersonal communication

cultural information
sociological information
psychological information
interpersonal communication
   competency
flexibility skills
empathy
role taking
problem solving
cultural obstacles
environmental obstacles
personal obstacles
relational obstacles
language obstacles
ethics

You have probably been giving and getting messages about communication most of your life. Have you ever stopped to think what communication is really all about? Phrases you've probably heard are:

"If we could just learn to communicate better, that would solve all of our problems."

"If you don't have something nice to say, don't say anything at all."

"Speak when you're spoken to."

"Silence is golden."

"They really must be in love, they seem to have no trouble communicating."

"What we have here is a breakdown in communication."

When you say that communication has taken place, what do you mean? How would you define *communication,* and what would you list as its important characteristics? Would you care how many people were involved? Would it matter where the activity took place? Is it important to accomplish some specific goal? Does it matter, as part of your definition, whether the participants are face-to-face or communicating through some electronic medium? Does it matter whether the messages are spoken or communicated without words? Is it important to consider what roles the participants assume—for example, whether one is a sender and the other a receiver? Is it relevant that the participants are from the same or different cultures? Before considering what interpersonal communication is, it is necessary to define the term *communication.*

DEFINING COMMUNICATION

Regardless of the culture of the participants or the location of their interaction, communication is a distinctly human process composed of six key elements that combine to create a number of unique characteristics. Although we may say that computers "talk" to other computers and that thermostats "communicate" electronically to switch on air conditioners, communication for our purposes is a human process, not a mechanical one. **Communication,** the process of sending and receiving messages through a channel, can include six elements: senders, receivers, messages, a context, a purpose, and feedback.

THE ELEMENTS OF COMMUNICATION

Communication can be likened to an archer, armed with bow and arrow, staring at a not-too-distant target. The archer is the **sender** (the person who devises and encodes the message), the arrow is the **message** (the information the sender devises for the receiver), and the target is the **receiver** (the person who takes in and decodes the message).

The archer is well aware that particular arrows suit particular targets in particular instances (for example, the arrow must match the wind condition). So, with the distance, the type of target, and a bull's-eye in mind, the archer selects a specific arrow. The particular instance makes up the **context** (the characteristics of the situation in which the communication takes place, such as the physical environment and the other people present), and hitting the bull's-eye is the **purpose** (the goal of the communication). If the definition of communication were to stop at this point, communication might be described as a **linear process**, beginning with the sender and ending with the message being received—all in a one-directional flow.

Communication is more than just sending and receiving messages. If the arrow flies off and the result is noted, something has been added to the process. Observing whether the bull's-eye is hit provides the feedback necessary for the archer to note success or failure. **Feedback** in communication is the process of sending information about the effect of a message—information the speaker uses to **adapt**, to adjust a message based on feedback. For example, the archer, noting that his or her arrow has missed the bull's-eye, could make tactical changes, such as selecting a different type of arrow or taking the wind conditions into consideration. Thus, too, the communicator, noting that his or her message has not had the anticipated effect, might reformulate the message by using different words. Adding feedback and adaptation change communication from a linear process that flows from sender to receiver to an **interactive process**, one that flows from sender to receiver, then receiver to sender, and so on.

Communicating with other human beings—especially in face-to-face situations—differs from our archery example because human communication has some unique characteristics. Archers' targets cannot run, hide, duck, fake a reaction, lie, manipulate, or scream when hit. People can!

THE CHARACTERISTICS OF COMMUNICATION

To get a complete view of human communication, we need to trade in the archer metaphor and, with it, both the linear and interactional models. Communication may be more than one person sending a message to another person, and more than having the other person send a message back. Consider this dialogue:

LAURA: Carmen, hand me the sheet of paper on the desk. *(Carmen hands Laura a sheet of paper.)*

LAURA: Not that one, the yellow one. *(Carmen puts her hand on a yellow sheet of paper.)*

CARMEN: This one?

LAURA: Not that one, the yellow one with the flowers in the margin. *(Carmen hands Laura the desired paper.)*

LAURA: Thank you.

Laura and Carmen have participated in an interaction in which, presumably, one served as the sender, the other as the receiver, and they switched roles several times until the desired outcome was achieved. In other words, based on the feedback, Laura and Carmen made adjustments in the cooperative pursuit of accomplishing their joint goal. In the process, they demonstrated four key characteristics of human communication:[1]

1. Messages are simultaneously sent and received.
2. Messages cannot be erased or taken back.
3. Communicators respond to messages proactively—that is, they respond based on their unique backgrounds.
4. The meaning of any message depends on the situation.

Adding these four characteristics to the definition of communication changes it from an interactional to a **transactive process**, one in which each characteristic of the communication process affects and is affected by the others.

Messages Are Simultaneously Sent and Received

The communication process doesn't mechanically alternate between sender and receiver. In reality, as Laura was making her initial request, she was simultaneously functioning as a receiver by watching Carmen's reactions. She functioned as a sender and a receiver at the same time. Carmen, while functioning initially as a receiver, was simultaneously functioning as a sender by giving Laura feedback. The word *communicator* is used to indicate this simultaneity—Laura and Carmen were neither senders nor receivers exclusively, but *communicators*.

Messages Cannot Be Erased

Notice that each message in Carmen's and Laura's conversation is built on what preceded it. Messages cannot be erased, but they can be modified and adjusted with subsequent messages. Laura continued to deal with Carmen's lack of understanding by modifying her directions until she accomplished her goal. She did this by clarifying.

Suppose that, in the heat of an argument with a friend, you blurt out the one insult that you know will hurt the other person most. And, as soon as you complete the offending message, you want to plead, "I take it back, I didn't mean it!" However, there is no such thing as "taking it back." You and your partner may choose to behave as if the message were erased, but, in reality, you both know that it exists and continues to exist in your memories.

Communication Is Proactive

Carmen and Laura's dialogue shows that communication is a **proactive process**—that is, you respond to any message based on your total history. If Carmen had not understood English, or had not recognized the color yellow, or had not cared to cooperate, then her reaction would have been different. Carmen's reaction to Laura's request demonstrated that she was not merely a passive recipient of Laura's messages: She selected what to hear, amplified and ignored portions to suit her taste, and remembered what she considered relevant based on her past experiences.

Meaning Depends on Context

The meaning of a given act of communication cannot be separated from its context. The context has three aspects: the people who are interacting, their physical surroundings, and their social relationships.

The context depends on the people communicating. If Carmen is only five years old, Laura will probably adapt her message to that age level, perhaps by using simpler language. If, in describing the yellow-toned sheets of paper, Laura had said, "Hand me the canary paper," a five-year-old Carmen might have looked for paper in the shape of a bird, because of her literal understanding of the word *canary*.

The link between people and meaning becomes even clearer when we add the component of culture. What happens when a foreign language is spoken or culture-bound idioms are used? Imagine having English as a second language and hearing someone say, "Give me a buzz," or "I think Jim is spaced." In these instances the background of the participants, more than the language they are using, determines meaning.

The number of people present also affects how a message is interpreted. For example, if Laura and Carmen are surrounded by other people, Carmen might comply with the request rather than question why. If they are alone, however, Carmen might be more willing to refuse or to question why she should do what Laura requests. If Carmen comes from a culture that stresses politeness when in the company of strangers, she would be less apt to confront Laura unless they were alone.

Where you are further affects the meanings you attribute to the messages you receive. If Carmen and Laura are at home, Carmen would probably assume Laura wants the paper to write on; however, if they were in a stationery store, she might assume that Laura wants to look at the paper to consider buying it.

Different social situations have different rules, and communication messages are interpreted based on the rules. If Carmen and Laura are taking a test and one of the rules is "No talking," Carmen might interpret Laura's request as an invitation to cheat. In contrast, if they are in a classroom working together on a project, Carmen might interpret the request as part of the normal process of sharing. How Carmen responds depends on the rules she has learned from her cultural conditioning.

Some acts of communication derive their meaning totally from the context. If taken literally, the message "Hi, how are you?" is an inquiry about the state of your health. You know, however, that within the context of passing an acquaintance on

TABLE 1.1 ELEMENTS OF COMMUNICATION PROCESSES

Linear Communication

Sender, Message, Receiver

Interactional Communication

Sender, Message, Receiver, Feedback, Adaptation

Transactional Communication

Sending and Receiving Messages Simultaneously, Contextual, Proactive Responses, Nonerasability of Messages the street, it means "Hello," or "I see you're around." It is not really asking for a health-related response. In fact, if you were actually to describe how you felt, you might startle the other person. In a physician's office, however, the same message would have a totally different meaning. In this context, your doctor would think you were strange if you gave the automatic response, "Fine, thanks, and how are you?" instead of a detailed, health-related one.

Your culture affects how you interact with others, how you interpret your physical surroundings, and how you form your social relationships. Understanding your culture—and the diversity of cultures with which you come into contact—provides a basis for deriving meaning from your communication interactions.

THE ROLE OF CULTURAL DIVERSITY IN INTERPERSONAL COMMUNICATION

Now, more than ever before, your interpersonal relationships involve people from cultures different from your own. Some of those cultures might be as near as across the street, while others might be contacted only when you voyage to other countries. Regardless of the location and setting, people are members of a "global village," interacting with new "villagers" whose perceptions and communication styles differ from those of the dominant culture. For example, you find that some people talk in whispers while others use loud voices. Why? Some people paint their entire bodies while others only apply color to their lips. Why? Some people touch their friends when they greet them while others bow their heads. Why? The answer to all of these questions is the same. People learn to think, feel, communicate, and strive for what their culture considers appropriate. Whether or not the other person is from your own culture or one that is alien to you, her or his cultural experiences greatly influence how she or he responds to you and your message.

People respond to the world in light of the messages they received growing up, and your culture, by confining you to a specific geographical area, determined the form, pattern, and content of these messages. If you were born into a culture that does not display outward signs of emotion in public, you probably do not display outward signs of emotion in your interpersonal relationships.[2]

Culture mandates who talks to whom about what and for how long. You were not born knowing a language, how to select "in" clothing, how to spend your time, or the most appropriate ways to show respect. Your culture presented you with a blueprint for how you should live your life and how you should communicate about it.

The inseparable nature of communication and culture is perhaps most manifest in the definition of culture. "**Culture** is the deposit of knowledge, experience, beliefs, values, attitudes, meanings, hierarchies, religion, timing, roles, spatial relations, concepts of the universe, and material objects and possessions acquired by a group of people in the course of generations through individual and group striving."[3] What this definition indicates is that people acquire their culture through various channels of communication and express their culture through these same channels.

People who share a common culture also share similar meanings. And, as cultures differ from one another, the communication practices and behaviors of individuals reared in those cultures also differ. For example, in one culture people may believe that deep affection and feelings of love need not be expressed verbally, yet in another culture verbal expression of one's feelings is expected: two different cultures, two different styles of interpersonal relationships. To better understand the powerful influence of culture on communication requires examining the characteristics of culture.

Lord Chesterfield once wrote, *"Human nature is the same everywhere, the modes only are different."*

CHARACTERISTICS OF CULTURE

Culture is not innate, it is learned. You were not born knowing how to speak your native language or whether you should kiss on the mouth or the cheek—you had to be taught.[4] What is fascinating about cultural learning is that it takes place on so many levels. For example, you may have learned part of your sex role by *seeing* who gets served first at the dinner table or who drives the family car whenever the family takes a trip. You learned rules of proper behavior when your parents *told* you to say "thank you" when you received a compliment. In both of these

SIBLING REVELRY

by Man Martin

examples learning took place, yet the methods of learning—one by observation and the other by lecture—were quite different.

The messages and behaviors that a culture deems most important come from a variety of sources and are constantly being reinforced. Parents, schools, peers, the media, religious leaders, folktales, and even art repeat the same message. If you were brought up in the United States, think for a moment of the many times and numerous ways you were "told" the importance of being popular and well-liked. Your culture even supplied you with the specific behaviors you needed to accomplish these two goals, such as buying the "right" car or using the "right" toothpaste. Being popular and well-liked are not universally important goals; thus, if you were brought up in another culture, these two stars to reach for would not be part of your constellation of needs.

Another characteristic also has its roots deep in the communication process —*culture is transmissible from person to person, group to group, and generation to generation.* Because we use symbols we can pass on both the content and patterns of a culture. For example, North Americans can use spoken words as symbols and tell others about the importance of winning and being "number one"—they can use car phones, fine wine, clothing, or jewelry as symbols to show others about success and status.

Each person, regardless of individual culture, is born to a massive battery of information and behaviors just waiting to be mastered. In North America each generation is told that individualism is a key value. For the Japanese and Mexican cultures the message is that the group supersedes the individual. In North American culture one is expected to be assertive ("If you don't stand up for your rights, others will walk all over you"). In Asian cultures interpersonal harmony is stressed ("The nail that sticks up is the first to feel the blow of the hammer"). In North America some forms of touching in public are considered normal behavior. In many Asian cultures touching in public is considered highly inappropriate.[5] Examples are endless and each leads to the same conclusion: The content and communication patterns of a culture are subjective and transmissible.

Although it may seem paradoxical, *culture is a dynamic system that changes over time; however, the deep structure of a culture resists change.* As cultures come in contact with each other they are bound to change. As Japan and the United States have more commerce we observe Americans borrowing Japanese methods of quality control while the Japanese use American marketing practices. When Mexicans come to the United States for work they often have to change their use of time. In their country people work hard and for long hours but treat themselves to an extended rest period during the middle of the day. Once in the United States, they often find that lunch is brief and the work day ends much earlier. In both examples you can see how people can be forced to adapt to new cultures. However, you need also to remember that the deep structure of culture is less susceptible to change. The Japanese and Mexicans might alter their work environment, but it is doubtful if either of them is going to change their view of the family or their notion of obligation.

The final characteristic is one that is very important to all students of interpersonal communication: *Members of a culture tend to be ethnocentric.* **Ethnocen-**

trism is a tendency to put a person's own culture and societal patterns at the core of all evaluations.[6] Feelings of "we are right" and "they are wrong" infect nearly every aspect of our interpersonal relationships with others. For example, how do you regard people who are different from you? In most instances you evaluate by applying the standards of your culture to each "foreign" group. While this is a very natural tendency, it also means that many of your evaluations are limited, arbitrary, and possibly false and misleading. It is truly a naive view of the world to believe and behave as if one culture, regardless of what it might be, has discovered the true, ultimate, and only set of norms. It is important as you encounter people from other cultures to avoid letting nearsighted views overshadow rationality.

KNOWLEDGE CHECKUPS AND SKILL DEVELOPMENT ACTIVITIES

This book provides you with a number of opportunities to check your knowledge and practice or develop some skill. *Knowledge Checkup* and *Skill Development* activities are integrated into each chapter and coordinated with the other activities to help you enhance your communication competencies. The Knowledge Checkups help you apply your understanding of the material covered in the reading or gain information about yourself, while the Skill Developments help you practice or develop some specific skill. Knowledge and skill are not separate but work together to provide you with a firm basis to become a competent communicator. Knowledge Checkup 1.1 will help you apply your understanding of the elements and characteristics of human communication to a dialogue between two people.

KNOWLEDGE CHECKUP 1.1

RECOGNIZING THE ELEMENTS AND CHARACTERISTICS OF HUMAN COMMUNICATION

Throughout this text you will be asked to complete a variety of self-evaluation checkups. Keep two things in mind as you respond to each. First, the value of the results depends on the honesty of your responses. Second, the results are pieces of information that will help you understand yourself and assess your knowledge and skills. They should alert you to the additional information and skills you need to become a more competent communicator.

Read the following dialogue and identify the elements and characteristics of human communication:

(Roberto and Sylvia are standing in line at a movie theater, waiting to purchase tickets.)

ROBERTO: I'm really glad we got the chance to get out of the house tonight. The kids were driving me crazy.

SYLVIA: After spending all day at the hospital examining children, I was more than ready to relax.

ROBERTO: Just because you're an intern on thirty-six hour shifts doesn't make you any more tired than I am!

SYLVIA: Don't let your male chauvinist attitude about my being a doctor get in the way of our seeing the movie!

ROBERTO: Don't give me that male chauvinist garbage! That's just your easy answer! I'll see you at home!

1. Who is the original sender?
2. Who is the original receiver?
3. Describe the effects of the context on the creation and interpretation of each person's message.
4. Describe the feedback in the dialogue.
5. What possible effect might the nonerasability of language have on this conversation?
6. Given the proactive nature of human communication, what assumptions can you make about Roberto and Sylvia?
7. What recommendations would you make to Roberto and Sylvia to help them communicate more competently with each other?
8. What influences from your own culture can you trace in your answers to these questions?

DEFINING INTERPERSONAL COMMUNICATION

Once you are familiar with the basic elements of communication and appreciate the role of culture in human interaction, you can begin to observe how in a very specific way interpersonal communication operates in your daily life.

There are two ways to define interpersonal communication. The first approach considers the situation in which communication takes place. The second considers the quality of the communication and is the one stressed in this book.

THE SITUATIONAL DEFINITION

The situational approach to defining interpersonal communication assesses the elements of the situation in which the communication takes place. Using this approach, interpersonal communication is defined as the communication that occurs when a small number of communicators have high access to each other.

Highest possible access occurs when communicators can, for example, see, touch, and hear each other. Lowest possible access occurs when communicators cannot directly see, touch, or hear each other. Access grows as direct contact increases. For example, letter writing offers less access to a person than does the telephone, which provides less access than does a face-to-face meeting.

This approach to defining interpersonal communication is limiting. It does not distinguish whether two people who are communicating are friends or strangers; whether they are pursuing personal goals or mutual goals; whether they love, hate, or are indifferent to each other; or whether they are work partners or lovers. These characteristics of the communication process are ignored because this approach to defining communication does not consider the *quality* of the communicators' relationship.

THE QUALITATIVE DEFINITION

The qualitative approach defines **interpersonal communication** as communication based on the recognition of each communicator's uniqueness and the use of that uniqueness in the development of individual messages as that person communicates with others.

A relationship is not interpersonal or noninterpersonal, but *tends toward* one or the other.[7] The more the participants use personal information about each other (Dale knows that Pat's favorite food is Mexican), adhere to rules that they themselves have established (Dale and Pat have a way of signaling "let's leave this party" that others do not see), define interaction styles based on their individual characteristics (Dale is usually too enthusiastic about new ideas, so Pat asks questions that bring Dale "back to reality"), and strive to reach individual and mutual goals (Dale and Pat help each other study so they can get good grades, although they want good grades for different reasons), the more strongly interpersonal their relationship becomes.

The qualitative approach to defining interpersonal communication assesses the characteristics of the communication process.[8] As individuals communicate in an interpersonal relationship, they (1) make predictions about each other's responses based on their understanding of each other, (2) establish rules for interacting that are unique to their relationship, (3) define their roles based on their own unique characteristics, and (4) strive to satisfy their individual as well as mutual goals and needs.

Predicting Responses

The tendency in interpersonal relationships is for people to use distinguishing information about each other to predict the effects of what they say. This information may be cultural, sociological, or psychological. **Cultural information** includes such things as the customs and beliefs of the culture from which the person comes. For example, if you know that someone is a North American and do not know anything else, you may predict that the person believes in democracy, equality, and striving for a decent standard of living.

Admittedly, cultural information is but one factor people use in making predictions; however, because it provides the overall context for sociological and psychological information, it is of crucial importance in interpersonal communication. For example, the groups you belong to (sociological information) are available to you because you are a member of a specific culture. Some cultures have fraternities and sororities, others do not. Some cultures have the Hell's Angels, some do not. In short, what is accessible to you depends, to a large extent, on what culture you are born into and live in.

Sociological information is suggested by the groups to which a person belongs or with which a person identifies. People often derive their values, ethics, and attitudes from their religious, social, work, political, and gender groups. For example, teachers are thought to value education, the importance of ideas, and their work, and to put less value on financial rewards. Democrats are stereotyped as "caring for the common person," whereas Republicans "look out for the rich." Women are stereotyped as "nurturing, caring, and sharing," whereas men are "task-oriented, emotionally controlled, and interested in sports."

Psychological information, the character traits that make an individual unique, encompasses such things as the particular individual's experiences, feelings, attitudes, beliefs, values, personality characteristics, and typical emotional responses. For example, among a man's psychological traits may be his love for his children, his enjoyment of detective novels, his compulsive dedication to jogging, and his need to be loved. Although a great many men may love their children, enjoy detective novels, and so on, it's the unique combination of this particular person's psychological traits that may be used most effectively to predict his responses to what you have to say.

The more you possess and use psychological information to make predictions about a relational partner, the more interpersonal your communication and the greater the degree of interpersonalness of your relationship. You see the other person as unique—as more than a representative of a particular culture or particular groups—and you deal with her or him as a unique individual. You may even be capable of seeing the individual's real self—without the smoke screens and facades. An individual's psychological self is the self that goes beyond the superficial and reflects genuine interests, beliefs, and perceptions.

Establishing Rules

Rules for communicating in an interpersonal relationship tend to be unique to that relationship. Rules may be set by cultural tradition or established by groups to which the communicators belong; they also may be set by the participants in the relationship. The more the rules are set by the participants, the more interpersonal the relationship tends to be. As people share more and more psychological information—get to know each other—they learn the other's likes, wants, and idiosyncrasies, and use this information to develop rules for interacting.

Defining Roles

In an interpersonal relationship, the roles tend to be defined by individual choices. Roles in a relationship also may be defined by the situation—as when your manager appoints you to form a task group or the task group chooses you to be its leader. Roles also may be defined by the individuals in the relationship. The more the roles are defined by the individuals based on their unique characteristics, the more personal the communication and the greater the degree of interpersonalness in the relationship. For example, noninterpersonal communication is common in families in which the roles of parent and child are set by cultural stereotypes, in which, "the parent is always right and the child must always obey." In such families parent–child communication tends to be noninterpersonal because the uniqueness of both individuals is not taken into consideration when they attempt to communicate.

Satisfying Goals

The goals for communicating in an interpersonal relationship include the satisfaction of both personal and mutual needs. The goals that guide a particular relationship may be based both on what the communicators have in common and on their uniqueness. In any relationship there are some times when mutual goals—those that stress the common needs of the participants—hold top priority and other times when individual goals—those that stress the uniqueness of the participants—take precedence. Interpersonal communication tends to take into account both mutual and individual goals while the partners continue to acknowledge each other's uniqueness.

Skill Development 1.1 will help you use the defining characteristics of interpersonal communication to assess where a relationship falls on a continuum, with "noninterpersonal" as one endpoint and "interpersonal" as the other.

SKILL DEVELOPMENT 1.1

ASSESSING RELATIONSHIP INTERPERSONALNESS

Select three important relationships to assess—these might include your work or school relationships, friendship relationships, or family relationships. For each relationship, complete the four items using the following scale:

Mark the item **5** if it is definitely true.

Mark the item **4** if it is mostly true.

Mark the item **3** if it is neither true nor false.

Mark the item **2** if it is mostly false.

Mark the item **1** if it is definitely false.

First relational partner _____

Second relational partner _____

Third relational partner _____

	RELATIONSHIPS		
	1	2	3

1. My relationship partner and I use psychological informa- ____ ____ ____
tion almost exclusively as the basis for predicting each oth-
er's responses.

2. Most of the rules we use for communicating in our rela- ____ ____ ____
tionship are unique to our relationship.

3. Our roles in the relationship are defined almost exclusively ____ ____ ____
by our individual characteristics.

4. Our goals for communicating include the satisfaction of ____ ____ ____
both personal and mutual needs.

TOTALS: ____ ____ ____

The possible range of your scores is 4 to 20. Four indicates noninterpersonal and 20 indicates interpersonal. Scores between 4 and 20 indicate degrees of interpersonalness. Scores of 12 and lower tend toward noninterpersonal, while scores of 13 and higher tend toward interpersonal.

Is one of your relationships more interpersonal than the others? In what ways is it more interpersonal?

Do your relationships differ on each of the four dimensions of interpersonal communication or are there one or more dimensions on which they score the same? What does this indicate about your relationships?

Does the other person's cultural background affect how she or he responds to you and your messages?

Beyond these examples, how many, if any, of your relationships are characterized by a high degree of interpersonal communication?

THE FUNCTIONS OF INTERPERSONAL COMMUNICATION COMPETENCY

Each time you communicate, you have a purpose, and you are most likely to accomplish your purpose if you communicate competently. **Interpersonal communication competency** is the ability to use your knowledge, skills, and motivation to achieve your interpersonal goals appropriately and effectively. For example, if your goal is to gain information, you will increase your likelihood of success if you do a good job of listening, asking questions, and summarizing information. If your goal is to form a relationship, the degree to which you are knowledgeable, skillful, and motivated to initiate conversations and express your opinions and feelings will influence your success.

Interpersonal communication has numerous functions, such as establishing human contact, exchanging information to reduce uncertainty in your life, sharing and changing attitudes and behaviors, and understanding yourself and the world around you.

These functions are not separate. All may occur in any interpersonal communication interaction. Think back to your first days at college. You needed to know where your classes met, where the bookstore was located, and how to register for courses. How did you find these things out? You probably asked questions, called the campus help line for information, and discussed your problems with other new students. By communicating competently, you discovered the people, places, and things that made up your world, and you reduced your uncertainty as you learned about your environment.

Suppose that you are thinking about taking a particular professor's class. You have heard through the grapevine that she has exciting classes and is a tough grader. You want to test the accuracy of those rumors before signing up. So you find people who have actually been in her class and then make statements such as, "I heard that Professor X is an easy grader," and watch and listen to their responses. Through this process, you hope to separate facts about Professor X from opinions that may not have been based on actual experience—this is an element of being a competent communicator.

Competent interpersonal communication also enables you to share your understanding of the world in an effort to get others to see your point of view. For example, if you believe that it is good to have a weekend to study before a test and you can persuade your classmates and professor to see the situation in the same way, you have a chance at getting the test moved from Friday to Monday.

THE COMPONENTS OF INTERPERSONAL COMMUNICATION COMPETENCY

Interpersonal communication competency, the ability to achieve your interpersonal communication goals, has three components: knowledge, skills, and motivation.[9] To reach competency, first you need to understand the situation, yourself, and the skills it takes to be effective. Second, you need to harness your knowledge and put the skills to use; doing so takes practice and experience with the appropriate behaviors. Third, you must be motivated to communicate competently: Knowing what to do and developing the appropriate skills aren't enough—you must want to put them to use.

KNOWLEDGE

Once you decide to communicate, you need to analyze the who, what, and where of the situation. Who are the participants? Are they like me? What are their cultural backgrounds? What are your objectives for the interaction? Where is the communication taking place?

To answer these questions you must know who you are, who the other person is—including psychological information that makes her or him unique—how anxiety-arousing the situation is for both of you, the nature of your relationship (including the rules), and the various means available for presenting your ideas.

For example, assume a friend asks what you are doing in your communication class. You believe your relationship has a high level of interpersonalness and you decide to tell your friend about the defining elements of interpersonal communication.

What you know about the topic and what you think your friend knows about the topic will determine, in part, what you choose to say. Where you talk will affect how softly or loudly you speak (hushed tones are required if you talk in the library, but a normal tone is possible if you are in the student lounge). Your relationship also affects the choices you make. For instance, if your friend shares your caring feelings, you might use your relationship for examples; otherwise, you might choose examples from relationships with which you are both familiar but in which neither of you is an active participant.

Knowing *who, what,* and *where* forms the basis for deciding what skills are necessary to communicate competently. *Knowing* what skills are necessary is not the same as *being able to perform* them. Knowledge and skills are separate aspects of communication competency, although the skills you employ will be based on your knowledge of what the situation requires.

SKILLS

How competent do you think you are in using communication skills? The following Knowledge Checkup will help you determine what skills you already have and what skills need further development.

KNOWLEDGE CHECKUP 1.2

HOW COMPETENTLY DO YOU COMMUNICATE?

Carefully consider the following list of communication skills.[10] Your self-assessed communication competence is most accurate if you are able to think back over past situations in which you communicated with others and generalize from those situations to derive your answers. To further establish the validity of your self-analysis, it may be helpful to get feedback from people who know you well and with whom you communicate often. Then, based on the scales, indicate how often you use each skill and how satisfied you are with your ability.

SCALE FOR *HOW OFTEN*

5 = all or most of the time (91–100 percent of the time)

4 = often (71–90 percent)

3 = sometimes (31–70 percent)

2 = rarely (11–30 percent)

1 = never or almost never (0–10 percent)

SCALE FOR *HOW SATISFIED*

5 = very satisfied

4 = somewhat satisfied

3 = neither satisfied nor dissatisfied

2 = somewhat dissatisfied

1 = very dissatisfied

	HOW OFTEN	HOW SATISFIED
1. I listen effectively.	_____	_____
2. I use appropriate words for the situation.	_____	_____
3. I use appropriate pronunciation for the situation.	_____	_____
4. I use appropriate grammar for the situation.	_____	_____
5. I use effective eye contact.	_____	_____
6. I speak at a rate that is neither too slow nor too fast.	_____	_____
7. I speak fluently (avoiding "uh," "like, uh," "you know," awkward pauses, and silences).	_____	_____
8. My movements, such as gestures, enhance what I say.	_____	_____
9. I give appropriate spoken and unspoken feedback.	_____	_____

10. I use vocal variety when I speak (rather than speaking in a monotone). _____ _____

11. I speak neither too loudly nor too softly. _____ _____

12. I use appropriate facial expressions. _____ _____

13. I understand my communication partner's main ideas. _____ _____

14. I understand my communication partner's feelings. _____ _____

15. I distinguish facts from opinions. _____ _____

16. I distinguish between speaking to give someone information and speaking to persuade someone to think, feel, or act a particular way. _____ _____

17. I recognize when my communication partner does not understand my message. _____ _____

18. I express ideas clearly and concisely. _____ _____

19. I express and defend my point of view. _____ _____

20. I organize messages so others can understand them. _____ _____

21. I use questions and other forms of feedback to obtain and clarify messages. _____ _____

22. I respond to questions and other forms of feedback to provide clarification. _____ _____

23. I give understandable directions and instructions. _____ _____

24. I summarize messages in my own words. _____ _____

25. I describe another's viewpoint. _____ _____

26. I describe differences of opinion. _____ _____

27. I express my feelings and opinions to others. _____ _____

28. I initiate and maintain conversations. _____ _____

29. I recognize and control my anxiety in communication situations. _____ _____

30. I involve the other person in what I am saying. _____ _____

TOTALS _____ _____

Compare your totals with these ranges:

HOW OFTEN

> 135–150 = Communicate skillfully all or most of the time
> 105–134 = Often communicate skillfully
> 75–104 = Sometimes communicate skillfully
> 45–74 = Rarely communicate skillfully
> 30–44 = Never or almost never communicate skillfully

HOW SATISFIED

> 135–150 = Very satisfied with my communication skills
> 105–134 = Somewhat satisfied with my communication skills
> 75–104 = Neither satisfied nor dissatisfied with my communication skills
> 45–74 = Somewhat dissatisfied with my communication skills
> 30–44 = Very dissatisfied with my communication skills

Each item in the self-analysis describes a skill that is a component of communication competence. Your effective performance of these behaviors increases your potential for being a competent communicator.

Finally, even if you scored close to 150 on both parts of the self-quiz, you will find that there is still much to learn and put into practice! And, don't be discouraged if you scored lower than you would have liked. The purpose of this text and of your communication course is to help you develop the knowledge and skills you need to improve your competency as a communicator.

MOTIVATION

To be a competent interpersonal communicator, you must want to communicate competently. You may be motivated by such possibilities as forming a new relationship, gaining desired information, influencing someone's behavior, engaging in joint decision making, or solving a problem.

In addition to potential benefits, every communication encounter has potential drawbacks. To communicate competently, you must be motivated to overcome such drawbacks. For example, you may have learned from past experiences to fear certain communication situations. Talking with a friend may pose no problem, but talking with an authority figure, such as a boss or professor, may cause you to fidget and show other signs of nervousness. To compensate for negative feelings, you must be strongly motivated to take the necessary action to communicate.

The amount of confidence you have in your ability to communicate will determine, in part, the strength of your motivation to communicate. If, for example, you think of yourself as shy, you are unlikely to initiate conversations with strangers. The reward for interacting may be clear to you, but your self-perceived lack of social skills decreases your motivation.

How motivated are you to communicate competently? Without some motivation to communicate competently, neither this book nor a course in communication will be useful. Look back at each of the thirty items in Knowledge Checkup 1.2 and ask yourself how motivated you are to perform the behavior described by each item at a high level of proficiency. For example, how motivated are you to "listen effectively," "use appropriate words," and "use appropriate pronunciation"?

Look at those items in Knowledge Checkup 1.2 for which you indicated low satisfaction (ratings of 1 or 2). Now examine the *how often* scores for those items. You may find that the skills with which you are most dissatisfied are the same ones you avoid using. You may be saying to yourself, "If I haven't developed that skill enough, I'm not going to risk using it."

By studying the information presented in this text, including the activities, you will begin to understand the components of competent interpersonal communication and develop the necessary skills. This combination should increase your motivation to communicate and to communicate competently.

THE QUALITIES OF COMPETENT INTERPERSONAL COMMUNICATORS

Competent interpersonal communicators have six qualities:

1. Competent interpersonal communicators act appropriately—they follow the rules.

2. Competent interpersonal communicators are effective—they communicate in ways that help them achieve their goals.

3. Competent interpersonal communicators are adaptable—they adjust their communication to the situation.

4. Competent interpersonal communicators recognize roadblocks to effective communication—they note potential obstacles and work to overcome them.

5. Competent interpersonal communicators understand that competency is a matter of degree—they realize that a given act of communication is rarely completely competent or incompetent, but probably somewhere between these two extremes.

6. Competent interpersonal communicators are ethical—they adhere to standards of right and wrong based on their culture, personal views, and circumstances.

COMPETENT INTERPERSONAL COMMUNICATORS ARE APPROPRIATE

For interpersonal communication to be appropriate, a communicator must recognize and follow the rules that guide interaction in a particular circumstance.[11] Every culture has rules for how to greet, interact, and leave interpersonal situations. These vary from a greeting and departure procedure of handshaking, to bowing, to kissing on the cheek. Cultural interaction rules may dictate no direct eye contact, or short durations of looking at each other, or staring. A person who fails to follow the rules is often perceived as abrasive or bizarre, and may be subject to negative reactions. Of course, because different situations call for different rules, what may be appropriate in one situation may be inappropriate in another. For example, a rule in your family may have been "No foul language." Thus, if you tripped over a bicycle when your family was around, it would have been inappropriate to scream out a four-letter obscenity. In contrast, if the same thing happened with a group of friends, your swearing might not break any rules and would therefore be acceptable. Similarly, a male job hunter might be refused employment in a clothing store for middle-class businessmen if he came to an interview wearing jeans and an earring, but a store aimed at upscale, fashion-conscious youth might be very pleased to hire him.

Many of the rules of appropriateness that you have learned stem from your cultural experiences. For example, in North American culture the interpersonal rules for doing business often call for a relaxed, friendly, and casual manner. First names may be used and status differences discouraged ("Just call me Nancy"). These rules do not hold for all cultures. The Japanese culture, for example, typically maintains a protocol of high respect for formality.[12] First names are seldom used and small talk is avoided. The Latin American and Arab rules for the business context usually include small talk on nonbusiness matters as part of business dealings. It is considered bad manners to "get down to business" before friendships have been developed, pleasantries exchanged, and coffee drunk.[13]

COMPETENT INTERPERSONAL COMMUNICATORS ARE EFFECTIVE

Effective communicators set goals related to their needs, wants, and desires, and communicate in ways that help them achieve these goals. For example, if you want to persuade a personnel director to hire you, you will tell her about all the experiences and education that qualify you for the position.

Competent interpersonal communicators create appropriate and effective messages for the contexts in which they find themselves. In Knowledge Checkup 1.2, questions 2, 3, 4, 5, 6, 7, 8, 10, 11, 12, 16, 18, 20, and 30 highlight these characteristics of competent communication. How satisfied are you with your ability to create appropriate and effective messages?

Reprinted courtesy of *Rocky Mountain News*

COMPETENT INTERPERSONAL COMMUNICATORS ARE ADAPTABLE

Adaptable communicators recognize the requirements of a situation and adjust their communication to their goals.[14] For example, when asked what competent communication is, a professor would use one set of examples in speaking to a student and a different set when speaking to a colleague.

Adaptation has three components. The first two—recognizing the requirements of a situation and adapting your communication behavior to suit the setting —have already been discussed. The third component is realizing that your values affect the way you adapt.

You may strongly believe that people should accept you as you are. But if you are inflexible in such beliefs, you will limit the number of contexts in which you can communicate competently. As long as you stay in situations that do not require adaptation, everything will be fine. But outside those situations—whether you are searching for a job, attempting to influence others, or meeting someone for the first time—your unwillingness to adapt will make it more difficult to accomplish your goals.

Being competent means having the ability to adjust and fashion your communication behavior to fit the setting, the other person, and yourself.[15] Knowing that you act differently in a classroom than you do at work, or that one culture may value time while another values activity, is but the first step in the adaptive process. The real key is being able to take this information and use it to alter the way you present yourself. This is what is meant when we say that competent interpersonal communicators are adaptable.

Being able to adapt moves from the simple to the complex as we move from close friends to strangers. The reason is obvious: We have more information about and clearer profiles of our friends than we do of strangers. Adaptation also is more intricate as we progress from members of our own culture to individuals from other cultures. The reason for this difficulty is once again a lack of information about our communication partner.

As illustrated in Knowledge Checkup 1.2, competent communicators have a large repertoire of behaviors available to them. They learn to pick and choose appropriate techniques based on the situation (including its participants) and their intentions for the interaction. Especially important for competency are **flexibility skills**, skills that enhance your versatility and resourcefulness, such as being aware that people from various cultures hold various beliefs and you may have to adjust. These include **empathy**—seeing things from the other person's point of view; **role taking**—engaging in behaviors that fit a situation and do not conflict with your sense of self; and **problem solving**—analyzing a problem and generating appropriate solutions.

COMPETENT INTERPERSONAL COMMUNICATORS RECOGNIZE OBSTACLES TO EFFECTIVE COMMUNICATION

An obstacle that keeps you from accomplishing your communication goal may take one of five forms: cultural, environmental, personal, relational, or language.

Cultural obstacles are the result of people's differences in background and experience. You have been taught rules for communicating within your family, in school, at work, and in society at large. When your rules and someone else's rules clash, there is a cultural obstacle. For example, you might believe each member of a family should have a say in making the rules that effect them, whereas the person you're speaking with believes that the father is the rule maker. Consider the problems that could arise if you were discussing career choices. You might not fully understand your friend's statement, "My father would never let me become a flight attendant."

Environmental obstacles occur when something in the physical surroundings impairs your ability to send or receive messages. For example, loud, piped-in music may make it difficult to hear what your friend is saying, or on a hot, humid day you may find it difficult to concentrate.

Personal obstacles stem from your likes and dislikes, what you think is important and unimportant, what you do and do not want. When your personal attitudes, values, and beliefs get in the way of your listening, they become personal obstacles. Have you ever noticed that who is speaking to you may matter as much as what is said? Do certain conversations bore you? Do certain topics set your thoughts off on a tangent? Do certain words trigger embarrassment or anger? Do you sometimes have too many things on your mind to concentrate on communicating? If you answered yes to any of these questions, personal obstacles have created barriers to effective communication.

Relational obstacles may result from differences in status and power, differences in the way people define their roles in a relationship, and differences in the ways people perceive their relationships. The titles *boss, parent, professor, police officer, judge,* and *president* all connote status and power. Unless you are one boss talking to another boss, or one parent talking to another parent, status differences exist. There even may be a status difference between two bosses or two parents. Status differences may determine who has the right to initiate conversations, give directions, make decisions, and reward or punish.

Each person in a relationship may define his or her own role differently. For example, a student who defines a teacher's role as "authoritarian" in a class where the teacher defines her role as "guide" will encounter relational obstacles because the student will expect to be told what information he is responsible for, while the instructor will want the student to ask questions about course content.

Individual participants also may define their relationship differently. For instance, in the case of two persons who are dating, one individual may see the relationship as more of a friendship, while the other may consider the relationship to be more intimate. Their different definitions will affect any discussion of the relationship, such as future plans, and conflict is likely to occur.

The different meanings people give to words and the way they organize those words create **language obstacles.** Meaning is not inherent in a word but in the person who interprets the word. What does the word *gross* mean to you? To a shipper it means 144 of an item. To a teenager it may mean obnoxious or offensive. To a surveyor it may mean imprecise. And yet to another person, it may mean that someone's language is foul or that someone is unattractive.

Grammatical structure may either help or hinder you in communicating ideas. Say the following two sentences aloud:

What's the latest, dope?

What's the latest dope?

In the first question, by pausing at the comma, you insult the other person while asking for information. In the second question, by not pausing, you merely ask for information.

COMPETENT INTERPERSONAL COMMUNICATORS RECOGNIZE THAT COMPETENCY IS A MATTER OF DEGREE

Competency is not something you either have or do not have; it comes in degrees.[16] Each component of competency can be thought of as occurring *more* or *less*. For example, *effectiveness* refers to communicating in ways that help you achieve your goals. If you always achieve your goals, your behavior may be considered completely effective. If you never achieve your goals, your behavior may be considered completely ineffective. Between these extremes are degrees of effectiveness, such as achieving your goals some of the time.

This notion of degree holds true for being appropriate, being adaptive, and being aware of obstacles to effective communication. As an interpersonal communicator, you need to recognize that you are not going to be competent all of the time. By increasing your knowledge of the communication process, and by learning and practicing communication skills, however, you will increase the number of instances in which you communicate competently.

COMPETENT COMMUNICATORS ARE ETHICAL

Ethics are rules for conduct that distinguish right from wrong. Competent communicators are ethical—that is, they adhere to their standards of right and wrong. Your definition of what is right or wrong, what is ethical or unethical, depends on at least three considerations. The first is the culture in which you were raised. Your culture has taught you what your standards should be. For example, North American culture stresses the importance of honesty above most other values.[17]

Second, who you are and how you have interpreted "should" messages from your family, school, religion, friends, television, and movies also determine your personal code of right and wrong. If you have been taught that cheating is wrong, you won't do it, no matter how desperate you are for a good grade on a test. But if you have been taught that you should always get high grades, you may not think of copying from a neighbor's exam as right or wrong, but only as another means of obtaining your goal.

If all you had to work with were cultural and personal "shoulds," it would be relatively easy to make ethical choices. However, a third consideration, the situation in which you find yourself, complicates matters. For example, if a job interviewer asks whether you have ever been fired, should you admit that you were once dismissed from a position? One "should" message tells you to get a good job while another says not to lie. If you believe that you won't get the job if you tell the truth, what will you tell the interviewer?

Because the range of variables that influence an individual's ethics is so wide, there are very few absolutes when it comes to communicating ethically. Perhaps the only one may be: Don't purposely hurt or limit another person's choices. Give others, regardless of their background and culture, what you would want for yourself —freedom from external restraint and the ability to decide your own course of action. These aspirations are universal.

YOU AS AN INTERPERSONAL COMMUNICATOR

Interpersonal communication competency refers to both particular behaviors and overall impressions. You may be perceived as competent in a particular situation or at performing particular skills.[18] For example, you may communicate well with your coworkers (a particular situation) and you may also have been told by one of your instructors that you are a good listener (a particular skill). This does not automatically mean that you are equally competent in other situations or equally skilled in other areas of communication.

Your overall impression of your own or someone else's interpersonal communication is based on three factors: observation of behaviors (you note what someone else does), judgment of the appropriateness of the behaviors (you apply your notions of right and wrong and good and bad to judge what you observe), and past shared experiences (you include in your understanding of the other person's behavior your shared background, including what you have done together, talked about, and so on). These factors must be dealt with simultaneously. No single behavior, judgment, or aspect of the history of an interaction by itself creates the overall impression.[19] Rather, the combination of all the behaviors, judgments, and history leads to the conclusion that someone is a competent communicator.

Take another look at your answers to Knowledge Checkup 1.2. Now that you have a general understanding of the defining characteristics of the interpersonal communication process, the importance of communicating competently, and the qualities of competent interpersonal communicators, see if there are any answers you would like to change. What are your strengths? What are your weaknesses? What goals will you set for your knowledge, skills, and motivation as a communicator?

As you progress through this book, you will gain the understanding and skills you need to communicate appropriately and effectively in interpersonal relationships. As your understanding and skills increase from reading the text and completing the examples in this book, so will your chances of being perceived as a competent interpersonal communicator.

  COMMUNICATION COMPETENCY CHECKUP

Communication Competency Checkups will help you summarize the material in each chapter. The goal of this communication competency checkup, as well as those at the end of other chapters, is to guide you in putting your skills and knowledge to use.

Each person is a potential partner for your interpersonal communication.

1. Describe your communication strengths and weaknesses using the results of Knowledge Checkup 1.2. Based on your description and the information in this chapter, formulate goals for increasing your effectiveness as an interpersonal communicator.

2. Define *communication* and *interpersonal communication.*

3. Explain each component of competent interpersonal communication and illustrate each with personal examples.

NOTES

1. C. David Mortensen, *Communication: The Study of Human Interaction* (New York: McGraw-Hill, 1972).

2. David Matsumoto, "Cultural Influences on Facial Expressions of Emotion," *Southern Communication Journal* 56 (1991): 128–137.

3. Larry A. Samovar and Richard Porter, *Communication Between Cultures* (Belmont, CA: Wadsworth Publishing Company,

1991), p. 51. For an extensive discussion on culture as it relates to communication, see: Larry A. Samovar and Richard E. Porter, *Intercultural Communication: A Reader* (Belmont, CA: Wadsworth Publishing Company, 1991).

4.　E. Adamson Hoebel and Everett L. Frost, *Culture and Social Anthropology* (New York: Wiley, 1974), p. 58.

5.　Peter Andersen, "Explaining Intercultural Differences in Nonverbal Communication," in Larry A. Samovar and Richard E. Porter (Eds.), *Intercultural Communication: A Reader* (Belmont, CA: Wadsworth Publishing Company, 1991), p. 289.

6.　Robley D. Rhine, "William Graham Sumner's Concept of Ethnocentrism: Some Implications for Intercultural Communication," *World Communication* 18 (Spring 1989): 2.

7.　Gerald R. Miller and Mark Steinberg, *Between People* (Chicago: Science Research Associates, 1975).

8.　Ibid.

9.　Brian Spitzberg and William Cupach, *Interpersonal Communication Competence* (Beverly Hills, CA: Sage, 1984); Brian H. Spitzberg, "An Examination of Trait Measures of Interpersonal Competence," *Communication Reports* 4 (1991): 22–29.

10.　These communication skills were determined by a task force of the Speech Communication Association (SCA), and endorsed by the organization's Educational Policies Board, to be minimal competencies for communicators. They were stated as an SCA guideline in "Speaking and Listening Competencies for High School Graduates." The full report on these competencies appears in Ronald E. Bassett, Nilwon Whittington, and Ann Staton-Spicer, "The Basics in Speaking and Listening for High School Graduates: What Should Be Assessed?" in *Communication Education* 27 (1978): 293–303. These competencies were further refined and expanded in Richard L. Quianthy (Project Director), *Communication Is Life: Essential College Sophomore Speaking and Listening Competencies* (Annandale, VA: Speech Communication Association, 1990).

For additional information on communication competency assessment and other measurement instruments, see: Brian H. Spitzberg, "Communication Competence: Measures of Perceived Effectiveness," in Charles H. Tardy (Ed.), *A Handbook for the Study of Human Communication* (Norwood, NJ: Ablex, 1988), pp. 67–105; and Brian H. Spitzberg and H. Thomas Hurt, "The Measurement of Interpersonal Skills in Instructional Contexts," *Communication Education* 36 (1987): 28–45.

11.　M. V. Redmond, "The Relationship Between Perceived Communication Competence and Perceived Empathy," *Communication Monographs* 52 (1985): 377–82.

12.　Diana Rowland, *Japanese Business Etiquette* (New York: Warner Books, 1985), p. 12.

13.　Susan A. Hellweg, Larry A. Samovar, and Lisa Skow, "Cultural Variations in Negotiation Styles," in Larry A. Samovar and Richard E. Porter (Eds.), *Intercultural Communication: A Reader* (Belmont, CA: Wadsworth Publishing Company, 1991), p. 187.

14.　Brian H. Spitzberg and H. Thomas Hurt, "Measurement of Interpersonal Skills in Instructional Contexts," *Communication Education* 36 (1987): 28–45, and Spitzberg, "An Examination of Trait Measures," 1991.

15.　Rod Hart, R. E. Carlson, and William F. Eadie, "Attitudes Toward Communication and the Assessment of Rhetorical Sensitivity," *Communication Monograph* 47 (1980): 1–22.

16.　Spitzberg, "An Examination of Trait Measures," 1991.

17.　Milton Rokeach and Sandra Ball-Rokeach, "Stability and Change in American Value Profiles, 1968–1981," *American Psychologist* 44 (1989): 775–84.

18.　Spitzberg, "An Examination of Trait Measures," 1991.

19.　Brian H. Spitzberg, "Communication Competence: Measures of Perceived Effectiveness," in Charles H. Tardy (Ed.), *A Handbook for the Study of Human Communication* (Norwood, NJ: Ablex, 1988), pp. 67–105.

FOR FURTHER INVESTIGATION

Backlund, Philip. "Essential Speaking and Listening Skills for Elementary Students." *Communication Education* 34 (1985): 185–95.

Bassett, Ronald E., Nilwon Whittington, and Ann Staton-Spicer. "The Basics in Speaking and Listening for High School Graduates." *Communication Education* 27 (1978): 293–303.

Berlo, David K. *The Process of Communication: An Introduction to Theory and Practice.* New York: Holt, Rinehart and Winston, 1960.

Bochner, Stephen, ed. *Cultures in Contact.* New York: Pergamon Press, 1982.

Brislin, Richard W. *Cross-Cultural Encounters: Face-to-Face Interaction.* New York: Pergamon Press, 1981.

Dance, Frank E. X. "The 'Concept' of Communication." *Journal of Communication* 20 (1970): 201–10.

Dance, Frank E. X., and Carl E. Larson. *The Functions of Communication: A Theoretical Approach.* New York: Holt, Rinehart and Winston, 1976.

Farb, Peter. *Word Play.* New York: Bantam, 1974.

Gudykunst, William B., and Stella Ting-Tommy. *Culture and Interpersonal Communication.* Newbury Park, CA: Sage Publications, 1988.

Kim, Young Y. *Communication and Cross-Cultural Adaptation.* Philadelphia: Multilingual Matters, Ltd., 1988.

Miller, Gerald R. "On Defining Communication: Another Stab." *Journal of Communication* 16 (1966): 88–98.

Miller, Gerald R., and Mark Steinberg. *Between People.* Chicago: Science Research Associates, 1975.

Muchmore, John, and Kathleen Galvin. "A Report of the Task Force on Career Competencies in Oral Communication Skills for Community College Students Seeking Immediate Entry into the Work Force." *Communication Education* 32 (1983): 207–20.

Quianthy, Richard L. (Project Director). *Communication Is Life: Essential College Sophomore Speaking and Listening Competencies.* Annandale, VA: Speech Communication Association, 1990.

Rubin, Rebecca B. "Assessing Speaking and Listening Competence at the College Level: The Communication Competency Assessment Instrument." *Communication Education* 31 (1982): 19–32.

Samovar, Larry A., and Richard E. Porter. *Communication Between Cultures.* Belmont, CA: Wadsworth Publishing Company, 1991.

Samovar, Larry A., and Richard E. Porter. *Intercultural Communication: A Reader,* 6th ed. Belmont, CA: Wadsworth Publishing Company, 1991.

Samovar, Larry A., Richard E. Porter, and Nemi C. Jain. *Understanding Intercultural Communication.* Belmont, CA: Wadsworth Publishing Company, 1981.

Singer, Marshall R. *Intercultural Communication: A Perceptual Approach.* Englewood Cliffs, NJ: Prentice-Hall, Inc., 1987.

Spitzberg, Brian H. "Communication Competence: Measures of Perceived Effectiveness." In Charles H. Tardy (Ed.), *A Handbook for the Study of Human Communication.* Norwood, NJ: Ablex, 1988. Pp. 67–105.

Spitzberg, Brian, and William Cupach. *Interpersonal Communication Competence.* Beverly Hills, CA: Sage, 1984.

Spitzberg, Brian H., and H. Thomas Hurt. "The Measurement of Interpersonal Skills in Instructional Contexts." *Communication Education* 36 (1987): 28–45.

Watzlawick, Paul, Janet H. Beavin, and Don D. Jackson. *Pragmatics of Human Communication: A Study of Interactional Patterns, Pathologies, and Paradoxes.* New York: Norton, 1967.

CHAPTER 2

Conceiving the Self

COMMUNICATION COMPETENCIES

This chapter defines and examines self-concept. Specifically, the objective here is for you to learn to:

- Identify the important elements that make up your self-concept, including your social identity, personality characteristics, values, physical characteristics, and ego extensions.
- Describe two principles of self-concept development—reflected appraisal and social comparison.
- Distinguish the person you *are,* the person you *wish you were* or think you *should be,* and the person you *present to others.*
- Assess how you feel about yourself—your level of self-esteem.
- Recognize the effects that high and low self-esteem have on communication.
- Use several techniques for increasing your self-esteem.
- Appreciate cultural differences in the concept of self.

KEY WORDS

The key words in this chapter are:

individual cultures
collective cultures
self-concept
social identity
personality characteristics
androgynous
values
physical characteristics

ego extensions
reflected appraisal
significant other
generalized others
social comparison
idealized self
actual self
should self

You just received a telephone call from a famous film director who has indicated plans to make a movie about your life. The screenwriter wants your input on several facets of the script. You are asked the following questions and told that since the director and producers are interested in the *real* you, you should answer spontaneously without pausing to think of the "best" answer.

What should be the title of this film epic?

The director asks you to describe yourself in order that he understand you better. How do you describe your physical appearance and how you feel about it; how do you get along with other people, your usual emotional states; and what do you believe in and value?

Who should play you?

Where should the production be filmed?

What kind of background music, if any, should be used?

Who should play some of your immediate family members?

What four or five major events in your life are the most significant and must be included in the film?

You hang up the receiver, lean back, close your eyes, and visualize the film. How do you feel about the final product? What did you learn about yourself from watching the movie of your life?

As you probe your sense of who you are, keep in mind that in Western cultures a preoccupation with self is very natural. Western media, art, literature, government, and psychology all focus on the importance of the individual, and a great deal of time is spent thinking about and pursuing personal happiness. Most conversations are about the self. In fact, the word "I" is used more than any other word. This emphasis on the "I" however, is not common to all cultures, just **individual cultures**, those that stress the importance of being identified as an individual. In **collective cultures**, those that subjugate the self to the group, people will not have the same model of self as those from individual cultures. For example, in much of Asia the concept of "self" is not as important as the concept of "group." In these cultures, the "us, not I," is the predominant personal concept.[1]

WHO YOU ARE: YOUR SELF-CONCEPT

Who you are is the foundation for all your communication. The individual needs, interests, and strengths that distinguish you from others are revealed in your communication.[2] Although English is your common language, you and the people around you often use different words to express similar experiences. These differences reveal something about how each of you sees the world. For instance, you may see a sunset and comment that it is getting late, whereas a photographer may see it and notice the stunning contrast between light and dark.

The meanings you attribute to the words you hear are also slightly different from others' interpretations—again reflecting your uniqueness. You may even use a special vocabulary to express who you are and what you do. For example, if you're a computer enthusiast, you may use the words *input* and *output* to explain things unrelated to computers.

Who you are includes how you feel about yourself, and, in turn, how you feel about yourself is reflected in how you communicate. If you think of yourself as shy, you may avoid raising your hand in class or speaking at a meeting; if you think of yourself as a good listener, you may encourage others to talk to you.

Who you are (the *I-am* me), what you would like to be (the *I-wish-I-were* me), and the person you present to others (the *here-I-am* me) form the foundation for how you communicate. Thus, improving your communication competency begins with an examination of who you are, how you came to be that person, and how your self-perception affects how you communicate.

THE PERSON YOU ARE

Your self-exploration began with the production of the movie of your life. Now, continue the process by answering the question "Who am I?" in Knowledge Checkup 2.1.

WHO AM I?

Complete each sentence:

1. When I look at myself in a full-length mirror, I see ＿＿＿＿＿＿＿

＿＿＿＿＿＿＿＿＿＿＿＿＿＿＿＿＿＿＿＿＿＿.

2. My friends would probably describe my relationships with them as ＿＿＿＿

＿＿＿＿＿＿＿＿＿＿＿＿＿＿＿＿＿＿＿＿＿＿.

3. As a family member, I see myself as ＿＿＿＿＿＿＿＿＿＿＿

＿＿＿＿＿＿＿＿＿＿＿＿＿＿＿＿＿＿＿＿＿＿.

4. My talents include ＿＿＿＿＿＿＿＿＿＿＿＿＿＿.

5. My greatest strengths are ＿＿＿＿＿＿＿＿＿＿＿＿.

6. My weaknesses or inabilities that bother me are ＿＿＿＿＿＿＿＿＿

＿＿＿＿＿＿＿＿＿＿＿＿＿＿＿＿＿＿＿＿＿＿.

7. I was ＿＿＿＿＿＿＿＿＿＿＿＿＿＿＿＿＿＿＿.

8. I was ＿＿＿＿＿＿＿＿＿＿＿＿＿＿＿＿＿＿＿.

9. I was ＿＿＿＿＿＿＿＿＿＿＿＿＿＿＿＿＿＿＿.

10. I am ＿＿＿＿＿＿＿＿＿＿＿＿＿＿＿＿＿＿＿.

11. I am ＿＿＿＿＿＿＿＿＿＿＿＿＿＿＿＿＿＿＿.

12. I am ＿＿＿＿＿＿＿＿＿＿＿＿＿＿＿＿＿＿＿.

13. I would like to be ＿＿＿＿＿＿＿＿＿＿＿＿＿＿.

14. I would like to be ＿＿＿＿＿＿＿＿＿＿＿＿＿＿.

15. I would like to be ＿＿＿＿＿＿＿＿＿＿＿＿＿＿.

You are the sum total of your past, present, and future. It may be said that you are what you are based on your verb "to be"—your *I have been, I am,* and *I shall be.* Knowledge Checkup 2.1 has allowed you to recount your perceptions of these three tenses. The varied responses you give describe who you are and provide information about your **self-concept**—the totality of your thoughts and feelings about yourself. Your responses most likely describe the *content* of your self-concept—your social identity, values, personality characteristics, physical characteristics, and ego extensions.[3]

Social Identity

Your **social identity**, the groups or categories to which you belong, begins with your birth. You are classified by gender, race, culture, religion, and family role (brother, sister, only child, youngest, firstborn), and given a name. Your birth certificate discloses the categories into which you were placed—the categories that provided you with an immediate social identity. For example, birth certificates typically identify your sex, race, whether you're a twin or triplet, when and where you were born, your parents' names, and your parents' birthplaces. All this information provides a social context for knowing who you are.

As you grow up, you add new classifications for yourself. You become a member of various groups and clubs. The groups to which you belong reflect your cultural identity (based on shared language, history, values, or territory), your religious beliefs, your political ideology, your interests, your work, and other aspects of how you view yourself.

What you are also includes what you were but are not now, such as an athlete, a baby sitter, or an officer of a club. Some former social identities you may want to conceal; others you may want to use to gain status. For example, you may not want your current friends to know that you were once married, or you may seek recognition by referring to your past activities as a manager of a local health club.

Different cultures place different emphasis on how much importance is given to defining ourselves by our social affiliations. Cultures such as those of North America that value individualism place less stock in social organizations than do collective cultures. The Japanese, for instance, often judge others and themselves by their company affiliations.[4] They are so proud of whom they work for that they will wear company pins attached to outer garments. And in China there is a saying that "If you know the family you need not know the person." This proverb highlights the high value that culture places on using others to define oneself, quite different from the United States, where the culture stresses who the individual is and that person's uniqueness.

Personality Characteristics

The content of your self-concept is more than your social identity. The many personality characteristics you use to describe yourself also contribute to your self-concept.

Personality characteristics are the qualities that constitute a person's character that are relatively stable across a lifetime, and that make him or her distinctive.[5] For example, you may consider a friend "happy and easygoing" and a teacher "stern." Before investigating some of the more than twenty thousand identified personality characteristics, complete Knowledge Checkup 2.2.

BEM SEX-ROLE INVENTORY[6]

Indicate the degree to which each statement is true of you.

Write **1** if the statement is never or almost never true of you.
Write **2** if it is usually not true of you.
Write **3** if it is sometimes but infrequently true of you.
Write **4** if it is occasionally true of you.
Write **5** if it is usually true of you.
Write **6** if it is always or almost always true of you.

_____ **1.** I am self-reliant.

_____ **2.** I am cheerful.

_____ **3.** I am independent.

_____ **4.** I am affectionate.

_____ **5.** I have a strong personality.

_____ **6.** I am sympathetic.

_____ **7.** I act as a leader.

_____ **8.** I am eager to soothe hurt feelings.

_____ **9.** I am analytical.

_____ **10.** I am warm.

The ten personality characteristics you just considered describe two types of personalities. The odd-numbered items represent a stereotypical "masculine" personality and the even-numbered items represent a stereotypical "feminine" personality. Add your responses to the odd items to obtain your "masculine" score. Then add your responses to the even items to obtain your "feminine" score. Total scores above 22 in either category are considered high and scores below 22 are considered low.

If you scored high on masculine and low on feminine, you would be classified by this instrument as having those personality characteristics that research shows are indicative of a person called "masculine." If you scored low on masculine and high on feminine, you would be classified by this instrument as "feminine." High scores on both lead to classification as "androgynous," a balance of both masculine and feminine personality characteristics, and low scores on both lead to classification as "undifferentiated." It is important to note that both males and females fall into all four personality categories and that these classifications exist apart from your biological-sex categorization.

A person who describes herself or himself as **androgynous**—both highly masculine and highly feminine—has the largest repertoire of communication behaviors to call upon. For example, this person may behave both empathically and objectively, and both assertively and cooperatively, which increases the person's adaptability—one of the qualities of the competent communicator. Gender-typed individuals—masculine or feminine—exhibit a smaller range of communication behaviors and, therefore, are less adaptable than androgynous individuals.

Masculinity and femininity are only two of the many different personality characteristics that affect communication. For example, others that have been studied are:[7]

Self-monitoring—sensitivity to one's communication out of concern for being appropriate. For example, high self-monitors are more likely than others to initiate conversations (the appropriate response to awkward silences) and reciprocate intimacy (the appropriate response to another's intimate behaviors) than are low self-monitors.

Extroversion–introversion—outgoing and focused on the world outside the self versus focused on the inner world of the self. Extroverts speak more than introverts and spend less time pausing. Introverts tend to display fewer nonverbal actions, such as gestures, than do extroverts.

The notion of extroversion–introversion is quite interesting when placed in a cultural context. In many cultures extroversion, at least as we know it in North America, hardly exists. In most Asian cultures, and even among many Native American Indian cultures, children are raised to be compliant and docile. Signs of extroversion are shunned as a communication style. When Asians or Native Americans confront a North American they are often uncomfortable if that person is emotionally open and shares ideas about himself or herself easily. And, of course, the reverse is true, resulting in North Americans perceiving Asians as standoffish and emotionally distant.

Dominance–submissiveness—controlling and authoritarian versus yielding and obedient. People with a dominant personality communicate more assertively and confidently than those with a submissive personality. They also participate more in groups and interrupt more.

Need for affiliation—concern with being included in others' activities. People with a high need for affiliation prefer to interact at closer distances and maintain more eye contact than those with a low need for affiliation.

Need for approval—concern with receiving praise and other positive feedback. People with a high need for approval pay attention to others' nonverbal vocal characteristics, such as pauses, more than do those with a low need for approval.

Other examples of personality characteristics include the extent to which you desire social relationships (e.g., some people prefer many friends; others prefer few friends or even to be alone), concern with making a good impression (e.g., some people are very concerned with acting properly and politely so that others see them as well mannered; others care little about following society's rules of etiquette), relaxed versus tense (e.g., some people exhibit few nonverbal indications of anxiety; others may seem to fidget constantly, bite their fingernails, and stammer when they speak, thus displaying their apprehension), conservative versus experimenting (e.g., some people are prone to conform to established habits; others try new things and are risk takers), and trusting versus suspicious (e.g., some people are willing to trust others until that trust is proven wrong; others are suspicious until the trust is earned).[8]

It is important to keep in mind that the personality characteristics discussed reflect a strong Western orientation. Because personality is a learned trait it shifts from culture to culture. For example, not all cultures teach their members to seek approval. In fact, cultures that stress introspection over interaction, such as in India, believe that it is a sign of weakness to receive one's happiness from others.

Values

Values reflect the importance you attach to different ways of behaving, such as being honest, as well as the goals to which you aspire, such as a peaceful world. Values motivate you to behave and to communicate one way or another. Knowledge Checkup 2.3 is designed to help you clarify several values.

KNOWLEDGE CHECKUP 2.3

DISCOVERING YOUR VALUES[9]

Rank the items within each set of values from most important to you **(1)** to least important to you **(9).**

It is important to be:

_____ Ambitious (hardworking, aspiring)

_____ Broad-minded (open-minded)

_____ Capable (competent, effective)

_____ Clean (neat, tidy)

_____ Courageous (standing up for your beliefs)

_____ Forgiving (willing to pardon others)

_____ Helpful (working for the welfare of others)

_____ Honest (sincere, truthful)

_____ Loving (affectionate, tender)

_____ Responsible (dependable, reliable)

It is important to have:

_____ A comfortable life (a prosperous life)

_____ A world at peace (free of war and conflict)

_____ Equality (brotherhood, equal opportunity for all)

_____ Family security (taking care of loved ones)

_____ Freedom (independence, free choice)

_____ Happiness (contentedness)

_____ Salvation (being saved, eternal life)

_____ Self-respect (self-esteem)

_____ Sense of accomplishment (lasting contribution)

_____ Wisdom (a mature understanding of life)

Which values are most important for you? Your important values affect how you communicate. In national surveys conducted over thirteen years, people across the United States were asked to rank these values.[10] For the "important to be" values, *honest,* on the average, was ranked first, *responsible* second, *ambitious* third, *forgiving* fourth, *broad-minded* fifth, *courageous* sixth, *helpful* seventh, *loving* eighth, and *capable* ninth. For the "important to have" values, *a world at peace,* on the average, was ranked first, *family security* second, *freedom* third, *self-respect* fourth, *happiness* fifth, *wisdom* sixth, *sense of accomplishment* seventh, *a comfortable life* eighth, and *salvation* ninth. A few differences between males and females were found. Males ranked *capable* and *a comfortable life* higher than females did, and females ranked *salvation* higher than males did.

These results—stable over the thirteen years—are averages; each value received every possible ranking. How you compare with the national results isn't important. What's important is for you to realize what values are important for you, understand how they help define who you are, and affect how you communicate.

The values you selected were, of course, the result of your cultural and social background; individuals from other cultures would probably not have selected the same factors. An understanding of your own and others' cultural values can help you make predictions about how your interpersonal partner might respond to you and your messages. Knowing, for instance, that much of Latin America values patience and an unhurried pace to life, might enable you to slow down and be calm when you are interacting with a person from that culture.[11] The same principle holds true in reverse when you are dealing with individuals who typically demand punctuality, such as the Swiss or the Germans—you must be on time for appointments and meet deadlines or you will be perceived negatively, no matter your intentions.[12]

You may have been told, "Big boys don't cry." Other cultures also tell their members what to value. The Chinese, who value social harmony, say, "The first man to raise his voice loses the argument." Arabs and people in other cultures who value fate over scientific reasoning say, "One does not make the wind blow, but is blown by it." The Irish value an easygoing manner and, accordingly, tell their people, "Life is a dance, not a race."

What is the relationship between your ranking of particular values and your behavior? For example, if you ranked *honesty* first, ask yourself if you have ever cheated on a test or kept extra change you received by mistake from a salesperson. Your behavior should be consistent with the values you hold as most important.

If you value honesty highly, you are more likely to communicate directly and openly, especially if you also value being courageous. Of course, if you value being ambitious more highly than being honest, you might stretch the truth during a job interview to increase your chances of getting hired. The issue gets more complicated if you consider how much you value self-respect. Will you respect yourself if you stretch the truth during the job interview?

Completing questionnaires like Knowledge Checkup 2.3 and observing your communication behavior should help you determine what your values are and which are most important to you. Knowing your values is the first step toward analyzing them and their relationship to how you behave. You will then be better equipped to change your values or your behavior as you see fit.

Your social identity is relatively unambiguous—you know the groups to which you belong; personality characteristics and values, however, are less discernible. You may be certain you're a student, but unsure about your warmth, true intelligence, or honesty. Your social identity is more easily verified than your psychological one. You may have a driver's license that clearly identifies you as a driver, but where in your wallet or purse is a document to prove that you're gentle, humorous, or forgiving?

Physical Characteristics

Your **physical characteristics**, your body's traits, make up another category of elements that contribute to your self-concept. While the characteristics may be clear—indeed, you are a certain height and weight and have eyes a particular color—how you feel about individual body parts and your body in general may be less certain. Born without a notion of self, your first identity was a physical one. Lying in your crib, you noticed hands that came and went from view. One day, you realized that the hands were *you*—and, still without being aware of it, your physical self-concept began to form. Your physical self remains important even now, which may be why you diet, lift weights, run, or apply makeup. How you feel about yourself affects whether you do these things or not and whether or not you do these things also affects how you feel about yourself.

Ego Extensions

Your self-concept extends beyond social, psychological, and physical characteristics to elements in your environment. You experience environmental elements, **ego extensions**, as part of yourself. Something is an ego extension if you refer to it as *my* or *mine,* feel pride or shame for it, and accept praise or blame for it as your own. For example, if you refer to the school you graduated from as "my school," if you are proud of its history and traditions, and if you consider criticism of it a personal attack, your school qualifies as an ego extension.

Your ego extensions may take many forms. Included may be your car, family members, country, state, city, neighborhood, and job. For example, if a teacher gives you a failing grade on a research paper and says, "This is terrible, but don't take it personally—I'm criticizing your work, not you," you may not be able to remain objective if you perceive the paper as an ego extension of you.

Your self-concept is complex, containing your social identity, personality and physical characteristics, values, and ego extensions. How is it that your particular self-concept came to be what it is?

The Sources of Self-Concept

Two primary theories explain how particular elements come to form your self-concept.[13] The first, reflected appraisal, suggests that you are influenced by the communication you receive from others, especially when it focuses on you. The

UNDERACHIEVERS ANONYMOUS

"A membership drive? Aren't three of us enough?"

Used with permission of Bob Vojtko and the Cleveland Plain Dealer.

second, social comparison, contends that you learn about yourself by comparing yourself to others.

Reflected Appraisal **Reflected appraisal** holds that your view of yourself is consistent with the view others hold of you, and that you have come to view yourself as you do *because* of the views of others. Some consistency between your self-perceptions and others' perceptions of you is essential for getting along in society.[14] Think of the problems you would encounter if, because you thought of yourself as intelligent, outgoing, and an effective communicator, you wanted to lead a team project, but the group members saw you as below average in intelligence, withdrawn, and a poor communicator.

At the root of reflected appraisals are the messages others send you about yourself. Not all messages carry the same weight, however. An appraisal from your best friend probably matters more to you than an appraisal from a relative stranger. To take someone's opinion seriously, you must usually perceive the person as a **significant other**, that is, someone whose opinion of you matters or whose judgment you trust. Friends normally exert more influence than strangers, and members of your family usually exert more influence than outsiders, because you consider friends and kin qualified appraisers who should have your best interests at heart.[15]

For an appraisal to be accepted as true, it must first be personal. The other person must know a great deal about you and adapt an appraisal specifically to you. Second, an appraisal must be consistent with past appraisals so that you do not dismiss it as a mistake or an anomaly.

Part of reflected appraisal is the notion of projecting another's appraisal. Without the other person present, you can *imagine* what her or his evaluation will be. The *little voice* that warns what your professor will say if you fail a test, or what your religious leader will think if you act improperly, exists because you can assume another's point of view, see yourself as that person sees you, and imagine and use a reflected appraisal.

Who are your significant others? Skill Development 2.1 will help you identify them.

SKILL DEVELOPMENT 2.1

IDENTIFYING YOUR REFLECTED APPRAISALS

You can recognize your reflected appraisals and examine who your significant others are by completing four sentences:

1. Two people who know me best and have my best interests at heart are _____.

_____

2. Two people who, in my opinion, are competent to judge me are _____.

_____

3. The two persons whose comments seem to have the greatest influence on how I think about myself and how I behave are _____.

_____

4. If each person identified in my responses to 1, 2, and 3 described me to someone, each would say:

Person: _____   Description: _____

_____

Person: _____   Description: _____
                                          _____

Person: _____   Description: _____
                                          _____

Person: _____   Description: _____
                                          _____

Person: _____   Description: _____
                                          _____

Person: _____   Description: _____
                                          _____

Your answers to question 4 are the reflected appraisals that helped form your self-concept.

If you grew up in a traditional family setting, it is likely that you identified your parent or parents, or whoever brought you up, as part of your group of significant others. This is logical since they know you well, probably have your best interests at heart, and may be perceived by you as competent to judge you (after all, they were probably your first heroes—the strongest, smartest, able-to-do-anything magical giants with whom you lived). To begin to assess their influence on your self-concept, complete Knowledge Checkup 2.4.

KNOWLEDGE CHECKUP 2.4

RECOGNIZING YOUR MOST SIGNIFICANT OTHERS' INFLUENCES

PART I

Write down as many family sayings with which you were brought up as you can—any sentence, phrase, colloquialism, question, or command that was communicated to you *over and over again*. (For example, maybe a family saying was, "If you're going to do something, do it right, or don't do it at all.")

My family sayings were _____
_____
_____.

1. a. What do the family sayings tell you about how your family significant others viewed you? For example, if you were constantly told to clean up your room, is it possible they saw you as a slob, or lazy, or unmotivated to be clean?

   b. Do you see yourself in any of these ways?

2. a. How many of your family sayings have a positive message for you?

   b. How many have a negative message?

   c. How do these messages relate to how you see yourself now?

PART II

Imagine that you are one of your parents (or whoever brought you up) and that you meet one of your friend's parents. You stop, say hello, and then talk about your children. *As your parent,* what do you say about yourself? (Take a few minutes to think aloud about what "your child" has done with her or his life, how you feel about her or him, and whether your expectations for your child are being met.)

How does your "parents" conversation relate to how you see yourself now?

Reflected appraisal includes what you think the **generalized others**—people in general—consider correct or proper. In other words, your interpretation of the attitudes of society. From years of watching television, for example, you may have formed the belief that conflicts are unhealthy unless they can be resolved in thirty or sixty minutes (with commercial breaks). Consequently, when you are involved in a real conflict—one that takes more than thirty or sixty minutes to resolve—your self-appraisal may be: "I am a bad person for engaging in unhealthy conflict. I had better run away or give in, or shout so loudly that I get my way, and end this problem immediately." How you communicate will be based, in part, on an appraisal from generalized others.

Finally, you must remember that your style is not universal. Most Asian cultures have taught their members that direct conflict should be avoided. Loud voices and harsh words are not valued. In Indonesia there is even a proverb that reinforces the view that acrimonious mannerisms should be avoided: "Empty cans clatter the loudest." In short, only foolish people engage in aggressive behavior.

Social Comparison   According to the principle of **social comparison**, you compare yourself to others to learn about yourself, and you evaluate how you measure up by the standards set by those others.[16] For example, suppose you compare your height to that of your friends. If you are taller, and if being tall is valued by your friends, you can make two appraisals: You are taller than some people, and that is good.

Comparisons take at least two forms: *better or worse* and *same or different.* Assessments of traits such as intelligence, strength, and creativity typically define whether you are better or worse, while comparisons of religious background, social class, and home region typically tell whether you are the same or different.

Comparisons let you see yourself as smart or stupid, attractive or ugly, popular or unpopular, depending on whom you compare yourself with. To compare better, change your source of comparison—you don't always have to change yourself!

SKILL DEVELOPMENT 2.2

IDENTIFYING YOUR SOCIAL COMPARISON GROUPS

You can recognize your social comparison groups by answering four questions:

1. Select one area in which you compare yourself to others. In what area is the comparison made? (For example, is the comparison based on wealth, intelligence, or social skill?)

2. In the selected area, which people am I better or worse than?

3. In the selected area, which people am I the same as or different from?

4. What do my comparisons tell me about who I am? (For example, do I put myself down or inflate my ego by selecting unrealistic people with whom to compare myself?)

The information you gather through reflected appraisals and social comparisons becomes the content of your self-concept. Because you are a complex, multifaceted, multidimensional being, the elements of your self-concept are voluminous. Once you have amassed your self-perceptions, you need to organize them.

Organizing the Elements of Your Self-Concept

The elements of your self-concept are not random and disorganized. Rather, they are ordered in a way that makes it possible for you to behave relatively consistently. The order can be pictured as a circle with elements that are most important to you at the center and ones that are less important toward the outside (Figure 2.1). For example, thinking of yourself as a loyal friend may be more central to your self-perception than thinking of yourself as a conscientious student.

Consider the following situations:

1. You have to stay on campus over spring break to research a term paper. Your parents call to remind you that a family gathering is taking place and that you're expected to attend. Your mother asks whether you will be coming home. Going home means not getting your research done. What would you tell her?

2. You apply for a job and get called for an interview. Two of the questions you're asked concern your prior work experience and your academic

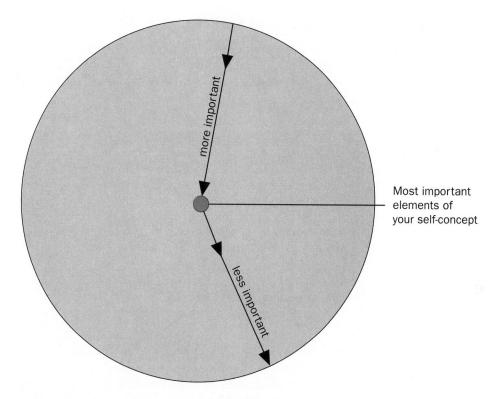

FIGURE 2.1

performance. You believe that if you tell the truth the odds are you won't get the job—which you need to pay for your college fees. What do you do?

You can determine the relative importance of the elements in your self-concept by examining your responses to hypothetical situations *as well as by observing your behavior in real-life situations.* In the first scenario, if you tell your mother you're coming home, you may value family security more than individual accomplishment. In the second scenario, if you tell the interviewer that you have a lot of experience and did very well in school, you may value ambition above honesty.

Communication problems may arise when two people who have the same elements in their self-concepts rank the elements differently. For example, you and a friend may hold honesty as an important value, but you may believe in "honesty at all costs" while your friend believes in being honest as long as honesty doesn't hurt anyone. Right versus wrong is not the issue as you communicate. Rather, difficulties arise because you have honesty at different places in your circle of self-perceptions—such as when you want to share your real feelings with a third person about her behavior and your friend suggests you withhold the truth because it could hurt her.

THE PERSON YOU WISH YOU WERE

The extent to which you think of yourself as a failure or a success, a good person or a bad one, depends largely on your notion of who you would like to be. At least three images form your desired self-concept: the *idealized self*, the *actual self*, and the *should self*.

The Idealized Self

Your **idealized self** is how you perceive yourself as "perfect." Elements of this image emerge when you say, "If I were _____, then everything would be OK." When you feel overwhelmed by problems, you may temporarily invoke your idealized self. If you feel the need to be successful, you may dream that you can do anything and accomplish anything. And if you feel the need to be loved, you may dream of being attractive and desirable. Although the idealized self is not obtainable, it influences how you judge your own and others' abilities to communicate.[17]

The idealized self that a person wants to be, like many goals, has its roots deep in our culture. For example, if you have "being attractive and desirable" as an objective, realize that people from Japan, China, and Mexico believe that the family is the primary value and the idealized self might seek to become a better son or daughter.

The Actual Self

Your **actual self,** a more realistic image than your idealized self, conforms more to your capabilities and the restrictions of your environment. Even young children know the difference between an idealized image and the actual one. They clearly recognize the self-picture that is possible and, therefore, worth striving for. Thinking about an idealized image, such as being a basketball star, may be fun (if sometimes frustrating), but many children's real efforts are spent pursuing an actual image, such as becoming a teacher, a lawyer, or a businessperson. A child who is asked, "If you could be anything, what would you want to be?" may answer "Superman" or "Wonder Woman," but that same child would probably admit that being Superman or Wonder Woman isn't really possible because it is understood that the idealized self is simply a pleasant dream.[18]

Comparing yourself to your idealized image is bound to leave you feeling inadequate. Comparing yourself to your actual image, however, is more fruitful because the actual self may possibly be achieved.

The Should Self

The third component of the desired self-concept is the **should self**, which contains all the "oughts" and "shoulds" that serve as your moral guidelines. These standards, against which you constantly measure yourself, come from your family, culture, school, friends, and the mass media. Your "shoulds" represent the moral standards of society; transgressing them usually results in guilt or anger with yourself.

"Shoulds" result not merely from your socialization, but also from the unique demands you place on yourself. Getting *A*'s may not be a society-wide "should," but *you* may think that there is no alternative, that anything less than an *A* represents failure. You may be convinced that eating more than one scoop of ice cream is disgustingly self-indulgent, or that sleeping for more than eight hours is inexcusably lazy, or that watching television is a waste of time. In addition to all the "shoulds" that you acknowledge, you may generate hundreds more. Every "should" increases the likelihood that you will view yourself as a bad person at some time.

The should self is another area where you need to be aware of cultural differences. For example, in cultures where religion determines a complete way of life, such as Hinduism, Islam, and Orthodox Judaism, the "should" list might include feelings of guilt for not spending more hours each day praying, for being a member of a group with an alternative lifestyle, or for performing a forbidden act, such as practicing birth control.

Knowledge Checkup 2.5 will help you recognize some beliefs you have about what "should be."

KNOWLEDGE CHECKUP 2.5

IDENTIFYING YOUR "SHOULD" STATEMENTS [19]

Read the following statements and indicate the extent to which you agree or disagree with each.

If you strongly agree, mark the statement **5.**

If you agree, mark the statement **4.**

If you neither agree nor disagree, mark the statement **3.**

If you disagree, mark the statement **2.**

If you strongly disagree, mark the statement **1.**

_____ **1.** It is important that others approve of me.

_____ **2.** I hate to fail at anything.

_____ **3.** I want everyone to like me.

_____ **4.** I avoid things I cannot do well.

_____ **5.** I find it hard to go against what others think.

_____ **6.** It upsets me to make mistakes.

Sum up your responses to items 1, 3, and 5: _____ —this is your *everyone should approve of me* score. Sum up your responses to items 2, 4, and 6: _____ —this is your *I should be perfect* score. Scores of 12 and higher are high, indicating strong belief in the should statement; scores of 6 and below are low, indicating little if any belief in the should statement, and scores of 7 through 11 indicate moderate belief in the should statement.

Believing that everyone should approve of you, when this is clearly impossible, and believing that everything you do should be perfect, another clear impossibility, guarantees that you will dislike yourself at some time. Later we'll look at how to combat illogical should statements.

THE PERSON YOU PRESENT TO OTHERS

Regardless of the person you are and the person you would like to be, the only person others know is the one you present to them. Most of us distinguish actors from the characters they play; however, others do not distinguish you from the person you portray. As Kurt Vonnegut wrote in his novel *Mother Night,* "We are what we pretend to be, so we must be careful about what we pretend to be."[20]

The person you think you are and the person you would like to be, together with your "shoulds," form the foundation for all your behavior. Acting in ways that do not fit your conception of yourself is difficult and often uncomfortable. If you must behave in ways that contradict how you see yourself, you are likely to distance yourself from the image you are presenting. For example, if you consider yourself shy, you might offer a toast at a dinner party by saying: "Well, gee, this

isn't something I do a lot. In fact, this is the first time. I feel really awkward about standing up here." You would reflect that being the center of attention is not part of how you see yourself.

Additional factors influence the person you present to others: the perceived requirements of the situation, others' expectations, and the goals for communicating.

The Requirements of a Situation

Your perceived requirements of a situation stem from the situation's immediate demands, the rules governing the situation, the demands of similar past situations, and the implications of your behavior for similar situations in the future. For example, one rule of thumb for child rearing is: "Be consistent in what you tell your child—don't change from situation to situation." Consider the following dialogue:

CHILD: I want some ice cream.

PARENT: No. You know that one of our rules is no junk food before dinner.

CHILD: I want ice cream. I want ice cream! I want ice cream!!

The immediate demand for the parent is to respond to the child's request for ice cream. Should an exception to the rule be allowed, or should a firm *no* be repeated? Situations that parallel the current one include the many times the child asked for cookies, cake, or candy and was refused. If the parent refuses the child's request for ice cream, this behavior would be consistent with past situations and the child might eventually learn to accept the house rule. But if the child is allowed to have some ice cream, then this probably opens the door to a flood of future requests and nagging for snack-time goodies.

The parent's message to the child reflects his or her definition of a good parent: "A good parent should not allow a child to eat junk food before dinner." In addition, this message reflects his or her analysis of the implications of responses for future interactions. The result may not please the child, but it is appropriate from the parent's perspective.

Others' Expectations

What you think people expect of you also affects how you behave. "People" includes both those with whom you are interacting and significant others who are now absent but helped form your self-image. Your goal may be to be consistent with what both groups expect of you. Those expectations may be unclear, especially for a new situation, and the expectations of one group may differ from the expectations of the other group. For example, ambiguity and conflict commonly mark dating situations, especially when dating first begins. Consider these inner thoughts of two young teenagers on a first date:

HE: She wants me to put my arm around her shoulder—she expects that.

SHE: My mother knows his mother and she told me that he's a nice guy. I'm sure he won't try anything.

HE: Should I put my arm around her?

SHE: I get the feeling he wants to put his arm around my shoulder. That's OK with me!

HE: If I put my arm around her and she slaps me, what will I do? But if she expects me to put my arm around her and I don't, what will she think? And if I do and she slaps me, what will happen? And if I don't and she thinks I'm the village idiot, will that mean I'll never see her again? And what will my mother think if it gets back to her that I put my arm around her friend's daughter and she slapped me? And what if it gets back that I didn't, and should have, and my mother's only son is an idiot?

SHE: I think he thinks that I think that he shouldn't put his arm around me. Then he must think I'm a prude.

And so the evening goes. No one is sure what to do. No one knows what image to live up to, what expectations to fulfill, or even what the expectations are.

People from different cultures often have different and sometimes conflicting expectations. These expectations can result in misunderstandings. For instance, a female student from Japan went out on a date with a North American student. After a lovely evening at a concert the Japanese student was sitting *silently*, respectfully enjoying the company of her date and thinking about the concert. He, however, *expected* her to talk—to make conversation to show she was having a good time. Not understanding the differences in cultural expectations, he said to her, "I'm very sorry you didn't have a nice time tonight." She *expected* silence, he *expected* to talk.

The Goals for Communicating

Several objectives also determine the self you present to others, which further complicate the issue of how to behave. First are the goals you have for interacting: You may want to get hired for a particular job, impress a professor with your intelligence, or have your love reciprocated. There are as many goals as there are people and interactions. How you communicate reflects what you want, either directly or indirectly.

Second is your objective to remain consistent with your image of yourself and avoid doing anything that might lower (or raise)[21] your self-evaluation: If the teenage boy does put his arm around the teenage girl and she slaps him, his view of himself as a nice guy will be challenged and he may well lose some respect for himself. On the other hand, if he doesn't try to put his arm around her and later finds out that she wouldn't have screamed, he will probably feel just as downcast.

Third may be your objective of "trying on" a social identity. All of us test new behaviors and experiment with new elements of our self-concept, although adolescence is the heyday for such testing. Is the teenage male too forward? The only way he can find out is to try on the behavior and see how it feels. If it's comfortable and others seem to approve, he may decide to keep it as an element of his self-concept. Is the teenage girl assertive? The only way she can find out is to tell her date that she wants him to put his arm around her, and see how it feels to have communicated assertively.

No one can make you feel inferior without your consent.
—Eleanor Roosevelt

HOW YOU FEEL ABOUT YOURSELF: YOUR SELF-ESTEEM

To get a quick idea of how you feel about yourself, answer the questions in Knowledge Checkup 2.6.

KNOWLEDGE CHECKUP 2.6

ANALYZING YOUR GENERAL SELF-ESTEEM [22]

Indicate the extent to which you agree or disagree with each statement.

Write **1** if you strongly disagree with the statement.
Write **2** if you disagree.
Write **3** if you neither agree nor disagree.
Write **4** if you agree.
Write **5** if you strongly agree.

_____ **1.** I am generally satisfied with myself.

_____ **2.** I feel that I have a number of worthy qualities.

_____ **3.** I am able to do things as adequately as most people.

_____ **4.** I think of myself in mostly positive ways.

_____ **5.** I have few regrets about my life.

_____ **6.** I wouldn't change much if I had the chance to live my life over again.

_____ **7.** I feel like a useful person.

Add up your responses to the seven items. The higher your score, the higher your self-esteem. Scores of 21 and higher suggest positive self-esteem, while scores below 21 suggest low self-esteem.

Although the test is short, it should give you a general idea of how you feel about yourself. You may disagree with the results and say something like, "Sure, I have a high score, but so what? I still hate the way my nose hooks and I don't do well in foreign language courses," or "My low score doesn't take into account that I'm a great pianist and play guard on the varsity basketball team." Such statements reflect the relationship between your general attitude toward yourself, as measured by the test, and your attitude toward parts of yourself. You may like some elements of your self-concept and not others. Thus you may take pride in your social abilities yet be embarrassed by your math deficiencies.

Knowledge Checkup 2.7 will help you analyze how you feel about yourself by posing specific, as opposed to general, questions.

KNOWLEDGE CHECKUP 2.7

ANALYZING YOUR SPECIFIC SELF-ESTEEM[23]

Indicate the degree to which each item is true or false for you.

If it is completely false, mark the item **1.**
If it is mostly false, mark the item **2.**
If it is partly false and partly true, mark the item **3.**
If it is mostly true, mark the item **4.**
If it is completely true, mark the item **5.**

_____ **1.** I am satisfied with my weight.

_____ **2.** I am satisfied with my looks.

_____ **3.** I am satisfied with my height.

_____ **4.** I am satisfied with my moral behavior.

_____ **5.** I am satisfied with the extent to which I am religious.

_____ **6.** I am satisfied with my relationship with a Supreme Being.

_____ **7.** I am satisfied with my family relationships.

_____ **8.** I am satisfied with how well I understand my family.

_____ **9.** I am satisfied with how I treat (treated) my parents.

_____ **10.** I am satisfied with how sociable I am.

_____ **11.** I am satisfied with the extent to which I try to please others.

_____ **12.** I am satisfied with the way I treat other people.

SCORING:

Add items 1, 2, and 3: _____. This is your *physical self-esteem score.*

Add items 4, 5, and 6: _____. This is your *moral-ethical self-esteem score.*

Add items 7, 8, and 9: _____. This is your *family self-esteem score.*

Add items 10, 11, and 12: _____. This is your *social self-esteem score.*

Scores in any category between 12 and 15 indicate high self-esteem; scores between 3 and 6 indicate low self-esteem; and scores from 7 through 11 indicate moderate self-esteem.

Is your self-esteem higher in some areas than others? How are differences in your scores reflected in how you interact with other people?

Whether you should focus on the overall evaluation or the individual assessments depends on what you want to know about yourself. Regardless of where you focus, keep in mind that generalizing from smaller parts to the whole or from the whole to smaller parts can mislead you: If you feel good about your work in school, avoid the generalization that you feel good about yourself in general. If you are upset with yourself in general, avoid concluding that you do not think highly of your singing ability. Instead, consider the whole and its parts together to gauge how justifiable is your self-esteem.

Your level of self-esteem tends to be reflected in your communication.[24] As you might suspect, communicators with high self-esteem, at least in North American cultures, are at a distinct advantage. Individuals who like and accept themselves tend to remain open-minded when they encounter new ideas, opinions, and beliefs. They also can change their minds more easily than people with low self-esteem because they are confident and unthreatened by others' ideas. As a result, their interactions are supportive and friendly, which leads to greater involvement with other people and the possibility of more intimate relationships. Consider the following dialogue between an employee who has low self-esteem, and the employee's boss.

BOSS: I'd like you to tackle the Long account.

EMPLOYEE: I already worked on it.

BOSS: I'd like you to try out some new ideas. I have some suggestions that you might consider.

EMPLOYEE: What's wrong? Didn't you like what I did?

BOSS: It's not that. I just think a new approach . . .

EMPLOYEE: Well, I just don't see how to go about it any other way. I'm sorry you have a problem with me.

The employee's reactions indicate an inability to accept change and an unwillingness to consider alternatives. The request for change was perceived as a personal attack, and rather than talk with the boss to discover what was desired, the employee responded defensively and created a poor impression.

People with high self-esteem also tend to show sensitivity toward others and have empathy, the ability to see things from another's perspective. Both of these characteristics hone the accuracy of a person's perceptions and contribute to effective conflict resolution. The ability to see a conflict from the other person's perspective strongly influences whether a mutually agreed-upon solution will be found.

Self-esteem also directly affects language. People with high self-esteem tend to have rich vocabularies and confident-sounding voices, whereas people with low self-esteem tend to use language filled with clichés and jargon. When things go wrong, the person with low self-esteem may say, "It never rains but it pours," or "Why does it always happen to me?" whereas the person with high self-esteem will probably give a clear description of the situation and its consequences. Language reflects feelings about the world, whether it is a place to trust others, act spontaneously, and be happy, or a place to withdraw, act defensively, and feel unhappy.

ENHANCING YOUR SELF-ESTEEM

Your communication reflects how you feel about yourself. The discussion so far reveals that one sure way to improve your communication is to increase your self-esteem. Among the methods of raising your self-esteem are confronting your "should" messages, focusing on the positive, and eliminating your self-put-downs.

CONFRONTING YOUR "SHOULD" MESSAGES

A prime source of low self-esteem is the "should" image you hold. If your self-esteem is low, you can boost it by discovering your "should" messages, assessing their reasonableness, and then refuting unreasonable ones. For example, to confront the message "I should get *A*'s in all my classes" you might say: "Earning *A*'s in all my classes is desirable, but expecting to may be unreasonable. I am better at some things than others. I can reasonably expect to get *A*'s in some courses and not others. I can't reasonably expect to earn all *A*'s, although I will strive for them."

Analyzing and refuting unreasonable "should" messages, such as those uncovered in Knowledge Checkup 2.7, provides information that clarifies your strengths and weaknesses and the demands you place on yourself. It also lays the foundation for enhancing your self-esteem because you begin to set realistic goals.

Because "should" messages reflect a culture's values, they are bound to differ from culture to culture. The message "I should be more assertive" is out of place in Asian cultures; and, "I should have more friends" is not common in cultures that stress solitude over interaction. Therefore, in setting interpersonal expectations, you should recognize that your "should" messages may not be someone else's shoulds.

SKILL DEVELOPMENT 2.3

CONFRONTING YOUR "SHOULD" MESSAGES

1. Complete each of the following sentences.

a. To be a good family member, I should _____

_____.

b. To be a good friend, I should _____

_____.

c. To be a good student, I should _____

_____.

d. To be a good person, I should _____

_____.

2. What unreasonable or reasonable demands does each "should" statement in question 1 make?

3. How do the unreasonable demands prevent you from feeling better about yourself?

4. Refute each "should" statement in question 1 and substitute a more realistic goal. (Discover the incorrect thinking that supports each should statement and replace it with more reasonable thinking.)

FOCUSING ON THE POSITIVE

All communication is open to interpretation, and your interpretation of a specific event can either increase or decrease your self-esteem. Assume that you are asked to lunch by a coworker, Jamie. You could say to yourself, "I guess Jamie likes my company and would enjoy having lunch with me—perhaps to discuss something important." You could also say, "Jamie probably needs a favor and thinks I'm the sucker who will do it. That little schemer probably doesn't care about me at all and is using lunch to set me up." The first interpretation enhances your self-esteem; the second decreases it.

The next time you find yourself in an ambiguous situation, try to analyze how much your interpretation reflects or affects your self-esteem. Do you tend to interpret situations positively or negatively? If you tend to interpret situations negatively or make negative statements, your self-esteem is likely low. If your interpretations or statements are predominantly positive, your self-esteem is likely high.

If you want to change, you must first recognize your problem. Skill Development 2.4 is designed to help you analyze and correct unfounded negative interpretations.

SKILL DEVELOPMENT 2.4

ANALYZING YOUR NEGATIVE INTERPRETATIONS

To determine whether you are interpreting a situation negatively, ask the following questions:

1. Is what I am saying really true?

2. Am I being unfair?

3. Is there something bothering me that has nothing to do with this issue?

4. Am I responding to the other person or using her or him as a scapegoat?

If your analysis indicates that you view matters negatively, consider focusing on the positive. Make the choice to change your interpretation.

ELIMINATING YOUR SELF PUT-DOWNS

A third method for enhancing your self-esteem is to attack your self put-downs. We are all experts at putting ourselves down; in fact, no one can do a better job than we can. We know all our weaknesses, including the ones most vulnerable to attack. The book *Vulture: A Modern Allegory on the Art of Putting*

Oneself Down describes self-put-downs in terms of vultures.[25] Consider, for a moment, the real vulture, an unattractive bird with sharp claws and a pointy beak whose favorite activity is picking on the weak, the helpless, and, preferably, the dead. It dives into the flesh and picks away at it.

The imaginary, psychological vulture, is similar to that bird: It is ugly and hungry, eager to pounce on its psychological food—your self-concept. Every self put-down is a call to the bird to attack. It screams to the bird that you are weak, helpless, and have an ailing self-concept. What do you call yourself when you lock your keys in the car? What do you call yourself when you trip over the edge of the carpet? Every self-put-down—"Idiot!" "Klutz!"—summons the vultures!

Put-downs may be either obvious or subtle. The obvious ones have a clear physical referent, like the keys dangling in the ignition of the locked car or the frayed edge of the carpet on which you tripped. The subtle put-downs impose limitations on you that, though not obvious, are destructive. Some typical ones are:

"I could never jog five miles a day."

"I could never write a paper longer than ten pages."

"I could never stick to a diet for more than a week."

"I just can't stop smoking."

Vultures tend to congregate in six areas. There are *intelligence vultures* ("I'm dumb," "I'm no good in math," "I'm no good at foreign languages"); *creativity vultures* ("I'm not imaginative," "I can't draw as well as she can," "I can't sing like he sings"); *family vultures* ("I'm the odd-ball in the family," "I should do more for my parents," "My brother is the favorite child"); *relationship vultures* ("I'm no good at meeting people," "I can't make friends," "I'm boring"); *physical vultures* ("I'm too short/tall/fat/thin," "My ankles are fat," "My teeth are crooked"); and *sexual vultures* ("I'm not sexy," "I'm boring in bed").

The results of self put-downs are obvious: You avoid the areas where the vultures lurk, including math classes, drawing, your family, and relationships, and you wear clothes that hide this or that part of your body. You act and communicate how you feel. The goal of Skill Development 2.5 is to help you kill off your vultures!

SKILL DEVELOPMENT 2.5

KILLING OFF YOUR VULTURES[26]

To kill off your vultures, follow this five-step process:

1. Pat yourself on the back by saying something good and true about yourself. You can surely think of something for which to compliment yourself.

2. Pat someone else on the back by saying something good and true about her or him. Not only will you feel good about yourself for complimenting another person, but you'll also find that compliments beget compliments.

3. Recognize your self-put-downs. This is hard because you probably utter so many put-downs every day. To make sure you catch them all, you may want to ask a friend for help. Be sure to identify both the obvious and the subtle ones (and don't argue when your friend points them out). This step is crucial: You can't cure what you don't recognize!

4. Block each put-down. As you hear it coming out, put your hand over your mouth (literally, if you have to). Soon you'll feel a negative statement coming and you'll be able to head it off before you say it.

5. Turn the put-down around: Put it in the past tense and eliminate its evaluative component. For example, when you trip over the edge of the carpet, say, "I used to be *clumsy,* but I'm not anymore. I *tripped,* that's all, and that's human."

As you work on raising your self-esteem, remember to be realistic: Don't expect too much too soon! Plan on some hard work. You view yourself as you do because you get some payoff (you get to sulk, or you get to feel sorry for yourself because people ignore you, or you get an excuse for being a poor student). Changing your self-concept and self-esteem means giving up the old rewards for new and better ones.

COMMUNICATION COMPETENCY CHECKUP

The goal of this Communication Competency Checkup is to guide you in putting your skills and knowledge about conceiving the self to use, and to help you summarize the material in this chapter.

The man getting ready to ring the doorbell is beset by a hoard of vultures. Put your skills and knowledge to use to help him resolve his problem.

1. What can you do to help him identify the elements of his self-concept that may be responsible for his problem?

2. With an understanding of the thoughts and feelings he has about himself, how would you identify his idealized self, his "should" self, and the self he presents to others? How would an understanding of these different aspects of self help him understand the present situation and his problem?

3. Develop three strategies for helping him improve his self-esteem: one for helping him confront his "should" messages and replace them with more realistic

goals; one for helping him recognize the unreasonableness of his negative interpretations and focusing instead on the positive aspects of the situation in which he finds himself; and one for eliminating his self-put-downs by substituting statements that recognize that being human means accepting imperfection.

4. Assume his date is from another culture. What specific advice could you give him to ward off possible culture shock?

NOTES

1. Akbar Javidi and Manoochehr Javidi, "Cross-cultural Analysis of Interpersonal Bonding: A Look at East and West," *The Howard Journal of Communications* 3 (Summer/Fall 1991): 131.

2. Mary Ann Scheirer and Robert E. Kraut, "Increasing Educational Achievement via Self-Concept Change," *Review of Education Research* 49 (1979): 131–50.

3. For detailed descriptions of the various ways the content of self-concept has been described, see: Ronald B. Adler, Lawrence B. Rosenfeld, and Neil Towne, *Interplay* (Fort Worth, TX: Harcourt Brace Jovanovich, 1992), chapters 2 and 3; William H. Fitts, *The Self-Concept and Self-Actualization* (Nashville, TN: Counselor Recordings and Tests, 1971), chapters 1 and 2; Morris Rosenberg, *Conceiving the Self* (New York: Basic Books, 1979), chapter 1; and L. Edward Wells and Gerald Marwell, *Self-Esteem: Its Conceptualization and Measurement* (Beverly Hills, CA: Sage, 1976), especially chapter 3.

4. Diana Rowland, *Japanese Business Etiquette* (New York: Warner Books, 1985), p. 91.

5. Thomas M. Steinfatt, "Personality and Communication: Classical Approaches," in *Personality and Interpersonal Communication,* James C. McCroskey and John A. Daly (Eds.) (Newbury Park, CA: Sage, 1987).

6. Adapted from Sandra L. Bem, "The Measurement of Psychological Androgyny," *Journal of Consulting and Clinical Psychology* 42 (1974): 155–62. The original inventory developed by Bem contains sixty items: twenty masculine, twenty feminine, and twenty neutral (neither masculine nor feminine exclusively).

7. For a summary of research conducted on communicator characteristics, see Howard Giles and Richard L. Street, Jr., "Communicator Characteristics and Behavior," in *Handbook of Interpersonal Communication,* Mark L. Knapp and Gerald R. Miller (Eds.) (Beverly Hills, CA: Sage, 1985), pp. 205–62.

8. Harrison G. Gough, *Manual for the California Psychological Inventory* (Palo Alto, CA: Consulting Psychologists Press, 1956); Allen L. Edwards, *Manual for the Edwards Personal Preference Schedule* (New York: The Psychological Corporation, 1959); Raymond B. Cattell, *16PF* (Champaign, IL: The Institute for Personality and Ability Testing, 1969).

9. Adapted from an instrument developed by Milton Rokeach, in *Understanding Human Values* (New York: Free Press, 1979). The original questionnaire contains eighteen "to be" and eighteen "to have" values.

10. The values here were those ranked one through nine by the national samples from 1968 through 1981. See Milton Rokeach and Sandra Ball-Rokeach, "Stability and Change in American Value Profiles, 1968–1981," *American Psychologist* 44 (1989): 775–84.

11. Edward T. Hall, *The Dance of Life* (New York: Doubleday, 1983), pp. 66–67.

12. Ibid., pp. 106–7.

13. Morris Rosenberg, *Conceiving the Self* (New York: Basic Books, 1979).

14. William B. Swann, Richard M. Wenzlaff, Douglas S. Krull, and Brett W. Pelham, "Allure of Negative Feedback: Self-Verification Striving Among Depressed Persons," *Journal of Abnormal Psychology* 101 (1992): 293–306.

15. William Fitts, *The Self-Concept and Self-Actualization* (Nashville, TN: Counselor Recordings and Tests, 1971).

16. Morris Rosenberg, *Conceiving the Self* (New York: Basic Books, 1979).

17. Charles, Pavitt, "Biases in the Recall of Communicators' Behaviors," *Communication Reports* 2 (1989): 9–15.

18. Rosenberg, *Conceiving the Self,* 1979.

19. Items are based on descriptions of several of the irrational beliefs discussed in Albert Ellis and Robert Harper, *A New Guide to Rational Living* (North Hollywood, CA: Wilshire Books, 1977).

20. Kurt Vonnegut, Jr., *Mother Night* (New York: Dell Books, 1966), p. v.

21. According to Swann et al.'s research, "Allure of Negative Feedback," 1992.

22. Adapted from the *Rosenberg Self-Esteem Scale,* in Morris Rosenberg, *Conceiving the Self* (New York: Basic Books, 1979).

23. Adapted from items presented in the *Tennessee Self-Concept Scale* (Nashville, TN: Counselor Recordings and Tests, 1964).

24. Don E. Hamachek, *Encounters with Others: Interpersonal Relationships and You* (New York: Holt, Rinehart, and Winston, 1982).

25. Sidney B. Simon, *Vulture: A Modern Allegory on the Art of Putting Oneself Down* (Niles, IL: Argus Communications, 1977).

26. The steps to killing off vultures are adapted from those presented by ibid., pp. 34–44.

FOR FURTHER INVESTIGATION

Austin-Leff, Genelle, and Jan Sprague. *Talk to Yourself.* Boston: Houghton-Mifflin, 1976.

Barnlund, Dean C. *Communication Styles of Japanese and Americans.* Belmont: Wadsworth Publishing Company, 1989.

Bem, Sandra L. "Sex Role Adaptability: One Consequence of Psychological Androgyny." *Journal of Personality and Social Psychology* 31 (1975): 634–43.

Centi, Paul J. *Up with the Positive, Out with the Negatives: How to Like the Person You Are.* Englewood Cliffs, NJ: Prentice-Hall, 1981.

Cole-Whittaker, Terry. *What You Think of Me Is None of My Business.* La Jolla, CA: Oak Tree Publications, 1979.

Dyer, Wayne W. *Your Erroneous Zones.* New York: Avon Books, 1976.

Fitts, William. *The Self-Concept and Self-Actualization.* Nashville, TN: Counselor Recordings and Tests, 1971.

Gergen, Kenneth J. *The Concept of Self.* New York: Holt, Rinehart and Winston, 1971.

Gergen, Kenneth J. "The Happy, Healthy, Human Being Wears Many Masks." *Psychology Today* 5 (May 1972): 31–35, 64–66.

Goffman, Erving. *The Presentation of Self in Everyday Life.* Garden City, NY: Doubleday, 1959.

Gudykunst, William B., and Sara Ting-Toomey. *Culture and Interpersonal Relationships.* Newbury Park, CA: Sage, 1988.

Hall, Edward T. *Beyond Culture.* New York: Anchor Books, 1977.

Hamachek, Don E. *Encounters with the Self,* 2d ed. New York: Holt, Rinehart and Winston, 1978.

Hamachek, Don E. *Encounters with Others: Interpersonal Relationships and You.* New York: Holt, Rinehart and Winston, 1982.

McCall, G. J. "The Self-Concept and Interpersonal Communication." In *Interpersonal Processes: New Directions in Communication Research,* Michael E. Roloff and Gerald R. Miller, eds. Newbury Park, CA: Sage, 1987.

McCroskey, James C., and John A. Daly. *Personality and Interpersonal Communication.* Newbury Park, CA: Sage, 1987.

Rokeach, Milton. *Understanding Human Values.* New York: Free Press, 1979.

Rosenberg, Morris. *Conceiving the Self.* New York: Basic Books, 1979.

Samuels, Shirley C. *Enhancing Self-Concept in Early Childhood: Theory and Practice.* New York: Human Sciences Press, 1977.

Servas, J. "Cultural Identity and Modes of Communication." In *Communication Yearbook 12,* John A. Andersen, ed. Newbury Park, CA: Sage, 1989.

Simon, Sidney B. *Vulture: A Modern Allegory on the Art of Putting Oneself Down.* Niles, IL: Argus Communications, 1977.

Weinberg, George. *Self Creation.* New York: Avon Books, 1978.

CHAPTER 3

The Self and Others

COMMUNICATION COMPETENCIES

This chapter examines the self and others. Specifically, the objective of this chapter is for you to learn to:

- Describe how you perceive objects and people.
- Explain the role of self-fulfilling prophecies in your interactions with others.
- Apply several techniques for increasing your perceptual accuracy.
- Learn how to express your emotions.

KEY WORDS

The key words in this chapter are:

perception
selective perception
snap judgments
selective organization
selective interpretation
self-fulfilling prophecy

empathy
emotion
labeling
stuffing
Three T's Emotional Expression
    Method

Read the following events concerning graduation at Somewhere State College.

When it came to graduation ceremonies, Leslie was not interested in wearing a cap and gown. A call to the Dean of Students' office confirmed that a cap and gown were not required to attend graduation. In order to be sure, Leslie called back a second time, spoke to another person, and was given the same information. Leslie attended graduation wearing nice clothes, but without a cap and gown. Shortly before Leslie got in line for the march into the stadium, the Dean of Students came up and asked if there was a problem. Learning that Leslie did not intend to wear a cap and gown (and agreeing that there was no rule requiring one), she offered to supply one—free. Leslie said, "Thank you, this is not a matter of money, I just prefer not to wear one." A few minutes later the college's Vice President approached Leslie, offered a cap and gown, and pointed out the possible embarrassment to everyone when Leslie went on stage to accept the diploma without the traditional collegiate garb. "I understand," Leslie said, "but I consider a cap and gown the symbol of what's wrong with education: pomp and ceremony without a real concern for learning." After some discussion, the Vice President offered to get Leslie's diploma and present it to her before the regular ceremony began. Leslie, indicating no desire to embarrass anyone, agreed. The Vice President gave Leslie the diploma and Leslie went off to sit in the stands and watch the ceremony.

What particulars of this graduation event do you consider the most important? How do you put these particulars together to explain what happened?

If you were a member of the administration, how would you interpret the events? How would you interpret the events if you were a member of the planning committee? If you were a campus protester? A parent? A member of a minority culture? A member of a culture that valued collectivism? A member of a culture that valued individualism?

How do *you* interpret the story?

What does your interpretation of the story tell about how you perceive things? How you perceive the particulars of the story is reflected in how you communicate about the story, including your interpretation.

PERCEPTION

Perception is the process of becoming aware of objects and events, including yourself and others. How you perceive yourself forms the basis for your perception of the world, and how you perceive the world both affects and reflects how you communicate.

Perception is an *active* process; the world may offer an infinite variety of details, but it does so passively. You need to make sense of the random pieces of information that are presented: You need to determine what you will perceive, how you will organize it, and how you will interpret it. *You* are the *cause* of what you perceive; you are the one in control, the one who determines what you perceive.

The physical dimensions of perception are pretty much the same for all people. All six billion of us have sensory organs such as eyes, ears, and fingertips, which operate with varying degrees of effectiveness, that allow us to take the world outside of us and convert it into something we perceive. Sensations that bombard us move through our nervous system to our brains and there are given meaning. The meaning is affected by our individual and cultural differences. In North American culture, for example, we might respond positively to people who "speak their mind," yet this same behavior would produce an unfavorable perceptive interpretation in most Asian cultures that value cooperation and politeness more than individual assertiveness.

Based on this understanding of the concept of perception, on what features of Leslie's graduation ceremony did you *choose* to focus? How did you *choose* to put those pieces together to make a coherent story? What meaning did you *choose* to derive from the story?

SELECTIVE PERCEPTION

The data available to your senses are too many to be grasped in their totality. You therefore need to engage in **selective perception;** that is, you need to choose what to focus your attention on. What you choose to perceive—whether that choice is conscious or not—determines the subject matter of your communication.

Objects that are brighter or larger or easily distinguishable from their surroundings in some other way are more likely to attract your attention than are objects that seem to fade into the background. You focus on the Hawaiian shirt at a formal party, the tallest building on a street, the loudest person in a room, or Leslie without a cap and gown—because these things stand out. Of course, the choice to pay attention is yours: You can choose to concentrate on the sea of black tuxedos instead of the colorful shirt, the entire skyline instead of the skyscraper, the hum of voices instead of the outstanding one, or the uniform caps and gowns instead of the lone person without academic garb.

An object's distinctiveness is one determinant of selection; another is your purpose for selection. If you're hungry, restaurant signs attract your attention; if you're looking for a fight, possible insults receive your focus; and if you want company, people passing by may draw your notice.

The selection process is essentially the same whether you choose to focus on people or objects. What the person or object looks like in comparison to the context, together with your own needs, wants, and desires, determines where you focus your attention and what you select to perceive.

If the focus of your attention is a person or a personal characteristic, some-thing else happens: you make a snap judgment. When the Hawaiian shirt grabs your attention at a formal party, you may immediately decide that its wearer is a jerk or someone you want to know better.

Snap judgments, conclusions reached rapidly with little forethought, which usually relate to liking/disliking, are based on your past experiences with similar people or characteristics, or on cultural stereotypes. Snap judgments help you de-cide whether to continue focusing your attention on the person. If your initial judg-ment is positive, you'll choose to gather more and more cues about the person; if your judgment is negative, you'll dismiss the person from your attention and move on to other aspects of your environment.

The speed with which you make these judgments is often a reflection on your culture. Cultures that tend to be impulsive, such as those of North America, are quick to reach conclusions and take action. North Americans often admire John Wayne and Rambo because they are swift in taking action when faced with prob-lems, yet in many Asian cultures people frequently learn to be reflective and arrive at a course of action at a slower pace. For example, if Japanese and American chil-dren were asked to draw pictures of their families, the American children most likely would start drawing immediately, while Japanese school children would think about their pictures before they began sketching.

SELECTIVE ORGANIZATION

Once you've chosen what to attend to, your next task is to organize the infor-mation in a way that makes it possible to interpret. To understand the information you amass, you must be able to see how parts relate to each other, and how the parts interrelate to form the whole. **Selective organization** is the process of fitting together the information you selectively perceive to form a whole. Just as what to perceive is your choice, so is how to organize it.

General tendencies guide how you organize what you perceive. You tend to accentuate details that you consider essential and minimize those that seem less important to you; to fill in gaps so that details relate easily and logically to each other and to eliminate details that don't fit or make sense; and to put all the infor-mation you gather into a context that facilitates a recognizable pattern.

You would organize the material you heard while listening to a speech on af-firmative action quotas in one way if you were a lawyer specializing in affirmative action cases, in another way if you were a person discriminated against, and yet in a different way if you were a student writing a term paper on affirmative action. If you were a lawyer, you would selectively perceive data related to legal issues and organize them into a coherent speech, filling in gaps left when the speaker handled other topics. You would probably place the information into a recogniz-able pattern such as "arguments in favor of X," or "arguments against X." If you were a victim of discrimination, you would focus on information related to your particular problem and, like the lawyer, fill in gaps and eliminate anything that seemed irrelevant; you also might create a pattern out of the pieces you accumulate, such as "useful" versus "useless" information. If you were a student new to the topic, you might take notes quickly, not sure what to focus on, but hoping that the speaker's tone of voice and method of organization would offer clues about what to report on later. Regardless of your purpose, you must organize the speaker's words—of ten without consciously thinking about it—so that meaning can be attributed to them. If a speaker does not organize a speech in a way that is meaningful to you, all you reap is a collection of unrelated, irrelevant facts.

The goal of filling in details (or eliminating them) is to create a unified whole of the information you receive. Look at the top line in Figure 3.1 as you hold your hand over the bottom line. What do you see? Now repeat the same process for the bottom line.

Although the letters are fully formed, you probably have no trouble organizing the top line into *A, B,* and *C,* and the bottom line into *12, 13,* and *14.* If you take another look at the middle figures in the two sequences, however, you may notice that both figures are essentially the same. Because you created a context out of the surrounding figures, you determined that the middle figure is a *B* in the first line and a *13* in the second line. The other possible sequences—*A, 13, C,* and *12, B, 14*—seem illogical because you have been raised in a culture where A's, B's, and C's, like 12's, 13's, and 14's, come in packages. The selective organization process is essentially the same for a person as it is for objects, letters, or numbers. For example, you commonly add details to people who are the focus of attention. Research shows that if you perceive someone as attractive, you add positive traits such as *kind, friendly, smart,* and *happy.* And you tend to add negative traits to complete the picture of someone who is less attractive.[1]

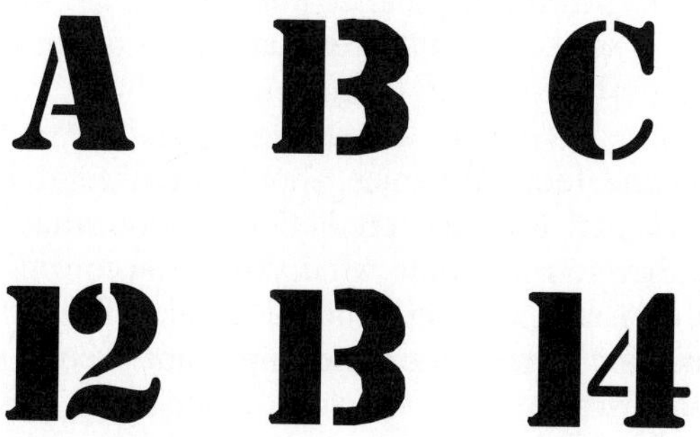

FIGURE 3.1

Ways of Organizing Perceptions of Others

There are two primary approaches to organizing impressions of other people. The first assumes that *traits interact with each other* to form the total picture of a person.[2] Traits are not independent of each other; rather, they combine and assume relative importance to form the overall impression. Consider the following list of characteristics you might perceive of someone:

intelligent
skillful
industrious
cold
determined
practical
cautious

What would be your overall impression of a person who possesses these traits? How do the traits interact to form your impression? One way to determine the answer is by simple substitution. For example, if you substitute *warm* for *cold,* does your impression change dramatically? Some traits are central to an overall impression, so changing any or all of them changes the impression. Your first response to the list might have been that this is an unhappy, stingy person who is unpopular. But after substituting *warm* for *cold,* you might think that this is a generous, happy, good-natured person.

Although the warm–cold trait is central when you evaluate a person's sociability, it becomes less important when you evaluate honesty. In such cases, the blunt–polite trait appears to be more central. Which traits are central depends on the nature of the evaluation.

The second approach to organizing your impressions takes form from *your ideas about the behaviors that characterize particular types of people or how people should behave in certain situations.* You have ideas about how certain types of people, such as extroverts, introverts, students, teachers, parents, and children should behave. You also have ideas about what certain events, such as lectures, wedding ceremonies, and football games, should be like. You use these ideas to organize what you see and to make predictions about what else you should or should not see. You therefore evaluate what you see according to how well it fits your idea of what the person or event should be like. For example, if you think graduation ceremonies are very serious and important events, you might attribute characteristics such as "immature" and "closed-minded" to Leslie for not wanting to wear the traditional graduation costume. If you think of them as frivolous and unimportant, you might attribute "strong-willed" and "clear-thinking" to Leslie.

Perceiving people is different from perceiving objects, if for no other reason than that you normally have many more things in common with another person than you do with an object. When the focus of perception is a person, you attribute qualities to the person that, for you, seem to go together. For example, *happy* and *independent* may be related in your mind, so that someone you perceive as happy you also perceive as independent. As with everything else, who you are determines what you attribute to another person. In someone you like, you see characteristics that you value for yourself; in someone you dislike, you see characteristics that you find objectionable for yourself. If you are proud of your ability to run long distances, you'll admire this trait in others. If you dislike your tendency to shout when you're angry, you'll dislike this trait in others.

FIGURE 3.2   THE HUMAN BRAIN WILL PERCEIVE HALF OF THESE IDENTICAL FACES AS GLUM, HALF, HALF AS HAPPY—EVEN WHEN THE DRAWING IS INVERTED.

It is important to keep in mind that most of the traits that you value are those that stem from your cultural background. If, for example, you like people who act young, behave aggressively, are competitive, and like to keep busy, it is because you learned that those were traits to be admired. On the other hand, if you had been brought up in another culture, you might not admire those traits.

SELECTIVE INTERPRETATION

Interpretation is just as much your choice as what you perceive and how you organize it. In **selective interpretation**, you choose how to explain the information you selectively perceive and selectively organize. How you interpret what you perceive depends on who you think you are, who you would like to be, and who you think you should be. It also depends on your knowledge and expectations of the people and objects in your environment as well as how you feel at the moment.[3,4] Many variables enter into your interpretation of what you perceive, which is why two individuals' perceptions are never the same. Just as no two people are identical, no two interpretations are identical.

How do you think the member of the administration interpreted the "problem" with Leslie (even using the word *problem* implies an interpretation)? Would the administrator think, "Why does this have to happen to me? Why can't these kids just cooperate?"

How do you think a member of the Student Planning Committee for Graduation would interpret the event? Would the committee member think, "This gives all students a black eye. Why can't some people just go along with graduation, even if they think it's stupid?"

How do you think a campus radical would interpret Leslie's behavior? Would the radical think, "Finally, someone stood up to the fascist administration!"?

And what about Leslie's parents? Would they sigh and think, "What did we do wrong raising Leslie?" (or, conversely, "What did we do right?"). What might the school administrators have done if Leslie was a member of a racial minority, a homosexual, or an international exchange student? And, how might Leslie as a minority or other-culture person have interpreted the administrator's behavior?

Skill Development 3.1 will give you some practice developing alternative interpretations for the same event.

SKILL DEVELOPMENT 3.1

DEVELOPING ALTERNATIVE INTERPRETATIONS

You have just finished working on a class or work project and Chris tells you, "I had a great time working with you. I hope we can work together again sometime."

Briefly explain how you would interpret Chris's remarks in each of the following circumstances.

1. You see yourself as a desirable person.

2. You see yourself as desirable, but you assume that your partner says something nice because doing so is good etiquette.

3. You see yourself as desirable, assume your partner says something nice because it is polite, and you have a bad stomach ache.

4. You feel that your interpersonal skills are weak and that you are boring.

After you selectively perceive and organize cues from another person—whether they are nonverbal or verbal—you attribute a motive to the person, make a general judgment, and finish by making a prediction. For example, in the answers to Skill Development 3.1:

"Chris wants to work with me again because Chris thinks I'm a nice person. I can expect Chris to like me more and more as we continue to get to know each other."

"Chris acted politely because Chris is a polite person who can be expected to behave politely in the future."

"Chris kept talking because Chris could see I was in pain and wanted to inflict further pain on me. Chris is a cruel person who can be expected to try to hurt me whenever the opportunity arises!"

"I know I'm boring, so it's obvious Chris is lying and I can expect Chris to lie to me in the future—except we'll probably never work together again."

Knowledge Checkup 3.1 will help you understand your own perception process—what you select to perceive, how you organize the information, how you interpret it—and what it reveals about you.

KNOWLEDGE CHECKUP 3.1

ANALYZING YOUR PERCEPTION PROCESS

Describe what you see in the picture on the following page. The picture is ambiguous. Because it presents a great deal of information that is unorganized and uninterrupted, there is no right or wrong way to perceive it.

1. What details of the picture do you select to perceive?

2. How do you organize the details you select to create a whole story?

3. How do you interpret the details that you select to perceive and organize?

4. What does your description of the picture—what you selectively perceive, selectively organize, and selectively interpret—tell you about yourself and your perception process? Do you believe that others will perceive the situation in the same way?

What you chose to see in the picture, how you chose to put the details together, and how you chose to make sense of the details reflect what is important to you. Were you more concerned with the two people than where they were? Did you describe their physical characteristics? Did you go into detail about their relationship, and, if you did, how did you describe the relationship? Did you perceive the scene as calm or tense? Is the person looking off, focusing on something, or just staring off into the distance? What does your perception of this picture tell about who you are?

THE SELF-FULFILLING PROPHECY

What you believe about yourself and others has a tendency to come true. This notion is called the **self-fulfilling prophecy.**[5] Consider, for example, the likely outcomes of the earlier interactions with Chris. If you believe that you are a good person and that Chris recognizes this (as in the first situation), you are likely to behave nicely the next time you two are together, which should increase the probability that Chris will, indeed, treat you nicely. If you believe that Chris was simply polite and didn't care about you as a person (the second scenario), you might treat Chris distantly and politely the next time you are together, which should increase the probability that you will be treated likewise. If you believe that Chris intends to harm you (the third case), you might be suspicious of Chris's every move, convinced that danger lurks in every behavior; if you continue behaving accordingly, Chris just might treat you unkindly. And if you believe that you are boring, you might avoid talking or enthusiastically listening to what Chris says, and Chris just might think you're boring.

People behave in ways that increase the probability that their beliefs about themselves and others will come true. Consider how self-fulfilling prophecy applies to the man in the following conversation. His basic belief was that he couldn't get any love. He was asked, "From whom can you get love? Anyone?" His responses, and the prompting questions, went like this:

"No, not *anyone.* The person needs to be a woman."

"Any woman?"

"No, she needs to be between eighteen and forty years of age."

"Any woman between eighteen and forty?"

"No, she needs to have long red hair."

"Any woman between eighteen and forty with long red hair?"

"No, she needs to have blue eyes."

"Any woman between eighteen and forty, with long red hair and blue eyes?"

"No, she also needs to be between 5'3" and 5'7"."

"Any woman between eighteen and forty, with long red hair and blue eyes, between 5'3" and 5'7"?"

"No, she also needs a college degree."

"Any woman between eighteen and forty, with long red hair and blue eyes, between 5'3" and 5'7", with a college degree?"

"No, she needs to have a degree in the helping professions, such as teaching or social work."

"Any woman between eighteen and forty, with long red hair and blue eyes, between 5'3" and 5'7", with a college degree in the helping professions?"

"No, there's one more requirement. She has to love me—first."

"And what's the problem?"

"I'm unlovable."

This man created his own experience of "getting no love" by making his requirements so strict that few women could possibly meet them. But if even one person matched his description, the final obstacle *guaranteed* that his prophecy would come true: He was unlovable. He could never perceive being loved because he *saw himself as unlovable.* So before his experiences could change, his self-perception needed to change. He was the cause of his experience.

Similarly, *you* are the cause of *your* experiences.

INCREASING PERCEPTUAL ACCURACY

Many issues need to be addressed before you can increase the accuracy of your perceptions. Given that *who you are determines what you perceive,* you may need to change even who you are in order to perceive things more accurately.

What you perceive is limited by what you believe. Picture yourself as a tube. At one end is a mesh screen through which you perceive your environment. If each thin wire in the screen were a belief, accumulating enough beliefs would mean that eventually nothing could get through. From the inside, all you could see would be your own screen. You would be trapped in your beliefs and they would cloud your view of reality. From inside the tube, everything would seem orderly, stable, and logical, resulting in the most dangerous of all beliefs: *What I see is what there is, and that is all there is.*

STRETCH YOURSELF

Increasing your imagination expands what you are capable of perceiving. The more you can imagine, the more you can perceive. Begin with your senses, because it is through your senses that you perceive things. Skill Development 3.2 will help you develop your sense awareness.

SKILL DEVELOPMENT 3.2

INCREASING SENSE AWARENESS AND SENSE IMAGINATION

INCREASING SENSE AWARENESS

1. Close your eyes.

2. Sit quietly for two minutes. Be aware of your surroundings, such as the sounds and smells.

3. Open your eyes.

4. What did you hear?

5. What did you smell?

6. What did you taste?

7. What were you touching or what was touching you?

8. What did you see?

9. Close your eyes again for two minutes. Again concentrate on what each of your senses is taking in.

10. Open your eyes.

11. What did you notice as you sat with your eyes closed the second time? How did you perceive things as you focused on each of your senses?

INCREASING SENSE IMAGINATION

1. What does winter *taste* like?

2. What is the *color* of worry?

3. What does time *feel* like?

4. What does a rainbow *sound* like?

5. What is the *smell* of silence?

To increase the accuracy of your perceptions, you need to break the habit of using your senses in usual ways and stop making common, automatic associations. Expand your imagination!

REMAIN OPEN-MINDED

To ensure accurate perceptions, you must be receptive to new information, assumptions, beliefs, and opinions, even when they seem to contradict your own positions. Increasing your perceptual accuracy requires, above all else, open-mindedness.

Being open-minded means recognizing that there may be more to see than you see, more to touch than you touch, more to hear than you hear, more to smell than you smell, more to taste than you taste—more to know about one subject, one person, or one world than you alone could ever know.

Being open-minded also means recognizing that you may perceive things that aren't there, eliminate inconvenient pieces of information, and otherwise push, pull, stretch, and bang the world to fit your preconceived notions.

Finally, being open-minded means recognizing that you may draw conclusions too quickly, state them too assuredly, and assume that if an answer works for you, it must work for everyone.

You can increase your open-mindedness by making yourself available to new and varied experiences. Your object is to gain additional information about your world. Below are suggestions to help you increase your open-mindedness:

1. *Talk to people.* The more you interact with others, the more you will learn and the greater your personal storehouse of varying perceptions will grow. Because each person sees the world differently, talking to others and listening to what they say provides you with a new perspective to consider.

2. *Share your perceptions and listen to the feedback you receive.* Avoid being defensive when you check your perceptions. Keep in mind that your view is a personal interpretation. You are entitled to your perception just as others are entitled to theirs. Your perception is right for you as others' perceptions are right for them. Be aware, however, that others may work very hard to make their perceptions your own, and you may also try to make your perceptions theirs.

3. *Deal with contradictions—don't ignore them.* Contradictions are often predictable once you recognize their origin, that is, that you are different from others as each of us is different from everyone else—so gather the contradictions, look at them, reconcile them when you can, and understand why you can't when you can't.

4. *Continue gathering information on a subject,* even after you have reached a decision. Recognize that what you know is only a fraction of what there is to know. Stay open to new information.

To be open-minded, you must accept change and be willing to adjust your thoughts and beliefs. There is no point in gathering new information if you don't intend to evaluate it and act on it.

INCREASE EMPATHY

To improve your perception of other people, you must strive to increase your **empathy**, your ability to experience the world as others do. Of course, you can never see things exactly as someone else would, but trying is important.[6] When you empathize with another person, her or his experience becomes clearer to you, you begin to understand her or his reasons for behaving and feeling in particular ways, and you start to develop an understanding of these things as *the other person understands them.* The goal, although unachievable, is something like the Vulcan mind-meld that Mr. Spock performs occasionally on *Star Trek.* Placing his fingertips on another's head, he and the other become one, and Spock comes to know the other person (or, in some cases, the other thing) as the other person knows *himself or herself.*

Although earthbound creatures cannot perform a Vulcan mind-meld, attempts to achieve empathy may be made in other ways. For example, groups of handicapped students have invited those who can walk to "spend the day paralyzed from the waist down," or those who can see to "spend the day blind," or those who

can hear to "spend the day hearing impaired." With the help of wheelchairs, blind-folds, and earplugs, the participants enlarge their own perception of the world.

Incorrect assumptions about another person also may be revealed by engag-ing in role reversal. Switch positions with someone with whom you have an ongo-ing argument, regardless of what the argument is about, and try to see the situation from the other's perspective. What does this person think, feel, and want? How does this person see you in the situation and interpret your behaviors? Empathy for the other person's position should provide insights that allow you to resolve your differences.

You might well imagine how difficult it is when the other person is from an-other culture. Empathy demands that we be able to infer the feelings and needs of another person. To do this we must, of course, know something about the other person. If the person is your best friend you have a great deal of knowledge about the ways he or she expresses himself or herself. Should that person be from an-other culture, one that is very or even slightly different from your own, it is diffi-cult to know the meaning of many specific actions. If your friend is Italian, and you're not, you might consider him very talkative when he gets upset, and you can use that data to engage in role reversal and imagine how you feel when you are upset. If your friend is from a culture where silence has meaning, such as Korea, and you are not Korean, you can still strive to understand that behavior and, therefore, take on a particular role. Some people find it easier to empathize than others.[7]

To overcome some of the problems associated with having empathy with someone from another culture you need to develop these five skills.[8] First, recognize that there are *differences in the way people express themselves.* Some individuals might shout in the company of strangers while others have learned to keep their emotions in check. Second, *know yourself and how you respond to the unknown.* Do you feel comfortable when confronted with ambiguous situations or do you work to overcome feelings of frustration? Third, try to *gather information about the other person so that you can understand the meaning behind his or her actions.* Do members of the other's culture value openness or is the person part of a private culture? Fourth, using the information you have, *try to put yourself in the other's place*—from the point of view of his or her culture. Finally, *take some action that demonstrates empathy.* For example, if touching is acceptable behavior for the other person, you might consider touching him or her; if touching is not acceptable, you might consider refraining from any touching but tell the other person you care, or send a card.

Unless you are a member of a helping profession—a psychologist, social worker, or nurse, for instance—your ability to empathize may not extend too far beyond the people with whom you share your most personal relationships. Empathy requires open-mindedly gathering information about the other person over long periods of time. The questions posed in Skill Development 3.3 should help you gather the information necessary to assess the degree of empathy in one of your friendship relationships.

SKILL DEVELOPMENT 3.3

ASSESSING EMPATHY IN FRIENDSHIP

The following questions can help you determine the degree to which empathy is part of a friendship. Select the closest personal friendship you have and respond to the questions based on that friendship.

1. Does your friend understand most of what you say?

2. Does your friend understand how you feel?

3. Does your friend appreciate what your experiences feel like to you?

4. Does your friend try to see things through your eyes?

5. Does your friend ask you questions about what your experiences mean to you?

6. Does your friend ask you questions about what you're thinking?

7. Does your friend ask you questions about how you're feeling?

Have your friend answer the same questions. Compare your answers. The results might well contribute to greater empathy in your relationship.

EMOTIONS

Perhaps the most important determinant of your perceptions and reactions are your emotions. **Emotions** are feelings accompanied by physiological changes, such as increased respiration, and overt nonverbal manifestations, such as crying, shrugging, or smiling. Although physiological changes and overt manifestations are the primary components of emotions, a third aspect often is found: labeling. **Labeling** takes place when someone experiences particular physiological changes and overt manifestations and verbally declares the feelings being felt or displayed.[9] For example, "I'm feeling angry" may be declared when experiencing increased respiration, flushed face, tense and blaring voice, and a raised fist.

KNOWLEDGE CHECKUP 3.2

IDENTIFYING YOUR EMOTIONS

Check the statements on the list that represent a feeling or reaction you've had with some regularity:

_____ **1.** I've spent a sleepless night fuming because someone criticized me.

_____ **2.** I've gotten a headache or stomachache thinking about something that I have to do, such as taking a test, giving a speech, or meeting a stranger.

_____ **3.** I've had fantasies in which I've attacked a person who I feel has taken advantage of me, such as a boss, parent, or teacher.

_____ **4.** When someone I care for is inconsiderate to me, I cry, get the feeling I want to hit the person, or feel my body get rigid.

_____ **5.** If I feel I have been snubbed, I fall silent or withdraw physically or emotionally.

_____ **6.** I repress my anger or other strong feelings because I'm afraid others won't like me if I let my true feelings out.

FAILURE TO EXPRESS EMOTIONS

If you answered yes to any of the statements in Knowledge Checkup 3.2, you have been a victim of pent-up emotions. All human beings experience a wide range of emotions, although many choose to express a very limited number of them. Knowledge Checkup 3.3 provides you with the opportunity to acknowledge those emotions you express most often. What are some of your favorite emotions? (Your favorite emotions are those you *do,* not necessarily those you would *like* to do, *can* do, or *will* do.)

EMOTION CHECKLIST

Check the emotions that you communicate most often.

_____ anger	_____ anxiety	_____ apathy
_____ bewilderment	_____ calmness	_____ comfortable-ness
_____ concern	_____ confidence	_____ confusion
_____ creativity	_____ cruelty	_____ curiosity
_____ depression	_____ desperation	_____ disappoint-ment
_____ eagerness	_____ enviousness	_____ excitement
_____ fearfulness	_____ flirtatiousness	_____ friendliness
_____ gentleness	_____ gladness	_____ guilt
_____ happiness	_____ hopefulness	_____ hostility
_____ hurt	_____ impatience	_____ feeling incom-petent
_____ feeling infe-rior	_____ insecurity	_____ feeling iso-lated
_____ jealousy	_____ lovability	_____ lovingness
_____ being melan-choly	_____ optimism	_____ paranoia
_____ playfulness	_____ possessive-ness	_____ pridefulness
_____ rejection	_____ sadness	_____ security
_____ seductiveness	_____ shyness	_____ silliness
_____ stupidity	_____ feeling sui-cidal	_____ supportive-ness
_____ supportive-ness	_____ sympathy	_____ tenderness

_____ being terrified _____ being touchy _____ feeling ugly

_____ being unsure _____ feeling useless _____ feeling violent

_____ weariness

If your favorite emotion isn't on this short list of all the possibilities, add it here:

_____

Although there are a large number of emotions that may be expressed, people typically express very few.[10] If you have one emotion you like to express a lot, it may be your "tool," your proven way to get things you want. For example, when you were a child, crying may have helped you get your parents to give you what you want, and so now, many years later, you find that when you don't get your way you tend to cry. Many people use anger the same way—as a means to achieve an end that worked when they were children.

If you have a small number of emotions that you express, you are limiting the ways you can communicate the many and complex feelings you can experience. Limiting yourself this way poses a roadblock to communicating effectively.

Some people may limit themselves almost exclusively to one or two emotions, such as anger and disappointment, or happy and energetic, and some may strive to eliminate the expression of their emotions altogether. There are several reasons why people limit which emotions they experience and how often they express them. These reasons typically reflect a North American and Western European attitude. If you are North American, they should help you recognize why you and your communication partners respond as you do and why people from other cultures may respond differently.

First, *emotions are hard to understand.* They aren't logical. Rather, they are felt, and feelings often can't be diagnosed, analyzed, or fully understood. Because of the nature of emotions, many people are afraid of them, just as they are afraid of other things they have difficulty understanding and being logical about. This fear of emotions leads to a decrease in expressing them.

Second, *people are often unaware of their emotions because they are taught to desensitize themselves to how they are feeling.* For example, you may be feeling anger, but your companion convinces you that you're only "upset," or you may be feeling overjoyed, but your friends label your emotion as "happy." Eventually, if you accept others' perceptions, you become less sensitive to the extremes of your emotions, and this decreased sensitivity may lead to decreased awareness of them.

Third, *many of us are taught, as part of the socializing process conducted by our parents, religious institutions, schools, and the media, that many of our emotions are bad and must be controlled.* You may even have been taught to stuff your feelings. **Stuffing** is the process of pushing emotions inside rather than confronting and expressing them. For example, many North American boys are taught that it is not manly to cry, and many North American girls are institutionalized to believe that it is "unladylike" and "improper" to express anger. Holding back these strong emotions often has unfortunate consequences, including masking the feelings with alcohol and drugs.

Fourth, *people may fail to express their emotions for fear of exposing themselves.* The reasoning goes like this: "If you know how I feel, you may use this information against me, or think I'm bad or stupid or wrongheaded." In order to protect yourself, you control your honest feelings so you do not give yourself away.

Fifth, *many social and career roles limit the honest expression of feelings.* In some cases the social expectations even describe which feelings are OK and which aren't—for instance, crying is OK at a funeral but not at a Marx Brothers movie. Certain professions limit the emotions that may be expressed. Doctors and nurses who are *too* sad or happy, and police officers who are anything but cool and detached, run the risk of being perceived as unprofessional.

Sixth, *many people are told not to embarrass others by displaying their feelings, feelings that would naturally be expressed through hearty laughter, loud vocal expressions, and physical touching.* Ironically, if you constantly stuff your feelings your body often rebels. If you store up the hurts, the angers, and the glee, eventually the feelings will come out in other ways. Unexpressed feelings can manifest themselves physically through headaches, neck tightness, ulcers, heart attacks, high blood pressure, impotence, and insomnia. The need for an emotional outlet can lead to eating binges, physical and verbal abuse, and the need for excessive sexual activity. These reactions are your body's way of saying, "I don't like what you're doing to me. You are denying me my natural right to feel. I won't be denied!" They are the body's way of saying, "By repressing your talent for expressing emotions, you're killing yourself."

Besides the physical reactions, the failure to experience emotions and to express felt emotions leads to an ever-increasing emotional incapacity. If you have been brought up in a family where you were restricted from letting out your felt emotions—"Stop being a sissy," "Be brave, keep up that stiff upper lip," "Stop that whining"—eventually, the denying and ignoring leads to your being desensitized to your own and others' emotions and you become unable to identify your own and other's feelings. The problem feeds on itself, growing larger and larger until a potentially rich emotional life becomes emotionally bleached and stagnant. With emotions, as with many other aspects of life, the problem is that you must "use it or lose it."

Finally, it should be clear that nearly all of the reasons why we often fail to express our emotions can be traced to our cultural, social, and psychological background. And it also should be clear that these reasons are multiple and complex. That is, a reluctance to let others see what is going on inside of you could stem from a cultural value that stresses self-restraint or cultural definitions of sex roles that allow certain people to do one thing and deny that role to members of the opposite sex. For example, in Northern American culture a woman can cry in public, but men have been taught not to do so. In China, children are conditioned to use the face to conceal rather than reveal emotion. They are raised to be stoic, and while they might experience a wide range of emotions, they have learned to bridle those emotions—at least in public.[11]

IDENTIFYING YOUR EMOTIONAL REACTIONS

Place a check mark before any of the following ways you deal with your emotions:

_____ 1. I react immediately if I feel a strong emotion, such as happiness, anger, or hurt.

_____ 2. I withdraw rather than tell someone how I feel, whether positive or negative.

_____ 3. I scream and yell.

_____ 4. I cry.

_____ 5. I feel like crying, but I don't.

_____ 6. I get so mad I can't think straight.

_____ 7. I find someone I feel comfortable with and talk out my feelings.

_____ 8. I talk to myself and try to get rid of my feelings.

_____ 9. I go and do something—physical exercise, write poetry—to get my mind off what's affecting me.

_____ 10. I laugh heartily.

_____ 11. I stuff my feelings for fear of hurting other people's feelings or getting negative reactions.

_____ 12. I physically or verbally attack the person who I feel is causing my emotional hurt.

_____ 13. I find someone to aggress against whether or not she or he is the person who I feel is causing my emotional hurt.

_____ 14. I determine whether this is a matter that must be dealt with now or can be put off until later.

_____ 15. I recognize that I am in control of myself and I don't have to get angry, feel out of control, or show my feelings to others.

Review your answers: What did you learn about yourself as an expresser of emotions? Are you a stuffer? Do you express your anger in hurtful ways—hurtful to yourself and others? Have you been desensitized to your emotions?

BENEFITS OF EXPRESSING EMOTIONS

With all the available reasons why people fail to express their emotions, or why they choose to express very few of the emotions they experience, it seems necessary to make the case for why people *should* express their emotions. The benefits of expressing emotions in North American culture fall into three areas: physical health, intimacy, and conflict resolution.

Physical Health

There is ample evidence that expressing emotions often promotes physical health. For example, it can help reduce stress and this, in turn, can help reduce high blood pressure, heart disease, ulcers, and the ability of the body to respond to infections.[12]

Another benefit of expressing emotions comes from the physiological changes that are the hallmark of strong emotions, such as an increased heartbeat, quicker respiration, and the release of adrenalin. People who express their emotions and who experience these physiological changes regularly recover from them more quickly than those who repress the expression of their emotions. The result for those who do not express their emotions is a continual state of physiological tension, rather than the tension-followed-by-release experienced by the others.

Increased Intimacy

Given the importance of emotions to how people interpret and respond to the world around them, people who do not share their emotions may deprive others of important information—information about who they are and how they see things. Without this information, obstacles to intimacy may be erected. This does not mean, of course, that every emotion should be blurted out thoughtlessly—competent communicators recognize that it is best when the expression of emotions takes into account the relationship partner, the situation, and the goals of communicating.

Intellectual, emotional, and physical intimacy stagnate without a continual flow of information about how each partner feels—the emotions each experiences—as intimacy is communicated. Without knowing the emotions experienced by the relationship partner, intellectual information becomes hollow, loses its coloration, becomes devoid of the feeling that communicates how the information is experienced emotionally by the relationship partner. Similarly, emotional intimacy is halted when emotions remain unexpressed—and the partners cease to grow emotionally. Finally, without sharing the emotions felt when being physically intimate, that aspect of a relationship cannot grow. It takes knowing the emotions experienced by each partner to understand the physical aspects of the relationship that each likes and dislikes, and to plan for a richer and fuller physically intimate relationship.

Conflict Resolution

Without communicating how you feel, you condemn yourself to those things that annoy you—whether it be a coworker who smokes or a friend who rarely shows up on time—and those that bore you—whether a marriage or a job. Although sometimes the best alternative may be to attempt to take your emotions in check (for example, the outcome may be a *worse* situation for yourself), it requires communicating how you feel to set in motion the changes necessary to end being annoyed or bored (or any other negative emotion you may be experiencing). Although expressing your emotions has risks involved—the smoking coworker may rudely tell you to mind your own business and continue smoking—not expressing yourself is the same as giving up on ever changing your situation.

To resolve conflicts effectively also requires knowing how each person involved in the resolution process feels about the problem and any suggested solutions. If one person feels more strongly about the problem than the other, and this is not communicated, assumptions will be made that will affect how each person communicates: Each will assume the other cares as much as she or he does. Similarly, without a clear understanding of how each person feels about suggested solutions, the odds of the best solution being selected are decreased. Incorrect assumptions about the emotions the other person is experiencing set the groundwork for poor conflict resolution.

There are obvious risks involved when you express your emotions. Be prepared for some consequences you may not have planned on. Second, the advice on the advantages of expressing emotion demonstrates a North American orientation, which is not universally accepted. For example, in regard to the emotion of anger the Buddha once wrote, "Expressing anger is like spitting into the wind—you are the one who suffers." Think about how different this advice is than the expression "Tell it like it is."

Helping Others Express Their Emotions

When those around us are expressing emotions, or turn to us for assistance in expressing emotions, we often are at a loss as to how to act. What do you tell someone who is disappointed, depressed, or unhappy? Typically, rather than allowing the person to feel as she or he wishes, advice is given such as, "Cheer up," "Every cloud has a silver lining," "Tomorrow will be a better day," "Things will get better." When someone is angry, you may say, "Simmer down," "There's no point in getting angry," or "Be objective." In other words, you may try to get the person to "feel better," which usually means, feel in a way that *you're* more comfortable handling. This is not usually an effective technique.

In the process of getting the person to feel differently, we often cut off one possible way of allowing her or him to deal with the emotion—by talking it out.

Misperception a Common Cause of War, Scholar Argues

Some misperception almost always accompanies the outbreak of war and any explanation of a war that ignores such misunderstanding is likely to be incomplete, says a political scientist at Columbia University.

Writing in a special issue (Spring 1988) of the *Journal of Interdisciplinary History* devoted to the subject of the origin and prevention of major wars, Robert Jervis notes that two kinds of misperception are most commonly linked to the outbreak of war: Countries underestimate their opponents' capability or willingness to fight and thus enter into armed conflict more readily, assuming victory will be easy; or countries overestimate their opponents' hostility and thus overlook or ignore opportunities for bridging differences.

World War II offers the clearest examples of the former, says Mr. Jervis. On one hand, the British tended to underestimate the strength of the German economy, thinking it was stretched taut at the beginning of the war. On the other hand, Hitler underestimated Britain's determination. In 1939, he doubted whether Britain would fight, and in 1940, he expected the country to make peace.

The "World War II model"—underestimating an adversary's strength and determination—partly underlies deterrence theory, Mr. Jervis says. Deterrence theory argues that, as long as a country maintains a show of strength and the enemy knows that the strength and the will are there, such underestimation—and therefore war—is much less likely.

—ELLEN K. COUGHLIN

Proven methods for dealing with emotions are at the center of the **Three T's Emotional Expression Method**—tears, talk, and toil.

Encouraging someone to express his or her emotions through *tears* (or laughter, which is an emotional parallel to tears—have you ever laughed so hard you cried or encountered someone at a funeral getting a laughing jag?) is a constructive interpersonal device.[13]

Encouraging someone to express his or her emotions through *talk*—with you acting as a good listener, not an advice giver, counselor, or consoler—is another effective tool.

Toil, in the form of physical effort, is yet another way of allowing yourself or another person to get rid of pent-up emotion. A game of tennis, volleyball, a long walk, or jogging are all constructive emotional releases. When combined with talking or relieving the pressure through laughter or crying, you have a formula for healthy emotional release.

Ironically, not only do many people discourage the experiencing of "bad" feelings, they try to protect against the backlash of feeling "too good." When someone is happy, do you say, "Better watch out, something is likely to go wrong," or "Don't go overboard," or "Keep it in perspective"?

Discouraging others from feeling as they do tells more about the discourager than the person experiencing the particular emotion. It often indicates the discourager is uncomfortable, unsure what to do, how to react.

There are cultural implications regarding the three T's. For some cultures, all three would be discouraged rather than encouraged. For example, in many Asian cultures, showing tears is a sign of weakness, and cultures that stress meditation and contemplation perceive that talking only clouds true feelings. They often believe that speaking is a negative act.[14] And, for those who follow the Hindu tradition, activity keeps a person from discovering reality and truth. Hence, they urge their members to avoid engaging in activity, but, instead, to sit quietly and meditate.

EXPRESSING YOUR EMOTIONS

Some general principles for expressing your emotions provide the basis for the following six guidelines:

1. *Identify the feeling—name it:* "I feel angry," "I feel wonderful," "I feel embarrassed," "I feel frustrated." In order to accomplish this, identify what's happening in your body, what your face looks like, what your voice sounds like, what shape your feeling has, and what you get out of having the feeling.

2. *Admit what you are feeling.* Assess your emotion and its intensity, and then admit to yourself that you are angry, hurt, anxious, happy, or euphoric.

3. *Express your feelings in similes and analogies:* "I feel stepped on," "I feel like a cloud floating on air," "I feel squelched," "I feel like a raging river." Expressing your feeling this way helps you understand it and communicate it in ways that may help others understand how you feel.

4. *Repeat what kind of action the feelings urge you to do:* "I feel like hugging you," "I'd like to slap your face," "I feel like getting up and walking out." This helps to acknowledge the consequences of your emotions, which are a key to understanding the emotion's intensity.

5. *Put one or more of the "three t's"—tears, talk, toil—into action.* Cry or laugh, find someone to talk to, do something that will get rid of the emotion if you don't want to deal with it at this moment in time.

6. *Recognize your diminished capacity for clear thinking—try to avoid making important decisions while feeling emotionally stressed.* A stressful period is no time to fire someone, end a relationship, or deal with a delicate issue. Your rational judgment is impaired whether you are feeling an emotional high or low.

Skill Development 3.4 will help you identify and express your emotions.

SKILL DEVELOPMENT 3.4

EXPRESSING YOUR FEELINGS

Three days before the start of the new semester, your apartment mate and best friend for the past three years has told you of plans to leave to move in with someone else. You don't know who the other person is and what their relationship is. This means that you will be left alone to pay the total apartment rent or to find a new roommate quickly. All the people you know have already made their living arrangements for the new semester.

1. Identify what you are feeling:

2. Express what you are feeling:

3. Express your feelings in similes, analogies, or figures of speech:

4. Repeat what kind of action the feelings urge you to do:

5. Since you recognize your diminished capacity for clear thinking, what types of actions should you not immediately take?:

COMMUNICATION COMPETENCY CHECKUP

The goal of this Communication Competency Checkup is to guide you in putting your skills and knowledge about the self and others to use, and to help you summarize the material in this chapter.

1. Analyze the cartoon from the perspective of someone who finds it funny by applying the notions of selective perception, selective organization, and selective interpretation. Then do the same analysis for someone who does not find the cartoon funny. How could the same cartoon get two different reactions?

2. What could the man do to increase his perceptual accuracy?

3. Make a snap judgment regarding the man and the boys in the cartoon. What clues lead you to these judgments?

4. What traits could you apply to the man and the boys? What was the basis for this assignment?

5. Explain how the statement made by the man can be applied to the concept of self-fulfilling prophecy.

6. How does the principle of open-mindedness apply to your reaction to the man in the cartoon?

BIZARRO By DAN PIRARO

The "Bizarro" cartoon by Dan Piraro is reproduced by permission of *Chronicle Features*, San Francisco, CA.

7. Make an empathic statement to the man based on his comment.

8. How could the boys express their emotions to the man?

9. If the boys have trouble expressing their feelings, what could you do to help them?

10. Assume the man is not a North American. What are the cross-cultural implications of his statement?

NOTES

1. For a discussion of implicit personality theory, see Seymour Rosenberg and Andrea Sedlak, "Structural Representations of Implicit Personality Theory," in *Advances in Experimental Social Psychology,* vol. 6, Leonard Berkowitz (Ed.) (New York: Academic Press, 1972), pp. 235–39.

2. The original research that considered how traits interact to form total impressions and the importance of central traits in the process was conducted by Solomon Asch, in "Forming Impressions of Personality," *Journal of Abnormal and Social Psychology* 41(1946): 258–90.

3. T. N. Bradbury and F. D. Finchman, "Attributions in Marriage: Review and Critique," *Psychological Bulletin* 107 (1990): 3–33.

4. Valerie Manusov, "An Application of Attribution Principles to Nonverbal Behavior in Romantic Dyads," *Communication Monographs* 57 (1990): 104–18.

5. Robert Rosenthal, *Experimenter Effects in Behavioral Research* (New York: Irvington, 1976).

6. Benjamin J. Broome, "Building Shared Meaning: Implications of a Relational Approach for Teaching Intercultural Communication," *Communication Education* 40 (1991): 235–39.

7. T. Adler, "Even Babies Empathize, Scientists Find, but Why?," *APA [American Psychological Association] Monitor* 21 (June 1990): 9.

8. The notion that empathy is a *skill* that can be taught and developed is only one perspective of empathy. For a detailed discussion of empathy, particularly in intercultural encounters, see Benjamin J. Broome, "Building Shared Meaning: Implications of a Relational Approach to Empathy for Teaching Intercultural Communication."

9. S. M. Pfeiffer and P. P. Wong, "Multidimensional Jealousy," *Journal of Social and Personal Relationships* 6 (1989): 181–96.

10. Carol A. Sterns and Peter Sterns, *Anger: The Struggle for Emotional Control in America's History* (Chicago: University of Chicago Press, 1986).

11. Larry A. Samovar, Richard E. Porter, and Nemi C. Jain, *Understanding Intercultural Communication* (Belmont, CA: Wadsworth Publishing Company, 1981), p. 171.

12. A summary of the emotion–ailment link is available in Jane E. Brody, "Emotions Found to Influence Nearly Every Human Ailment," *New York Times* (May 24, 1983): C1, C8.

13. "Why Men Don't Cry," *Science Digest* 92 (June 1984): 24.

14. George A. Borden, *Cultural Orientation: An Approach to Understanding Intercultural Communication* (Englewood Cliffs, NJ: Prentice-Hall, 1991), p. 35.

FOR FURTHER INVESTIGATION

Albrecht, K. *Stress and the Manager.* Englewood Cliffs, NJ: Prentice-Hall, 1979.

Asch, Solomon E. "Forming Impressions of Personality." *Journal of Abnormal and Social Psychology* 41 (1946): 258–90.

Bersheid, Ellen. "Emotion and Interpersonal Communication." In *Interpersonal Processes: New Directions in Communication Research,* Michael E. Roloff and Gerald R. Miller, eds. Beverly Hills, CA: Sage, 1987.

Broome, Benjamin J. "Building Shared Meaning: Implications of a Relational Approach for Teaching Intercultural Communication," *Communication Education* 40 (1991): 235–39.

Delia, Jesse G. "Change of Meaning Processes in Impression Formation." *Communication Monographs* 43 (1976): 142–57.

Ellis, Albert, and Robert Harper. *A New Guide to Rational Living.* North Hollywood, CA: Wilshire Books, 1977.

Kelley, Harold H. "The Process of Causal Attribution." *American Psychologist* 28 (1973): 107–28.

Pines, Ayala M., Eliot Aronson, and Ditsa Kafry. *Burnout.* New York: Free Press, 1981.

Sillars, Alan J. "Attributions and Communication in Roommate Conflicts." *Communication Monographs* 47 (1980): 180–200.

Snyder, Mark E. "Self-Fulfilling Social Stereotypes." *Psychology Today* 16 (July 1982): 60–68.

Sylvester, Sandra. *Living with Stress.* Kansas City, MO: National Catholic Reporter Publishing, 1985.

Wells, Theodora. *Keeping Your Cool Under Fire.* New York: McGraw-Hill, 1980.

CHAPTER 4

Nonverbal Communication

COMMUNICATION COMPETENCIES

This chapter examines nonverbal communication. Specifically, the objective of this chapter is for you to learn to:

- Describe the nonverbal behaviors important in assessing strangers.
- Recognize the stereotypes associated with physical appearance, including body type, physical attraction, clothing, and jewelry.
- Interpret and control facial movements and eye behavior.
- Assess the effects of physical and psychological contexts on the interpretation of nonverbal cues.
- Describe the importance and uses of touch.
- Use vocal cues to express emotions and regulate social interactions.
- Describe the types and uses of body movements, and learn to mirror body movements of others to increase their perceptions of similarity to you.
- Recognize nonverbal messages that indicate deception.
- Use nonverbal behaviors to affect how you feel.

KEY WORDS

The key words in this chapter are:

nonverbal communication	paralanguage
ectomorphic	vocalics
mesomorphic	nonfluencies
endomorphic	silence
turn taking	stutter-start
physical context	body movements
psychological context	emblems
territoriality	illustrators
territorial invasion	regulators
territorial violation	affect displays
territorial contamination	adapters
personal space	gestures
intimate distance	postures
personal distance	congruency
social distance	clusters
public distance	

Think back to the last time you walked into a room filled with strangers. How did you decide to whom you would speak? What clues did you look for and how did you interpret them? Before a word was spoken, a great deal of information was exchanged. Which actions and characteristics did you focus upon?

Rank order the following items with respect to their importance for you in determining whether you approach someone or not. Rank the most important characteristic **1** and the least important **9.**

_____ Body shape, whether she or he is fat or thin, muscular or flabby, short or tall.

_____ The clothing the person is wearing, whether it is clean or dirty, in or out of style.

_____ Jewelry, such as a wedding band or college ring.

_____ Eye contact, such as whether the other person looks at you and how long eye contact is sustained.

_____ Facial expression, whether the person is smiling, frowning, or looking bored or puzzled.

_____ Distance, the space between you and the other person, such as how close you can get before the other person backs up or breaks eye contact.

_____ Voice, such as whether the person's voice sounds nasal, throaty, or resonant.

_____ Body movements, such as the person's gestures and stance.

_____ Touch, such as whether the person touches you, or how she or he responds to your touch.

These clues suggest the many forms of nonverbal communication. **Nonverbal communication** includes those actions and attributes of people _other than words_ and aspects of the environment that convey meaning.

How you use nonverbal symbols, and the meaning you give those symbols, have been learned as part of your cultural experiences. Based on cultural tradition, people from Thailand do not touch in public, while in Russia and France men and women embrace in public.[1] The Japanese feel uncomfortable when their partner uses too much eye contact. The Arabs, on the other hand, engage in a great deal of direct gazing.[2] These examples, and thousands of others, demonstrate that we have _learned_ our use of much of our nonverbal communication.

FUNCTIONS AND CHARACTERISTICS OF NONVERBAL COMMUNICATION

FUNCTIONS OF NONVERBAL COMMUNICATION[3]

You base first impressions almost entirely upon nonverbal information, such as body shape, clothing, jewelry, eye contact, and facial expressions. The importance of nonverbal behavior, however, does not stop with first impressions. Rather, nonverbal communication is always an important part of the total communication process, which includes both verbal and nonverbal messages.

Sometimes nonverbal communication works in conjunction with verbal communication. You may use nonverbal communication to *complement* your words, as when you point south while saying, "They went down the hall that way." A complementing nonverbal message conveys the same meaning as the verbal message and, therefore, completes or supplements the verbal message. Holding your hands about eight inches apart as you say, "The fish was about eight inches long," would be a complementary verbal and nonverbal message.

You also may use nonverbal communication to *accent* your words, as when you pause before making a point in order to emphasize the thought's importance or pound your fist on the table during an argument to add impact to your words.

Nonverbal messages also may be used to *regulate* both verbal and nonverbal communication. For example, signaling a waiter to come to your table is an attempt to regulate his actions. Similarly, if the waiter responds by holding up his pointing finger, he is regulating your waiting time. Also, putting your pointing finger to your lips to signal a noisy child to be quiet is an attempt to regulate her volume.

Besides working in conjunction with spoken words, nonverbal communication can *substitute* for spoken words. For example, nodding your head yes instead of verbally stating agreement or holding up two fingers in response to the question "How many scoops of ice cream do you want?" are both examples of substituting nonverbal for verbal messages.

Nonverbal communication can *contradict* your spoken words. For example, glancing away from your friend as you hesitantly say, "I like that sweater," provides the listener with a contradictory message: positive words and evasive eye movement.

CHARACTERISTICS OF NONVERBAL COMMUNICATION

In addition to complementing, accenting, regulating, substituting, and contradicting verbal behavior, nonverbal communication has several identifiable characteristics that highlight its usefulness.

Emotions and feelings are more accurately and easily communicated nonverbally than with words. Whereas words are best for conveying ideas, nonverbal communication is best for conveying feelings and emotions. For example, explaining the definition of communication to a friend may be quite easy with words. Consider the problems you would have if you were limited to nonverbal messages. Similarly, the emotions felt at a funeral of a loved one are communicated more concisely and effectively by crying than are attempts to put those emotions into words. This difference between verbal and nonverbal messages may stem from the fact that verbal messages need to be learned and most nonverbal messages are innate.

When considering how people express emotions and feelings nonverbally, you need to keep in mind the role of societal influence. For example, in many cultures outward signs of emotion are accepted as natural. People from the Middle East are expressive and animated. For the Japanese external signs are often considered a mark of rudeness and an invasion of privacy.[4] Think a moment about what the implications are of the English expression, "Keep a stiff upper lip."

Nonverbal behaviors are not easily controlled consciously. Because nonverbal behaviors are for the most part performed without thought, they are relatively free of distortion or deception, especially in comparison to the more easily controlled verbal messages. It is difficult to bring nonverbal behaviors under conscious control. For example, this is true of a blushing face, stammering, or jaw clenching when a person is nervous or embarrassed. The behavior is automatic, an unconscious reflex.

When verbal and nonverbal communication conflict, the nonverbal messages are characteristically the more accurate reflection of feelings. Because nonverbal behaviors are often below our level of awareness, and are not easily controlled, most individuals regard them as the more accurate indicator of a speaker's feelings. Because of the ease with which verbal communication can be manipulated, the presumption is that if someone is intent on covering up or lying, he or she can select the appropriate coverup words more easily than faking nonverbal behaviors. No amount of verbal protesting and stating, "I'm not embarrassed," can cover up looking away from the other person and shifting your weight from foot to foot.

Nonverbal communication is more effective than verbal communication for expressing messages in a less confrontive manner. If you think something you might say is likely to elicit rebuke or embarrassment you run less risk of these reactions if you avoid using words. For example, if you want to know whether your date likes you, and are unwilling to ask directly, gently taking hold of the other person's hand and gauging the response (pulling away or allowing the hand-holding) may provide you with the information you need. The nonverbal behavior, in this instance, is less invasive—both you and the other person can opt out of the situation without a confrontation.

Nonverbal behaviors indicate how you should interpret the verbal messages you receive. Consider the difference between someone saying, "I think I understand your directions to Mario's Restaurant," in a confident tone of voice and someone saying the same thing in a hesitant tone, accompanied by head-scratching and raised eyebrows. In the first situation you might feel pleased with your direction-giving; in the second one you probably should consider how to restate your message to make it clearer. The key to interpreting the content of verbal messages is the interpretation of their nonverbal underpinnings. In other words, do the cues such as tone of voice, facial expression, and stance, complement or contradict the words?

There are cultures that rely heavily on verbal language and others that put more stock in nonverbal messages. Anthropological studies show that cultures can be classified and placed on a continuum according to the emphasis they put on words versus nonverbal messages as tools for carrying meaning.[5] At one end of the continuum are the German, French, Scandinavian, North American, and English societies which believe that verbal messages are extremely important. The Japanese, Chinese, and Koreans, on the other hand, believe that the meaning is found in the physical context. People know what is being felt without having to talk. The Korean language actually contains the word "nunchi," which literally means "being able to communicate through the eyes."[6]

The functions and characteristics of nonverbal communication are displayed in a variety of ways. People communicate nonverbally through physical appearance, face and eyes, context of communication, touch, voice, and body movements.

PHYSICAL APPEARANCE

Your physical appearance includes everything that's visible to others, from the top of your head to the bottom of your feet, including your body shape and the clothing you wear. How much importance do you place on your own physical appearance? How much importance do you place on the physical appearance of others?

BODY SHAPE

If you are like most people, one of the first pieces of data you use to size up another person is body shape, whether the person is **ectomorphic**—thin and frail-looking; **mesomorphic**—muscular and well-proportioned; or **endomorphic**—fat and round.[7] Each body shape encourages different stereotypes: "Thin people are so *tense*"; "Fat people are very *lazy*"; and "Muscular people are so *confident.*" Knowledge Checkup 4.1 will provide you with the opportunity to assess how well you feel the stereotyped personality characteristics predict your own body type.

KNOWLEDGE CHECKUP 4.1

BODY SHAPE SELF-ANALYSIS[8]

Complete the sentences by choosing from the words provided.

1. Most of the time I feel _____, _____, and _____.

calm	relaxed	complacent	anxious	cheerful
confident	energetic	impetuous	shy	thoughtful

2. When I work or study, I seem to be _____, _____, and _____.

efficient	enthusiastic	reflective	meticulous	precise
serious	competitive	sluggish	cooperative	placid

3. Socially, I seem to be _____, _____, and _____.

outgoing	considerate	talkative	cool	tolerant
warm	sympathetic	awkward	assertive	kind

4. For letters A through C, underline the one word of the three selections that most clearly describes the way you are:

A. withdrawn   sociable   active

B. dependent   dominant   detached

C. enterprising   affable   tense

Do you see yourself as an ectomorph, a mesomorph, or an endomorph? Here are the personality traits stereotypically associated with each body type. Circle the ones you selected.

Ectomorph	Mesomorph	Endomorph
anxious	assertive	calm
awkward	cheerful	complacent
considerate	competitive	cooperative
cool	confident	kind
meticulous	efficient	placid
precise	energetic	relaxed
reflective	enthusiastic	sluggish
serious	impetuous	sympathetic
shy	outgoing	tolerant
thoughtful	talkative	warm
withdrawn	active	sociable
detached	dominant	dependent
tense	enterprising	affable

Did you circle a majority of adjectives in any one list? How do the adjectives you circled suit your body type? Like any stereotype, the generalization may not apply to a particular example—in this case, you.

The consequences of being tall or short are well documented. Tall people have a distinct advantage over their shorter peers. For example, men 6 feet 2 inches and taller receive starting salaries about 12 percent higher than those under 6 feet; short actors often get the "short end of the stick" by being cast as buffoons, arch villains, or "small tough guys." Many jobs, from flight attendant to police officer, have traditionally required a certain minimum height.

Problems even extend to health. Researchers have found that men 5 feet 7 inches and shorter in North America may be 70 percent more prone to heart attacks than men 6 feet and taller. This may be due to the stress felt by shorter men in a society where being tall is valued.

BODY IMAGE

How you *feel* about your appearance has greater influence on your interaction with other people than how you actually look. If you are uncomfortable with your appearance, you are likely to avoid interaction with others or at least assume that you deserve negative reactions. Teenagers suffering from acne may confine themselves to the house on weekends or assume that dating is out of the question, just as adults who put on a few pounds may skip a party, wanting to lose weight before appearing "in public." Knowledge Checkup 4.2 will help you learn how you perceive your own appearance.

KNOWLEDGE CHECKUP 4.2

APPEARANCE SATISFACTION

How satisfied are you with the way your body looks?

If you are extremely satisfied, mark **7.**

If you are satisfied, mark **6.**

If you are slightly satisfied, mark **5.**

If you are neither satisfied nor unsatisfied, mark **4.**

If you are slightly unsatisfied, mark **3.**

If you are unsatisfied, mark **2.**

If you are extremely unsatisfied, mark **1.**

_____ hair	_____ eyes	_____ nose
_____ mouth	_____ back	_____ chest/breasts
_____ stomach	_____ hips	_____ sex organs
_____ teeth	_____ chin	_____ cheeks

_____ lips	_____ muscle tone	_____ shoulders
_____ arms	_____ elbows	_____ forearms
_____ wrists	_____ hands	_____ fingers
_____ thighs	_____ knees	_____ calves
_____ buttocks	_____ height	_____ weight

_____ overall facial attractiveness

_____ overall body appearance

How does your feeling about a particular body part affect how you behave, including what clothes you select to wear? What is the relationship between how you feel about your own body parts and the body parts you find attractive in others?

Generally, the more physically attractive you perceive yourself to be, the more positive your self-concept is. This explains why physically attractive people tend to be more independent and more resistant to pressure to conform than are less attractive people. Attractive females, for example, are generally more confident, and attractive males are generally more assertive and less critical than their less attractive peers.[9]

Also, if others perceive you as physically attractive, they are more likely to evaluate you positively. Attractive people are thought to be kinder, stronger, sexier, more interesting, poised, modest, sociable, and outgoing than unattractive people. Physically attractive people are given more help, receive more awards, and are perceived as more credible (and are therefore more persuasive) than their physically unimposing counterparts.[10]

On the other hand, attractiveness may not always be an asset. Research reveals that a businesswoman perceived as attractive may suffer unpleasant and unfair consequences from the perception. Because of her appearance, others may consider her unintelligent, self-centered, and fickle. Others may assume that she gained her power through her appearance rather than her ability. Being perceived as attractive also may make a businesswoman the target of coworkers' jealousy, gossip, and sexual harassment.[11] Some individuals, both men and women, are subject to PQS—*prom queen syndrome*. Individuals who are extremely attractive are often perceived to be unreachable, untouchable, and undatable by others because it is believed that the overly attractive person is "all dated up," "wouldn't go out with an ordinary someone like me," or "is so attractive that I'd be uncomfortable with everyone paying attention to them." In reality, those with PQS are often undated and lonely because of those misconceptions.

It is easy to imagine the influence of culture on attractiveness and the judgment of beauty. In North America, for example, we tend to value the appearance of slender women, but in many other cultures the definition of what is attractive calls forth a series of different images.[12] In Eastern Europe, for example, women who are heavyset often are deemed more attractive than lean and thin females. In fact, being skinny is associated with physical weakness.

CLOTHING AND OTHER ARTIFACTS

Most of us assume that people wear clothes for protection and modesty, but that isn't always the case. For example, according to the observations of Darwin, the natives of Tierra del Fuego never wore clothes in spite of severe weather conditions; and modesty in some cultures—particularly those that are not westernized—is not related to wearing, or not wearing, clothes.[13]

If protection and modesty are not the primary reasons for wearing clothes, there must be other important reasons why people wrap themselves in cloth, leaves, bark, or skins. These reasons include communication. Others take note of what you wear—just as you observe what they wear—to assess your current economic and social levels; your social, economic, and educational background; your level of success, social position, and sophistication; your value system, and your trustworthiness and moral character. For example, a person who is wearing a uniform identified with a particular charity (e.g., the Salvation Army) can collect more donations than someone without the uniform. This is probably so because the person is perceived as being trustworthy.[14]

Although it may not be fair—or wise—to judge people by their clothes and accessories, these judgments are a fact of life.

There is some evidence that your clothing preferences do, indeed, say something about your personality. Knowledge Checkup 4.3 provides you with the opportunity to assess your clothing preferences.

KNOWLEDGE CHECKUP 4.3

CLOTHING QUESTIONNAIRE[15]

Indicate the extent to which each of the following statements accurately or inaccurately reflects your clothing preferences. Use this scale:

   5 = very accurate

   4 = fairly accurate

   3 = neither accurate nor inaccurate

   2 = fairly inaccurate

   1 = very inaccurate

1. I like close-fitting clothes.

2. I usually dress according to the weather rather than for fashion.

3. When buying clothes, I am more interested in practicality than attractiveness.

4. I see nothing wrong with wearing clothes that reveal a lot of skin.

5. The people whom I know always notice what I wear.

6. It is very important to be in style.

7. There is nothing like a new article of clothing to improve my morale.

8. I buy clothes for comfort rather than appearance.

9. If I had more money I would spend it on clothes.

10. I like clothes with bold designs.

Add responses to 5, 6, 7, 9 ("clothing consciousness") _____

Add responses to 1, 4, 10 ("exhibitionism") _____

Add responses to 2, 3, 8 ("practicality") _____

CLOTHING CONSCIOUSNESS:

Males—(scores from 16 to 20): generally conforming, believe that people can be easily manipulated and that clothing is a means to manipulate others; deliberate; guarded; deferential to authority, custom, and tradition; (4–8): generally aggressive, independent, and outgoing; dependable.

Females—(16–20): generally inhibited, loyal, anxious, kind, sympathetic, and conforming; (4–8): forceful, dominant, clear-thinking; independent.

EXHIBITIONISM:

Males—(12–15): aggressive, confident, unsympathetic; moody, unaffectionate, outgoing, and often impulsive; (3–6): nondisclosive; believe others are easily manipulated.

Females—(12–15): radical, high moral self-concept, generally detached in relationships; (3–6): timid, sincere, accepting of others, patient.

PRACTICALITY:

Males—(12–15): generally inhibited; not leadership oriented; cautious, low motivation for establishing friendships; (3–6): success-oriented, forceful, mature, serious.

Females—(12–15): clever, enthusiastic, guarded, confident, outgoing, not oriented toward leadership positions; (3–6): self-centered and independent.

What you wear matters more in some situations than in others and matters more to some people than to others. Your friends probably allow you more latitude in style and color than does your employer, and your choice of clothing for an informal party may be less consequential than your choice of clothing for a business luncheon.

What you wear in a business setting is important; what you wear to a job interview is crucial. An interviewer's first impression of you at an interview comes from what you wear.[16] If that initial impression is unfavorable, your opportunities may be immediately closed off. Dressing too differently from your interviewer may result in a poor evaluation, as may dressing in anything but conservative garb, which, for men, includes dark suits and solid white shirts with power ties of red or yellow; and, for women, a dark or medium-toned skirted suit, white or pastel blouses, closed-toed pumps, and modest jewelry. Whether or not you are comfortable with your appearance, you can control—at least to some extent—how the interviewer perceives you by choosing your clothes carefully.

Societies also vary in their use of clothing as a form of communication. The Germans and Japanese value formality and encourage men to wear business suits and women to be groomed in dresses. In the Arab world, robes and veils are part of the attire and since modesty is also valued, women cover most of their bodies to reflect that value.

Unlike clothes, which may merely suggest characteristics, certain accessories communicate specific messages. Wedding bands, college rings, and religious symbols all convey particular and relatively unambiguous messages. Jewelry also may be used to communicate social status and economic level, such as a Timex versus a Rolex watch. A college student with a bookbag slung over the shoulder conveys an image of normality, while that same person toting a leather briefcase most probably would be seen as different, atypical.

You react to what you wear just as others do: You may find that putting on your jogging outfit gets you ready, both physically and mentally, to run; putting on your favorite dress-up outfit helps get you in the mood for a sophisticated party. Your mood affects what you choose to wear, and what you choose to wear in turn affects your mood. Dress how you *want* to feel and, sure enough, you just might feel that way!

Find out your own style of dressing by completing Knowledge Checkup 4.4. Are you communicating what you want to with what you wear?

KNOWLEDGE CHECKUP 4.4

YOU ARE WHAT YOU WEAR

Assess your clothing habits by responding to the following seven questions. Circle the word that best describes you:

1. My clothes generally tend to be:
   a. bright-colored
   b. solids
   c. loose
   d. muted colors
   e. prints
   f. tight-fitting

2. The style of clothes I generally select is:
  a. trendy
  b. high style
  c. traditional
  d. comfortable

3. When I dress in the morning, I:
  a. put on whatever I grab
  b. plan my wardrobe carefully

4. I alter the clothing I wear according to the type of social situation I am going to be attending. Yes_____ No_____

5. I mainly wear one outfit or style of clothes (e.g., sweats or jeans most of the time). Yes_____ No_____

6. I normally wear jewelry to convey specific messages (e.g., engagement ring, religious medals), rather than purely for decoration.
Yes_____ No_____

Review your answers. Write two statements that describe how your clothing and artifacts probably impress others:

_____

FACE AND EYES

Except in circumstances when you're trying to deceive someone, you communicate more about your emotions with your face—especially your eyes—than with any other part of your body.[17] You also depend more on other people's facial cues than on any other nonverbal behavior to ensure successful interactions. Facial cues may communicate five dimensions of meaning:

    1. The extent to which communication is experienced as pleasant or unpleasant, good or bad (Does this person find interacting with you a pleasant experience?)
    2. The level of interest in the communication (Is this person interested in you or what you're saying?)
    3. The intensity of involvement in the communication (Is this person involved in your interaction?)
    4. The spontaneity of the response (Is this person controlling his or her facial expressions or behaving naturally?)
    5. The extent to which communication is understood (Does this person understand what you're saying?)

    Looking at others' faces has early roots. Early in life you learned to search out the faces that meant warmth and security; soon after your birth, you recognized and were attracted to the faces of those who cared for you. Later you learned that this part of the body communicated even more useful information. Now you spend a lot of time looking at faces because faces identify people more than any other aspect of the body. Even young children, when they're asked to draw themselves, typically produce a large head with eyes, nose, mouth, and ears attached to a small body with little more than stick arms and legs. The head is what is important: It is what you speak to and what speaks back to you.

Because the face can be so revealing, you have probably learned a number of adaptive techniques or ways of manipulating your facial expressions to communicate a desired message. You can *qualify* your expressions by adding a second facial expression to change the impact of the first one. For example, after looking angry and yelling "I can't stand it any longer!" you might look sad or confused in order to communicate, "I'm hurt and sad, as well as angry, and I want to talk about this."

You can *modulate* your facial expressions to communicate feelings stronger or weaker than the ones you're actually experiencing. For instance, to make the statement "I'm really upset with you" more intense, you could squint your eyes to show that you really mean what you're saying.

You can *falsify* your facial expression by showing an emotion when none is felt (you may have no particular feeling about your friend's new coat, but to maintain your friendship you look excited); evidencing little or no facial expression when you experience a particular feeling (you may feel angry about your friend's lateness, but keep your expression neutral to avoid an argument); or covering a true emotion by displaying a false one (you may express pleasant surprise when your parents unexpectedly show up to cover your real feeling of dismay).

People throughout the world use facial expressions to display emotion and express intimacy. People have learned, usually unconsciously, specific cultural norms regarding the amount and variety of facial expressions to reveal. For example, in many Mediterranean societies, signs of grief, sadness, and even joy are, by our standards, greatly exaggerated. Crying at a North American funeral may be typical of that culture, just as grief wailing may be typical of a Mediterranean country. The Chinese and Japanese, on the other hand, do not readily show signs of emotion. Even the expression "save face" is a reminder that the face can reveal and/or conceal feelings.[18] Besides national cultural differences in the use of the face, there are, in our own society, gender differences. When compared to men, women use more expression, smile more, and are apt to return a smile more when someone smiles at them.[19]

Although overall facial expressions are interesting, the eyes hold perhaps the greatest fascination. Everyday expressions confirm the emphasis on sense of sight: You don't say "I feel/smell/hear/taste what you mean," or "I'll feel/smell/hear/taste you later," but "I *see* what you mean" and "I'll *see* you later." Old friends, of course, are a "sight for sore *eyes.*" The evil eye, a glance that can inflict harm, must, of course, always be guarded against! Looks can kill—at least figuratively!

Perhaps the most reliable measure of interest is pupil size. Findings from studies focused on pupil size confirm that pupils enlarge when you're interested in a subject and contract when you're uninterested. By noticing others' pupil size—certainly not something they can easily control—you can often gauge their level of interest.[20]

You also use your eyes to regulate the flow of conversation. Typically, a speaker looks away from the other person, glances back now and then to check for feedback, and then establishes full eye contact to indicate when it's time for **turn taking,** indicating that it's the other person's turn to talk.

Facial cues can communicate the emotion you're experiencing, but your eyes indicate its intensity. For example, your face may communicate interest and happiness, but the intensity of that expression comes from your eyes.

Culture modifies how much eye contact people engage in and who is the recipient of the contact. In most Western societies our communication partner is expected to look us in the eye, with a 3- to 10-second duration being most comfortable. Think about how you react when someone looks away while you're talking to him or her, or doesn't look at you at all. Arabs look directly in the eyes for long periods of time, while Asian cultures teach their children to focus their eyes on their superior's Adam's apple or tie knot.[21] People raised in rural Mexico will lower their eyes as a sign of respect. Native Americans are yet another group that feels uncomfortable with unbroken eye behavior. So strong is that orientation that Navajos tell a folktale about a "terrible monster called He-Who-Kills-With-His-Eyes." The legend teaches the Navajo child that "a stare is literally an evil eye and implies a sexual and aggressive assault."[22]

Communication between black and white Americans is yet another area where cultural differences show. When speaking, blacks tend to employ much more continuous eye contact than do whites. However, the opposite is true when blacks are listeners.[23]

In our society, gender also affects eye contact usage. Women tend to look more at their communication partner than men do, look at one another more, hold eye contact longer, and appear to value eye contact more than men.[24]

Paying attention to the facial expressions and eye behavior of others can increase your sensitivity to the communicative function of the face. Skill Development 4.1 should help you increase your skill.

SKILL DEVELOPMENT 4.1

INCREASING YOUR SKILL AT INTERPRETING FACIAL EXPRESSIONS

1. What emotions are being communicated by facial expressions in each picture?

2. What levels of interest and involvement are communicated facially by each person in each picture?

3. In each picture, what intensity of emotion is revealed by the facial expressions?

4. What nonverbal information did you use to answer questions 1 through 3?

5. Did anything besides facial expressions help you answer the questions?

6. Can you locate any cultural information in these pictures?

CONTEXT OF INTERACTION

Because meaning is contextual, nonverbal behaviors have little meaning outside the situation in which they occur. For example, nonverbal behaviors that communicate sorrow—slumped body, hand pressed against forehead, downward glance, and sighs—can also communicate overwhelming happiness. You are more likely to interpret the behavior as sorrow if the physical context is a hospital and more likely to interpret it as happiness if the context is a game show and the person's score indicates she just won $10,000. Some context is needed to interpret the behavior correctly.

Two contexts are important: physical and psychological. The **physical context** is composed of objects and their arrangement in the environment. It may include architecture, furniture, room color, and temperature. The **psychological context** includes a person's thoughts and feelings toward aspects of the physical context. For example, a student may feel that the seat she occupies in a classroom is "her space."

PHYSICAL CONTEXT

Close your eyes—now, describe the exact setting where you are now sitting (e.g., if you are in a room—what are the colors of the walls and floor, what is the texture of the ceiling, what is the color of the clothing of the person closest to you; if you are outside—what color is the nearest building to you, what is the nearest physical object, what color is it?). If you are typical, you probably couldn't accurately describe the details of the things and people around you. Most of us are unaware of the environment, yet it has a great effect on us.

A physical context may be analyzed along a number of dimensions. For example, a physical context may be assessed according to its degree of *formality* (most business offices usually are formal), *comfort* (family rooms are normally warm and comfortable), *privacy* (bathrooms are supposed to be private), *familiarity*—how usual or unusual it is (modern office buildings are traditionally strikingly unusual), and *closeness*—how close it encourages you to be with others (family rooms are supposed to be arranged so that people can feel close).

To create a desired effect (formal or informal, comfortable or uncomfortable, private or public, familiar or unfamiliar, close or distant), you may adjust a room's color, temperature, and furnishings. For example, red is perceived as hot and full of vitality, whereas pale blue and green are cool and calm. Brown is unhappy, purple can be depressed or dignified and gives off the most energy of the shades of a color wheel. White is neutral, which may account for its widespread use in a variety of shades and settings.[25]

Color and temperature interact. For example, a white room seems cooler than a red room when the temperature is identical. If your goal is comfort, keep in mind that perceptions of attractiveness decrease as temperature and humidity increase. Cool temperatures are better for working and warm ones for relaxing, although *cooler* and *warmer* are relative terms.

Next to raising or lowering the thermostat, the easiest way to change the environment is with furnishings and lighting. Rooms with indirect lighting, comfortable furniture, and carpeting and drapes are perceived as attractive, and increase feelings of happiness and energy; rooms with direct lighting, few sound-absorbing furnishings, and uncomfortable furniture cause occupants to feel tired and bored.[26]

Players in Black May Be Spoilsports

By Marilyn Elias
USA Today

Sports teams wearing black uniforms draw more penalties and may play more aggressively just because they wear black a Cornell University study shows.

"It seems that black carries an aggressive message, both for those looking at the color and those wearing it," said psychologist Thomas Gilovich. He and colleague Mark Frank found:

- Penalty records of NFL and NHL teams from 1970–86 show teams in black are penalized significantly more. Also, teams that switched to black uniforms developed markedly worse penalty records.
- When amateur referees and fans view videos of non-pro teams, they judged black-uniformed teams as

more aggressive than teams wearing white and making the same moves.

- When offered a choice of competitive games to play, men given black uniforms select more aggressive games.

"The excessive penalties amassed by black-uniformed teams stem from their own aggressiveness and harsher treatment by the referees," Gilovich says.

"Not so fast," argues Los Angeles sports psychologist Saul Miller, consultant to more than a dozen (multicolored) teams in the NFL, NHL, NBA and both baseball leagues.

"The referee action suggests a perceived difference in terms of aggressive behavior. We don't know that the players really act more aggressive."

Chairs, for example, can greatly influence others' responses to a room: High-backed chairs covered with expensive cloth are more formal than low-backed ones in corduroy; soft, cushioned chairs are generally more comfortable than ones without cushions; several chairs indicate that a room is not private, that it is open to more than one person at a time; and grouping chairs close together, facing each other, encourages interaction.

Skill Development 4.2 will help you compare two environments. Specifically, you will describe those aspects of each setting on which you base your perceptions of formality, comfort, and so on, and discuss the differences in the use to which each setting is suited.

SKILL DEVELOPMENT 4.2

ASSESSING TWO ENVIRONMENTS

Analyze the following two settings with regard to their formality, comfort, privacy, familiarity, and closeness: a fast-food restaurant and a library reading room (or area) with which you are familiar. Indicate which part of the environment—color, temperature, furnishings, or lighting—you used as the basis for your assessment. For example, if you describe the fast-food restaurant as uncomfortable, specify why. Is it the uncushioned chairs, the bright lighting, the lack of soundproofing, the colors?

	Fast-Food Restaurant	Library Reading Room
1. Formality:		
2. Comfort:		
3. Privacy:		
4. Familiarity:		
5. Closeness:		

Given your analyses of each environment, compare them with respect to the purpose of each. Does each environment communicate its purpose clearly? What changes would you make to each environment to make its purpose clearer and to increase the probability that it will be used "appropriately"?

PSYCHOLOGICAL CONTEXT

Psychological context may be divided into territoriality and personal space.

Territoriality is a feeling of ownership toward some fixed area. It may not be strictly logical to lay claim to certain areas of your environment, but you do it

HERMAN®

"He's not very sociable."

anyway. You *feel* that the room you sleep in is *your* room and the roses you tend are *your* roses. Because you feel that pieces of your environment belong to you, you feel protective toward them, personally insulted if someone makes an unkind remark about them, and sad or irate if something happens to them.

To lay claim to a piece of territory requires that you mark it with your ownership. You may leave an "occupied" sign on an airplane seat, drape your coat over the back of a chair in a restaurant, or spread your books on a desk in the library to indicate that the place is yours and that you will be returning to claim it—*so others keep off!* You may also formally mark your territory with your name or some representative symbol, such as a club's emblem or your initials. "This room belongs to _____ " is a popular sign for those who want to emphasize that trespassing will not be tolerated.

You also may mark the boundaries of your territory. For example, a fence may separate your property from your neighbor's; painted lines separate your parking space from the next ones; and a closed door clearly separates your room from the rest of the residence.

In a business setting, territory shows status. For example, the boss usually has a private office and the privilege of entering subordinates' work areas without knocking first. Similarly, the people with the most power and prestige most often get the largest and best-located offices.

Knowing your own and others' feelings about fixed areas of the environment —who lays claim to what—can help ensure smooth interactions. What territory do you claim and defend in public environments, such as your school, classroom, or workplace. What private environments such as your home or car, do you claim and defend?

Even the manner in which we organize our seating is swayed by culture. North Americans, when in group situations, usually talk to the people seated or standing in front of them instead of those beside them. Thus, seating arrangements are often face-to-face. The Chinese, on the other hand, often experience uneasiness when they are face-to-face and hence prefer side-by-side arrangements.

People from cultures that value conversation (such as the French, Mexicans, and Italians) often feel uncomfortable in North American homes when they go to sit down and find that the furniture is pointed toward the television set and not other people.

Problems arise if there is **territorial invasion** (someone tries to take over your territory and throw you out, as often happens when siblings fight over space in a shared bedroom); **territorial violation** (when someone uses your territory without your permission); or **territorial contamination** (when someone makes your territory "impure," such as when an overnight guest sleeps in your bed).

Your reaction to an invasion, violation, or contamination can take several forms. You may decide to withdraw—a fight may not be worth your effort, or it may be all too clear you would lose. You might mark your boundaries more clearly, in hopes that the other person would withdraw and others recognize the territory as yours. Or, you might choose to fight—if the territory is important to you, you might respond to an intruder with threats and, in the end, violence.

How you respond depends on *who* enters and uses your territory (a friend is less threatening than a stranger), *why* she or he enters or uses it (for instance, a "mistake" is less important than a "planned attack"), *what* territory is entered or used (you may care more about your bedroom than your seat in class), and *how* it is entered or used (for example, an invasion is more threatening than a violation). Knowledge Checkup 4.5 will help you recognize your definition of and responses to someone using your territory.

KNOWLEDGE CHECKUP 4.5

ANALYSIS OF TERRITORIAL DEFENSE

You and a friend are eating pizza at a local restaurant when, all of a sudden, she or he reaches across the table, picks up your slice of pizza, and takes a bite.

1. Is this an invasion, violation, or contamination?

2. How would you react? Would you withdraw, remark your boundary, or fight?

3. Explain your responses to 1 and 2 with reference to the who, why, what, and how of the situation.

Unlike territory, which remains fixed, your personal space goes where you go. **Personal space** is an invisible bubble of space around you—a body buffer zone. It is larger in front than in the back, and varies in overall size depending on where you are and with whom you're interacting. Your personal space probably contracts when you're with friends—you let friends get closer to you than strangers before you begin to feel uncomfortable.

In your next conversation with an acquaintance, try an experiment. As you talk, slowly, subtly, move closer to the other person and watch what happens. Most likely, the person will back away, countering each of your movements forward with a movement backward without consciously being aware of what is happening.

As the experiment demonstrates, you hardly notice your personal space until someone violates it. Crowded elevators and theaters are uncomfortable partly because your space requirements are not met. When doctors and nurses touch you, they breach your space bubble and may leave you feeling exposed and vulnerable. Such violations may trigger a variety of nonverbal defensive reactions: You may shift your body away from the intruder, cut off eye contact to gain distance (a popular technique in elevators), or show nervous reactions, such as tightening your jaw, making downward or sideways glances, stroking your face, or tapping your fingers.

You protect your personal space because it serves several important purposes. Most importantly, it buffers you from others who might pose a threat. It also gives you room to breathe, move about, and act as you choose, free from crowding. It satisfies your psychological need to be separate from other people. Finally, given that distance communicates intimacy—closer is more intimate than farther—personal space allows you to regulate your intimacy.

Personal space requirements vary with age, gender, and personality, among other things. For example, as people get older their space requirements tend to increase; interacting females generally require less space than interacting males; and introverts and people with low self-esteem usually require more than the average space between themselves and others.

Our response to any physical context not only reflects individual perceptions but deep-rooted cultural characteristics. For example, people from societies that emphasize privacy and the individual over the group (such as in England, North America, and Australia) demand more space than do those from communal cultures (such as in Latin America and the Mediterranean).[27] You can well imagine the potential for discomfort when a member of a culture that requires a great deal of space is confronted with members of a society that stands or sits close together.

Perhaps the most important overall determinant of spatial distancing is the relationship between the participants, including both the activity in which they are engaged (for instance, some sports require close contact) and their feelings for each other.

Personal space can be broken down into four zones:

1. **Intimate distance,** from touching to 18 inches, is reserved for intimate activities, including passing secrets, making love, and having confidential conversations.

2. **Personal distance,** from 18 inches to 4 feet, is used for discussing personal subjects.

3. **Social distance,** from 4 to 12 feet, requires a louder voice than intimate or personal distance and is thus used for more impersonal conversations, such as business transactions.

4. **Public distance,** 12 feet and beyond, is usually used for small group meetings and for hailing people. Distances farther than 25 feet limit communication to shouts and broad nonverbal gestures.[28]

Increasing your sensitivity to your own and others' personal space requirements as well as knowing the norms and expectations for using the space in your environment increase your ability to communicate skillfully. Recognizing how people use space and react to violations of space should help you to respond quickly and appropriately when problems of perceived inappropriate behavior arise.

Love: Arm's Length Away

By Kim Painter
USA Today

Unhappy husbands literally keep their distance from their wives, a new study shows.

Researchers at Brigham Young University in Provo, Utah, asked 108 married couples to walk toward each other and to stop at a comfortable chatting distance.

The couples also took tests to assess happiness.

Results: When the husband was satisfied, couples stood 11.4 inches . . . apart; unhappy men stood 14.8 inches from spouses.

Wives' feelings didn't seem to affect distance.

The reason, says Provo researcher and therapist C. Russell Crane: "Husbands control the distance. If they're unhappy, they don't let their wives get as close. . . . They're protecting their space, keeping their emotional distance."

Findings from related studies:

▪ Adults in Greece and the Soviet Union give children more affectionate touches than USA adults.

▪ Those who touch a lot are less wary, more satisfied with their bodies and looks than those who don't.

Knowledge Checkup 4.6 provides you with the opportunity to apply the information on personal space in an analysis of a common setting.

PERSONAL SPACE ANALYSIS

The following activity requires you to, first, observe how people use space in a particular setting and, second, to note reactions to violations of spatial expectations.

1. Select either a department store or your college bookstore. Observe the interaction distances that seem usual between clerks and customers, and between customers in a checkout line.

2. What are the average distances between the people you observed?

3. How do people respond when one person comes too close to another or when one person touches another? How do people react to these violations of their space? How could they avoid violating each other's personal space?

4. Think back to a foreign film or a film that contains interaction between North Americans and people of another culture, as well as people from the same culture. Or try to observe people who are from a culture other than your own. Describe their use of spatial distance during conversations.

TOUCH

Touch is the most relevant sense at the beginning of your life—it is how you first orient yourself to the world. By the time you learn to speak, however, sight and sound predominate and touch becomes less important. Nonetheless, the need for touch remains, although opportunities for touching and being touched decrease. The elderly may be the most touch-deprived members of Western society and, therefore, the loneliest.

Your skin is a sensitive receiver of communication: Pats, pinches, strokes, slaps, punches, shakes, and kisses all convey meaning. Touches may signal a particular relationship. Some are *professional-functional* ones, as when a doctor performs a physical examination. *Social touches,* such as handshakes, fulfill norms associated with greeting, acknowledgment, and parting. *Friendship touches,* such as shoulder-patting and hugging, convey the message that "We're friends," "I like you," or "I appreciate you." *Intimate touches,* such as kisses, can communicate love, while sexually arousing touches can increase the physical and emotional pleasures of lovemaking.

The messages that touch communicates depend on how, where, and by whom you're touched.[29] Slight variations in touch can communicate great differences of emotion. A person may touch your shoulder lightly to say "Listen to me," apply slight pressure to say "Seriously consider what I say," or squeeze forcefully to communicate "You'd better do as I tell you!"

The same type of touch on different parts of your body communicates different messages. A slap across your face may evoke fear or anger, while a slap on the back may cause happiness. Similarly, lightly stroking your hand may communicate concern, while the same touch on your head may communicate affection.

In addition to receiving messages, your skin also sends them. Polygraphs, for example, operate on the assumption that changes in your internal state are reflected in changes in your skin, and that these changes can be measured to determine whether you're lying.

The importance of touch for children has been well documented.[30] In general, the more caring (not abusive) touching an infant receives, the higher the probability that he or she will become a well-adjusted child, adolescent, and adult. Lack of touching during infancy has been implicated in health problems (such as allergies and eczema), academic problems (such as learning disabilities and low scores on intelligence tests), and decreased capacity for mature, sensitive tactile communication in adulthood (such as problems with showing affection by hugging). Feelings of trust and liking for others, on the other hand, have been linked to positive early tactile experiences. Parents who avoid touching their children, or touch them only on certain "neutral" body parts, often communicate that some parts are "better" than others, some are "more important" than others, and some parts are "bad." The action may result in an adult being alienated from her or his body.

Most people, except those who have been abused, raped, or brought up in low- or no-touch families, associate touching with positive messages. Handshakes, probably the most common type of touch, connect people and help begin interactions on a note of shared status. Many cultures worldwide use touch to express affectionate greetings; for example, Americans kiss, Eskimos rub noses, and Burmese press their mouths and noses to another's cheek and inhale deeply.[31]

Regardless of many of the positive messages associated with touch, many individuals avoid touching and being touched. Knowledge Checkup 4.7 provides you with an opportunity to assess your touch avoidance.

KNOWLEDGE CHECKUP 4.7

ASSESSING YOUR TOUCH AVOIDANCE[32]

Read the following statements concerning touch and indicate the extent to which you agree with each statement.

If you strongly agree, mark the statement **1.**

If you agree, mark the statement **2.**

If you are undecided, mark the statement **3.**

If you disagree, mark the statement **4.**

If you strongly disagree, mark the statement **5.**

_____ **1.** I often put my arms around friends of the same sex.

_____ **2.** I like it when members of the opposite sex touch me.

_____ **3.** I like to touch friends of the same sex as I am.

_____ **4.** I find it enjoyable when my companion and I embrace.

_____ **5.** Touching a friend of the same sex does not make me uncomfortable.

_____ **6.** Intimate touching with members of the opposite sex is pleasurable.

SCORING:

Add your responses to items 1, 3 and 5. This is your same-sex touch avoidance score. _____

Add your responses to items 2, 4 and 6. This is your opposite-sex touch avoidance score. _____

Add the two sums together to obtain your touch avoidance score. _____

Same-sex and opposite-sex scores of 14 and 15, and a total score of 27 and above, indicate a high propensity to avoid touch. Same-sex and opposite-sex scores of 3 and 4, and a total score of 9 and below, indicate a high propensity to touch. Same-sex and opposite-sex scores between 5 and 13, and a total score between 10 and 26, indicate neither a high nor low propensity to touch.

Touch avoidance relates to several other communication behaviors. For example, the more a person avoids touch, the more likely it is that she or he will avoid verbal communication. In addition, touch avoidance is related to self-disclosure: People who disclose little also tend to touch little, and those who are willing to self-disclose also tend to touch a great deal. Also, men and women differ in their touch avoidance—men are more likely to be same-sex touch avoiders, while women are more likely to be opposite-sex touch avoiders.[33]

Avoiding touching is often associated with a negative attitude. We communicate dislike, disrespect, and refusal by not touching. Because we normally close a deal with a handshake, refusing to shake hands equates with refusing to complete a deal.

USES OF TOUCH

Touch is most useful for communicating intimacy, involvement, warmth, reassurance, and comfort. Touch has proven therapeutic power that nurses and other health care professionals employ to help their patients emotionally as well as physically. The therapeutic benefits of touch may derive in part from the effect that touch has on a recipient's willingness to talk. Because touch implies reassurance and caring, it encourages self-disclosure.

Touch helps to persuade people. For example, a study showed that a request for the return of a quarter left in a phone booth met with greater success when the new booth occupant was touched on the arm than when not touched. Similarly, requests to sign a petition received almost twice as many positive reactions when touch was involved—even when it is "accidental," as when fingers touched when a piece of paper was passed.[34]

Touch is also useful for communicating power relationships. Generally, the person who initiates the touch is perceived as more powerful, more dominant, and of higher status than the one who is touched. In interviews, for example, while an initial greeting handshake is mutual and customary, the handshake that ends the interview is the prerogative of the interviewer, the person with more power in the situation. The interviewer may or may not offer to shake hands, but the lower status interviewee may be perceived as "pushy" if he or she makes the offer.

EXPECTATIONS FOR TOUCH

Cultural background largely determines expectations about touch. For example, the least touchable cultures include Canadians of Anglo descent, Germans, Chinese, and the English. There even appear to be distinctions in these groups, with the upper class being the least touched and touching. The most touch-oriented cultures include Latin Americans, Russians, and Netsilik Eskimos. North American culture falls between the extremes. Although North American culture may be classified as nontouch, it is less extremely so than the Chinese or German cultures.[35]

Regardless of cultural background, touch is expected in some situations and not in others. For example, you are more likely to touch others when giving them information or advice, asking a favor, expressing worry, or sharing an intimacy. You also are prone to touch a communication partner if you or the person is excited. You are less likely to touch another person when you are asking for information or advice, giving an order, agreeing to do something, or participating in a casual conversation. Casual, friendly settings, such as parties, are apt to encourage more touch than are formal work settings; private settings are more conducive to touching than public places.

Whether your expectations about touch are violated depends on several considerations: Where is the touch? How long does it last? How much pressure or intensity is used? What is your relationship with the person touching you? What are the circumstances—for example, are other people watching?

Reactions to being touched in the wrong place or by someone you don't like can range from politely ignoring the gesture to starting a fight.[36] If someone offers a limp handshake, you probably won't respond visibly, although you may form a particular impression of the person; if someone punches you in the arm, however, you are likely to respond with a punch of your own, a verbal attack, or a smile.

Being sensitive to responses to touch can help improve your relationships. You can use touch to increase your persuasiveness, appear powerful, and communicate warmth, intimacy, and comfort—but only if your touch doesn't violate the other person's expectations.

Knowledge Checkup 4.8 calls for an analysis of your responses to being touched by acquaintances and close friends, as well as the touch you engage in with family and friends. Think carefully as you do the Checkup—people tend to overestimate how often they are touched.[37]

KNOWLEDGE CHECKUP 4.8

ANALYZING YOUR TOUCH BEHAVIOR[38]

1. How often do people in your immediate family touch each other?

very frequently   frequently   seldom   never

2. Pick two people with whom you interact regularly, a close friend and an acquaintance from work or school.

   a. How often do you and your close friend touch each other?

      very frequently   frequently   seldom   never

   b. How often do you and the acquaintance touch each other?

      very frequently   frequently   seldom   never

   c. What parts of the body are you most likely to touch when you touch your mother? Father? Same-sex friend? Opposite-sex friend? (Place a check mark on those parts of the body in Diagram 4.1.)

   d. On what parts of your body are each of these people likely to touch? (Place an X on those parts of the body in Diagram 4.1.)

3. The numbers on Figure 4.2 identify various parts of the human body. (Note that the figure and identifying numbers and letters on the left represent the front of the body, and the figure on the right represents the back of the body.) Using those numbers, answer the following questions. Use as many numbers as are applicable.

   a. What part of the body (front and back) are you most likely to touch:

      your closest same-sex friend _____

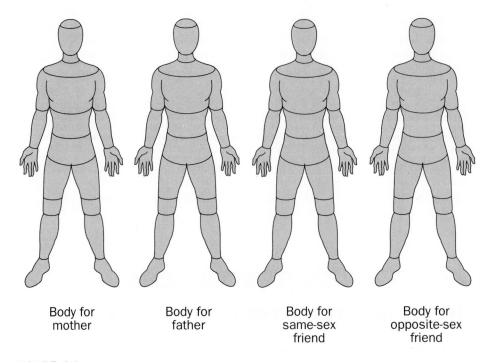

Body for
mother

Body for
father

Body for
same-sex
friend

Body for
opposite-sex
friend

FIGURE 4.1

From Joseph A. DeVito, *The Nonverbal Communication Workbook*, Copyright © 1989 by Waveland Press, Inc.,
Prospect Heights, Illinois. Reprinted with permission from the publisher.

your closest opposite-sex friend _____

a stranger of the same sex _____

a stranger of the opposite sex _____

b. What parts of your body are each of these people likely to touch?

your closest same-sex friend _____

your closest opposite-sex friend _____

c. What parts of the body do you feel should *never* be touched by another person other than yourself? _____

4. Write a two- or three-sentence statement about your touch behavior based on
your responses to questions 1–3.

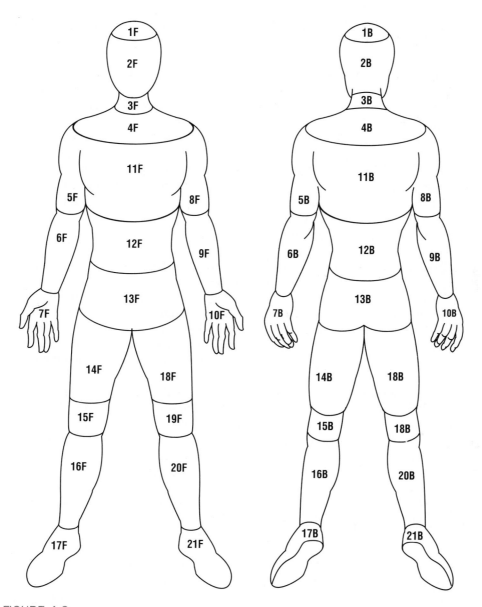

FIGURE 4.2

VOICE

Independent of the words you speak, your voice communicates a great deal about you. All by itself, your voice offers strong clues to your age, emotional state, education, home region, and status. **Paralanguage** or **vocalics**—variations in loudness (loud or soft), pitch (low or high), rate (fast or slow), quality (the particular resonance of your voice—for example, flat, breathy, nasal, throaty, or tense), articulation (slurred or clipped), duration (time it takes to emit a particular sound), and pronunciation (what syllables are stressed)—give your vocal cues their unique character.

For example, when we express anger, we speak loudly, quickly, and with wide variations in pitch (although mostly high). When we communicate affection, we speak softly, slowly, in a low pitch, and with vibrancy. The vocal expression of joy is similar to the one for anger except that the voice is not quite so blaring. Sadness is expressed much as affection is except that pauses in the expression of sadness are irregular.

People's stereotyped reactions to different voice qualities indicate the importance of controlling your vocal behavior. For example, breathiness in males is associated with youth and an artistic temperament, and in females with prettiness, petiteness, and shallowness. Wide variations in pitch for both males and females is associated with being dynamic and extroverted, and an increased rate for both connotes animation and extroversion.[39] Of course, stereotyping by voice has its pitfalls: basing your mental picture of a blind date on a telephone conversation may lead to surprises when the two of you meet face to face.

Two other aspects of vocal behavior that affect perceptions are nonfluencies and silence. **Nonfluencies**—vocal behaviors that interrupt or disturb the flow of messages, such as "uh," "you know," and "stuff like that," unnecessary repetition of words, stuttering, incomplete sentences, and corrections—are usually associated with low credibility and lack of confidence. Keep nonfluencies to a minimum, or even eliminate them, to appear more competent.

Culture affects vocalics. For example, Arabs tend to speak loudly and with a great deal of gusto and enthusiasm. To them, loudness designates strength and sincerity, while speaking softly implies frailty. The Thai and Philippine societies, on the other hand, use so little volume it almost sounds as if they are whispering. For them, a soft voice reflects good manners.[40] When interacting with North Americans, people from the "quiet" societies often believe the loud volume means the American is angry, rude, or upset.

There are even paralanguage gender differences in our society. Men tend to speak louder, speak in lower pitch, and are less expressive, except in emotional extremes such as anger or withdrawal, than women.[41]

The American philosopher David Thoreau—*"In human intercourse the tragedy begins, not when there is misunderstanding about words, but when silence is not understood."*

Silence—not speaking or making nonverbal vocal sounds, such as "um," when you are interacting with another person—is more varied in meaning. Silence may communicate anger, attentive listening, grief, depression, respect, awe, or the message "leave me alone." Silence often strains a relationship. For example, you may be uncomfortable with long silences and strive to keep them short.

Skill Development 4.3 will help you practice using your voice to express emotions effectively.

EXPRESSING YOUR EMOTIONS EFFECTIVELY

Read the following sentence in different ways to communicate five emotions: anger, bewilderment, fear, happiness, and sadness. If a tape recorder is available, record your attempts.

There is no other answer. You've asked me that question a thousand times, and my answer is always yes.

1. Were you able to create five different meanings as you read the sentences? Which emotion was hardest to communicate? Which was easiest?

2. What variations in paralanguage did you make in each case to create the desired effect?

Vocal cues play a significant role in communication aside from conveying emotions: They *regulate* and *structure* interactions, much as eye contact does. For example, if someone tries to interrupt when you are speaking, you can maintain your role as speaker in two ways. You can either fill your pauses with meaningless vocalizations such as "uh, well" or "but, uh," or you can alter your pitch and volume to signal "Don't interrupt me now!" The other person will rarely take over the speaking role if you use either of these techniques.

If, on the other hand, you want to stop speaking and let the other person begin, you can employ several techniques. You can use ascending pitch and volume, as if you were asking a question, and pause afterward. Alternatively, you can use falling pitch and volume and stretch out your final words. Of course, just keeping quiet is a sure signal that you're through, but your signal may go unnoticed for an embarrassingly long time if the other person is only half-listening. Listeners give priority to cues other than silence because silence can be ambiguous: It can mean a variety of things including "I'm through" or "I'm thinking."

Sometimes when you are listening you want to say something, but the speaker is unwilling to relinquish control. After trying the usual nonverbal methods for communicating your desire to speak—raising your hand, moving forward and gesturing, raising your eyebrows, opening your mouth—you may be forced to use a vocal stutter-start. A **stutter-start** is the pronunciation of a word with a repetition of the first sound, such as "m-m-m-m-maybe," or the use of an elongated nonfluency, such as "uhhhhhh." You may, of course, interrupt directly and begin speaking, but then the other person is likely to interrupt you in return and to maintain the speaking role.

Another way to regulate a conversation is to encourage the other person to *continue* speaking. In addition to the nonvocal behaviors that communicate "I'm listening, please go on," such as head nods, sustained eye contact, and appropriate facial expressions, you may use encouraging vocalizations such as "uh-huh," "hmmmmm," "ahhhhh," and "ohhhhh."

USING VOCAL CUES TO REGULATE CONVERSATIONS

Read the dialogue and note the vocal cues used to regulate the conversation in these ways: (1) to maintain the role as speaker, (2) to get the other person to speak, (3) to take over as speaker, and (4) to get the other person to continue speaking. The conversation, between a student in a communication class and the instructor, takes place after class in the instructor's office.

STUDENT: I . . . well . . . had a little trouble understanding today's lecture on the voice. I . . .

INSTRUCTOR: What specifically did you have trouble with?

STUDENT: *(Leans forward and points at the instructor as if to speak.)*

INSTRUCTOR: *(Raising the pitch of his voice and speaking quickly.)* If you would ask questions in class, maybe you wouldn't have this problem.

STUDENT: B-b-b-but, I have trouble asking questions in front of the other students.

INSTRUCTOR: I used to have the same problem when I was a student. *(Leans back in chair, looks at student for several moments.)*

STUDENT: Gee, I would never have guessed that.

INSTRUCTOR: *(Lowering his pitch and speaking slowly.)* As I was saying, I used to have that problem until I realized that if I didn't understand something, and didn't ask, I would never get the information I needed.

STUDENT: I think I see what you mean.

INSTRUCTOR: Hmmmmmm.

STUDENT: But sometimes it's just hard for me.

INSTRUCTOR: *(Pitch rising as he speaks.)* But, you have to do it. *(Pause.)*

STUDENT: I guess you're right.

INSTRUCTOR: Uh-huh.

STUDENT: *(Pitch lowering, rate decreasing, and final two words stretched.)* I'm just going to have to do it.

INSTRUCTOR: If you give it a try, I'll work with you on it.

Your analysis of the dialogue may have revealed:

STUDENT: I . . . well . . . (**vocalized pause used to maintain his role as speaker**) had a little trouble understanding today's lecture on the voice. I . . .

INSTRUCTOR: (**interrupts to take over as speaker**) What specifically did you have trouble with?

STUDENT: *(Leans forward and points at the instructor as if to speak in an* **attempt to take over as speaker***.)*

INSTRUCTOR: *(Raising the pitch of his voice and speaking quickly.)* (**rising intonation to maintain his role as speaker**) If you would ask questions in class, maybe you wouldn't have this problem.

STUDENT: B-b-b-but (**stutter-start to take over as speaker**), I have trouble asking questions in front of the other students.

INSTRUCTOR: I used to have the same problem when I was a student. *(Leans back in chair, looks at student for several moments.)* (**uses silence to get other person to speak**)

STUDENT: Gee, I would never have guessed that. (**relinquishes speaker role**)

INSTRUCTOR: *(Lowering his pitch as he speaks slowly.)* (**falling intonation to maintain his role as speaker**) As I was saying, I used to have that problem until I realized that if I didn't understand something, and didn't ask, I would never get the information I needed.

STUDENT: I think I see what you mean. (**relinquishes role**)

INSTRUCTOR: Hmmmmmm. (**vocal encourager to get other person to continue speaking**)

STUDENT: But sometimes it's just hard for me. (**relinquishes role**)

INSTRUCTOR: *(Pitch rising as he speaks.)* (**rising intonation to maintain his role as speaker**) But, you have to do it. *(Pause.)* (**silence to get the other person to speak**)

STUDENT: I guess you're right. (**relinquishes role**)

INSTRUCTOR: Uh-huh. (**vocal encourager to get other person to continue speaking**)

STUDENT: *(Pitch lowering, rate decreasing, and final two words stretched.)* **(falling intonation and stretching final words to get the other person to speak)** I'm just going to have to do it.

INSTRUCTOR: If you give it a try, I'll work with you on it. **(Finality)**

Many interpersonal problems may arise because of the different uses societies make of silence. Those imbued with Eastern traditions do not feel uncomfortable with the absence of noise and talk, and are not compelled to fill every moment with words like most North and South Americans feel compelled to do. There are numerous Asian sayings that reflect this cultural bias such as, "Out of the mouth comes evil" and "A flower does not speak."[42]

BODY MOVEMENTS

Body movements are motions such as gestures; head, arm, finger, leg, and toe movements; and changes in posture or trunk position. Some self-help books on nonverbal behavior suggest easy and clear interpretations of body movements. Merely by focusing on body movement, the writers contend, you can successfully understand and manipulate other people. Wrong! Although body movements provide a wealth of information, interpreting that information is not that simple. For example, according to some authors of popular books, crossing your arms on your chest, crossing your legs, and pointing your index finger are all supposed to signal defensiveness. Rubbing your eyes, touching your nose, and glancing sideways are all supposed to communicate suspicion. Rubbing your hand through your hair or taking short breaths is supposed to indicate frustration.

Although any of these examples *may* be true at particular times and in particular circumstances, they are overgeneralizations. It's hard to interpret body movements without paying careful attention to the specific situation, including your relationship with the other person and the cultural context in which you're interacting. The same gestures may mean different things in different cultures. For example, what North Americans recognize as the "A-OK" gesture (making a circle with one's thumb and index finger), meaning "everything is fine," is a vulgar sexual threat in the Mediterranean area and a sign for money in Japan and Korea.[43]

Not only the gesture, but the size, intensity, and frequency of our actions can take on communicative importance. Jews, Italians, Middle Easterners, and South Americans are noted as being animated when they interact. On the other hand, many North Americans, Northern Europeans, and Asians equate vigorous action with a lack of manners and restraint.

TYPES OF BODY MOVEMENTS

Body movements fall into five categories: emblems, illustrators, regulators, affect displays, and adapters.[44]

Emblems are movements that have direct verbal translations in a given culture, such as the thumbs-up gesture, the "come here" signal, and the waves that mean hello and good-bye in North America.

Illustrators—which, like emblems, are used intentionally—add to or support what is said, as when you hold your hands different distances from the ground to indicate the relative heights of two friends, or point to your car when talking about it.

Regulators, also used intentionally, influence who talks, when, and for how long. For example, moving close when greeting another person may initiate a conversation; moving backwards toward a door may signal the end of an interaction.

Less awareness and intentionality characterize affect displays and adapters. **Affect displays**, body movements that express emotions, are most commonly associated with the face—in fact, fear, anger, surprise, disgust, sadness, and happiness are six facial expressions that can be identified across all cultures. Other body movements also may express emotions. Foot-tapping, fidgeting, covering your mouth while speaking, and shifting your weight from foot to foot may indicate nervousness or boredom, depending on the context.

Adapters, which are seldom intentional, are body movements performed by habit. Your use of adapters often satisfy some physical need: You itch, so you

scratch; your hair needs grooming, so you pat it; or something is caught between two teeth, so you use a fingernail to dislodge it. Interestingly, these adaptive behaviors satisfy not only your physical needs, but also your psychological needs. For example, stroking your chin calms you down, perhaps by distracting you from a stressful situation. Therefore, adapters may indicate psychological states. For instance, scratching when there is no itch often indicates nervousness, and stroking your hair may be your way of calming yourself.

USES OF BODY MOVEMENTS

Body movements also may be categorized according to their uses. One use of body movements is to communicate a degree of pleasure or displeasure, liking or disliking. For example, you may lean forward, face the other person directly, and assume a position that mirrors the other person's position to communicate liking. You may communicate dislike by reversing these behaviors, as well as by crossing your arms in front of you and tensing your body. In general, movement toward something with an open body position (such as open arms) indicates liking, and movement away from something with a closed body position (such as crossed arms) indicates disliking.

Body movements also may communicate a level of interest or arousal. Closing your eyes momentarily may mean simply that you're tired, or it may mean there is a lack of interest.

Finally, body movements may be used to communicate feelings of dominance or submissiveness, powerfulness or powerlessness. Dynamic gestures and erect posture indicate feelings of power or dominance, whereas slow, hesitant gestures and a slumped posture indicate feelings of powerlessness or submission.

Gestures are movements made by a particular part of your body, such as your hands. Your hands provide some of your most expressive gestures: You wave hello and good-bye, suggest that someone is mixed-up by moving your index finger in a circle while pointing to the side of your head, and suggest that you're thinking by rubbing your chin. Gestures also can communicate emotions. For instance, you drum your fingers to indicate impatience or boredom, or hit a table to emphasize that you really are angry.

Consider the gestures that accompany these sentences:

Me? What did I do?

Take it! I give up!

You can trust me on this one.

Whew! That was a tough job!

Clearly, gestures can communicate very specific pieces of information.

Postures, movements that involve your whole body, are useful for communicating general attitudes. For example, the angle at which you turn your body toward another person may reveal your desire to include or exclude her or him. Turning your back on someone is typically interpreted as rejection, whereas standing face-to-face is seen as acceptance. Whether or not you mirror another's movements may indicate your liking or perceptions of similarity. Films of group therapy sessions, when slowed down and viewed carefully, often reveal an intricate dance: People mirror the behaviors of individuals they like or want to encourage to like them, and exhibit opposite body movements to individuals they dislike or reject.

The changes in posture are subtle and rarely consciously performed. You may notice similar behavior in the way a seated group of people cross their legs. One change can set off a chain reaction—those who have positive feelings for the person who moved shift to a similar position, while the others quickly move to an opposite position.

Skill Development 4.4 provides you with the opportunity to compare what happens when you mirror and don't mirror another person's body movements.

SKILL DEVELOPMENT 4.4

INCREASING PERCEPTIONS OF SIMILARITY

If you want to examine perceptual differences based on body movements, interact with a person who does not know you well (and thus does not know your usual body movements) and mirror that person's movements. Use similar gestures, posture, eye contact, facial expressions, touch patterns, and vocal characteristics. Note any reactions. Does it seem that this person likes you and feels comfortable with you?

Repeat the activity with another person, only this time use dissimilar gestures, posture, and so on. Note the reactions.

How do the reactions differ in the two situations? What does this imply about how mirroring behavior can be used as a persuasive device?

NONVERBAL CLUES TO DECEPTION

Commonplace lies, like giving your professor a false explanation of why you missed class, may not make you feel anxious. The consequences of being found out are not serious, and the length of time you must maintain the deception is relatively short. By the same token, you will find it more difficult to catch someone else in a minor deception than in a complex fabrication.

Many nonverbal clues may suggest that someone is telling a lie. But because the clues are deviations from **congruency**—a person's typical nonverbal behavior—you need to know the typical behavior in order to assess the situation. Some people, however, are more sensitive to nonverbal clues to deception. For example, young people and women are more accurate at detecting lying than men.[45]

Some of the more reliable clues to deception, in North American society, are vocal: Liars tend to hesitate and pause, speak rapidly, and "sound nervous" (change paralanguage frequently). Several gestures, including shrugging, a lot of self-touching, and frequent hand movement, may also tip you off. Also, liars tend to look away from you much of the time, avoid your gaze after brief eye contact, and experience pupil dilation. In contrast, facial gestures are too easily controlled to offer many useful clues to lying. Unfortunately, if you suspect someone is trying to deceive you, your suspicion increases the probability that you will perceive the person as dishonest; however, your suspicion does not increase your accuracy of deception detection.[46]

If everyday lies are distinguished by low anxiety, uncommon lies are distinguished by the opposite. When stakes are high and lying must continue for a long time, liars often become extremely nervous. They tend to make very little eye contact, shift their eyes, move their feet a lot, fidget, shift their weight, twitch, and make nervous facial gestures, such as licking their lips. Careful observation will reveal that the pupils of their eyes dilate at the moment they tell their lie.

You cannot, however, identify a liar on the basis of a single behavior; only when telltale behaviors appear in **clusters**—in groups—should you begin to suspect that a speaker is not telling the truth. Because most of the behaviors that indicate lying can also indicate nervousness, be careful not to assume that nervousness *equals* lying. (How calm would you be if you were falsely accused of cheating on a final exam? As you explained your side of the story, would you behave as if you were nervous?)

FEELING = BEHAVIOR = FEELING

This discussion has emphasized how nonverbal behavior can reveal your emotions. That is, how you feel determines how you behave. The opposite is also true: How you behave often determines how you feel. *Acting* as if you're happy is a good way to become happy, just as *acting* as if you're tired is a sure path to feeling that way. You may have already learned that you can stop feeling tired and reenergize yourself when you're studying by sitting up straight, taking a deep breath, putting your shoulders back, and looking intently at the work you're doing and thinking you are not tired. You *act* alert, so you *feel* alert!

SKILL DEVELOPMENT 4.5

GOING FROM BEHAVING TO FEELING

Think of something that you believe very, very strongly. Orally describe your belief as you watch yourself in a mirror or picture yourself giving the presentation. Or, if you cannot do this, think back to the last time you were involved in an emotionally charged discussion.

Note how you behave: how you stand, how your face looks, how you gesture, what your voice sounds like, and what touch behaviors you exhibit.

Then select a topic about which you are neutral and, using all the behaviors you observed when you were intensely interested, talk or visualize about the neutral topic. After a few moments, note how you feel. Does the neutral topic now excite you?

People often wonder how they can energize themselves. Select any emotion and *act* as if you're experiencing it. Just *behave* the way you want to feel and you are likely not only to act, but feel it!

Nonverbal communication, which helps you transmit feelings and emotions, regulates your interaction with others, and works together with verbal communication to create messages, has many aspects. Physical appearance, facial gestures, eye behavior, touch, vocal characteristics, body movement, and the physical and psychological contexts within which each of these takes place all contribute to nonverbal communication. Although nonverbal communication often operates at a low level of awareness, understanding its role in communication and developing skills in this area of human interaction are crucial to your development as a competent communicator.

COMMUNICATION COMPETENCY CHECKUP

The goal of this communication competency checkup is to guide you in putting your skills and knowledge about nonverbal communication to use and to help you summarize the material in this chapter. After reading the cartoon, answer the questions on the following page.

"You are about to experience something rare in your life, Stan—rejection."

Drawing by Koren; © 1988 The New Yorker Magazine, Inc.

1. Based on the nonverbal information in the cartoon, what do you know about each of the three human characters—for example, their age, gender, emotional state, social status, and how they're interacting?

2. Is the woman's nonverbal behavior complementing or contradicting her verbal behavior? Explain your answer with reference to the touch behavior, the eye contact, and the posture you observe, as well as the tone of voice you presume the woman is using.

3. Describe the situation with respect to the couple's spatial relationship.

4. How could the woman communicate her verbal message using only nonverbal behaviors?

5. Pretend you are the woman and read the cartoon caption as if you were calm. Read it as if you were worried about what might happen if the man got angry. Read it as if you had noticed the man with the dog listening in. Read it as if this were the third time you needed to repeat the statement to the man with whom you are holding hands. How do the readings differ in loudness, pitch, rate, voice quality, articulation, and pronunciation?

6. If the man had been smiling before the woman spoke, what might have been his reason for smiling? If he was smiling after she spoke, how would you interpret this?

NOTES

1. Larry A. Samovar and Richard E. Porter, *Communication Between Cultures* (Belmont, CA: Wadsworth Publishing Company, 1991), p. 202.

2. Ibid., pp. 198–99.

3. Mark L. Knapp and Judith A. Hall, *Nonverbal Communication in Human Interaction,* 3d ed. (Fort Worth, TX: Holt, Rinehart and Winston, 1992), pp. 17–25.

4. Dale G. Leathers, *Successful Nonverbal Communication: Principles and Applications,* 2d ed. (New York: Macmillan, 1992), pp. 355–56.

5. Edward T. Hall, *Beyond Culture* (New York: Anchor Books, 1976).

6. Samovar and Porter, *Communication Between Cultures,* p. 199.

7. For a discussion on body types see: W. H. Sheldon, *The Varieties of Temperament* (New York: Hafner Publishing Co., 1942); *Atlas of Man: A Guide for Somatotyping the Adult Male at All Ages* (New York: Harper and Brothers, 1954); *The Varieties of the Human Physique* (New York: Harper and Brothers, 1940).

8. This material was adapted from an instrument developed by Cortes and Gatti. For the full instrument, see: J. B. Cortes and F. M. Gatti, "Physique and Propensity," *Psychology Today* 4 (May 1970): 42–44, 82–84.

9. Virginia P. Richmond, James C. McCroskey, and Steven K. Payne, *Nonverbal Behavior in Interpersonal Relations* (Englewood Cliffs, NJ: Prentice-Hall, 1987).

10. For summaries of the research on the role of physical attractiveness in human interaction, see Dale Leathers, *Successful Nonverbal Communication: Principles and Applications,* 2d ed. (New York: Macmillan, 1992); Loretta A. Malandro and Larry L. Barker, *Nonverbal Communication* (Reading, MA: Addison-Wesley, 1983).

11. Nancy Baker, *The Beauty Trap* (New York: F. Watts, 1984). For a summary

of research, see: "When Beauty Can Be Beastly," *Chicago Tribune,* 21 October 1985, sec. 4, p. 22.

12. Loretta A. Malandro, Larry Barker, and Deborah Ann Barker, *Nonverbal Communication* (New York: Random House, 1989), pp. 28–29.

13. Charles Darwin, *The Expression of Emotions in Man and Animals* (Chicago: University of Chicago Press, 1965; originally published, 1872).

14. Samuel G. Lawrence and Mike Watson, "Getting Others to Help: The Effectiveness of Professional Uniforms in Charitable Fund Raising," *Journal of Applied Communication Research* 19 (1991): 170–85.

15. Based on a questionnaire developed by Lawrence B. Rosenfeld and Timothy G. Plax. For the complete questionnaire, see: Lawrence B. Rosenfeld and Timothy G. Plax, "Clothing as Communication," *Journal of Communication* 27 (1977): 23–31.

16. For information on clothing to wear to interviews, see John T. Molloy, *Dress for Success* (New York: Warner Books, 1975); John T. Molloy, *The Woman's Dress for Success Book* (Chicago: Follett, 1977); L. B. Rosenfeld, "Beauty and Business: Looking Good Pays Off." *New Mexico Business Journal* (April 1979): 22–26.

17. Knapp and Hall, *Nonverbal Communication,* 1992.

18. Judee K. Burgoon, David B. Buller, and W. Gill Woodall, *Nonverbal Communication: The Unspoken Dialogue* (New York: Harper & Row, 1989), pp. 192–95.

19. Judy Cornelia Pearson, *Gender and Communication* (Dubuque, IA: Wm. C. Brown, 1985), p. 250.

20. For a discussion of pupilometrics, see E. H. Hess, A. L. Seltzer, and J. M. Shlien, "Pupil Response of Hetero- and Homosexual Males to Pictures of Men and Women: A Pilot Study," *Journal of Abnormal Psychology* 70 (1965): 165–68; and E. H. Hess and J. M. Polt, "Pupil Size as Related to Interest Value of Visual Stimuli," *Sciences* 132 (1960): 349–50.

21. Helmut Morsbach, "Aspects of Nonverbal Communication in Japan," in Larry A. Samovar and Richard E. Porter (Eds.), *Intercultural Communication: A Reader* 3d ed. (Belmont, CA: Wadsworth, 1982), p. 308.

22. "Understanding Culture: Don't Stare at a Navajo," *Psychology Today* (June 1974): 107.

23. Marianne LaFrance and Clara Mayo, *Moving Bodies: Nonverbal Communication in Social Relationships* (Monterey, CA: Brooks/Cole, 1978), p. 188.

24. Barbara Westbrook Eakins and R. Gene Eakins, *Sex Differences in Human Communication* (Boston: Houghton Mifflin Company, 1978), pp. 150–52.

25. Judee K. Burgoon, David B. Buller, and W. Gill Woodall, *Nonverbal Communication,* p. 130.

26. Maslow and Mintz compared reactions to photographs of faces made in a "beautiful" room (one with windows, attractive draperies, and indirect lighting), an "average" room (a professor's office), and an "ugly" room (a storage area with a single overhead light bulb). See A. H. Maslow and N. L. Mintz, "Effects of Aesthetic Surroundings: I. Initial Effects of Three Aesthetic Conditions Upon Perceiving 'Energy,' and 'Well-Being' in Faces," *Journal of Psychology* 41 (1956): 247–54; and N. L. Mintz, "Effects of Aesthetic Surroundings: II. Prolonged and Repeated Experience in a 'Beautiful' and 'Ugly' Room," *Journal of Psychology* 41 (1956): 459–66.

27. Carol Dolphin Zinner, "Beyond Hall: Variables in the Use of Space," *The Howard Journal of Communications* 1 (Spring 1988): 32.

28. Edward T. Hall, *The Hidden Dimension* (Garden City, NY: Doubleday, 1966).

29. Judee Burgoon and Joseph B. Walther, "Nonverbal Expectancies and the Evaluative Consequences of Violations," *Human Communication Research* 17 (1990): 232–65.

30. R. Heslin and T. Alper, "Touch: The Bonding Gesture," in *Nonverbal Interaction,* John M. Wiemann and Randall P. Harrison (Eds.) (Beverly Hills, CA: Sage, 1983), pp. 47–75; Ashley Montagu, *Touching: The Human Significance of the Skin* (New York: Harper & Row, 1971).

31. For a discussion of this and other

affectionate greetings see Peter Farb, *Word Play* (New York: Alfred A. Knopf, 1974).

32. This instrument is adapted from the eighteen-item questionnaire developed by Andersen and Leibowitz. For the complete instrument, see Peter A. Andersen and K. Leibowitz, "The Development and Nature of Touch Avoidance," *Environmental Psychology and Nonverbal Behavior* 3 (1978): 89–106.

33. Joseph A. DeVito, *The Nonverbal Communication Workbook* (Prospect Heights, IL: Waveland Press, 1989), p. 140.

34. Chris R. Kleinke, "Compliance to Requests Made by Gazing and Touching Experimenters in Field Settings," *Journal of Experimental Social Psychology* 13 (1977): 218–23; Frank N. Willis and Helen K. Hamm, "The Use of Interpersonal Touch in Securing Compliance," *Journal of Nonverbal Behavior* 5 (1980): 49–55.

35. For a summary of studies on cross-cultural touch behavior, see Robert G. Harper, Arthur N. Wiens, and Joseph D. Matarazzo, *Nonverbal Communication: The State of the Art* (New York: John Wiley, 1978).

36. Burgoon and Walther, "Nonverbal Expectancies," 1990.

37. Stanley Jones, "Problems of Validity in Questionnaire Studies of Nonverbal Behavior: Jourard's Tactile Body–Accessibility Scale," *Southern Communication Journal* 56 (1991): 83–95.

38. A modification of DeVito, *The Nonverbal Communication Workbook,* p. 142.

39. David W. Addington, "The Relationship of Selected Vocal Characteristics to Personality Perception," *Speech Monographs* 35 (1968): 492–503. David W. Addington, "The Effect of Vocal Variations on Ratings of Source Credibility," *Speech Monographs* 38 (1971): 242–47.

40. Samovar and Porter, *Communication Between Cultures,* p. 206.

41. Pearson, *Gender and Communication,* p. 257.

42. Samovar and Porter, *Communication Between Cultures,* p. 225.

43. Robert G. Harper, Arthur N. Wiens, and Joseph D. Matarazzo, *Nonverbal Communication: The State of the Art,* p. 64.

44. Paul Ekman and Wallace Friesen. "The Repertoire of Nonverbal Behavior: Categories, Origins, Usage, and Codings," *Semiotica* 1 (1969): 49–98.

45. Devorah A. Lieberman, Thomas G. Rigo, and Robert F. Campain, "Age-Related Differences in Nonverbal Decoding Ability," *Communication Quarterly* 36 (1988): 290–97; Steven A. McCormack and Malcolm R. Parks, "What Women Know That Men Don't: Sex Differences in Determining the Truth Behind Deceptive Messages," *Journal of Social and Personal Relationships* 7 (1990): 107–18.

46. For an excellent summary of the literature concerning deception, see Pamela Kalbfleisch, "Deceit, Distrust and the Social Milieu: Application of Perception Research in a Troubled World." *Journal of Applied Communication Research* 20 (1992): 308–34.

FOR FURTHER INVESTIGATION

Andersen, Peter A., and K. Leibowitz. "The Development and Nature of Touch Avoidance." *Environmental Psychology and Nonverbal Behavior* (1978): 89–106.

Borisoff, Deborah, and Lisa Merrill. *The Power to Communication: Gender Differences as Barriers.* Prospect Heights, IL: Waveland Press, 1985.

Burgoon, Judee K., David B. Buller, Jerold L.

Hale, and Mark A. DeTurck. "Relational Messages Associated with Nonverbal Behaviors." *Human Communication Research* 10 (1984): 351–78.

DeVito, Joseph A. *The Nonverbal Communication Workbook.* Prospect Heights, IL: Waveland Press, 1989.

Druckman, D., R. M. Rozelle, and J. C. Baxter. *Nonverbal Communication: Survey,*

Theory and Research. Beverly Hills, CA: Sage, 1982.

Edinger, J. A., and M. L. Patterson. "Nonverbal Involvement and Social Control." *Psychological Bulletin* 93 (1983): 30–56.

Ekman, Paul, and Wallace V. Friesen. *Unmasking the Face: A Guide to Recognizing Emotion from Facial Clues.* Englewood Cliffs, NJ: Prentice-Hall, 1975.

Ekman, Paul, Wallace V. Friesen, and J. Baer. "The International Language of Gestures." *Psychology Today* 18 (May 1984): 64–69.

Goffman, Erving. *Relations in Public.* New York: Basic Books, 1971.

Hall, Edward T. *Beyond Culture.* New York: Anchor Books, 1977.

Hall, Edward T. *The Dance of Life: The Other Dimension of Time.* New York: Anchor Press, 1983. Pp. 108–18.

Henley, N. M. *Body Politics: Power, Sex, and Nonverbal Communication.* Englewood Cliffs, NJ: Prentice-Hall, 1977.

Hickson, Mark, III, and Don W. Stacks. *NVC: Nonverbal Communication—Studies and Applications,* 2d ed. Dubuque, IA: Wm. C. Brown, 1989.

Jones, Stanley E., and Elaine Yarbrough. "A Naturalistic Study of the Meanings of Touch." *Communication Monographs* 52 (1985): 19–56.

Knapp, Mark L., and Judith A. Hall. *Nonverbal Communication in Human Interaction,* 3d ed. New York: Holt, Rinehart and Winston, 1992.

LaFrance, Marianne, and Clara Mayo. *Moving Bodies: Nonverbal Communication in Social Relationships.* Monterey, CA: Brooks/Cole, 1978.

Leathers, Dale G. *Successful Nonverbal Communication: Principles and Applications,* 2d ed. New York: Macmillan, 1992.

Lieberman, Devorah A., Thomas G. Rigo, and Robert F. Campain, "Age-Related Differences in Nonverbal Decoding Ability." *Communication Quarterly* 36 (1988): 290–97.

Malandro, L. A., and Larry L. Barker. *Nonverbal Communication.* Reading, MA: Addison-Wesley, 1983.

McCormack, Steven A., and Malcolm R. Parks, "What Women Know That Men Don't: Sex Differences in Determining the Truth Behind Deceptive Messages." *Journal of Social and Personal Relationships* 7 (1990): 107–18.

Mehrabian, Albert. *Silent Messages: Implicit Communication of Emotions and Attitudes,* 2d ed. Belmont, CA: Wadsworth, 1981.

Molloy, John T. *The Men's and Women's Dress for Success Book.* Englewood Cliffs, NJ: Prentice-Hall, 1976.

Mulac, Anthony, Lisa B. Studley, John W. Wiemann, and James J. Bradac. "Male/Female Gaze in Same-Sex and Mixed-Sex Dyads: Gender-Linked Differences and Mutual Influence." *Human Communication Research* 13 (1987): 323–44.

Richmond, Virginia P., James C. McCroskey, and Steven K. Payne. *Nonverbal Behavior in Interpersonal Relations.* Englewood Cliffs, NJ: Prentice-Hall, 1987.

Rosenfeld, Lawrence B., and Jean M. Civikly. *With Words Unspoken: The Nonverbal Experience.* New York: Holt, Rinehart and Winston, 1976.

Rosenfeld, Lawrence B., Sallie Kartus, and Chett Ray. "Body Accessibility Revisited." *Journal of Communication* 26 (1976): 27–30.

Rosenthal, Robert, and Bella M. DePaulo. "Expectancies, Discrepancies, and Courtesies in Nonverbal Communication." *Western Journal of Speech Communication* 43 (1979): 76–95.

Schlenker, B. R. *Impression Management.* Monterey, CA: Brooks/Cole, 1982.

Stewart, Lea P., Pamela J. Cooper, and Sheryl A. Friedly. *Communication Between the Sexes: Sex Differences and Sex-Role Stereotypes.* Scottsdale, AZ: Gorsuch Scarisbrick, Publishers, 1986.

Thayer, Stephen. "Close Encounters." *Psychology Today* 22 (March 1988): 31–36.

Thourlby, W. *You Are What You Wear.* New York: New American Library, 1978.

Weimann, John M., and Randall P. Harrison, eds. *Nonverbal Interaction.* Beverly Hills, CA: Sage, 1983.

CHAPTER 5

Verbal Communication

COMMUNICATION COMPETENCIES

This chapter examines verbal communication. Specifically, the objective of the chapter is for you to learn to:

- Understand the relationship between language and meaning.
- Distinguish between abstract and concrete language, denotative and connotative meaning, and private and shared language.
- Identify and overcome barriers to verbal interaction caused by language problems.
- Improve your use of language to ensure clear communication.
- Recognize and avoid sexist and racist language.
- Recognize and appreciate intercultural differences in the use of verbal language.

KEY WORDS

The key words in this chapter are:

verbal language	allness
argot	static evaluation
denotation	bypassing
connotation	relative words
semantic differential	euphemisms
private language	clichés
shared language	emotive words
jargon	nonemotive words
polarization	distorted language
indiscrimination	qualifiers
stereotypes	oxymoron
facts	sexist language
inferences	racist language
fact–inference confusion	

Lisa and Eric just attended a college production of the musical *West Side Story.* As you listen in on their conversation, keep the following question in mind: Do their language differences reflect differences in what each values and who they are?

LISA: Well, what did you think of the show?

ERIC: I thought the guy playing Tony had a great voice, but it overshadowed Maria's singing. The chorus had some blending problems, and the orchestra drowned the singers out during the solos.

LISA: I thought the story conflict between the two gangs developed a real sense of the growing conflicts caused by the chaotic sociological underpinnings of our society.

ERIC: Did you notice that during the entire production the guy playing Baby John was singing flat?

LISA: This production had a lot of the same qualities as *Romeo and Juliet* since it dealt with the same social and cultural issues. I thought it was wonderful.

ERIC: A musical production can't be good if the singers and the orchestra aren't perfect! I think they needed more time rehearsing.

LISA: Oh well, everybody has to have some opinion, even if it isn't right!

Eric and Lisa appear to be talking *at* each other and not *with* each other. The barriers to interpersonal communication that they are experiencing—and ways to overcome those barriers—are part of the subject matter of this chapter.

THE IMPORTANCE OF VERBAL COMMUNICATION

Before you went to school you accomplished the most complex feat you will ever accomplish: You mastered the basics of **verbal language**, the ability to communicate using the words and grammatical system of a particular society. You discovered how to use the words in the way people around you use them. You learned to create sentences that fit the rules for how sentences should be created in your culture's language. You learned to say "put the pen on the table, and not "the pen on the table put." You learned to use words to mean what others in your culture generally mean—you said "dog" and not "bird" when you pointed at a four-legged, furry animal that barked.

If you were fairly typical, by age four you had learned enough basic vocabulary to survive for the rest of your life.[1] You learned meanings for words like *love, good,* and *right* that are too subtle for dictionaries to explain fully. You learned rules for combining words that are so complex that researchers and philosophers have yet to spell them out in a comprehensible way. Did you ever stop to think about how you are able to put together sentences that you have never heard before and understand statements that are new to you? You knew how to use language to satisfy your need to understand the world, to express yourself, and to form relationships—all by the age of four, all without the aid of formal schooling!

What is so engrossing about the way in which we learn to talk is that while so much of the learning process is universal, there is also a great deal of it that is culture-specific. Language represents the experiences within a geographic or cultural community. Through social interaction our culture teaches us both the symbol (be it a sound or written marks) and what that symbol stands for. We hear the sound symbol "dog" and we have a cultural picture in our heads of what the symbol means. Members of different cultures will usually have different sounds and/or marks, and they may also have different pictures in their heads for what the symbols mean. "Dog" in some parts of the world, such as Hong Kong, China, and Korea, is considered food—quite a different word picture than is used in North American culture. What is the picture in heads throughout the world for such words as *freedom, affirmative action,* and *God*? Obviously, these terms, and many others, have different connotations. Cultures differ and so do the words they use and the meanings they give to words.

Language is a powerful and useful tool. You use it to organize information you gather; to relate to people and events you experience; to regulate your own behavior, as when you talk to yourself while choosing a course of action; and to regulate the behavior of others, as when you try to persuade your friends to see one movie instead of another. Consider what it would be like to lose your ability to communicate verbally. How would you make sense of new information if you couldn't use words to place the information into categories? How would you keep track of where you should be if you couldn't use words to remind yourself? How would you interact with others? Life would be difficult, frustrating, and probably not as productive as it could be—for you as well as for those you encounter.

Language is your primary tool for survival. Understanding obstacles to its use and developing ways to overcome them can help you communicate more effectively. But there is still another reason for studying verbal communication: *Your language reflects who you are and how you perceive yourself.*[2] What differences do you presume between Lisa and Eric based on their conversation? Do they "see" the same things?

Your language both reflects and affects what you perceive. It was argued more than sixty years ago that we are prisoners of our language, that what we experience is largely due to the language habits of our community. The Sapir-Whorf hypothesis states that the language we use guides how we see and interpret the environment and shapes our ideas; also, a people's language serves as a key to understanding their culture.[3] To understand a person's verbal communication is to understand how that person sees the world, how that person thinks—the reality in which that person's culture lives.[4]

Calvin and Hobbes

by Bill Watterson

Many examples support the Sapir-Whorf hypothesis. For one, Eskimos have no single word for snow but a great many discrete words for different kinds of snow. The Masai of Africa have seventeen terms for cattle. Arabic has over 6,000 words for what most Americans call a camel. And Americans have a wide vocabulary for distinguishing types and models of cars. This reflects the importance of snow for Eskimos, cattle for the Masai, camels for Arabs, and cars for Americans. The point isn't that Americans cannot see the distinctions in snow that Eskimos see, but that they do not see them because such subtleties about snow aren't important to them. The vocabulary you use reflects your interests and concerns, the way you look at the world, and the distinctions among objects, people, and events that are important to you.

Grammar, too, serves as evidence for the Sapir-Whorf hypothesis. How you think about something is reflected in and affected by the grammar you use. In English, for example, you would say, "the white wine" (the specific, white, comes first, and the general, wine, follows), while in French you would say, *"le vin blanc"* (the general, wine, comes first, and the specific, white, follows).[5] As with differences in vocabulary, differences in grammar do not necessarily reflect inabilities to think differently, but rather preferences for what is important to a particular language community.

We can observe an extension of the Sapir-Whorf hypothesis by looking at the language patterns of some of the many co-cultures in the United States. These groups have evolved an **argot**—a special vocabulary that mirrors their experiences— experiences that are often different than those of the mainstream culture. An understanding of these unique vocabulary systems is important because you might hear private words and phrases that sound foreign and alien to you. Secondly, these specialized vocabularies, as noted by the Sapir-Whorf hypothesis, can offer insight into the experiences of these co-cultures.

Members of the male gay co-culture, because they may live two lives—one among the dominant culture and one among members of their own co-culture—has developed a rather extensive argot. A fellow gay is often referred to as "a member of the family." In this case, "family" means the brotherhood of homosexual men. A bisexual may be labeled as "AC/DC," much like electrical alternating current. In asking whether a fellow gay has come out to society the question is asked, "Have you told your story?" Even coming out signifies no longer hiding the person's sexual preference. And, in asking whether a vacation resort has a gay clientele, the question may be couched as, "Is it festive?"[6]

Street gangs have acquired a rich vocabulary that reflects their experiences. "Claim" or "turf" is an area that each gang maintains as belonging to them. Again, these are "logical" words to describe the idea or action: "claim," a marking off of territory, "turf," a piece of territory. "Signs" are hand signals used to communicate to other gang members. Based on the bridge between the argot and the implied meaning, what do you think gangs mean by "homeboy," "buster," and "claimer"? A "homeboy" is a member of the same gang, a "buster" is someone who doesn't stand up for the gang, and a "claimer" is someone who wants to be a member of the gang but has not yet proven himself or herself.

The argot of African Americans mirrors their environment, perceptions, and values. "Feel draft" expresses some African Americans' feelings of racism in white people. A person who attempts to emulate or to please the whites is frequently referred to as a "Tom" or an "Oreo." "Tom" refers to the subservient slave, Uncle Tom, in *Uncle Tom's Cabin,* "Oreo" paralleling the cookie—dark on the outside and white on the inside. "The man," referring to anyone who has power, harks back to slavery days when "the man or master" had all the power.[7]

Concepts concerning argot and the Sapir-Whorf hypothesis include the concept that there are many co-cultures in any society that have extensive argot. Second, the argot of each co-culture is composed of a vast number of words. Third, argots are regional. African Americans in Los Angeles might well have different terms than the African Americans in San Diego, even though the two cities are only 120 miles apart. Fourth, argots are subject to change. A term that is used one month is apt to be discarded the next. In fact, because most co-cultures feel alienated from the dominant culture, they are constantly changing their argot.

Many studies linked ethnic identification with ethnic language use. For example, Mexican Americans who were strong ethnic identifiers were found to be frequent users of Spanish language media.[8] Stronger support for the relationship between language use and ethnic identification also was found in a study of Welsh speaking individuals living in England: Language maintenance was found to be a function of ethnic identification.[9]

LANGUAGE AND MEANING

Language is symbolic; that is, words have no meaning in themselves but are arbitrary letter combinations that stand for or represent something. The word "pizza" is not edible and the word "water" is not drinkable. There is nothing pizza-like about the word pizza, and nothing liquid-like about the word water. If there were a

logical connection between a symbol and what it symbolized, wouldn't it seem silly for the word "big" to have fewer letters than the word "small"? Why would "ten," "diez," and "dix" all mean the same thing (and why have none of the three ten letters)?

The relationship between a symbol and what it symbolizes is arbitrary, agreed upon by the people who use the symbol. Learning a language is, in part, learning the rules for how meanings and symbols are connected.

If the connection between a symbol and the object, idea, or event that it refers to were simple, communicating would be rather easy. Every time you said the word "car" it would mean the same thing to you as it meant to the person with whom you were talking. But because the relationship between a word and what it symbolizes is arbitrary, meanings are in the people who use the words, not in the words themselves. No meaning is inherent in any symbol. People attach a specific, personal meaning to every word they use. For example, for you, the word "car" may mean a 1985 Ford Thunderbird, even though the same word could refer to many different automobiles. For someone else, car might mean a different specific automobile, such as the one she owns, or all autos of a particular make, such as Chrysler. And if the person is from a nonmotorized culture, the word "car" might be a funny-sounding word without meaning.

Just because meanings are in people, not in words, does not imply that communication is impossible. You daily talk to people; you are reading this book right now. How is this possible? Even though each of us has his or her own dictionary, people with a common language also *share* a dictionary. This common dictionary is what makes it possible to communicate. You can speak to others and read this book because of societally shared meanings. Language is dynamic. In addition to shared meanings and individual meanings, new words with new meanings and old words with new meanings constantly are created. For example, the *New American Heritage Dictionary of the English Language* has about 16,000 new entries.[10] Some of these are new words, having been created by newspapers and trade magazines (e.g., political managers are referred to as "handlers," and "input" refers to entering information into a computer); others evolved through the everyday speech of people (e.g., "igg" meaning "to ignore," and "suss" meaning "to discover"); others came about through necessity—the need to label new inventions and identify newly evolved attitudes (e.g., "telephone tag" evolved following the proliferation of answering machines; "mini-van" to describe a cross between a car and a truck; and "pro-choice" and "pro-life" to describe attitudes toward abortion).

The specific meaning you attribute to a symbol—which reflects something about who you are and your culture—differs according to how concrete or abstract the symbol is, its denotations and connotations, and whether the language is private or shared.

ABSTRACT AND CONCRETE SYMBOLS

Symbols differ in the degree to which what they refer to is concrete or abstract. Concrete symbols are highly specific and refer to one thing. Abstract symbols, on the other hand, are general and may refer to many things. For example, consider a football team that has been named the Cleveland Browns by its owner. The name Cleveland Browns is a concrete symbol because it refers to one particular team—a reality that can be verified. As we move from this concrete symbol to more abstract ones, we move from the reality of the particular football team to more general concepts. A useful model of this movement from concrete to abstract is the ladder of abstraction, with its first rung the most concrete and its final rung the most abstract. A progression for Cleveland Browns from most concrete to most abstract, from the first rung to the last rung on the ladder of abstraction, is illustrated in Figure 5.1:

The symbol that stands for the particular object—the name that refers to the particular object, "Cleveland Browns"—is the most concrete level of language possible. It appears on Rung 1.

A description of the physical characteristics of the object is also concrete, but not as concrete as the symbol for the particular object, so it appears on Rung 2. "Professional football team" may seem fairly concrete, but it is still a broad category that encompasses a variety of teams.

"Football team" is more abstract because this category expands to semiprofessional, amateur, collegiate, academic, and peewee teams.

"Athletic team" is still more abstract because this term may refer to teams that play any sport, such as baseball, basketball, or soccer.

The category "team" is the most abstract term when contrasted with the label "Cleveland Browns" because it includes all groups of people who designate themselves or are designated as a team, including work, social, and sport teams. Thus, it occupies the highest rung on the ladder of abstraction.

Team

Athletic Team

Football Team

Professional Football Team

CLEVELAND BROWNS

FIGURE 5.1 LADDER OF ABSTRACTION

The more abstract a symbol is, the greater the probability that different people attach different meanings to it. A person who tells his friend, "It's important to have many friends," may run into trouble with the friend's interpretations of "many" and "friends" because both words are abstract. "Many" could mean three to some people and twenty to others, and "friend" could mean anything from a passing acquaintance to an intimate confidante. The speaker may have something particular in mind, but so will the friend, and the differences between them may be great.

People's tendency to assign different meanings to the same symbol is only one problem with abstract language. People also use the same abstract word to mean different things on different occasions. You might use the abstract word "love" to refer to one set of feelings when talking about the person with whom you are romantically involved and another set when talking about a good friend. A problem could arise if a listener is unaware that "love" is being used to refer to two different feelings, one, deep emotional commitment (referring to your romantic partner) and the other, friendship (referring to your friend). One way to resolve this problem is to use less abstract symbols, such as "when I am with you I get the feeling I never want to leave," versus "I like it when we're together."

As you move up the ladder of abstraction, more and more meanings may be attributed to the symbols you use. But to communicate clearly, both you and the person with whom you're communicating must have similar notions of what your symbols refer to. Thus, the less abstract your language is, the higher the probability that you and the other person will agree on meaning. Telling the doctor, "I don't feel well," is not as useful as giving a detailed, concrete description of where, when, and for how long you have had pain.

Knowledge Checkup 5.1 will help you construct a ladder of abstraction and compare more and less abstract words and descriptions for the same object.

KNOWLEDGE CHECKUP 5.1

CONSTRUCTING A LADDER OF ABSTRACTION

Select the specific name of your favorite food, car, movie, or campus organization and place it on the bottom rung of the ladder of abstraction. Complete each step of the ladder with one or more words until you are at the most abstract level.

_____   most abstract level

_____

_____

_____

_____   most concrete level

1. What happens to meaning as you move up the ladder of abstraction? What happens when you move down the ladder?

2. How can the ladder of abstraction help you communicate more clearly?

DENOTATION AND CONNOTATION

The meaning of a symbol is affected not only by its level of abstraction but also by its denotations and connotations. **Denotation** refers to the usual associations that members of a particular language community have for a symbol. **Connotation** refers to the secondary associations for the symbol that are more personal and may not be shared by every member of the language community. For example, a denotation for home may be shelter, while connotations could include warmth, pleasant retreat, place back in the city, or where my folks live.

Denotations

An examination of any dictionary will confirm that most words have several denotations. The most commonly used 500 words in English have approximately 14,000 definitions. Of course, the more denotations a word has, the more ambiguous it is.

The word "team," used earlier in the ladder of abstraction, has several denotations in addition to "an athletic group." It refers to a clique, assemblage, association, band or collection of people, crew, and an organization. Individuals unfamiliar with English may be unaware of any given word's multiple denotations. Assuming that only one denotation exists, a word may be used incorrectly in varying contexts. For example, a denotation for "got" is "obtained." A new English speaker who knew this denotative connection could say, "I obtained up this morning at 7 A.M." The speaker failed to recognize that not all denotations are equal and interchangeable.

Connotations

The connotations of a word refer to the attitudes or feelings people have for the word or what it symbolizes. What are your connotations for the word "car"? Is it something good or bad? Fast or slow? A plaything or a workhorse? Necessary or frivolous? If you have had good experiences with cars—no accidents and few repairs—you are likely to have positive associations with the symbol. Problems with cars in the past are likely to give rise to negative connotations. There can be as many connotations as there are people who use the word, whereas the number of denotations is limited.

The following words refer to the same thing, but their connotations may be different. What is your reaction to each word? What are your connotations?

fired

released

axed

dehired

let go

deselected

involuntarily separated

The connotations you have for a word are more likely to determine your response than the denotations, probably because you learned the connotative meanings for many words before you learned their denotations. For example, in your family you may have learned that bills are an annoyance before you ever understood what bills were. The process of reacting first and learning the denotation second is a hard habit to break.

Because connotations are more subtle and varied than denotations, new English speakers have a great deal of difficulty mastering this aspect of language. Words such as "love," "hate," and "democracy" have a great number of connotations. For example, you may "love chocolate," "love your dog," "love your mother," "love going to the movies," and "love the way your car drives." The word "love" is the same, but the connotations are seemingly different. Grasping the subtlety of these differences requires familiarity with a culture that takes time to develop.

One device used for measuring connotative meaning—the attitudes and feelings you have toward a concept or term—is called the **semantic differential**, a tool that measures a person's reactions to an object or concept by marking spaces between a pair of adjectives, one positive and one negative, with each space representing an attitude position.[11] For example, rate the concept *"my high school education"* on the following scales by circling the number that best reflects your feelings. The endpoints 1 and 7 are defined by the adjectives. The numbers between them represent less extreme positions. For example, on the first scale, 1 = bad, 2 = somewhat bad, 3 = slightly bad, 4 = neither good nor bad, 5 = slightly good, 6 = somewhat good, and 7 = good.

bad	1	2	3	4	5	6	7	good
not satisfying	1	2	3	4	5	6	7	satisfying
boring	1	2	3	4	5	6	7	exciting
tense	1	2	3	4	5	6	7	relaxed

You can get a sense of whether your connotations for the concept *"my high school education"* are positive or negative simply by adding your responses to the four scales and comparing your sum with the highest score possible, 28, and the lowest score possible, 4. If your sum is close to 28, your connotations are positive. On the other hand, if your score is close to 4, your connotations are negative.

PRIVATE AND SHARED LANGUAGE

Private language refers to language whose meanings are agreed upon by one segment of a larger language community; **shared language** refers to language whose meanings are agreed upon by all members of the language community. Private language may consist of both specialized words and specialized meanings for common words. For example, "input" and "output" may not mean much to people unfamiliar with computers; "ollies" may defy definition by anyone who doesn't ride a skateboard; "vertebral subluxation" may confuse those outside the chiropractic profession; and, although you have probably suffered from cephalalgia, only your doctor would call a headache by this name. Typically, also, as people develop a more intimate relationship they also develop a more private language.[12]

Specialized words are often called **jargon.** They have two purposes. First, they serve as shorthand for those familiar with them. The third cervical vertebra can be shortened to the specialized symbol C3 to save chiropractors time when talking to each other and to patients familiar with their vocabulary. Specialized words also help identify those who use them as members of the same group. With the right vocabulary, you can sound like a lawyer, doctor, teacher, mechanic, or plumber because each profession has its own language. Who would say the following? (And what does it mean?)

> That the sense of smell used by these cattle was established because of the marked audible variation in inhalation intensity as the animals grazed.

The sentence, which means "We knew the cattle used their sense of smell while grazing because we heard them sniffing," is from the book *Ethology of Free Ranging Domestic Animals.* The sentence won an Obscure Prose in Scientific Literature Award from the *Veterinary Record.* The meaning of each word is clear, but the joint meaning of the words would make sense only to someone specializing in cattle care.

In addition to using specialized words, specialized language may use common words in special ways. What meanings would you assign to the following words and phrases in classified advertisements to sell houses?

> Owner will sacrifice.
>
> Must sell.
>
> Cozy, intimate.
>
> Secluded.

The first two probably mean "for sale," the third probably means "very small," and the fourth probably means "very far from the nearest city." Although the common meanings of these words are clear, their specialized meanings in this context may not be so obvious.

Try to imagine how difficult it would be for someone who spoke English as a second language to determine the real meaning for argots and idioms. If you were just learning to speak English, and you translated one word at a time, what would you make of these sentences?

> "She has a buzz on."
>
> "Do you want to go window shopping?"
>
> "It's raining cats and dogs."
>
> "Give me a ring."
>
> "The joke laid an egg."
>
> "It's just a ballpark figure."
>
> "Couch potato."
>
> "Don't jump down my throat."

What meaning would you assign to the following sentences, knowing that the speaker is a typical teenager living at home:

"My room is clean."

"I have nothing to wear."

"Everybody's wearing it."

The first probably means "The mess you saw earlier has been stuffed into my closet." The second probably means "The particular shirt I want to wear isn't here." And the third probably means "The person I've chosen to set the standards for what I should wear was wearing it yesterday."

Problems arise when either specialized words or specialized usages come into play. When you encounter a specialized word, you know that whatever it means to you—if anything—it probably does not mean the same thing to the other person. Specialized usage, however, can go undetected unless other information is available. The statement "My room is clean" seems clear enough, but it will probably remain incorrectly interpreted until a closet door is opened!

Shared language—words that have similar meanings for those who are communicating—is the basis for effective communication. Problems occur when language is too abstract, when connotations differ widely, or when language is private and you happen to be the outsider. Under these circumstances, the meanings attributed to the words and phrases could be different enough to render communication ineffective.

Knowledge Checkup 5.2 provides you with the opportunity to grapple with the meanings of words from a private language.

KNOWLEDGE CHECKUP 5.2

SPECIALIZED COMMUNICATION VOCABULARY

Define the following words or phrases:

1. PERT

2. semanticity

3. primacy effect

4. ethos

5. preening behavior

If you were trying to solve a problem by dividing it into small steps in order to best analyze and evaluate the solutions, you'd be implementing the Program Evaluation and Review Technique *(PERT).*

Semanticity is the feature of human language that refers to the fact that some, but not all words, have specific meanings.

The *primacy effect* is the condition by which what comes first exerts greater influence than what follows.

To the Greek philosopher Aristotle, *ethos,* ethical proof, depended upon the speaker's perceived goodwill, knowledge, and moral character.

If you've ever watched people fix their hair and straighten their clothes, you've seen *preening behavior,* aimed at making oneself more attractive or more desirable to another person by rearranging one's hair or clothing.

BARRIERS TO SUCCESSFUL COMMUNICATION: OUR IMPERFECT LANGUAGE

Barriers to successful communication are inherent in language.[13] Language is a tool created by people and, like any tool, it has limitations. Among the most common barriers to successful communication are polarization, indiscrimination, fact-inference confusion, allness, static evaluation, and bypassing.

POLARIZATION

Polarization is the tendency to describe people, ideas, and events in either–or terms. When you use polarized language, an idea is either ridiculous or wonderful, a new acquaintance is either friendly or aloof, and a movie is either the best you've seen or the worst. The problem stems not simply from your wanting to make events seem more dramatic, but from the English language. Our language tends to consist of well-defined extremes and few words to describe the points in between. Time how long you need to write the opposite of each of the following words:

cold

tall

relaxed

illegal

You probably need only a few seconds to come up with the four opposites: hot, short, tense, and legal. But now see how long it takes you to come up with the midpoint for each pair.

If you were able to identify true midpoints at all, it probably took you a lot longer than it did to think of opposites. And you may have noticed that some of your midpoints, which may be one word or whole phrases, are not specific to a particular pair of opposites. Average, OK, usual, normal, and *neither–nor* constructions (neither hot nor cold, neither short nor tall) are cited as typical midpoints for most pairs. What was your midpoint for legal and illegal? A midpoint exists or we wouldn't need courts.

A problem with many word pairs is that there is no real midpoint to refer to. For example, if you're not happy, you're sad—and any response that falls between the two extremes is usually interpreted as sad. If, in response to your question "How are you?" someone said "OK," "average," "usual," or "neither terrific nor terrible," you would probably think he or she was not doing well.

Although there are instances when *either–or* language is appropriate—either you are reading this book or you're not, either you had lunch yesterday or you didn't—such language still denies that there are degrees of virtually everything. You might be reading this book but not concentrating, which is different from reading intently, just as an apple and a cup of coffee for lunch is different from a three-course meal. There are degrees of reading and degrees of eating lunch.

The tendency of our language to polarize can have dramatic results. For example, if you call yourself a healthy person and you get ill (which is not unusual), you may begin to call yourself unhealthy because our language lacks a midpoint between the two. Such a change in labels could affect your behavior. For instance, you might avoid skiing because you fear that going out in cold weather will make you sick.

To avoid the problems of polarization, be aware that the world comes in shades between the colorful extremes of our language. People and events are rarely one thing or another. Be aware that reality is often the middle ground, somewhere between the dramas of the polarized extremes.

By increasing your vocabulary to include midpoints, you can avoid limiting yourself to polarized opposites. Skill Development 5.1 is designed to give you practice in communicating midpoints.

FINDING MIDPOINTS BETWEEN EXTREMES

Describe the midpoint for each of the following pairs of words.

1. beautiful _____ ugly

2. fat _____ skinny

3. responsible _____ irresponsible

4. dark _____ light

Did you find it difficult to describe midpoints. Also, do you think your midpoints and those of others' are the same?

INDISCRIMINATION

No two people, ideas, events, or processes are identical. However, to deal with the world as if everything were unique would be an overwhelming task. Our language helps us to categorize things that are similar by providing general nouns, such as *house* (when no two houses are the same) and *cat* (when no two cats are the same). Difficulties arise when we focus only on the similarities between things, because then we lose or ignore the differences. The problem is one of **indiscrimination**, the failure to see things as unique and individual.

Stereotypes, oversimplified images of things or people, whether related to gender, age, race, or some other feature, are examples of the process of indiscrimination. Stereotypes are based on similarities, whether positive or negative, and once an individual is placed in a general category, all the presumed similarities are attributed to him or her. Stereotypes are quick ways to organize information about people. If stereotypes are incorrect, the qualities that make the person unique are lost. For example, a seventy-five-year-old person may have nothing in common with other seventy-five-year-olds except for age. The category "senior citizen," however, includes a host of presumed similarities among the people so labeled, such as inflexibility and loss of memory.

Another problem with indiscrimination is that once a person, idea, or event is categorized, the tendency is to keep her/him/it pigeonholed. New information may be ignored or denied to keep the classification intact. The goal is to keep life simple, neat, and well organized, even though life is often complex, messy, and chaotic.

The process of indiscrimination is one reason why first impressions are so important to relationships. We use the first pieces of information we receive to categorize the other person—for example, by race, height, weight. Then we use subsequent information to fill out the categories rather than to change them. Our first impression thus tends to stick.

To avoid the problem of indiscrimination, be aware that no two people, ideas, objects, events, or processes are identical, even if they share the same category—or are called by the same name—because of some similarities. Keep in mind that differences are as important as similarities, and that there is always more to know about everything. Avoid hardening of the categories.

SKILL DEVELOPMENT 5.2

COMMUNICATING DIFFERENCES

1. List five characteristics that individuals who share the title *actor* have in common.

2. List five characteristics that differentiate one *actor* from another.

3. Describe two *actors* you know or know about.

4. What is useful about nouns such as *actor*?

5. What problems occur when nouns such as *actor* are used?

FACT–INFERENCE CONFUSION

Facts are statements based on observations; they relate directly to what you see, hear, touch, taste, or smell.[14] **Inferences** are conclusions that are suggested by observations but not based on them. For example, the statement "Amir is six feet tall" can be verified by measuring Amir's height in stocking feet: It is a fact. The statement "Amir is handsome," however, is an inference. Several facts may be put together and the conclusion drawn that Amir is handsome, but there can be no direct observation of the conclusion that he is "handsome."

Fact–inference confusion, the tendency to respond to something as if it were observed when, in reality, it is merely a conclusion, occurs because our language makes no grammatical distinction between facts and inferences.[15] The two statements, "Amir is six feet tall" and "Amir is handsome," are grammatical equivalents. The tendency, then, is to interpret inferences as facts, so that "Amir is handsome" has the same truth value as "Amir has brown eyes."

Problems occur when you state inferences as if they are facts, because while you and others may agree on the truth of facts, there is no guarantee of agreement on the truth of inferences. You may state an inference as a fact and expect others to treat it as such, but you may run into misunderstandings if you fail to recognize that the inference is really a subjective opinion. For example, "Amir is handsome" may seem like a fact to you, given that Amir is six feet tall and has brown eyes and black hair, and that these are your criteria for handsomeness. However, someone else, while agreeing with the facts of Amir's physical traits (six feet tall, brown eyes, black hair), may consider blue eyes and blond hair the necessary criteria for handsomeness. Thus, for this person, Amir is not handsome.

Knowledge Checkup 5.3 will provide you with some experience distinguishing facts from inferences.

KNOWLEDGE CHECKUP 5.3

DISTINGUISHING FACTS FROM INFERENCES [16]

Read the following story, assuming that all the information is accurate and true. Then, for each statement, indicate **T** (true), **F** (false), or **?** (don't know).

A certain West Coast university scientist chartered a ship for exploration purposes. When a large white bird was sighted, the scientist asked permission to kill it. He stated that white albatrosses are usually found only off the coast of Australia. He wanted the bird as a specimen for the university museum. The crew protested against the killing of the bird, calling the scientist's attention to the old sea superstition that bad luck followed the killing of a white albatross. Nevertheless the captain granted permission to kill the bird and the bird was killed. These mishaps happened after the bird was killed: The net cables fouled up three times, a rib was broken when Jackie Larson, a scientific aide, fell down a hatch ladder, and the scientist became seasick for the first time in his life.

1. The scientist had never been seasick before.   T F

2. The purpose of the voyage was primarily pleasure and sight-seeing. T F

3. The scientist asked the captain for permission to kill the bird.   T F

4. Jackie Larson broke his rib.   T F

5. The white albatross was sighted near Australia.   T F

KEY

1. T—The story specifies that "The scientist became seasick for the first time in his life."

2. F—The story specifies that "A . . . scientist chartered a ship for exploration purposes."

3. ?—We do not know whom the scientist asked.

4. ?—We do not know if Jackie Larson broke a rib or if it was the ship's rib. In addition, we don't know if Jackie Larson is a male or a female.

5. ?—We do not know where the ship was when the sighting was made.

Statements 3, 4, and 5 are inferences because they are not based on observations, but only suggested by them. Statements 1 and 2 are facts because they are based on observation.

Be aware that factual statements can be made only after an observation and are limited to what is observed, whereas inferences can be made anytime and go beyond what is observed. Also, although facts have a high degree of certainty, inferences vary in their probability—some being highly probable and others being highly improbable. Recognize facts and inferences for what they are and avoid confusing them. When confronted with an inference, ask yourself, "What is the probability that this inference is true?" An inference should spark questions and a search for the facts, if any, that support it.

ALLNESS

Allness is the assumption that when you say something, you've said all there is on the subject. The much-told story and poem about six blind men and an elephant is an excellent illustration of this concept. Never having felt an elephant before, each blind man examines a small part and, based on the little information gathered, attempts to describe the entire beast. The first blind man touches the elephant's side and describes it as a wall; the second touches the tusk and describes it as a spear; the third touches the trunk and likens the elephant to a snake; the fourth touches the knee and describes the elephant as a tree; the fifth touches the ear and says the elephant is like a fan; and the sixth touches the tail and likens the elephant to a rope. Each is right and each is wrong.

The point to the poem is that we are all similar to the blind men when it comes to describing anything in the world. We see only a small part of something and, based on insufficient information, assume we can describe all of it. Whether it's another person, an idea, or an event, we know very little in comparison to what can be known. What you say about something is what you choose to say at the moment, or all you know about it at the moment, and not all there is to know. Our language, however, does not reflect this.

Be aware that whatever you or someone else says about something, there is more that can be said. Keep an open mind and realize that our finite language is being used to describe infinitely complex things.

STATIC EVALUATION

Everything in the world is continuously changing, continuously in process, but our language tends to remain static. The result is called **static evaluation**, the inability of our language to account for constant change. When you meet a person for the second time you act as if she or he is the same person, but in reality that person has changed, just as you have changed. Since the first meeting each of you has gotten older and has had experiences that have changed you. Although changes may be minor, they exist. Our language rarely takes these changes into account. Statements are fixed in time, whether past, present, or future, even when the subject of the statement changes.

Each student's Permanent Record in education is testimony to the problem of static evaluation. If a student is evaluated negatively by one teacher, subsequent teachers who read the evaluation may take it for the current reality. The former teacher's point of view becomes imposed on new situations and the student has an uphill battle to persuade others that he or she has changed. To confront this problem, some schools now restrict teachers from reading Permanent Record folders before a student completes the class, except for medical information.

Be aware that everything that is said applies to a particular time. A new perspective, or at least a healthy skepticism of the old perspective, is necessary to keep up with changes. When you communicate, let others know the time frame for what you're saying and ask others for their time frames. Skill Development 5.3 will help you eliminate static evaluation from your communication.

SKILL DEVELOPMENT 5.3

ELIMINATING STATIC EVALUATION

Combating the problem of static evaluation requires dating your communication —specifying the time frame for a particular message. Rewrite the two statements to eliminate their static evaluations, making up the details that you need. For example, "Shana is a great athlete" could be recast as "Shana is the only student ever to graduate from Brush High School who was awarded ten athletic letters and chosen to five all-conference teams."

1. Nico is a faithful friend.

2. Roxanne likes to run.

BYPASSING

At one time or another, you've probably told someone how to locate a particular address only to find out later that your directions didn't work, that the person was unable to find the right street (e.g., your definition of "go a little way" means a quarter of a mile to you but only 100 feet to your listener). You thought you were clear, and you probably were—for you. Most people speak until their message is perfectly clear to themselves, which does not mean that it is clear to the other person! Those speakers are likely to be bypassing. **Bypassing** occurs when you assume incorrectly that your meaning for your words is the same as another person's. However, as you learned earlier, different people assign different meanings to the same words because meanings are in people, not in words.

To avoid the problem of bypassing, don't assume that your meaning is shared merely because the other person nods encouragingly and seems to understand. Ask questions when you are unsure whether your meaning and another's are the same.

USING LANGUAGE EFFECTIVELY

Barriers to successful communication may begin with the limitations inherent in our language, but they do not end there. The way we use language—the words we select and the way we put them together—poses more problems. Among the most common communication problems are the use of unclear language and the use of language that creates negative impressions. If you are aware of the problems you face when selecting words to communicate, you increase your chances of communicating effectively.

UNCLEAR LANGUAGE

Given the arbitrary relationship between symbols and their referents, different words may refer to essentially the same thing. The "Triangle of Meaning,"[17] Figure 5-2, displays the relationship of a thought or reference, a symbol (word), and a referent (what the word refers to). The dotted line between the symbol and referent indicates an indirect relationship between a word and what it is supposed

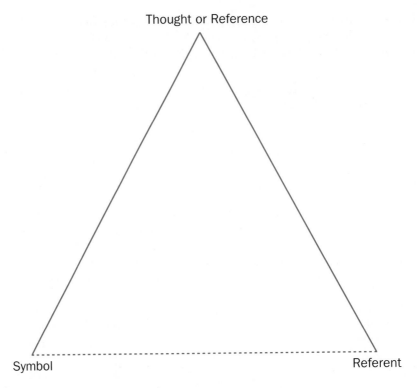

Thought or Reference

Symbol   Referent

FIGURE 5.2   OGDEN AND RICHARDS' TRIANGLE OF MEANING

Based on C. K. Ogden and I. A. Richards, *The Meaning of Meaning* (New York: Harcourt Brace Jovanovich, 1923), as presented in Ronald B. Adler, L. B. Rosenfeld, and Neil Towne, *Interplay,* 5th ed. (Fort Worth, TX: Harcourt Brace Jovanovich, 1992), p. 130.

to represent. For example, the thought "carbonated water with flavoring" relates to the word "soda" and to the object (a flavored carbonated drink). The word "soda," however, bears no direct relationship to the physical object. If it did, you could drink the letters S-O-D-A. In addition, the carbonated drink also can be referred to by the symbols, "pop," "Coke," "fizz," and "drink." Because of this arbitrary relationship between a word and a thing, meaning may be unclear. A glance at *Roget's International Thesaurus* proves that every idea can be expressed in many different ways. Each way, however, presents a slightly different slant, much like our earlier list of synonyms for the word "fired." The most widespread examples of unclear language include relative words, euphemisms, clichés, emotive words, distortions, qualifiers, and oxymorons.

Relative Words

Relative words gain their meaning by comparison and clarification. Unless the point of comparison is specified, relative words lack clarity. For example, consider the following questions: Is your car fast? Are you smart? Are you tall? Is your school a good one? It's impossible to define *fast, smart, tall,* and *good* without knowing the basis for comparison: Fast compared to a new Jaguar? Smart compared to Albert Einstein? Tall compared to professional basketball player Michael Jordan? Good compared to Harvard? A competent communicator is specific with respects to the comparison, for example, "My car is fast. It goes from 0 to 60 in 10 seconds."

Whenever you evaluate something without indicating your criteria, the meaning for your words is likely to differ from another person's meaning. An easy class for you may not be easy for someone else, and a good restaurant for you may not please your friends. To what other classes are you comparing the class? What is your basis for comparison? Is it the amount of homework? How lively the class meetings are? How strict the grading is? With what other restaurants are you comparing the restaurant? What is your basis for comparison? Is it the prices? The way the food is prepared? The amount served?

Euphemisms

Euphemisms are inoffensive words or phrases substituted for possibly offensive language. The goal of a euphemism is to soften the blow of what you have to say. Unfortunately, softening often leads to an unwanted side effect: lack of clarity.

How can you tell a friend his sweater is ugly? Telling him outright may be too blunt, but what happens when you use the words "unique," "interesting," or "makes a fashion statement"? And how do you respond to a friend who asks how you like her new furniture when you hate it? Do you call it "original"? How about "tasteful"? Or do you change the subject?

The Pentagon has created several memorable euphemisms. For example, "combat" is "violence processing" and "civilian casualties" are "collateral damage." Educational institutions have their own fair share of euphemisms. For example, the term "remedial English" has been replaced with "developmental English," the "remedial reading room" has become "the skill-development center," and "pay raises" have become "salary adjustments."

Although politeness and attempts to help people feel better about themselves are laudable, when a euphemism distorts meaning, it needs to be replaced with more accurate, more direct language. If you use "I" language to assume responsibility for your opinions, you can say what is on your mind without resorting to unclear language. For example, you may tell the friend whose sweater you find ugly, "I like sweaters that are less colorful." Such a statement lets him know that you don't like the sweater and why, and that the opinion is yours.

Clichés

Clichés are trite expressions that convey a common or popular thought. They lack originality and impact because of overuse. When what are now clichés first began being used, they had particular meanings based on what they were actually describing. In time, the original meaning disappeared and only the sentiment was left. For example, "put to the acid test" dates back to a time when gold was in wide circulation and users questioned whether they had the genuine ore. Nitric acid was applied, and if the sample was false, the acid decomposed it. Do you know the original meaning of the phrase "have an ax to grind"? According to one story, a man approached a boy and persuaded him, by flattery, to sharpen his ax. The boy sharpened the ax but received no thanks. From that point on, whenever the boy saw someone flattering someone else, he wondered whether the flatterer had an ax to grind, that is, some hidden purpose in mind.

Although the meaning of a particular cliché may be clear to the person using it, others may not understand its point. For example, although the meanings of "play it by ear" and "stiff upper lip" may be clear to you, how would a person learning English as a second language interpret those phrases? To avoid possible misunderstanding when speaking with people whose background is different from your own and who may thus be unfamiliar with some of your phraseology, either avoid clichés altogether or clarify them.

Emotive Words

Emotive words seem to be descriptive but actually communicate an attitude toward something or someone. Depending on your likes or dislikes, you select the words that communicate your attitude. Clarity is sacrificed when the word is used as a description rather than an expression of a point of view. For example, a 1956 Chevrolet may be called a "car" (neutral attitude), a "jalopy" (negative attitude), or a "classic" (positive attitude). Notice that the description "1956 Chevrolet" are **nonemotive words**, that is, these words do not communicate an attitude toward the object.

Someone who saves money may be called "thrifty" (positive) or a "tightwad" (negative). A small house may be called "cozy" (positive) or "claustrophobic" (negative). Such emotive words seem to describe something, but what they describe is less important than the speaker's attitude.

The shared meanings of emotional words are often so powerful that people may use them to alter the reality of what is being discussed. Reflect for a moment on the emotional language used as part of the abortion controversy. One side talks of the "unborn child" while the other states "undeveloped fetus." If you think of the images created by these words you have two very different pictures of the same concept.

Listen for emotive and nonemotive words and separate them from what the speaker is describing. The clearest meaning occurs when what is described and how the speaker feels about it are both known.

Distortions

Communication is least clear when language is used to distort meaning. Attempts to exaggerate (or to minimize) the value, importance, or worth of something usually involve **distorted language.**

Advertisers use phrases such as "gives you more" without explaining more of what. They tell you "you can be sure" without mentioning what you can be sure of.

They describe drinks as "the real thing" and cigarettes as having "real taste" without defining the word *real*. And they describe products as "new" and "improved" without explaining what's new or how they're improved.

Qualifiers

Qualifiers, words that clarify or limit the meaning of an idea, may be used to make a claim more accurate, but questions remain about the meaning. For example, a dishwashing product may leave dishes virtually spotless, but what does a "virtually spotless" dish look like? Other qualifiers that may distort meaning include "up to" ("up to ten days' relief"), "as much as" ("as much as a full day's supply"), "like" ("feels like real wood"), "fights" ("fights cavities"), and "helps" ("helps prevent tooth decay"). The hope is that the qualifier will be forgotten and the residual message, the information you remember, will be that the dishes will be spotless, relief will last ten days, the supply will last a full day, the product is real wood, the toothpaste stops cavities, and the toothpaste prevents tooth decay. Do not ignore exaggerations or qualifiers when assessing the meaning of messages you receive; also, try to avoid using distortions in your own messages.

Oxymorons

Oxymorons are self-contradictory phrases. For example, how can someone be "cruel to be kind" and how can something be "almost unique"? Have you ever

heard a book hailed an "instant classic," a trip described as a "working vacation," a milk substitute called a "nondairy creamer," a person described as being "vaguely aware," and a guess at your car's repair cost called an "exact estimate"? Each phrase contains two words that contradict each other, resulting in a lack of clarity. Oxymorons confuse rather than clarify, so rather than assume what a speaker means, ask questions. Substitute more precise language for oxymorons in your own language. For example, "cream substitute" is more precise than "nondairy creamer."

RECOGNIZING UNCLEAR LANGUAGE

Read the following paragraph from a hypothetical teacher evaluation. Identify the uses of relative words, euphemisms, qualifiers, clichés, emotive words, distortions, and oxymorons.

> I am very pleased to evaluate the instructor who is being considered for a full-time position. It is my opinion that his approach to teaching is quite interesting. Although some might claim that he has an ax to grind in the classroom, I find his teaching style clean as a whistle. His lectures are spontaneously planned, giving them a quality that is virtually unmatchable. The acid test of whether he should be hired is that he is a grade-A teacher.

The unclear language you should have spotted is: "I am very pleased to evaluate the instructor who is being considered for a full-time position. It is my opinion that his approach to teaching is quite interesting" (*relative term*—interesting compared to what?). "Although some might claim that he has an ax to grind" (*cliché*) "in the classroom, I find his teaching style clean as a whistle" (*cliché*). "His lectures are spontaneously planned" (*oxymoron*—how can a lecture be both spontaneous and planned?), "giving them a quality that is virtually unmatchable" (*distortion*—what is a virtually unmatchable quality?). "The acid test" (*cliché*) "of whether he should be hired is that he is a grade-A" (*emotive word*) "teacher."

Sexist Language

Sexist language expresses stereotyped sexual attitudes or a sense that one gender is superior to another. Traditionally, English has been a sexist language. For example, words used to describe males—*independent, logical, aggressive, confident, strong*—often have positive connotations, whereas those used to describe females—*dependent, illogical, gullible, timid, weak*—often have negative connotations. Men and women are too often viewed as opposites.[18]

Hi & Lois

Reprinted with special permission of King Features Syndicate.

In addition, the word *man* often is used generically to refer to people in general, as in *mankind.* Sexist language implies that the world is made up of superior, important men and inferior, unimportant women.

Contrast the different stereotypical descriptions of the same behavior in men and women:[19]

He's curious; she's nosy.

He's a bachelor; she's a spinster.

He's suffering a midlife crisis; she's menopausal.

He's firm; she's stubborn.

He's ambitious; she's clawing.

He's versatile; she's scattered.

He's concerned; she's anxious.

By contrast, a nonsexist language either makes no reference to gender or does not imply superiority of one gender over another. For example, references to people in general include women and men, so the word "mankind" is inappropriate. Words such as "humanity," "people," and "humankind" are both more accurate and nonsexist.

Nonsexist Communication

You can eliminate sexist language in three ways. The first calls for circumventing the problem by eliminating gender-specific terms or substituting neutral terms. For example, using the plural *they* eliminates the necessity for *he, she, she and he,* or *he and she.* Eliminate derogatory terms, such as "chick" and "stud." When no gender reference is appropriate, substitute neutral terms to solve the sexism problem. For example, given that both men and women work for the postal system, substitute *letter carrier* for *mailman.* Of course, some terms refer to things that could not possibly have gender; make those terms gender-neutral. For example, a *manhole* is a *sewer lid* and something *man-made* is *synthetic.*

The second method for eliminating sexism is to mark gender clearly—to heighten awareness of whether the reference is to a female or a male. For example, rather than substitute letter carrier for mailman, use the terms mailman and mailwoman to specify whether the letter carrier is a man or a woman. Other examples include:

Saleswoman and *salesman* (rather than *salesperson*)

Congresswoman and *congressman* (rather than *congressperson* or *member of congress*)

Chairman and *chairwoman* (rather than *chair* or *chairperson*)

Policeman and *policewoman* (rather than *police officer*)

Inherent in this second approach is the notion that there is nothing sacred about putting he before she. Use both orders interchangeably—*she and he, him and her,* and *hers and his.* Adding *she, her,* and *hers* after *he, him,* and *his,* without changing the order, continues to imply that males are the more important gender and should come first.

The third method for eliminating sexism is to increase your awareness of its occurrence. Becoming aware of sexism in your own language can serve as the stimulus for change. And becoming aware of sexism around you, such as in advertising and the media, can stimulate you to articulate your opposition to its presence.[20]

SKILL DEVELOPMENT 5.4

ELIMINATING SEXIST LANGUAGE[21]

Rewrite the following sentences to make them gender-neutral.

1. The average student is worried about his grades.

2. Ask the student to hand in his work as soon as he is finished.

3. Writers become so involved in their work that they neglect their wives and children.

4. The class interviewed Chief Justice Rehnquist and Mrs. O'Connor.

5. I'll have my girl type the letter and get it out to you.

Rewritten, gender-neutral sentences:

1. "The average student is worried about grades" eliminates the *his* form altogether.

2. "Ask students to hand in their work as soon as they are finished" uses the plural to eliminate the singular *he.*

3. "Writers become so involved in their work that they neglect their families" eliminates the assumption that writers are men.

4. Either "The class interviewed Chief Justice Rehnquist and Justice O'Connor" or "The class interviewed Mr. Rehnquist and Ms. O'Connor" treats both the male and the female justices in a parallel manner.

5. "I'll have my secretary type the letter and get it out to you" eliminates the stereotyped image of secretaries as women and avoids language that is patronizing.

Racist Language

Racist language expresses stereotyped racial attitudes or feelings of superiority of one race over another. Whereas sexist language in the United States has traditionally divided the world into "superior" males and "inferior" females, racist language usually divides the world into "superior" and "inferior" racial groups. All the same sexist assertions about women have been made for so-called inferior racial groups. For example, (fill in any group) are less intelligent and more childlike and emotional than (fill in any group). As with the word "male," connotations of the word "white" are positive—"clean," "pure," "innocent," and "bright"—and connotations of the word "black" are negative—"dirty," "dark," "decaying," and "sinister," as are those for "yellow"—"chicken," "afraid," and "sickly."

Racist language reflects indiscrimination; that is, it fails to make important distinctions among people who may have only one characteristic in common. Members of a racial group may differ more from each other than they do from members of other racial groups. Remarks that encompass entire groups of people should be eliminated from your communication. Avoid abstractions and be concrete: Refer to your own experience and to the particular limitations of your own experience.

To communicate effectively, you must understand how meaning and language are connected, that is, what words symbolize and how the thoughts they stimulate relate to each other. You must also understand barriers to successful communication and gain appropriate skills to overcome those barriers. Language may have problems that reflect its imperfection, and you may not always put this imperfect tool to the best use, but effective verbal communication can be a reality. By combining your understanding and skill with your motivation, you can become a competent communicator.

COMMUNICATION COMPETENCY CHECKUP

The goal of this Communication Competency Checkup is to guide you in putting your skills and knowledge about verbal communication to use, and to help you summarize the material in this chapter.

The man in the short-sleeved jacket is unobtrusively listening in on a conversation while waiting for the elevator. The two communicators, the man with the

FOR BETTER OR FOR WORSE copyright 1987 & 1989 Lynn Johnston Prod., Inc. Reprinted with permission of UNIVERSAL PRESS SYNDICATE. All rights reserved.

curly hair, and the man with the mustache, are having a discussion about something.

1. Analyze the conversation in terms of the abstractness versus concreteness of the language.

2. What are the denotations and connotations of the conversants' words?

3. From the perspective of the two men talking as well as from the perspective of the man listening in, is the language private or shared?

4. What barriers to successful communication exist between the speakers and the eavesdropper?

5. Language is an imperfect tool, as the eavesdropper apparently realizes. If the eavesdropper were hired as a communication consultant, what specific advice could he give the conversants regarding their use of language? What do they need to understand about language in terms of (a) the relationship between language and meaning, and (b) barriers to verbal interaction? What specific skills do they need to develop in order to overcome barriers to verbal interaction?

NOTES

1. For an excellent discussion of language learning see, Rita C. Naremore and Robert Hopper, *Children Learning Language: A Practical Introduction to Communication Development* (New York: Harper & Row, 1990). For classical studies of language acquisition, both verbal and nonverbal, see, J. Piaget, *The Child's Conception of the World,* trans. Marjorie Wordon (New York: Harcourt Brace, Inc., 1928); B. F. Skinner, *Verbal Behavior* (Englewood Cliffs, NJ: Prentice-Hall, 1957); and J. S. Bruner, *Child's Talk: Learning to Use Language* (Oxford: Oxford University Press, 1983).

2. Anita Vangelisti, Mark Knapp, and John Daly, "Conversational Narcissism," *Communication Monographs* 57 (1990): 251–74; and Karen Foss and Belle Edson, "What's in a Name, Accounts of Married Women's Name Choices," *Western Journal of Speech Communication* 53 (1989): 356–73.

3. Benjamin L. Whorf, *Language, Thought and Reality,* J. B. Carroll (Ed.) (Cambridge, MA: Technology Press of Massachusetts Institute of Technology, 1956); Harry Joijer, "The Sapir-Whorf Hypothesis," in Larry A. Samovar and Richard E. Porter (Eds.) *Intercultural Communication: A Reader* (Belmont, CA: Wadsworth Publishing Company, 1991), p. 245.

4. Stephen W. Littlejohn, *Theories of Human Communication,* 4th ed. (Belmont, CA: Wadsworth, 1992), pp. 190–214.

5. For a discussion of the issues raised in this section, see, Sarah Trenholm, "The Problem of Signification," in *Human Communication Theory* (Englewood Cliffs, NJ: Prentice-Hall, 1986), pp. 68–96.

6. For a discussion of gay communication, see, *Alternative Communications: Journal of the Caucus of Gay and Lesbian Concerns* (Annandale, VA: Speech Communication Association); and James Chesebro (Ed.), *Gayspeak: Gay Male and Lesbian Communication* (New York: The Pilgrim Press, 1981). For an extended bibliography on gay communication, see: Daniel Ross Chandler, "The Rhetoric of Gay Liberation: An Interdisciplinary, Annotated Bibliography for Communication Studies" (Annandale, VA: Speech Communication Association, 1988).

7. For a discussion of Black English, see, Naremore and Hopper, *Children Learning Language,* pp. 67, 155, 157–58; Clarence Major, *A Dictionary of Afro-American Slang* (New York: International Publishers, 1971); W. Labov et al., *A Study of the Nonstandard English Used by Negro and Puerto Rican Speakers in New York City,* Final Report, U.S. Office of Education Cooperative Research Project No. 3288 (Washington, DC: U.S. Office of Education, 1968); as well as the work of Howard A. Mims, Speech and Hearing Department, Cleveland State University, Cleveland, Ohio.

8. H. Giles and P. Johnson, "Ethnolinguistic Identity Theory: A Social Psychological Approach to Language Maintenance," *International Journal of Sociology of Language,* 68: 69–99.

9. M. Y. Young and R. C. Gardner, "Modes of Acculturalization and Second Language Proficiency," *Canadian Journal of Behavioural Science* 22 (1990): 59–71; and M. S. Trueta, "Language and Identity in Catalonia," *International Journal of the Sociology of Language* 47 (1984): 91–104.

10. Jim Wise, "Word Game" [Durham, NC] *Herald-Sun* (September 6, 1992): E-1, E-8.

11. Donald K. Darnell, "Semantic Differentiation," in Philip Emmert and William D. Brooks (Eds.), *Methods of Research in Communication* (Boston: Houghton Mifflin, 1970), pp. 181–96.

12. Robert Ball and Jonathan G. Healey, "Idiomatic Communication and Interpersonal Solidarity in Friends' Relational Cultures," *Human Communication Research* 18 (1992): 307–35.

13. N. Coupland, H. Giles, and J. M. Wiemann, *Miscommunication and Problematic Talk* (Newbury Park, CA: Sage, 1991).

14. Based on definitions included in Joseph A. DeVito, *The Communication Handbook: A Dictionary* (New York: Harper & Row, 1986).

15. Ibid., pp. 112–13.

16. This test is adapted from William V. Haney, *The Uncritical Inference Test* (San Francisco: International Society for General Semantics, 1969), p. 2.

17. C. K. Ogden and I. A. Richards, *The Meaning of Meaning* (New York: Harcourt Brace, Inc., 1923).

18. See, Barbara Bate, *Communication and the Sexes* (New York: Harper & Row, 1988); and Judy C. Pearson, *Gender and Communication* (Dubuque, IA: Wm. C. Brown, 1985); and Laurie P. Arliss and Deborah J. Borisoff, *Women and Men Communicating* (Fort Worth, TX: Harcourt Brace College Publishers, 1993.)

19. For a discussion of male/female stereotypes and language usage, see, Deborah Borissof and Lisa Merril, *The Power to Communicate: Gender Differences as Barriers* (Prospect Heights, IL: Waveland Press, 1985); Lea Stewart, Alan D. Stewart, Sheryl Friedley, and Pamela Cooper, *Communication Between the Sexes: Sex Differences and Sex-Role Stereotypes* (Scottsdale, AZ: Gorsuch Scarisbrick Publishers, 1990); Karen Foss and Sonja Foss, *Women Speak: The Eloquence of Women's Lives* (Scottsdale, AZ: Gorsuch Scarisbrick Publishers, 1991); and Deborah Tannen, *You Just Don't Understand: Women and Men in Conversation* (New York: William Morrow, 1990).

20. Lana F. Rakow, "Don't Hate Me Because I'm Beautiful," *Southern Communication Journal* 57 (1992): 132–42.

21. Adapted from: *Guidelines for Nonsexist Use of Language in NCTE Publications,* rev. ed. (Urbana, IL: National Council of Teachers of English, 1985).

FOR FURTHER INVESTIGATION

Ananis, Michael. "Teenspeak: A Rudimentary Guide to a Secret Language." *Review* [Eastern Airlines in-flight magazine] (April 1987): 44–49.

Andrews, Lori B. "Exhibit A: Language." *Psychology Today* (February 1984): 28–33.

Arliss, Laurie P., and Deborah J. Borisoff. *Women and Men Communicating.* Fort Worth, TX: Harcourt Brace College Publishers, 1993.

Bate, Barbara. *Communication and the Sexes.* New York: Harper & Row, 1988.

Berryman, Cynthia L., and James R. Wilcox. "Attitudes Toward Male and Female Speech: Experiments on the Effects of Sex-Typical Language." *Western Journal of Speech Communication* 44 (1980): 50–59.

Dance, Frank E. X., and Carl E. Larson. *The Functions of Human Communication: A Theoretical Approach.* New York: Holt, Rinehart and Winston, 1976.

DeVito, Joseph. *Language: Concepts and Processes.* Englewood Cliffs, NJ: Prentice-Hall, 1976.

Froman, Robert. "How to Say What You Mean." *Etc.* 43 (1986): 393–402.

Guidelines for Nonsexist Use of Language in NCTE Publications, rev. ed. Urbana, IL: National Council of Teachers of English, 1985.

Haney, William V. *Communication and Interpersonal Behavior,* 5th ed. Homewood, IL: Irwin, 1986.

Hardy, William G., ed. *Language, Thought, and Experience.* Baltimore: University Park Press, 1978.

Hayakawa, S. I. *Language in Thought and Action,* 4th ed. New York: Harcourt Brace Jovanovich, 1978.

Amirson, Craig E. "An Introduction to Powerful and Powerless Talk in the Classroom." *Communication Education* 36 (1987): 167–72.

Kim, Young Y. *Communication and Cross-Cultural Adaptation.* Philadelphia: Multilingual Matter, Ltd., 1988.

Miller, Casey, and Kate Swift. *Words and Women.* New York: Anchor Press, 1976.

Mulac, Anthony, John M. Wiemann, Sally J. Widenmann, and Toni W. Gibson. "Male/Female Language Differences and Effects in Same-Sex and Mixed-Sex Dyads: The Gender-Linked Language Effect." *Communication Monographs* 55 (1988): 315–35.

Naremore, Rita C., and Robert Hopper. *Children Learning Language,* 3d ed. New York: Harper & Row, 1990.

Pearson, Judy C. *Gender and Communication.* Dubuque, IA: Wm. C. Brown, 1985.

Rothwell, J. Dan. *Telling It Like It Isn't.* Englewood Cliffs, NJ: Prentice-Hall, 1982.

Sapir, Edward. *Language: An Introduction to the Study of Speech.* New York: Harcourt Brace and World, 1955.

Trenholm, Sarah. "The Problem of Signification." In *Communication Theory,* pp. 68–96. Englewood Cliffs, NJ: Prentice-Hall, 1986.

Wood, Barbara. *Children and Communication: Verbal and Nonverbal Language Development,* 2d ed. Englewood Cliffs, NJ: Prentice-Hall, 1981.

CHAPTER 6

Listening

COMMUNICATION COMPETENCIES

This chapter examines listening. Specifically, the objective of this chapter is for you to learn to:

- Identify your own listening patterns.
- Define listening and summarize the four stages of the listening process.
- Describe the three levels of listening.
- Explain the importance of listening as part of the communication process.
- List some of the barriers to good listening.
- Apply several techniques for improving your listening skills, including methods for focusing your attention, organizing material, and providing feedback.
- Use empathic listening skills.

KEY WORDS

The key words in this chapter are:

listening	internal distractions
hearing	egospeaking
empathy	daydreaming
redundancy	paraphrasing
overloaded	chunking
red flag	ordering
green flag	reordering
external distractions	empathic listening

In Center Harbor, Maine, local legend recalls the day when Walter Cronkite [at that time, television's leading news anchorman] steered his boat into port. The avid sailor, as it's told, was amused to see in the distance a small crowd of people on shore waving their arms to greet him. He could barely make out their excited shouts of "Hello Walter . . . Hello Walter." As his boat sailed closer, the crowd grew larger, still yelling "Hello Walter . . . Hello Walter." Pleased at the reception, Cronkite tipped his white captain's hat, waved back, even took a bow. But before reaching dockside, Cronkite's boat abruptly jammed aground. The crowd stood silent. The veteran news anchor suddenly realized what they'd been shouting: "Low water . . . low water."[1]

Like Cronkite, do you hear what you want to hear, or do you hear the words actually spoken? There appears to be enough research evidence to indicate that if you are typical, you are probably guilty of tuning out, yielding to distractions, becoming overly emotional, faking attention, or even dozing with your eyes open—all when you're supposedly listening.

The average North American spends 50 to 80 percent of his or her day listening but actively hears only half of what is said, understands only a quarter of that, and remembers even less. Our attention span rarely lasts more than 45 seconds. Most people use only 25 percent of their native ability to listen.[2]

Listening, like so many communication variables, is influenced by culture. Some cultures, many in the Far East, "are biased in favor of lengthy silences."[3] For these cultures, the amount of time spent talking and listening is far less than in cultures that value conversation. People in Japan and other Asian cultures, for example, are more likely to spend less time talking on the job than do North Americans. It has been suggested that this relates to higher productivity on the job. You only need to think of the Asian saying, "By your mouth you shall perish," to see that the emphasis is not on interaction, but on being still.

Not all cultures have the same attention span. In Buddhism, for instance, there is a concept called being "mindful." This means giving whatever you are doing your *complete* and *full* attention. It involves training the mind to focus on the moment, to keep it, as Buddha wrote, from thrashing around like a fish placed on the shore.[4] If your cultural orientation is to being alert, being in the present, you will certainly be able to listen more effectively than someone who is thinking about the past or the future while someone else is talking.

How well do you listen based on your cultural needs? That is, how well do you take information gathered through your sense of hearing and give it meaning?

WHAT IS LISTENING?

Listening is the active process of receiving, attending to, and assigning meaning to sounds, and remembering. It is active because it involves taking information from speakers, processing it, giving meaning to it, and, when appropriate, encouraging the continuation of communication by giving appropriate feedback.

Listening is the most important of our communication skills. There is no other skill that could make you as well informed and desirable as a companion. Listening is the key skill for becoming a good communicator, an effective counselor, and a skilled leader.[5] Despite its great value, listening is probably the most underrated of the sensory skills. If you are typical, you probably received less than half a year of formal listening training in all of your elementary and secondary schooling.[6] Compare that short time to the usual six to eight years devoted to formal reading instruction, twelve years to writing, and one year to speaking. Most people spend only about 9 percent of their time writing, 16 percent reading, and 35 percent speaking, so for your most used skill, listening, you received the least training. Little emphasis is placed on listening training in the schools because people sometime assume that normal hearing equals good listening. In fact, hearing and listening are not the same. **Hearing** is merely the biological act of receiving sounds, while listening is a much more active process.

Listening is a learned skill. The effectiveness of your listening often depends on what is going on in your mind as well as what is going on around you. You must learn to participate both mentally and physically in the communicative transaction. You must learn to listen in different ways at different times. You have to realize that listening productively and effectively just doesn't happen. It takes work! You cannot turn on your listening any more than you can say, "I'm going to run ten miles today even though I've never exercised a muscle." You must train your listening skills through training—and people who have listening training become more effective listeners.[7] In addition, many of the people you will be spending time with are going to be coming from backgrounds and cultures that are different from yours. There will be occasions where you meet people who do not speak the same native language as you. As they speak languages different from your native language, your listening skills will be challenged.

THE REASONS FOR LISTENING

Listening is an important communication skill because it has so many uses. You listen for comprehension, appreciation, identification, evaluation, and to empathize and gain self-understanding.

COMPREHENSION

Comprehension involves grasping the meaning of the sounds you hear. Through comprehension you acquire information, ideas, and others' viewpoints. Comprehension is required in the classroom, at work, at home, and in social settings. By comprehending the messages you receive, you gain new ideas, learn new skills, test ideas, and expand your perspective.

APPRECIATION

You listen appreciatively to music, to the sounds of nature, and to the actor's voice. Appreciative listening differs from comprehensive listening because your purpose is not to gain information, per se, but to relax or to feel a particular way, such as peaceful, stimulated, or excited.

IDENTIFICATION

A doctor listens to the sound of a patient's heart to detect abnormality. A mechanic concentrates on the sounds of an engine to determine whether the car is running smoothly. You listen to the pitch of someone's voice to discern tension or relaxation. The sound of the wind, the roll of the thunder, and the crash of the waves all supply useful information about the probable severity of an oncoming storm. In identification you use the sound to identify something—the sound reveals the "something" to you.

EVALUATION

You evaluate what is being said by carefully analyzing whether the ideas are acceptable to you, meet your expectations, and are logical. You evaluate the messages of commercials, salespeople, friends, and family members. In a work environment, whether you are an employer or an employee, you constantly evaluate and are evaluated.

EMPATHY

One of the most overlooked and underrated uses of listening is **empathy**—the ability to experience the world as others do.[8] The easiest way to think of your role as an empathic listener is to picture yourself as a mirror. As someone explains her or his concerns, stressors, or conflicts, you reflect what you are hearing by restating the ideas in your own words. Usually, the person who seeks an empathic listener needs reflection, not advice. Empathic listening can reduce tensions, help solve problems, encourage cooperation, and promote open communication.

SELF-UNDERSTANDING

Listening to others' observations about you can lead to self-understanding and personal growth. Similarly, listening to yourself talk about who you are provides important data for self-analysis. Just by listening to yourself talk, you may discover that you feel more strongly about a topic than you had realized. You may become more intense than you would have predicted, or you may bring up arguments that you didn't realize were important to you.

INVESTIGATING YOUR LISTENING PATTERNS

Each of us follows a general pattern while listening. Use Knowledge Checkup 6.1 to investigate your perception of your personal listening patterns.

PAYING ATTENTION? TAKE THIS TEST AND SEE [9]

1. When conversing I find my mind wandering:
   a. Often.
   b. Occasionally.
   c. Rarely.
2. In general I do:
   a. Most of the talking.
   b. Most of the listening.
   c. As much talking as listening.
3. Someone has just told me a dramatic or humorous story about himself or herself. I:
   a. Ask for more details.
   b. Say, "That's nothing. Let me tell you what happened to me."
   c. Make a reflective expression such as, "That must have been terrifying," or "What a funny experience."
4. In a typical conversation I:
   a. Ask more questions than I answer.
   b. Answer more questions than I ask.
   c. Ask as many questions as I answer.
5. I interrupt people:
   a. Frequently.
   b. Occasionally.
   c. Almost never.
6. Someone is telling me a story or making a point about something. Midway I realize what he is driving at, so I:
   a. Let him finish before I talk.
   b. Finish the thought for him to show that I am tuned in to what he is saying.
   c. Let my mind wander until it's my turn to talk, since I know what is going to be said.
7. When talking to someone I use the word "you":
   a. More often than the word "I."
   b. Less often than the word "I."
   c. More or less the same as the word "I."
8. In a brief social conversation (under 10 minutes) I use the other person's name:
   a. Rarely.
   b. Once or twice.
   c. As many times as possible to make him or her feel appreciated and recognized.

9. When other people are talking, I look them in the eye:
   a. Most of the time.
   b. Some of the time.
   c. Infrequently, since I don't want to make them feel uncomfortable.
10. I consider a proper communicating distance with someone I don't know well to be:
    a. One arm's length.
    b. Two arms' length.
    c. Three arms' length.
11. When it's my turn to talk, I change the subject matter:
    a. Often.
    b. Occasionally.
    c. Almost never.
12. When someone is explaining something technical or complicated I:
    a. Say, "Let me see if I understand what you're saying," and rephrase the explanation in my own words.
    b. Interrupt the person along the way to be sure I am getting it all.
    c. Act as if I am following what he or she says, even if I am not, so I won't look or sound stupid.
13. Whenever possible, I:
    a. Lean somewhat away from the other person so he or she won't feel crowded.
    b. Lean toward the other person to indicate my interest.
    c. Neither lean toward nor away from the other person.
14. Around new people I tend to be:
    a. Reserved.
    b. Friendly.
    c. Ready to express my opinions as a way to get the conversation moving.
15. As someone speaks, I usually:
    a. Remain quiet and neutral.
    b. Add my "two cents' worth" as I go along to keep the conversation lively.
    c. Nod, smile and acknowledge what is being said as it is being said.

ANSWERS INDICATING GOOD LISTENING SKILLS ARE:

1—C; 2—B or C; 3—A or C; 4—C; 5—C; 6—A; 7—C; 8—B; 9—A (?); 10—B; 11—C; 12—A; 13—B; 14—B; 15—C.

SCORING:

13 to 15 right answers—you perceive yourself as an accomplished listener.

10 to 12 right answers—you perceive yourself to be a better listener than most people, but need to fine-tune your skills somewhat.

7 to 9 right answers—you perceive your listening skills to be seriously lacking and need a great deal of polishing.

0 to 6 right answers—you perceive your listening skills to be extremely poor and need immediate first aid.

Bear in mind that people are often unaware of their true listening behaviors and your answers may not reflect how you really behave. You can check your answers by having someone with whom you interact regularly fill out the form reflecting on your behavior—not his or her own.

The explanations of the statements in Knowledge Checkup 6.1 are:

1. Everyone's mind wanders from time to time, but if you find it happening often, you probably are not paying attention or using effective listening techniques.

2. Doing most of the listening can be all right if you are in business situations and can even be a social plus if done in moderation. If taken to the extreme, however, it can mean you aren't giving others enough feedback or may be making them uncomfortable by giving the impression you are holding back—letting them reveal themselves without being willing to reveal much about yourself.

3. A good listener lets the other person know she or he heard what was said and is interested and concerned.

4. When you ask as many questions as you answer, it is an indication that you are an active listener, that you know how to listen effectively, that you probe to clarify unclear information, and that you ask for expansions of ideas.

5. If you frequently interrupt people, you deny yourself the opportunity to receive an entire message. You also may be perceived as an impatient and rude listener, thus encouraging the other person to cut short his or her message. This can result in a hurried and incomplete statement.

6. You may be wrong about what you think the other person was about to say. Listening the person out ensures getting the entire message.

7. If you use the word "I" too much it may mean that you are only listening long enough to get a topic you want to speak about and, thus, are egospeaking (only interested in presenting your point of view and not in gaining the information obtained through concentrated and complete listening).

8. It's important to use the other person's name once or twice in a brief conversation in order to etch it into your memory.

9. Looking the other person in the eye concentrates your attention on that person and allows you to obtain the nonverbal clues often necessary to gain the subtleties of a speaker's intent. When you employ intense eye contact to facilitate listening, remember to keep in mind the differences between cultures. Specifically, be aware that in many cultures people feel uncomfortable when there is sustained eye contact. This is why there is a question mark next to item 9's answer.

10. If you get physically too close to people, they may feel intimidated and feel uncomfortable communicating. Thus, they might cut short their message, causing you to lose some or all of the meaning. On the other hand, standing too

far away may make people feel you are not interested and, again, cause them to alter their message process. In the United States, an arm's length away seems to be comfortable for most senders and receivers. Remember, however, that this is a North American pattern, and not necessarily the same in other cultures.

11. Changing the subject matter drastically may indicate a lack of interest on your part and may be a clue that you're not listening intently to the speaker.

12. Constant interruptions before the other person has a chance to complete a thought can be distracting to you as a listener and confuse the speaker. A confused speaker is likely to cut her or his message short before completing it.

13. In North American culture it's appropriate to lean toward the speaker. It shows interest and also allows you to have direct visual contact in order to obtain the full verbal and nonverbal intent of the message.

14. Being highly opinionated stifles communication and may cause listening problems.

15. Remaining quiet and neutral often doesn't give the speaker feedback, so he or she may not know if you don't understand. Effective feedback alerts the speaker to the necessity to make adjustments—clarification of terms, adding examples, restructuring the message—in order to aid you in understanding.

Based on this general knowledge about listening and your role as a listener, it is important that you understand some specific principles to guide your study of listening.

1. *Poor listening can be remedied.* Sharpening your listening skills requires patience and practice. Once you have learned the skills, you can put into practice what you need to become a skilled listener.

2. *There is no single "best" listening strategy.* Good listeners know how to decipher what various speakers mean in varying situations, and different situations require different listening strategies. Some speakers don't organize their ideas well; others do. Some realize that they must repeat their main ideas to ensure understanding; others ramble on without systematic repetition. Some people give you time to think about what they've said; others move rapidly ahead. Some speakers choose simple and clear words; others use language to confuse and confound. Regardless of the speaker's strengths and weaknesses, it is the listener's responsibility to adapt and to understand.

3. *Good listening depends on finding some personal benefit in the speaker's words.* Because listening is hard work, you need to find some reason for paying attention.

4. *When you listen, you must actively participate in the communication process.* You have a responsibility to interpret what's said, assess its value, decide how to use it, and respond accordingly.

5. *Listening is a problem-solving task.* You must constantly be alert to the question, "What does the speaker mean?"

6. *You need to monitor the way you listen.* Not all situations require the same concentration of energy. Listening to a soap opera on television does not require the same level of concentration as listening to a teacher's lecture.

7. *You need to learn to listen for thinking cues.*[10] It is important to recognize that you should use the pauses found in a speaker's natural speaking pattern to process what is being said. This means you should process the message as it is being said—use the pauses to think about the message rather than waiting for the next point.

Use the fact that most speakers use **redundancy,** repeating their ideas over again, in the same or different words, to help you listen. Realize that if you miss something once it may well be repeated later in the interaction. Stay alert to the redundancy when it is presented.

You can use the *rapid predict-then-confirm strategy* to help you listen effectively. As you listen to a speaker, predict what is coming up in a sentence and then wait to see if it occurs. Most of the time, your predictions will be correct. You may guess the exact words, but you should be able to identify and predict the general idea. Thus, you will be hearing prediction and confirmation based on recurring themes of the message, as well as the overall points and arguments. Be careful that you do not merely confirm your predictions by only listening to parts of the speaker's message.

THE STAGES OF LISTENING

The process of listening, of actively receiving sounds, usually proceeds through the stages of sensing, understanding, evaluating, and responding.

The Sensing Stage

First, through your senses you become aware of the message. For example, someone speaks, you hear the sounds, and, in some cases, you see actions that clarify or enhance the sounds.

The Understanding Stage

If the sounds are familiar, you interpret them and understanding takes place. If a person says "D-E-S-K" and if you understand standard American English, you combine the letters into the word "desk" and picture a piece of furniture at which a person sits while doing certain types of work. You comprehend the intent of the sounds as they combine. If someone points at a desk and says the word, you have a further clue to the intended message.

The Evaluating Stage

After you understand the message, you may go through a stage in which you appraise it. If a speaker says, "Let's sit down at the desk and talk," you may evaluate the message ("This is a good suggestion" or "This is a bad suggestion") and decide how you are going to respond ("I think I'll agree" or "I think I'll refuse").

The Responding Stage

In the responding stage, you do something with the message. For example, you may sit down at the desk, indicating that you understand the message, and choose to evaluate the invitation positively. Or you may say, "I don't want to sit down and talk right now," showing that you understand the message but do not want to accept the invitation. Even ignoring the message is a response, although an ambiguous one. It leaves the speaker wondering whether the message was received, whether it was understood, or whether the lack of response should be taken as an insult. Skill Development 6.1 will help you identify the listening stages you're in while attending a class.

SKILL DEVELOPMENT 6.1

IDENTIFYING LISTENING STAGES

Listed below are listening/response situations. Identify the listening stage represented by each circumstance.

1. You glance down at the floor where your notebook is placed. It holds your homework. Listening stage _____

2. At the start of a class session you are sitting looking out the window, hear your instructor's voice, and turn to face her. Listening stage _____

   _____

3. You pick up your notebook and take out the homework assignment. Listening stage _____

4. Your instructor says, "Take out your homework." Listening stage _____

   _____

ANSWERS:

1—evaluating stage, 2—sensing stage, 3—responding stage, 4—understanding stage

THE LEVELS OF LISTENING

There are three levels of listening, each representing a different degree of effectiveness (Fig. 6.1). At the third level is inefficient listening, at the second level is minimal listening, and at the first level is good listening. An investigation of the weakest to the best levels should allow you to understand what you must do to improve your listening.

Level 3 Listening

Level 3 listening is characterized by listening now and then. You tune in and tune out, aware of the presence of others but mainly absorbed in your own thoughts.

You may be more interested in what you want to say than in what the other person is saying, listening only for pauses that will let you take control of the conversation. You may sit passively and offer little feedback to the speaker. You may think about unrelated matters and make little effort to perceive the message. In short, you are not paying attention to the speaker. Level 3 listening can produce misunderstandings, hurt feelings, confused instructions, loss of important information, embarrassment, and frustration.

Level 2 Listening

In Level 2 listening, you hear words and sounds but do not actively try to grasp anything beyond surface meanings. Typical of this level is tuning out after you think you have enough information to guess the speaker's intent. As a result, you may grasp the basic meaning of the message, but miss the emotion and feeling and thus fail to comprehend the full content.

Level 2 listeners often seem emotionally detached from a conversation. Misunderstandings may occur because the listener often misses how the meaning of what is said is modified by the way in which it is said.

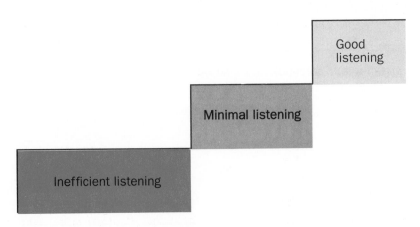

FIGURE 6.1   THREE LEVELS OF LISTENING

Level 1 Listening

Level 1 listening is active listening. You listen for main and supporting ideas, acknowledge and respond, give appropriate feedback, and pay attention to the speaker's total communication. In other words, a Level 1 listener is concerned about the content, the intent, and the feelings of the sender's message.

BARRIERS TO EFFECTIVE LISTENING

To become a good listener, you must be aware of the barriers that may interfere with the accurate reception of message.[11] Knowledge Checkup 6.2 will help you answer the question "How can I tell if I'm not listening?"

KNOWLEDGE CHECKUP 6.2

NONLISTENING SIGNALS

Which of the following are your signals that you aren't listening to the speaker?

1. I daydream.

2. I slouch down in the chair, if I am seated.

3. I glance at my watch, the ceiling, or the floor.

4. I play with some object, such as glasses, paper clip, or pencil.

5. I stare into space.

6. I drum my fingers on my arm or on a solid surface.

7. I cross my legs and bounce my foot.

8. I turn slightly away from the speaker.

9. I yawn, sigh, or show other signs of boredom.

10. I don't look directly at the speaker.

11. Add any nonlistening acts you participate in while attempting to listen:

_____

NONLISTENING CUES

You undoubtedly checked several items on the list. If you are aware of the behaviors that indicate you aren't listening, you can stop them and refocus your attention on the speaker. For example, if you observe yourself yawning and realize that you have quit listening because you're bored, stop yawning, focus on what the speaker is saying, and ask yourself, "Why is this material important for me?" Even if you don't find the material interesting, there may be important reasons for listening, such as to prepare for an upcoming test or to avoid appearing rude.

Overloading

You may not be engaging in good listening if you feel **overloaded,** that is, you feel as if you couldn't possibly listen anymore because you already have too much information to retain. You are capable of grasping and retaining only a limited number of ideas at any given moment. The human brain works like a computer in that it receives information, stores it, and then responds when the proper stimulus has activated the retrieval process.[12] Similar to a computer, the human brain can in effect overload and "blow a circuit." Receiving too much information at one time, being upset by certain messages, and feeling out of control because of the situation or the participants can cause poor listening. Sometimes you may need to tell the sender that you just can't listen any longer, or you may need to leave the receiving environment. Other times you may have no choice but to continue listening, even though it's difficult to concentrate.

Feeling overloaded can be avoided in several ways. As explained later in this chapter, learning how to focus your attention and organize material, besides improving your listening skills in general, can be particularly useful for overcoming feelings of overload.

Arguing with the Speaker's Logic

Another nonlistening cue occurs when you doubt the value of listening or start arguing with a speaker, either of which may happen if a speaker's ideas seem illogical or if the information doesn't seem valid. For example, you may react negatively when you hear the word "always" and know there are exceptions, or when you realize that no evidence supports a conclusion, or when the speaker states that "everyone knows" but doesn't specify who "everyone" is. Nonetheless, to stop listening, or to listen without paying close attention, may not be the best response. Keeping an open mind and withholding final judgment will enable you to gather new information, some of which may be useful. There is always time to reject what a speaker has to say after you listen!

Responding to Emotionally Loaded Words

How do you feel when someone says to you:[13]

"What you should have done was . . . "

"You have to . . ."

"Only someone stupid like you would . . ."

"If you had done it my way . . ."

"See, I told you that would happen!"

"You do this all the time [sigh]."

"You always . . ."

"Are you going to be on time for a change?"

A judgmental word or phrase—called a **red flag**—evokes strong emotions and interferes with your willingness and ability to listen. If, for example, you have strong feelings against abortion and your communication partner mentions that she is in favor of abortion, you may immediately turn off the rest of her message.

Red flags also include people who provoke strong negative reactions. For example, merely seeing someone with whom you're having an ongoing argument may be enough to trigger thoughts that interfere with your ability to listen. Your mind may concentrate on the last argument, how to approach the person, or how to escape with dignity.

Often our strong negative reactions to other people grow out of our stereotypes toward their ethnic or cultural background. We see the color of their skin, hairstyle, or attire and leap to react. These cultural red flags are as harmful as any you might use. They keep you from focusing on the content of the message.

Similarly, some topics may arouse negative emotions regardless of how they are discussed. For example, your feelings against the death penalty may be so strong that any mention of the topic—even by someone who agrees with you—interferes with your ability to listen.

In contrast, **green flag** words are words and phrases that stir up positive feelings, and they too may interfere with listening. If you are an avid sun worshipper and the person you are conversing with says that he has recently been in Hawaii, your mind might switch to a scene in which you are sunning yourself on a palm tree-covered beach. Green flags for college students may include spring break, a canceled exam, and graduation.

Green flags also include people who trigger strong positive emotions that interfere with your ability to listen. For example, meeting an old friend whom you haven't seen in years may cause such strong positive feelings that you fail to listen when she tells you she has only a few minutes to talk. Similarly, some topics may arouse positive emotions. For instance, your positive feelings toward parenthood may be so strong that you fail to listen to your acquaintance's reasons for deciding not to have children.

Both red and green flags lead you to stop actively participating in the listening act. Being aware of your red and green flags is the first step in combating their interference.

KNOWLEDGE CHECKUP 6.3

SENDING UP YOUR RED AND GREEN FLAGS[14]

PART I

Following are some words and phrases that may be emotionally charged. Take a moment to check the ones that are red flags for you.

_____ You should	_____ You have to
_____ You're supposed to	_____ You must
_____ You're a failure	_____ You're so stupid
_____ Slow poke	_____ What a waste
_____ You don't listen	_____ It's for your own good
_____ You're always doing that	_____ You never get things done on time

PART II

Identify red and green flags in each of the following categories. For each category, list five words or phrases that trigger you to react very positively or negatively.

TOPIC	**RED FLAG**	**GREEN FLAG**
Activities		
People		
Issues *(topics)*		

Once you are aware of some of your red and green flags, you can make a conscious effort to stop yourself from daydreaming or becoming irritated. You won't always be successful, but you can make progress.

Failing to Receive the Whole Message

Have you ever filled out an application form and found that on the line that said "Name" you wrote your first and last names in sequence before you saw that the directions said, "Print last name first"? This is an example of not allowing yourself to receive the whole message. You may also do this when you listen.

Read the following statement:

Jack and Jill went up the
the hill to catch a pile of water

Now go back. Did you read the double word *the?* Did you read *fetch* or *catch?* Did you read *pail* or *pile?* Because you are probably familiar with the nursery rhyme "Jack and Jill," you may not have needed more than the first three words to know what followed. If you knew the rhyme but caught all the deviations, you are probably alert to the importance of paying attention to an entire message. If not, you need to practice receiving entire messages before jumping to conclusions.

External Distractions

Listeners may have problems receiving a message if there are **external distractions**—people, objects, or events in the environment that divert attention. Have you ever had difficulty receiving a message when a lot of people were talking, when machinery, such as a dishwasher, was running, or when the television set was on? External distractions are not limited to environmental noise. You may be distracted by a speaker's clothing, dialect, pronunciation, or poor grammar—or by the general setting. One reason teachers avoid holding classes outdoors is that the many external distractions—people walking by, the weather, and so on—interfere with good listening.

External distractions are usually obvious and, once pointed out, easy to eliminate. A change of location may be enough to reduce noise or remove distractions, and recognizing that pronunciation and poor grammar are not good enough reasons to stop listening usually eliminates them as problems.

Internal Distractions

In comparison to external distractions, **internal distractions,** attention diverters that occur within you, are more difficult to recognize and often are more difficult to eliminate. A study of what students think about during a lecture found that only 20 percent actually pay attention to the message, and only 12 percent concentrate fully. The others are thinking erotic thoughts, reminiscing, and worrying.[15] Hunger, having the flu, and an itch on your left leg are all internal distractions.

Two products of internal distractions are egospeaking and daydreaming. **Egospeaking** is jumping into a communicative transaction because you have something you want to say, or because you feel that what you have to say is more important or more interesting than what the other person is saying. Egospeaking not only stops you from receiving the whole message, it irritates others because it is disrespectful. In addition, the moment you decide (consciously or unconsciously) to interrupt, you stop listening.

Once you realize what egospeaking is, you should be able to control it. Several physical clues will help you detect when you are about to egospeak. When most people start to interrupt, they literally jump into the conversation by raising their bodies, leaning forward, and moving their arms and hands upward, often pointing with a finger. If you catch yourself making such motions while someone else is talking, you are probably about to egospeak. Another way to detect that you are egospeaking is to listen to yourself. If you tend to enter conversations with such phrases as "That's interesting, but . . . ," or "Uh-huh, but what happened to me was . . . ," or if people ask, "What does that have to do with what we're talking about?" you are probably egospeaking. Egospeaking becomes a problem if it is a typical feature of your communication, because if you egospeak often, you are probably not getting as much out of listening as you could.

Daydreaming, being lost in your own thoughts, is another common barrier to effective listening. When you daydream you may still be hearing sounds, but instead of focusing on what is being said you are floating in mental space—thinking of what you'll make for dinner, an upcoming test, your weekend plans, or anything else that, at that moment, strikes you as more interesting than the speaker's message.

To stop daydreaming you need to recognize you are doing it, identify what set you off, and in the future try to avoid the action or situation that stimulated it. For example, were you slumping in your chair? Were you looking out the window? Did a green or a red flag send your thoughts flying? Keeping in mind that the speaker's message is important for you may help you avoid daydreaming.

For Better or For Worse®   **by Lynn Johnston**

MAKING LISTENING WORK FOR YOU

Several techniques can help you avoid or overcome barriers to effective listening. By learning to focus your attention, organize what you hear, receive the whole message, paraphrase the speaker's message, and provide the speaker with feedback, you can take an active role in the communication process and, as a result, become a more skilled listener.

FOCUSING ATTENTION

To be a good listener, you must know how to focus attention on the speaker. This focusing skill helps in two ways: It allows you to pick up nonverbal cues and it shows the sender that you are paying attention.

People who wear glasses often say that they can't hear as well without their glasses. Although this may strike you as odd, it is probably true because without their glasses, some receivers may miss a speaker's facial expressions, gestures, and body positions. As a result, they may miss much of the total message. By facing a speaker and watching carefully as she talks, you will catch both obvious and subtle cues about her intentions and emotions. Noting such factors as her breathing patterns, facial expressions, leg and arm positions, finger movements, and physical distance will help you to interpret her message.

Paraphrasing

Listening with the intent of **paraphrasing,** restating the speaker's message in your own words, will force you to focus on the message being presented. Indeed, one of the most effective ways of checking whether you have received a message is to repeat it back. Restating not only gives you a chance to check the ideas you have received, but also informs the other person that you are listening. Given how rare good listening is, paraphrasing to demonstrate your attentiveness can be a great compliment. In addition, if you force yourself to paraphrase, you will find you must listen to the entire message without interrupting.

Paraphrasing is an excellent device to use in a telephone conversation. Repeating the name and number of a caller who is leaving a message makes you focus on important details and note them accurately. Restating the details of an order, the directions for how to get someplace, or what a caller wants saves time in the long run by eliminating unnecessary mistakes.

Skilled paraphrasers repeat only the speaker's general idea—not the entire message. Paraphrasing starters include: "It sounds as if you . . . ," "You seem to be saying . . . ," "It appears to me that you believe . . . ," "What I perceive is . . . ," "What I heard you say was . . . ," and "So you believe that . . . ." When paraphrasing is done well, it is the best way to demonstrate that you are focusing on the speaker and listening thoughtfully.

The skill of paraphrasing is extremely important when you are interacting with people who may not speak the same native language as you do. Being able to reword their thoughts enables both people to check the accuracy of the message. Skill Development 6.2 will help you recognize accurate and effective paraphrases.

SKILL DEVELOPMENT 6.2

RECOGNIZING EFFECTIVE PARAPHRASING[16]

Select the effective paraphrase of the sender's message.

1. *Speaker:* "Sometimes I think I'd like to drop out of school, but then I start to feel like a quitter."
   a. "Maybe it would be helpful to take a break and then you can always come back."
   b. "You're so close to finishing. Can't you just keep with it a little bit longer?"
   c. "It sounds like you have doubts about finishing school but that you don't like to think of yourself as a person who would quit something you started."
   d. "What do you think the consequences will be if you drop out?"
2. *Speaker:* "I really don't want to go to a party where I don't know anyone. I'll just sit by myself all night."
   a. "You're apprehensive about going someplace where you don't know anyone because you'll be alone."
   b. "It would really be good for you to put yourself in that kind of a situation."
   c. "I can really relate to what you're saying. I feel awkward too when I go to strange places."

    d. "Maybe you could just go for half an hour and then you can always leave if you're not having a good time."
3. *Speaker:* "I get really nervous when I talk with people I respect and who I fear might not respect me."
    a. "I've really found it useful to prepare my remarks in advance. Then I'm not nearly as nervous."
    b. "You really shouldn't feel nervous with people you respect because in many ways you are just as good as they are."
    c. "You feel uncomfortable when you talk with people who you think may not regard you in a positive way."
    d. "Why do you think you get so nervous about people you respect?"

ANSWERS:

1—c, 2—a, 3—c

Taking Notes

Some people find that taking notes improves their listening because it requires them to concentrate on what the speaker is saying. Since an average sender speaks 150 words per minute (about half the number of words on a typed, double-spaced page) and an average receiver can grasp meaning at rates as high as 500 words per minute, listeners should have time to jot down a speaker's ideas.[17]

To make your notes most useful, concentrate on the main ideas and supporting evidence. Write down only what is necessary to remember the most important information, use key words, and avoid writing complete sentences or every word the speaker says. By putting the ideas in your own words, you can check your understanding and immediately review the speaker's message. Note taking is a skill that must be practiced. It should be an automatic part of your listening routine in class, while talking on the phone, and when you feel you can't concentrate on or remember a spoken message without some reinforcement.

Repeating

Another way to focus your attention and increase your comprehension is by repeating. For example, when a person is introduced to you, focus your attention on the name and immediately repeat it by saying something like, "It's nice to meet you, Marcia." Call the person by name several times during your conversation. Then, when departing, repeat the name again. The more you repeat the name and look at the person, the stronger your memory is likely to be.

Physically Paying Attention

Most people don't realize how much their bodies reflect whether they're focusing on what is being said. For example, when you're interested in what another person is saying, you lean forward and align your body with the speaker's body;

when you're enthusiastic about an idea, your posture straightens; and when you're disturbed by what is being said, your body tightens.

Good listeners recognize that sometimes they must change body position in order to focus more intently. Think of your body as an auto engine. If you drive a gearshift car, you know that at certain times you need to upshift or downshift. You need more engine power to get up a hill and less to cruise comfortably along a level highway. Similarly, in listening, you must upshift or downshift your body when it needs a change in power. Level 3 listening doesn't take a lot of effort; much like easy driving, third gear will do. Level 2 listening takes more power, and Level 1 requires great concentration and physical involvement. Sitting or standing upright with your eyes on the speaker are your most powerful listening positions. They force you to focus all your attention on the speaker and the immediate situation.

Right now, while you are reading this book, sit up straight, center all your attention on the words you are reading, ignore any outside sounds, and underline the key words on this page. You will find that your power of concentration increases immediately because you have, in effect, shifted into first gear. Stay in this position as long as necessary to grasp the material you are reading. Once you have identified the general trend, shift out of first gear. (It helps to know that in writing and speaking, the writer or speaker usually makes a statement and then clarifies by defining terms and giving examples. You may need first gear for the statement, second gear for the definition, and, if you understand what is being said, third gear for the examples.) Shift back to first when a new idea is presented. When you are not in first gear you can relax your body, but you should still stay alert (Level 2 listening, second gear).

Because active listening is hard work, it is tiring to maintain maximum alertness. Certain activities, such as appreciative listening, usually require only third gear. In contrast, listening for comprehension, as in class lectures, usually requires frequent shifting from gear to gear. Such shifts do not take place automatically. You must psychologically and physically shift gears for yourself during the act of listening.

ORGANIZING MATERIAL

You can help yourself remember what is said by using the organizing techniques of chunking, ordering, and reordering. (These techniques may be useful for listening to class lectures or technical information, but may not be practical in an ongoing conversation.)

Chunking

Chunking is the grouping together of bits of information insofar as they share a particular relationship. This allows you to condense information for easier recall. For example, while discussing a story in an American literature class, you could group the terms that describe each character so that later you remember each person's physical and emotional description rather than random details. Also, in conversation, as you and a friend talk about people you know in common, you can remember the names your friend tells you by placing the people in categories such as "major," "hometown," or "groups to which they belong."

Ordering

Ordering is the arranging of bits of information into a systematic sequence. Thus, in chemistry class you can more easily remember a process by organizing it into a step-by-step progression. For example, first, get the equipment for the experiment; second, get the necessary chemicals; third, study the lab manual to determine the order in which the chemicals are mixed; fourth, mix the chemicals. Similarly, planning a trip with a friend, you can organize your ideas by each day of the trip.

Reordering

Reordering is the changing of an existing system of organizing information so that a new or different sequence is developed. Reordering is useful when you have difficulty remembering material in the sequence in which it is presented. For example, rather than remembering the causes of World War I by dates, you might remember them according to the causes in each country going from west to east (England, France, Germany, and Austria-Hungary).

Skill Development 6.3 will give you some practice in chunking, ordering, and reordering.

SKILL DEVELOPMENT 6.3

CHUNKING, ORDERING, AND REORDERING

1. Chunk these: Wheaties, Bananas, Peaches, Cheerios, Frosted Flakes, Pineapple, Shredded Wheat, Strawberries.

2. Chunk these: hammer, saw, screws, wood, bricks, chisel, screw driver, nails, plaster board.

3. Order these: Christmas, Easter, Valentine's Day, Independence Day, Halloween, Labor Day.

4. Order these: France, Russia, Germany, England, Poland, India, Japan.

5. Reorder your answer for exercise 4.

6. Reorder these cities: Atlanta, Georgia; Baltimore, Maryland; Cleveland, Ohio; Dallas, Texas; Ft. Lauderdale, Florida; San Francisco, California.

POSSIBLE ANSWERS:

1. Fruits that are commonly put on cereals (bananas, peaches, pineapple, and strawberries) and cereals (Wheaties, Cheerios, Frosted Flakes, and Shredded Wheat).

2. The list contains tools used in construction (hammer, saw, chisel, and screw driver) and materials used in construction (screws, wood, bricks, nails, and plaster board).

3. The sequence Valentine's Day, Easter, Independence Day, Labor Day, Halloween, and Christmas, orders the holidays from earliest to latest in the year.

4. and 5. The sequence England, France, Germany, India, Japan, Poland, Russia, orders the countries alphabetically. Other methods for ordering them include spatial—going from west to east (England, France, Germany, Poland, Russia, India, Japan) or east to west, and from the country with the largest population total to the smallest, and vice versa.

6. Among the many possibilities would be to chunk the cities by north to south location, or east to west location, by alphabetical or reverse alphabetical order.

PROVIDING FEEDBACK

As a listener, a person can provide feedback to show listening attention or interest in the subject, to stop speakers from using unfamiliar vocabulary, to discourage them from digressing and speaking in circles, to alert them to the need for examples, to make them focus on the issue, to signal the need for specifics, to show empathy, and to suggest that thoughts need to be organized more comprehensively.

The focus of Skill Development 6.4 is on the methods others use to provide feedback that indicates they are listening to you.

SKILL DEVELOPMENT 6.4

LISTENING FOR FEEDBACK CUES

For each situation list several ways in which you could let others know you are listening to them, or others could let you know they are listening to you. As an example, answers are provided for the first situation.

Situation 1: You have just told your friend that you are going to Europe for the summer. She. . .

1. Nonverbal cues: *raises her eyebrows*

2. Verbal cues: *says "Wow!"*

3. Nonverbal and verbal cues combined: *nods and says "That's great"*

Situation 2: Your psychology professor calls you into her office and tells you that she would like you to be her research assistant next year. You. . .

1. Nonverbal cues: _____

2. Verbal cues: _____

3. Nonverbal and verbal cues combined: _____

Situation 3: Your communication professor is giving a lecture on rhetorical theory and you don't understand the relevance of the concept of *ethos.* You. . .

1. Nonverbal cues: _____

2. Verbal cues: _____

3. Nonverbal and verbal cues combined: _____

Situation 4: You have just told your best friend that your brother was hurt in an auto accident. He. . .

1. Nonverbal cues: _____

2. Verbal cues: _____

3. Nonverbal and verbal cues combined: _____

Look at the feedback cues you just listed. Do you use them when you are listening? Obviously, if they are encouraging when others use them on you, they will be encouraging when you use them on others.

Good listeners also use questions as feedback. By listening to a speaker's message carefully, you can determine the best question to ask to ensure that you understand the true intent. Do Skill Development 6.5 to practice this technique.

PROVIDING FEEDBACK

Here are some speakers' statements. Based on the problem, indicate two questions you would ask as feedback.

1. "Running that computer program is easy. You buck up the system, bring up the program, key in the material, and you're on your way." *Problem:* You don't understand what to do because you don't understand computer jargon.

2. "We went to the party and everyone was doing all kinds of stuff." *Problem:* You want to know specifically what was done.

3. "I believe that higher interest rates are good for the economy!" *Problem:* You want to know why the speaker has this belief.

4. "There are three reasons for changing the speed limit. I think those are enough cause for passing the law." *Problem:* You don't know what the reasons are.

DEVELOPING EMPATHIC LISTENING SKILLS

Empathic listening, listening to understand another person's message from her or his point of view, requires attention to both the content and the feeling of the message. You must establish rapport, communicate acceptance, and encourage the speaker to continue talking.

If you already are or plan to become a helping professional, working in psychology, social services, teaching, speech therapy, law, or medicine, you must have good empathic listening skills. Empathic listening requires that you understand the basic helping process model as illustrated in Figure 6.2.

Involving yourself in another person's life requires acting as a mirror to reflect his or her problems or needs. You then help the person to *explore* the situation. This is often accomplished by listening carefully and posing feedback questions that stimulate the other person to talk and think about his or her problem. The goal is to help the person to *resolve* the problem through either personal insight or a series of experiences that provide useful skills. In the *concluding step,* the listener summarizes the involving, exploring, and resolving steps and indicates possible future actions.

To be a good empathic listener, you should restate what is said and use verbal and nonverbal feedback to show that you understand. Only if the troubled person asks for advice and you are trained to help people achieve behavioral change should you get involved beyond reflecting. People who try to play "Dear Abby"

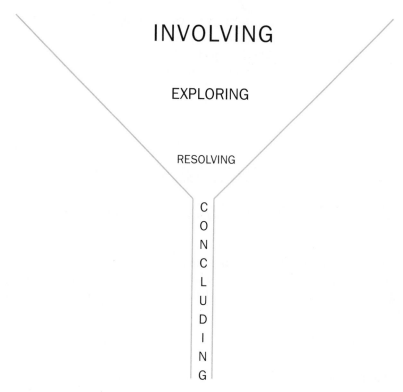

INVOLVING

EXPLORING

RESOLVING

C
O
N
C
L
U
D
I
N
G

FIGURE 6.2

without the appropriate training, no matter how good their intentions, often do more harm than good.

In empathizing you must listen not only to the speaker's words, but also to the feelings behind the words. You must see the world through the other's eyes, suspending judgment in order to understand the speaker's thoughts and feelings as the speaker experiences them.

To carry out the process, the empathic listener should keep these questions in mind: What is the real problem (why is the person asking for help)? What is the person feeling (about himself or herself, the problem, you, and the process of getting help)? How can you be helpful (what can you realistically do)?

Good empathic listeners reflect the actual situation rather than create new pictures. One of the most difficult things you, as an empathic listener, must do is to stop yourself from interrupting the emotional flow of a speaker who needs to express his or her feelings. Interrupting, giving advice, or even asking questions at an inappropriate time may thwart the effectiveness of the interaction.

Paraphrasing is an especially productive way to probe a speaker for more information. In addition, your feedback should describe rather than evaluate, be specific rather than general, and take into account the other person's needs. Try to avoid trite statements ("That's too bad," "This too shall pass," and "We all go through that"), but invite the person to tell more ("Would you like to talk about that?" "Tell me about it," and "I'd be glad to listen").

Noting how you respond to others' statements and actions can help you determine whether you listen empathically. Knowledge Checkup 6.4 will help you assess your usual response to others—whether you listen empathically or with some other style.

KNOWLEDGE CHECKUP 6.4

ASSESSING YOUR LISTENING RESPONSES[18]

Circle the letter that best describes your first response to the person in each situation. The goal is to tell how you would actually respond, not what the right response would be or how you would like to respond. Each is a work-related example. Put yourself into the situation, whether or not you have actually had the experience.

1. "I think I'm doing all right, but I don't know where I stand. I'm not sure what my boss expects of me, and she doesn't tell me how I'm doing. I'm trying my best, but I wonder who else knows that. I wish I knew where I stood."
   a. "Has your boss ever given you any indication of what she thinks of your work?"
   b. "If I were you, I'd discuss it with her."
   c. "Perhaps others are also in the same position, so you shouldn't let it bother you."
   d. "Not knowing if you're satisfying your boss leaves you feeling unsure, and you'd like to know just what she expects from you."
2. "The policy is supposed to be to promote from within the company. And now I find that this new person is coming in from the outside to replace my boss. I had my eyes on that job; I've been working hard for it. I know I could prove myself if I had a chance. Well, if that's what they think of me, I know when I'm not wanted."
   a. "You shouldn't have to climb over people to get what you want."
   b. "Getting ahead is very important in your life, even if it means hard work, and it won't be easy."
   c. "What in particular do you want to achieve?"
   d. "You should take some management classes to help you advance."
3. "I'm really tired of this. I come in in the morning and already I've got twice as much work as I can do. And then they say that 'this is a rush,' or 'hurry up with that.' I've got so many people asking me to do things that I just can't keep up, and it bothers me. I like my boss, and my work is interesting, but I could use a vacation."

    a. "With so many people asking you to get everything done, it's difficult for you to accomplish all of it, and the pressure gets you down."

    b. "Are all these requests from other people part of your job?"

    c. "You seem to have too much work. Why don't you talk it over with your boss?"

    d. "You probably are overworked because you're not organized."

4. "I work like mad to get rush projects completed! What's my reward for getting them out? Nothing! No thanks, no nothing. In fact, most of the time the so-called rush projects are sitting on people's desks unattended for days."

    a. "How often does this happen?"

    b. "You ought to tell them you don't like being treated this way."

    c. "It appears to me you feel like others are taking advantage of you and that you are being treated unfairly."

    d. "You shouldn't get so angry."

5. "He used to be one of the guys until he was promoted. Now he's not my friend anymore. I don't mind being told about my mistakes, but he doesn't have to do it in front of my coworkers. Whenever I get the chance, he's going to get his!"

    a. "To be told about your mistakes in front of coworkers is embarrassing, especially by a supervisor you once worked with."

    b. "If you didn't make so many mistakes, your boss would not have to tell you about them."

    c. "Why don't you talk it over with a few people who knew him before and then go talk to him about this situation?"

    d. "How often does he do this?"

Listed below are the possible responses for each of the five situations. If you circled answer *a* in situation number 1, circle 1a below (in the "asking for information response" category). If you circled answer *b,* circle 1b below (in the "recommendation response" category). Do this for your five responses.

Empathic response: 1d, 2b, 3a, 4c, 5a

Recommendation response: 1b, 2d, 3c, 4b, 5c

Asking for information response: 1a, 2c, 3b, 4a, 5d

Critical response: 1c, 2a, 3d, 4d, 5b

Underline the category in which you have the most circled answers. This is your general listening response style.

EMPATHIC RESPONSE STYLE

If your general response style is empathic, you are probably nonjudgmental as you listen. Empathic listeners tend to focus on the essential themes and feelings that are being expressed and at the same time try to build rapport and mutual understanding. Empathic listeners also demonstrate a good grasp of paraphrasing because their feedback reflects both the content and the feelings of the speaker.[19]

RECOMMENDATION RESPONSE STYLE

If your general listening response style is to make recommendations, you are probably an advice offerer who tells the speaker what to do and what not to do. You attempt to solve the problem or to do the thinking for the talker.

ASKING FOR INFORMATION RESPONSE STYLE

If your general listening response style is to ask for additional information, you probably want to clarify your understanding before you react. This approach is usually positive, but if you overuse it a speaker may feel grilled or that you aren't dealing specifically with the problem and how she or he feels. As a result, your delay may be perceived as disinterest or lack of involvement.

It is important to remember that some cultures will not answer your request for additional information. In the Japanese and Chinese cultures, as a way of saving face people often will say *yes* even when they mean *no*. And in many Latin cultures, where social harmony is important, people will often supply you with the response they think you want to hear rather than the "real" one.

CRITICAL RESPONSE STYLE

If your general response style is to criticize, you show a tendency to judge, approve, or disapprove of the messages you receive. Instead of focusing on content and emotion, you are probably listening for information that may be used to evaluate the speaker. Critical responses often cause conflicts because the speaker feels attacked and thus may lash out at you in frustration.

Hearing may be natural, but effective listening is not. It requires work: You need to evaluate your listening strengths and weaknesses; you need to recognize the barriers that interfere with your ability to be a good listener; and you need to develop the skills necessary to overcome those barriers. In addition, if you want to help others, you need to develop empathic listening skills. Given the large amount of time you spend listening, the work is well worth the effort.

COMMUNICATION COMPETENCY CHECKUP

The goal of this communication competency checkup is to guide you in putting your skills and knowledge about listening to use and to help you summarize the material in this chapter.

Reprinted with special permission of North America Syndicate.

The teacher seems to be indicating that Funky is not displaying good listening skills in class.

1. In the classroom, which reasons for listening should be motivating Funky?

2. Based on Funky's response, what listening level is he displaying?

3. Which barriers to effective listening seem to be keeping Funky from being an effective listener, both in the classroom and now while talking to the teacher?

4. What specific techniques could Funky use to improve his listening skills and therefore maintain attention throughout the class and in the type of interpersonal conversation illustrated here?

5. Name one of Funky's red flags.

6. Consider this situation: In the teachers' lounge an instructor was discussing a class she recently taught. She said, "I was really afraid that the way I presented the material would confuse the students." What would a fellow teacher with an empathic response style say? What would a person with a recommending response style say? What would a person with an asking-for-information response style say? What would a person with a critical response style say? How would the teacher probably react to each colleague's response?

NOTES

1. Don Oldenburg, "Sometimes People Only Hear What They Really Want to Hear," *Washington Post,* as reprinted in *Cleveland Plain Dealer,* March 18, 1987, G1, using materials developed by Robert Montgomery, in *Listening Made Easy* (New York, AMACOM, 1984).

2. Ibid.

3. Satoshi Ishii and Tom Bruneau, "Silence and Silences in Cross-Cultural Perspective: Japan and the United States," in Larry A. Samovar and Richard E. Porter (Eds.), *Intercultural Communication: A Reader* (Belmont, CA: Wadsworth, 1991), p. 314.

4. Larry A. Samovar and Richard E. Porter, *Communication between Cultures* (Belmont, CA: Wadsworth, 1991), p. 125.

5. Beverly D. Sypher, Robert N. Bostrom, and Joy Hart Siebert, "Listening Communication Abilities and Success at Work," *Journal of Business Communication* 26 (1989): 293–303.

6. For a discussion of several studies concerning how communicating time is divided (among listening, speaking, and writing, for example), see: Andrew D. Wolvin and Carolyn Gwynn Coakley, *Listening,* 4th ed. (Dubuque, IA: Wm. C. Brown, 1992), pp. 7–9.

7. Judi Brownell, "Perceptions of Effective Listeners: A Management Study," *Journal of Business Communication* 27 (1990): 401–15.

8. J. Bruneau, "Empathy and Listening: A Conceptual Review and Theoretical Directions," *Journal of the International Listening Association* 3 (1989): 1–20.

9. Adapted from Dr. Virginia Katz, University of Minnesota–Duluth, as cited in Oldenburg, "Sometimes People Only Hear."

10. Based on D. Aronson, "Stimulus Factors and Listening Strategies in Auditory Memory: A Theoretical Analysis," *Cognitive Psychology* 6 (1974): 108–32, as cited in Blain Goss, "Listening as Information Processing," *Communication Quarterly* 30 (Fall 1982): 306.

11. Steven Golan, "A Factor Analysis of Barriers to Effective Listening," *Journal of Business Communication* 27 (1990): 25–36.

12. For a discussion of the cybernetic process, see: Norbert Wiener, *The Human Use of Human Beings* (New York: Anchor Books, 1950).

13. Adapted from: Madelyn Burley-Allen, *Listening: The Forgotten Skill* (New York: John Wiley and Sons, 1982), p. 44.

14. Adapted from a handout by George Tuttle and John Murdock, "Approaches to Teaching Listening as a Communication Behavior in Businesses and Organization," a workshop at the Speech Communication Association Convention, Anaheim, CA, November 11, 1981, plus additional material from Burley-Allen, *Listening: The Forgotten Skill,* p. 42.

15. Cited by Ronald Adler, Lawrence Rosenfeld, and Neil Towne, *Interplay: The Process of Speech Communication,* 4th ed. (New York: Harcourt Brace Jovanovich, 1989), p. 182.

16. Based on a non-author-identified handout entitled, "Listening," Speech Communication Association, San Francisco, 1989.

17. David B. Orr, "Time-Compressed Speech–A Perspective," *Journal of Communication* 18 (1968): 288–92.

18. Burley-Allen, *Listening: The Forgotten Skill,* pp. 85–89.

19. For an extended discussion of empathic listening and response styles, see: William E. Arnold, *Crisis Communication* (Scottsdale, AZ: Gorsuch Scarisbrick Publishers, 1980). For a discussion of monologic and dialogic listening, see, Michael Beatty, *The Romantic Dialogue: Communication in Dating and Marriage* (Englewood, CO: Morton Publishing Company, 1986), Chapter 9.

FOR FURTHER INVESTIGATION

Arnold, William. *Crisis Communication.* Scottsdale, AZ: Gorsuch Scarisbrick Publishers, 1980.

Broome, Benjamin. "Building Shared Meaning: Implications of a Relational Approach to Empathy for Teaching Intercultural Communication." *Communication Education* 40 (1991): 235–49.

Burley-Allen, Madelyn. *Listening: The Forgotten Skill.* New York: John Wiley and Sons, 1982.

Drakeford, John W. "Tuning Out: The Most Debilitating Social Disease." *New Woman* (July 1983): 66–69.

Dyer, Wayne. *Your Erroneous Zones.* New York: Avon Books, 1976.

Goss, Blaine, "Listening as Information Processing." *Communication Quarterly* 30 (1982): 304–7.

Kinlaw, Dennis. *Listening and Communication Skills.* San Diego, CA: University Associates, 1981.

Raudsepp, Eugene. "The Art of Listening Well." *INC* (October 1981): 135.

Steil, Lyman. *Your Listening Profile.* New York: Sperry Corporation, 1980.

Steil, Lyman. "Secrets of Being a Better Listener." *U.S. News and World Report* (May 26, 1980): 65–66.

Wolff, Florence, and Nadine Marsnik. *Perceptive Listening,* 2d ed. Fort Worth: Harcourt Brace Jovanovich, 1992.

Wolvin, Andrew D., and Carolyn Gwynn Coakley. *Listening,* 4th ed. Dubuque, IA: Wm. C. Brown, 1992.

CHAPTER 7

Stress and Communication Anxiety

COMMUNICATION COMPETENCIES

This chapter examines stress and communication anxiety. Specifically, the objective of the chapter is for you to learn to:

- Distinguish stress from distress and eustress.
- Identify verbal and nonverbal behaviors that accompany distress and eustress.
- Describe the three stages of stress reactions.
- Recognize your personal sources of stress.
- Use both self-help stress management techniques and stress management techniques that require the assistance of other people.
- Identify the presence of personal communication anxiety.
- Define communication anxiety and identify its causes and effects.
- Assess the extent of your own communication anxiety and choose appropriate short-term or long-term methods of treatment.
- Utilize the Stress Management Model for buffering, controlling, and combating stress.

KEY WORDS

The key words in this chapter are:

stress	entrapment
eustress	time management
distress	empathic listening support
stressor	technical appreciation support
alarm stage	emotional support
adaptation or resistance stage	shared social reality support
exhaustion stage	communication anxiety
burnout	publicly anxious people
buffering	privately anxious people
controlling	rhetoritherapy
combat	systematic desensitization
self-defeating attitudes	positive visualization

It's 7:00 A.M. and a call from a friend jars you out of a restless sleep. He asks, "What's happening today?" It's Tuesday, which means three hours of classes and work after school. It also means taking a test and finding out about the raise you were promised. And to top it off, you need to resolve an argument you and your friend had yesterday.

How do your respond? Do you pull the blanket over your head and go back to sleep? Do you laugh or cry? Do you stare at your face in the mirror and wonder how you're going to survive? Or do you take a deep breath, exhale, and feel yourself getting excited by what is clearly going to be a challenging day?

STRESS AND COMMUNICATION

Stress is your body's reaction to any event that pushes it out of what you consider to be normal; it is your body's preparation to respond to the unusual. The stress process is sequential: (1) an *event* occurs, (2) you *perceive* it to have a particular effect on you, (3) the event is related to something you *need or want*, and (4) you determine how you *feel* about it.

For example, consider that Tuesday morning after a sleepless night. The test is your *event*. You *perceive* the test as making you nervous. You *want* a high grade on the exam so you can confirm that you know the course material, get a high grade in the course, and increase your chances of being accepted into graduate school. How do you *feel* about the test? If you have studied hard, know the material, and were successful on previous exams in the course, you may feel terrific and not even use the word *stress* to define the situation. On the other hand, if you're like most students, even if you studied, feel you have a general grasp of the material, and did fairly well on previous tests, you may feel anxious and use the word *stressed* to describe yourself.

The test evoked a reaction. If you were prepared and confident, then your reaction was actually **eustress**, or stress perceived as positive. If you were anxious about the test, it was **distress**, stress perceived as negative. The word *stress* can be misleading because it does not indicate whether your feelings are positive or negative. Interestingly, your body responds in the same way regardless of how you feel.

TABLE 7.1 4-Step Stress Sequence

Step 1: An event occurs

Step 2: You perceive it to have a particular effect on you

Step 3: The event is related to something you need or want

Step 4: You determine how you feel about it

As your instructor starts to pass out the test, perhaps a knot forms in your stomach, whether you perceive the situation negatively or positively.

There is nothing in any event that in and of itself makes it a **stressor**, a source of stress. What makes it a stressor is your perceptions. As a result, every event and situation is a potential stressor.

VERBAL REACTIONS THAT REFLECT FEELING STRESSED

Individuals who feel distress or eustress display a variety of predictable verbal behaviors. For example, when people feel their needs are being thwarted—as in conflict situations—they tend to attack the other person rather than to discuss the underlying issues. If asked for clarification or additional explanation, they tend to repeat exactly what was said the first time. And they often swear for emphasis. Consider the following conversation in which Robert is distressed:

JON: Where were you last night?
ROBERT: I told you I went to the library.
JON: I went to look for you.
ROBERT: I already told you! I went to the %#$&% library!!
JON: Okay, I was just asking.
ROBERT: I went to the $&*$#* library to study for that %$&@%#& test!

People who feel stress may appear self-engrossed because they lead the conversation to their own areas of expertise or interest. If they can't direct the topic of conversation, they often remain quiet. Or they may grow impatient and use a variety of interjections, such as "yes, yes, uh-huh, yes," to encourage the other person to hurry. For example, on the day of a test, that topic may consume all of your thoughts. Because you are anxious, talking with your friend becomes an either–or proposition: Either you talk about the test—and you use impatient interjections to get your friend to hurry up and get to the topic you wish to discuss—or you don't talk at all. Knowledge Checkup 7.1 provides you with the opportunity to assess your verbal communication reactions to stressors.

KNOWLEDGE CHECKUP 7.1

SELF-ASSESSMENT OF YOUR STRESS REACTIONS

Check each behavior that you personally experience when you feel pressured.

_____ verbally attack people
_____ repeat the same words over and over without variation

_____ talk obsessively about the source of stress
_____ make errors in grammar and pronunciation
_____ encourage others to speak quickly
_____ experience lack of quick recall, resulting in pauses
_____ talk only if you can talk about the source of stress

YOUR NONVERBAL REACTIONS TO STRESS

There are more nonverbal than verbal responses to stressors. Knowledge Checkup 7.2 gives you the opportunity to identify your nonverbal stress signs.

KNOWLEDGE CHECKUP 7.2

YOUR NONVERBAL SIGNS OF STRESS

Put a check mark next to as many of these nonverbal signs of stress as you experience:

_____ gritting teeth

_____ sweating palms

_____   tightened stomach muscles

_____   chewing on pencils

_____   shifting position in a chair

_____   moving, walking, and eating rapidly

_____   finger drumming

_____   fist clenching

_____   jaw clenching

_____   head scratching

_____   nail biting

_____   using facial expressions, such as repeatedly wetting the lips, clearing the throat, and wrinkling the forehead

_____   using eye movements, such as rapid blinking, squinting, and looking away

_____   pacing

_____   shifting weight

_____   wiggling

_____   eating too much or not at all

_____   drinking or smoking more than usual

_____   hands trembling

_____   withdrawal—avoiding interaction

_____   using a sarcastic or nasty tone

_____   engaging in vocal explosiveness—accenting key words when there is no reason to do so

_____   speeding up at the ends of sentences

_____   using higher voice pitch than normal

_____   overarticulating—enunciating words so clearly and precisely that it draws attention

STAGES OF STRESS REACTIONS

Our reactions to stress occur in three stages: alarm, adaptation or resistance, and exhaustion. By being aware of your reactions, you can begin to identify those situations that you consider stressful.

The Alarm Stage

In the **alarm stage** your body's systems are alerted to a potential threat. The primary physiological reaction is the production of adrenalin. This reaction causes your muscles to tense and get ready for action, your heart rate to increase, and your senses to become more acute. For example, when you see someone with whom you've had an argument, you may find yourself tightly clenching your jaw, feeling your heart pounding, and becoming aware that your palms are sweating. All of these reactions—which include a heightened awareness of yourself, the other person, and your surroundings—prepare you to meet the person.

The Adaptation or Resistance Stage

The second phase in reacting to stress is **adaptation** or **resistance.** You may adapt to a situation by accepting it and adjusting your behavior to meet its demands, or you may resist by denying or ignoring it. When you saw the other person walking your way you could have adapted by accepting that the meeting would happen, whether you liked it or not, and thinking about what to say, or you could have resisted by turning in another direction and walking away—essentially refusing to meet.

The Exhaustion Stage

The last stage is the **exhaustion stage.** After surviving a stressful situation, you feel physically and mentally drained. All you may want to do is rest or escape. After confronting someone with whom you're having a conflict you may feel a strong desire to sleep or avoid working any more that day.

Prolonged fatigue without signs of relief can lead to **burnout**—physical, emotional, and mental exhaustion. *Physical exhaustion*, characterized by feeling tired and weak, may lead to such things as increased illness, higher incidence of accidents, frequent headaches, and nausea. *Emotional exhaustion*, typified by feelings of helplessness, depression, and entrapment, may lead to continual crying, inappropriate laughter, and loss of emotional control. And, *mental exhaustion*, distinguished by negative attitudes toward yourself, your work, and life in general, may lead to work dissatisfaction, feelings of inferiority, and a damaged self-concept.[1]

RECOGNIZING YOUR STRESSORS

You don't have to look far to recognize your stressors. Although college is supposed to be one of the most enjoyable times of life, this is hardly the case for students who find themselves facing the tremendous pressures of learning, relational development, adjusting to new and conflicting ideas, holding down a job, caring for children, and the myriad of other possible stressors. The suicide rate is higher among college students than among nonstudents of the same age group, and many students drop out of school because they cannot cope with the strain. For students who do not drop out, the counseling center serves an important function: Between 5 and 10 percent of the college population seeks professional psychological help.[2] In the adult non-school population, people vary in their causes of stress. Women tend to feel more role conflict (home versus work) and men report more work-related stress.[3]

To deal with stress, you must first recognize your sources of stress. Knowledge Checkup 7.3 will help you analyze those aspects of your life that trigger stress reactions.

KNOWLEDGE CHECKUP 7.3

YOUR STRESS ANALYSIS

Answer the following questions. Each time you answer yes, give examples.

1. What are your current life goals? Do any of your important goals conflict with each other? (*Sample:* Yes, I want to work full-time so I can be financially independent, but I also want to be a full-time student who makes Dean's List each semester.)

2. What are your important values? Do your values conflict with those of people who are important to you?

3. Are there times when you can't get all your work done? Are there times when you are bored because there is not enough work to do?

4. Do you avoid saying no?

5. Do you give other people more importance in your life than you give yourself?

6. Are there certain people and/or events in your life that you perceive as stressors?

7. Do you feel it is necessary to alter your emotions to make them socially acceptable?

8. Do you eat foods that you consider unhealthful?

9. Do you find it difficult to get away from people or events that you perceive as stressors?

10. Do you get angry or depressed when you do not come in first in competitive activities?

11. Are any of your family relationships distressing?

12. Do you avoid taking the time to do nice things for yourself?

RESPONDING TO YOUR STRESSORS: SELF-HELP TECHNIQUES

Don't be disturbed if you answered yes to many or all of the questions in Knowledge Checkup 7.3. It only means that you are typical and that, like any other typical person, you need to take action to buffer, control, and combat your stress.

You use the technique of **buffering** when you anticipate a stressor and develop a plan that helps you deal with the situation before you experience distress. For example, because you anticipate that a possible group meeting in one course may be scheduled right after one already planned in another course, you begin preparing now for the meeting already planned and save study time to prepare for the possible meeting later.

Controlling takes place when the stress you feel is not strong enough to require combat, but you take action to ensure that it doesn't increase. This could occur when you determine, after several semesters of experience, how many close relationships you can participate in at one time without feeling overburdened. By getting close to no more than the predetermined number of people, you effectively control your stress.

When the stress becomes distress, it is necessary to **combat** it—to reduce or eliminate the negative feelings through self-help techniques or techniques requiring others. Among the self-help techniques you may use to buffer, control, and combat stress on your own are attitude changes, time management, and exercise. Techniques requiring others include self-help groups and professional help.

Attitude Changes

We are a society that regards perfection, speed, pleasing others, winning, and strength as highly desirable. Although no one could possibly live up to the North American ideal, to be less than perfect is to be considered flawed and undesirable. To be less than quick at doing everything is to appear insecure. Not to want to please others is to be self-centered. Not to win all the time is to be a loser. And not to be physically and emotionally strong is to be impotent and impaired.

Attitudes that include having to be perfect, fast, other-centered, winning, and strong all the time are self-defeating. Self-defeating attitudes increase the probability that you will perceive people and events as threatening and, therefore, increase your feelings of distress. Increased feelings of distress mean increased use of your verbal and nonverbal communication indicators of stress, such as biting your nails, shifting your weight from foot to foot, or speaking nonfluently. Self-defeating attitudes also increase the likelihood that your communication will reveal your low self-esteem. For example, you may avoid communicating with others, criticize yourself a great deal, or speak hesitantly for fear of being wrong.

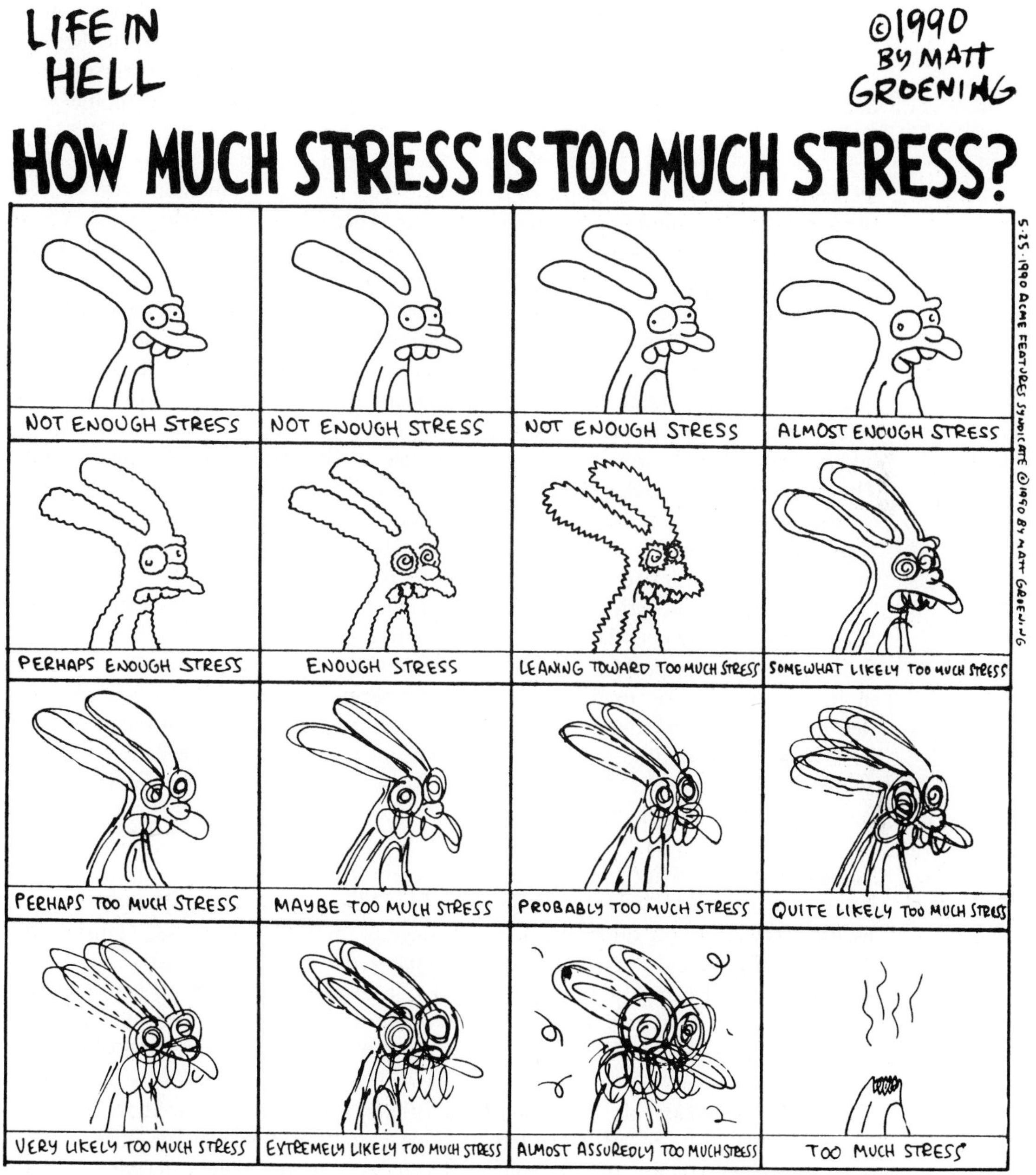

The most common anxiety-producing myths in our society are that we must be perfect, quick, pleasing, winning, and strong. Review your answers to Knowledge Checkups 7.1 and 7.2 to find out how susceptible you are to the stresses produced by these myths. Then consider the steps you can take to overcome your stressors.

Perfection   Questions 1, 7, and 10 in Knowledge Checkup 7.3 indicate whether you think it is necessary and important to be perfect. Though striving to do your very best is not in and of itself negative, it may become a stressor if you believe that anything less than perfection in everything you do means that you are a bad person.

Because no one is perfect, it is important to recognize that the possibility of achieving perfection is indeed a myth. Acknowledging the myth for what it is can aid you to catch the potential stressor before it becomes distressful. For example, in question 1 you might have indicated that one of your goals is to work full-time to be financially independent. Do you want to do this because being financially independent will make you the "perfect" spouse or the "perfect" daughter or son? The other goal is to make the Dean's List every semester. Do you think that being on the Dean's List will make you the "perfect" student? Neither one of these goals is in and of itself wrong. But problems arise when you attempt to achieve either or both of them in order to perceive yourself as perfect.

The stress associated with always striving for perfection may become self-defeating as energy gets drained in unproductive worry. In place of telling yourself that you have to be perfect, tell yourself that being imperfect does not mean being inefficient, ineffective, or incomplete. All people make mistakes and you are entitled to your share, no matter what you have been told. That does not mean you can goof off! The next time you hear your internal voice say, "Be perfect!," respond with, "I can be myself," "I can make mistakes," "I can be human," and, possibly most difficult of all, "I can accept failure."

Speed   Question 3 indicates whether you subscribe to the "hurry-up" myth. Do you feel you should always be doing something? Do you feel that you lack the time to do everything you ought to do? When your internal voice says, "Hurry up," "Stop wasting time," "You're not going to make it," or "You'll never get it done," respond with, "I can take the time I need," "I deserve some time to just do nothing," "I'll get it done, but at a pace that's comfortable," and "I'll examine the time available and come up with a plan to accomplish the project within the schedule."

> "I am five-years old. I am the best little boy in the world, told so day after day. The worst thing I have done to date is to consider—just to consider—ripping off the mattress tag that says DO NOT REMOVE THIS TAG Under Penalty of Law." John Reid, *The Best Little Boy in the World*, p.3

Pleasing Others   The most pervasive myth is that it is crucial to please others. In an attempt to please others, people often become nonassertive or passive—willing to let others have their way and let their own needs and wants go unfulfilled. By being passive you deny yourself the opportunity to express your wants, needs, and thoughts. Therefore, you increase your level of frustration and become distressed.

Questions 2, 4, 5, 6, 7, 9, and 11 in Knowledge Checkup 7.3 all relate to pleasing others. Often this myth becomes so important that you consider yourself selfish, inconsiderate, rude, and aloof if you put yourself first. It is natural for young children to want to please their parents, and because they are rewarded for complying, such behavior is reinforced. The attitude based on pleasing behavior thus becomes a way of life—a way of life that may make a person strive for goals that are emotionally and physically destructive.

Your emotion-conscious internal voice tells you to express your emotions in line with societal expectations. The messages might be, "Don't be impulsive," "Control yourself," "Act like a grown-up," and "A proper lady doesn't get angry, she cries." To cope, you may respond, "I can express how I feel so long as I don't hurt someone else," "Anyone can get angry and anyone can cry, it has nothing to do with gender," "I have the right to show my feelings and not fear them as weak-nesses," or "I can own my feelings."

Perhaps question 4 best summarizes this myth: Are you someone who can't say no? Before discussing this misconception, answer the following questions:

KNOWLEDGE CHECKUP 7.4

YOUR RESPONSIBILITY QUESTIONNAIRE

Indicate whether each statement is true or false regarding your *usual* behavior.

T F I believe other people can make me feel bad by what they say or do.

T F I believe other people can make me feel good by what they say or do.

T F I can make other people feel bad by what I say or do.

T F I can make other people feel good by what I say or do.

If you answered true to any of the questions, you are the victim of **entrapment**! Entrapped people believe that by saying yes they can make other people happy. In fact, you can't make anyone feel anything; only the other person can make himself or herself feel a particular way. Likewise, no one can make you feel anything; only you can choose how to feel. Your behavior may *invite* another person to feel a particular way—for example, calling someone stupid may invite the person to feel hurt—but it is up to the other person to decide whether to accept the invitation. Calling someone stupid may elicit feelings of anger, hurt, amusement, disbelief—any variety of feelings. The other person will choose how she or he will feel.

If your internal voice tells you, "Others can make you feel good or bad by what they say or do," substitute, "Wrong! Others may invite me to feel a particular way, but how I feel is my choice." Similarly, when you think you can make others feel a particular way, substitute the word *invite* for *make* and you will be a step closer to eliminating the myth that it is necessary to please others.

Winning   How important is it to you to be a winner? What will you do to win? How do you feel when you don't win? These are some of the issues implied in question 10. In North America, where there is an emphasis on individualism, people have the attitude that "Winning isn't everything; it's the *only* thing." If you are one of those people, your internal voice screams continuously, "Win, win, win," and "Second place is no place." To silence the voice, respond with, "I only have to do my best, winning isn't everything," "Not everything is a contest that must be won or lost." It is important to remember that if you have this attitude you might be interacting with people from cultures that stress collectivism, such as Mexico, Japan, and China. Many people from collectivistic cultures do not have the competitive voice driving them to win at any cost.[4]

Physical and Emotional Strength   Question 8 in Knowledge Checkup 7.3 relates to the myth of being physically and emotionally strong. The United States is in the midst of a health kick. It doesn't take much for a North American to feel guilty about his or her physical appearance: Gaining a pound, eating two scoops of ice cream instead of one (or better yet, none), not being a jogger or an aerobics enthusiast—any of these can set off a health-conscious internal voice: "You didn't exercise today," "Nobody loves a fat person," "Why do you think they call it *junk* food?" Although certain foods are indeed better for your health than others, it is often the guilt associated with eating poorly and not exercising that is the major stressor, and not the junk food or lack of exercise. Respond to the internal voice with messages such as, "Though I should be exercising now, I have to finish my work." (Do not lie to yourself! Lying to yourself doubles the anxiety: the original guilt plus the added guilt!)

Skill Development 7.1 will help you practice appropriate coping responses to self-defeating attitudes.

SKILL DEVELOPMENT 7.1

DEVELOPING COPING RESPONSES TO SELF-DEFEATING ATTITUDES

Here are a series of experiences you could have. Make a coping response to counterbalance your internal voice in each situation.

1. Your term paper is due next week. You have completed the research, but have not written the paper. A friend has an extra ticket for a concert and wants you to attend—the look on your friend's face indicates how important it is for you to go. You really need time to finish the paper. Your internal voice says, "It's really important to please one's friends—after all, that's what friends do." Your coping response is: _____

_____

2. A family member calls to say that your pet, whom you've had since you were six years old, has been hit by a car and will probably die. Your companion says, "Hey, it's only an animal."
Your coping response to your internal message to hold back tears is: _____

_____

3. Your instructor hands back your English theme. You worked hard on it and had it checked by the writing lab tutor, who told you it was excellent. To your surprise and disappointment, when the instructor hands back your paper you're told, "Weak paper. Did you read the assignment?" You've always been told to "respect your elders" and that "teachers are always right," so your first inclination is to leave the class and say nothing.
Your coping response is: _____

_____

Time Management

Very few people have unlimited time. If you are typical, you are under pressure to fill your precious hours with work, school, relationships, and other responsibilities. As a result, you are often caught in a web of conflicting demands that require you to use **time management**, to set priorities for the use of your time and then to decide what to do when and for how long. By managing your time effectively, you reduce the stress in your life and, therefore, reduce the number of verbal and nonverbal indicators that you are feeling stressed.

One way to manage your time is to divide responsibilities into three categories of importance. Suppose that you want to go to a movie with your friends but have a group project due tomorrow and a term paper due next week that you have started working on and are enjoying writing. In order of priority, the group project is a *have-to* (it's due tomorrow, so there's no putting it off), the paper is a *want-to* (even though you enjoy working on it, it isn't due for a week), and the movie is a *would like-to* (even though you want to do it more than the other two).

Once you understand your priorities and needs (remember you must do such things as eat and sleep, too), you can develop a schedule for managing your time. The goal is to buffer, control, or combat stress by avoiding overscheduling, underscheduling, conflicting schedules, and, most importantly, procrastination. Use the Time Management Model (Skill Development 7.2) to learn an approach to budgeting your time.

TIME MANAGEMENT MODEL

DIRECTIONS:

A. On a separate sheet of paper:
1. List your *have-to's* (things that *must* be done today) and the approximate amount of time that each activity will take. (Remember to include time for taking care of important relationships, sleeping, eating, classes, work obligations, and stress reduction—exercise and relaxation.)
2. List your *want-to's* (things you *should* do today) and the approximate amount of time that each activity will take.
3. List your *would like-to's* (things that you *would like* to do if you had some extra time today) and the approximate amount of time that each activity would take.

B. Using the calendar page:
1. Schedule the *have-to's* (A) in their order of importance.
2. If there is time left, schedule the *want-to's* (B) in their order of importance.
3. If there is time left, schedule the *would like-to's* (C) in their order of importance.

C. Follow the schedule!

DATE _____

AM	ACTIVITY
7	
8	
9	
10	
11	
Noon	
1	
2	
3	
4	
5	

6 _____

7 _____

8 _____

9 _____

10 _____

11 _____

MDNT _____

Just setting a schedule and sticking to it may become frustrating, so it is important to create a reward system for fulfilling your goal. If your schedule gives you an hour to study, set aside the last ten minutes to do something you will enjoy. It may be taking a short walk, watching a little TV, getting some ice cream, shooting a couple of baskets, or phoning a friend. Do whatever you feel will reward you for "being good." This technique allows you to look forward to the pleasure that will come from doing what, in some instances, you'd prefer not to do. It also works on the principle of costs and rewards in that you are getting something you need or want in exchange for doing something that takes effort. *Just be sure that after enjoying your reward, you return to your schedule and complete your tasks!*

Once you have implemented your schedule (and you may need to develop several, for example, one for weekdays and one for the weekends), evaluate the results and either continue with the schedule or make the necessary adjustments. Warning: Once you become skilled at time management, you will find it hard to waste time or use procrastination as an excuse for not getting things done. Are you ready to let go of these stressors? Or are they comfortable alibis for you?[5]

Exercise

You may have heard that exercise is an excellent way to protect yourself from the negative effects of stress.[6] Exercise serves three functions—none of which relates to the self-defeating attitude, "It is necessary to be strong."

First, exercise may help you to avoid stressors. Once you are aware of your verbal and nonverbal indicators of stress, you can act on them to ensure that a stressor doesn't become a distressor. If, for example, while typing a research paper, you realize that you can feel your body tightening, your palms starting to perspire, and that you are furiously pounding the keyboard, you can act on these messages—you are feeling stress. An exercise break, whether spent taking a short walk or tossing a ball, may relieve your initial stress reactions, refresh your energies, and enable you to get back to the task.

Second, exercise can help you escape from distress. Assume that you ignored your initial stress reactions and continued to work on the research paper. In a short time you will be experiencing distress: You are swearing at the instructor for assigning the paper, making typing mistakes, and finding it hard to sit still. Then, to make matters worse, your companion walks in with a smile and an energetic, "Hi, how's it going?" You can think of only two possible responses: kill or escape. Exercise is one way to escape.

Third, being involved in an ongoing exercise program allows an individual who has gone through distress to recover more quickly than would the sedentary person. If, instead of exercising to escape, you were to scream at your friend for five minutes, your level of physical fitness would determine how quickly your body returned to an unstressed condition after the outburst. Physiological reactions to stress are similar to those experienced while exercising. In both there is an increased heart rate and muscle activity. If the body is well exercised, its ability to cope with changes and recover is increased. (An additional benefit of exercise, such as walking, is that it gives you the opportunity to have long, uninterrupted talks with friends—which also helps reduce your stress!)

To improve your physical fitness as a coping behavior, an exercise program is needed. You may think that you are already short on time, but it is possible to introduce exercise into your daily life without making any drastic changes in your routine. Simply walk up the stairs rather than take the elevator, park your car in the farthest lot rather than the closest, walk or bike to the store rather than drive, do isometric exercises while watching television or sitting in class, take an exercise class to fulfill part of your graduation requirements, or join a lunchtime exercise program where you work. If you have more time, play tennis with friends, jog in good company, or exercise with supportive, caring people.

RESPONDING TO YOUR STRESSORS: TECHNIQUES THAT REQUIRE THE HELP OF OTHERS

It is often possible to work alone in buffering, controlling, and combating feelings of stress, but you may sometimes find it necessary to turn to others. When work, school, or relationship concerns overwhelm you, you may turn to friends and family for support. And when distress becomes extreme, you may find that outside sources of help are necessary, as illustrated in Figure 7.1.

Professional Help

Assistance in dealing with stress can be provided by professionals, such as social workers, counselors, and psychologists. Turning to these sources should be regarded as a sign of strength and willingness to take action, not as a sign of weakness. It takes courage to assume control of your life and not allow your past history or other people to control you.

Self-help Groups

Self-help groups are a common form of support for people with identifiable stress-related problems. Chronic drinkers may attend meetings of Alcoholics

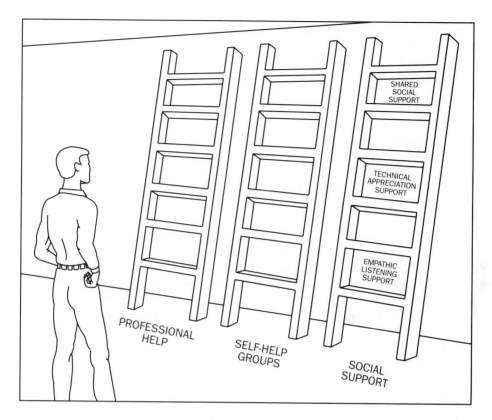

FIGURE 7.1 RESPONDING TO YOUR STRESSORS: TECHNIQUES THAT REQUIRE OTHERS

Anonymous, overweight individuals may turn to Overeaters Anonymous, and divorced or widowed parents may join Parents without Partners. A wide range of self-help groups are available, including ones designed to deal with the stress related to traumatic events, such as rape, incest, and child abuse. On the other hand, religious groups, hobby groups, and study groups also provide you with support by enhancing opportunities for interpersonal relationships and giving you time off from your stressors.

Social Support

Everyone needs social support to respond to everyday stressors: empathic listening support, technical appreciation support, emotional support, and shared social reality support.[7]

Empathic Listening Support We all need and appreciate **empathic listening support**—listening without offering advice, asking penetrating questions, or making judgments.[8] For example, after you've ended a long-term friendship, you may feel better if you can talk to someone who will reflect what you say and express concern and understanding, but will not judge you or tell you what to do. Truly empathic listeners are most helpful because they do not offer advice, tell the talker what to do or what not to do, try to solve the problem, or do the thinking for the talker ("Maybe you should call your friend"). They ask questions that encourage the other person to talk and think about the problem but avoid pushing the talker to reach conclusions ("How do you feel about this relationship?"). And they avoid making critical comments that express approval or disapproval of the other person's comments or actions ("I think you're a fool to end such a great relationship!")

When you're feeling stressed, you may actively seek out a good empathic listener to test your thoughts on.

Technical Appreciation Support   **Technical appreciation support** is the acknowledgment you need from another person when you have done a good job on something, whether concrete or abstract.[9] Unlike empathic listening, which may come from almost anyone you trust, technical appreciation, to be meaningful, must come from an expert, someone you respect and trust to be honest with you. For example, after you've worked hard on a paper about Jane Austen, the comment, "Good work," will be meaningful only if it comes from your instructor or some other expert in English literature. Friends or relatives who say the same thing may not have the same effect unless you perceive them as experts. Although you may appreciate a friend's or relative's comment, it is not technical appreciation but, rather, emotional support.

Emotional Support   **Emotional support** is provided by people who tell you that they are on your side whether or not they agree with what you are doing.[10] The key to emotional support is that it comes from someone who cares more about you as a person than about a particular piece of your work, a problematic relationship, or even the bad mood you're in! Thus, a father can give emotional support to a daughter who has just failed a test by communicating his caring for her personally regardless of the test and regardless of his own feelings about the bad grade. Skill Development 7.3 will help you practice giving emotional support.

SKILL DEVELOPMENT 7.3

GIVING EMOTIONAL SUPPORT

Read each situation and write one appropriate, emotionally supportive statement you could make. For example, your friend has been dating the same person exclusively for over a year. One night, after a date, your friend announces, "Dale told me it's all over between us." An emotionally supportive statement you could make is:

"It must be upsetting to date someone for so long and then realize the relationship might be over."

1. "I've been trying and trying, but I can't get the answer to this accounting problem."

   Emotionally supportive statement:

2. "If one more person criticizes me, I'll bite her head off."

   Emotionally supportive statement:

Shared Social Reality Support   **Shared social reality support** comes from people with whom you can check your perceptions of life and its complexities.[11] Such support can help you gain a perspective on your problems and aid you in developing reasonable courses of action. For example, students in the middle grades often call each other the minute they arrive home and talk for hours about what just happened in school. Their goal is to verify that they see things similarly.

COMMUNICATION ANXIETY

Before reading ahead, complete Knowledge Checkup 7.5, designed to assess your feelings of comfort and discomfort while communicating. The first part focuses on your communicating in general. The remaining parts focus on your feelings about communicating in specific settings.

KNOWLEDGE CHECKUP 7.5

CAGC: COMMUNICATION APPREHENSION IN GENERALIZED CONTEXTS QUESTIONNAIRE[12]

Indicate the degree to which each of the following statements applies to you.

Circle **1** if you strongly agree.

Circle **2** if you agree.

Circle **3** if you are undecided.

Circle **4** if you disagree.

Circle **5** if you strongly disagree.

There are no right or wrong answers. Many of the statements resemble each other. Do not be concerned about this. Work quickly so that you record only your first impressions.

GENERAL

1 2 3 4 5   **1.** When communicating, I generally am calm and re-laxed.

1 2 3 4 5   **2.** I find the prospect of speaking mildly pleasant.

1 2 3 4 5   **3.** In general, communication makes me uncomfortable.

1 2 3 4 5   **4.** I dislike to use my body and voice expressively.

1 2 3 4 5   **5.** When communicating, I generally am tense and nervous.

GROUP DISCUSSIONS

1 2 3 4 5   **6.** I am afraid to express myself in a group.

1 2 3 4 5   **7.** I dislike participating in group discussions.

1 2 3 4 5   **8.** I am tense and nervous while participating in group discussions.

1 2 3 4 5   **9.** Engaging in a group discussion with new people makes me tense and nervous.

1 2 3 4 5   **10.** I am calm and relaxed while participating in group discussions.

MEETINGS AND CLASSES

1 2 3 4 5   **11.** I look forward to expressing my opinions at meetings and classes.

1 2 3 4 5   **12.** Generally, I am nervous when I have to participate in a meeting and class.

1 2 3 4 5   **13.** Usually I am calm and relaxed while participating in meetings and classes.

1 2 3 4 5   **14.** I am very calm and relaxed when I am called upon to express an opinion at a meeting and class.

1 2 3 4 5 **15.** Communicating in meetings or classes generally makes me uncomfortable.

INTERPERSONAL CONVERSATIONS

1 2 3 4 5 **16.** While participating in a conversation with a new acquaintance I feel very nervous.

1 2 3 4 5 **17.** Generally, I am very relaxed while talking with one other person.

1 2 3 4 5 **18.** Ordinarily, I am very calm and relaxed in conversations.

1 2 3 4 5 **19.** I am relaxed while conversing with people who hold positions of authority.

1 2 3 4 5 **20.** I am afraid to speak up in conversations.

SCORING:

GENERAL

Total your scores for items 3, 4, 5. Score A _____

Total your scores for items 1, 2. Score B _____

$$(18 - \underset{\text{Score A}}{\underline{\hspace{2cm}}}) + \underset{\text{Score B}}{\underline{\hspace{2cm}}} = \underset{\text{Total}}{\underline{\hspace{2cm}}}$$

GROUP

Total your scores for items 6, 7, 8, 9. Score C _____

Indicate your score for item 10. Score D _____

$$(24 - \underset{\text{Score C}}{\underline{\hspace{2cm}}}) + \underset{\text{Score D}}{\underline{\hspace{2cm}}} = \underset{\text{Total}}{\underline{\hspace{2cm}}}$$

MEETINGS AND CLASSES

Total your scores for items 12, 15. Score E _____

Total your scores for items 11, 13, 14. Score F _____

$$(12 - \underset{\text{Score E}}{\underline{\hspace{2cm}}}) + \underset{\text{Score F}}{\underline{\hspace{2cm}}} = \underset{\text{Total}}{\underline{\hspace{2cm}}}$$

INTERPERSONAL CONVERSATIONS

Total your scores for items 16, 20. Score G_____

Total your scores for items 17, 18, 19. Score H_____

$$(12 - \underline{\hspace{2cm}}) + \underline{\hspace{2cm}} = \underline{\hspace{2cm}}$$
$$\text{Score G}\text{Score H}\text{Total}$$

Save your scores for each section. You'll learn how to interpret them as the chapter progresses.

A form of stress specifically related to communication is called **communication anxiety**—the *fear* of engaging in communication interactions. This term should not be applied to people who are merely quiet or choose not to participate in communication situations.

The messages that communicatively anxious people tell themselves are, "I lack the ability and/or confidence to share my true self with someone else," and, "I can't interact when I'd like to." Communication anxiety, sometimes called shyness, can be emotionally based and/or based on a lack of communication skills.

No matter which term is selected, once a person accepts the label, his or her attitudes and actions reflect the label. Often these people think that others don't take them seriously so they are afraid to seek help and advice. As a result, they become increasingly isolated, nonassertive, and withdrawn.

It is estimated that between 80 and 93 percent of all people feel some communication anxiety and that 15 to 20 percent of all college students have high levels of communication anxiety.[13]

COMMUNICATION ANXIETY AND YOU

Up until now the discussion of communication anxiety has centered on people in general. Let's examine your score on the first section of Knowledge Checkup 7.5 to see how you label yourself. As you consider the results, remember that this knowledge checkup is not an objective measure. Rather, it reflects your self-perceptions. According to a national sampling, a score of 14 or above in the General section of the questionnaire indicates that you perceive yourself as more apprehensive about communicating than the average person.[14]

Private and Public Communication Anxiety

Publicly anxious people are strongly hesitant about communicating with others and display their anxiety through such outward signs as avoiding eye contact, blushing, perspiring, and speaking in a quavering voice when forced to communicate in public settings.

While some people are publicly anxious, others are privately anxious. **Privately anxious people** mentally resist active communication, but will participate—often by forcing themselves. They seldom display the outward physical reactions of stress, such as fingernail biting, sweaty palms, or dry mouth, but still feel discomfort. Famous people who admit to being privately shy include Carol Burnett, Johnny Carson,[15] and even one of America's most prominent interviewers, Barbara Walters. Each has gained success by learning to cope with communication anxiety.

Situational Communication Anxiety

Another way to look at communication anxiety is to discern whether it is situational or general. Once again examine your scores for Knowledge Checkup 7.5. If you think of yourself as a communicatively anxious person but scored lower than 14 on the General section, you may have been surprised. There is a simple explanation: You may be anxious in some contexts but not in others. Look at your scores for the other segments of the questionnaire. If you received a score of over 16 for Group Discussion, or over 15 for Meetings and Classes, or over 13 for Interpersonal Conversations, you may have identified specifically where your anxiety lies. It is not uncommon for some people to display anxiety in only one context, whereas others display anxiety in several or all contexts.

CAUSES OF COMMUNICATION ANXIETY

There are several theories about what causes communication anxiety. Some researchers say it is caused by environmental factors, while some believe it is caused by genetic factors.[16]

Communication anxiety seems to come from being brought up in an authoritarian home, having attended authoritarian schools, and/or being the product of an authoritarian religion. These forces may have taught you to control what you say or emphasized the importance of being "seen but not heard." In addition, if your parents were communicatively anxious, there is a 70 percent chance that you are anxious because you are imitating their patterns.[17]

Lack of communication skills often results from attending schools that don't teach students how to organize ideas or develop effective speaking and listening skills. Or it may stem from parents who limited their children's exposure to the question-answer process and thus prevented them from playing with language and developing the basic communication skills. As a result of their restricted early years, communicatively anxious people—both women and men—tend to fear rejection, criticism, and imperfection.

THE EFFECTS OF COMMUNICATION ANXIETY

Most people with communication anxiety believe that they suffer negative consequences, that they have given up control of themselves to someone else or to an unknown force, that they are puppets whose strings are being pulled by their master, *fear*.

There are some demonstrated effects of communication anxiety.[18] In classroom situations, communicatively anxious students volunteer rarely, if at all.[19] They often drop classes that require oral communication or miss class when oral participation is necessary. These patterns can affect learning and grades.[20] Some anxious students even fail to graduate with only one course to complete—a required course in speech communication.

People with communication anxiety often choose college majors that require few, if any, oral presentations, such as research or technical fields. And in the workplace, if they must participate orally—whether one-on-one, in a group, or in a public setting—they miss promotions and pay increases because they are handicapped by their fear.[21]

DEALING WITH COMMUNICATION ANXIETY

If your scores on Knowledge Checkup 7.5 indicated that you are anxious in one or more communication contexts, you may be wondering what you can do. First, be assured that communication anxiety is not an incurable illness. In most people the problem is either psychological and related to feelings of insecurity, or stems from a lack of communication skills. In either case, remedies are possible.

Second, recognize that you must identify your particular needs in order to select the appropriate course of action. Skill Development 7.4 will help you assess both the situation and yourself the next time you're feeling communicatively anxious.

SKILL DEVELOPMENT 7.4

MATCHING NEEDS TO REMEDIES

The next time you feel communicatively anxious, ask yourself:

1. *What aspects of this situation make me uncomfortable?* Do I feel prepared to deal with the situation? Am I afraid of failing?

2. *What is happening to my body?* Am I feeling tense? Am I panicking? Do I have a mind block?

Knowing the factors that contribute to your communication anxiety and the extent of your reactions will help you assess the seriousness of your situation and plan an appropriate course of action. If your communication anxiety tends to be mild and infrequent, you can probably manage it by using short-term stress reducers. However, if you often feel communicatively anxious, if particular situations are always particularly stressful, and if you think of your anxiety as a serious handicap, you may want to seek a more permanent solution.

The success rate in teaching communicatively anxious people to cope with or alter their behavior is extremely high. But, like any attempt at changing personality or learning, the treatment or training will be effective only if you truly want help and diligently apply yourself. Three options, which are portrayed in Figure 7.2, are rhetoritherapy, systematic desensitization, and positive visualization.

Rhetoritherapy

If you find you lack the skills necessary to participate in a conversation, give a speech, or ask questions, you may benefit from **rhetoritherapy**—communication training.[22] Taking a basic communication course should help develop some fundamental skills. Enrolling in classes or workshops that teach techniques of assertiveness, public speaking, conversation, decision making, and group participation also should put you on the road to eliminating your anxiety. As you work through this book, for example, you are constantly required to test your newly found knowledge of communication techniques. If you have communication anxiety, as you start applying these skills in real-life situations you should find yourself feeling more and more confident.

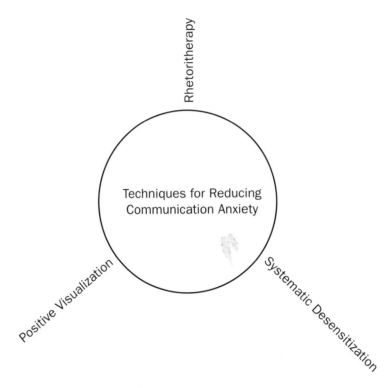

FIGURE 7.2   TECHNIQUES FOR REDUCING COMMUNICATION ANXIETY

Systematic Desensitization

If you tend to get extremely nervous when you think about communicating or actually try to communicate, you may benefit from **systematic desensitization**— a process in which you gain control over your anxiety by learning to recognize your stressors and use relaxation techniques to combat their effects.[23] In such a program, a competent professional (such as a psychologist, hypnotherapist, or trained communication practitioner) will (1) help you to identify your stressors, (2) teach you relaxation techniques, (3) set up situations that are more and more anxiety-provoking, and (4) teach you how to apply the relaxation techniques when an anxiety-provoking situation occurs.

Positive Visualization

Many people are immobilized by their fear of a communication situation. In **positive visualization**, a person prepares for the anticipated unpleasant experience by picturing the situation being carried out successfully.[24] Once the individual develops this "mental film," he or she repeats it over and over before the event so that the expected outcome will be positive rather than negative.

Positive visualization is, in effect, a constructive form of self-fulfilling prophecy. For example, if you fear meeting strangers, before your next introduction do the following: Close your eyes and picture yourself being introduced, shaking hands, saying your name, listening to the other person's name, asking a question, hearing the answer, saying good-bye, and feeling pleased about the whole experience. Envision this sequence repeatedly. You may be amazed to find that because you are prepared and are expecting positive results, the event will be much to your liking and less stressful than if you had predicted failure. Skill Development 7.5 provides an opportunity to practice positive visualization.

SKILL DEVELOPMENT 7.5

PRACTICING POSITIVE VISUALIZATION

A friend of yours asked you to participate in a fund-raising drive for the American Cancer Society. You agreed to help, think the drive is worthwhile, but you realize you have other priorities and should have said no. You decide to back out, but the person is a good friend. You think of what you are going to say and review it enough times until you feel comfortable with the language. The plea is prepared and you have rehearsed it. To further help you prepare and to help yourself relax, you are going to use positive visualization. Do the following: Close your eyes and visualize the friend. Picture yourself walking to the friend's apartment, saying "hello," and explaining the fact that you are overcommitted and must back out of your prior acceptance to help. Visualize yourself relaxed as you present your ideas. Next, see and hear the friend assenting to your reversal. You are feeling positive about what you did and the outcome of your having acted assertively.

In the future, whenever you are preparing for what you perceive might be a stressful communicative situation, use a similar positive visualization exercise.

THE STRESS MANAGEMENT MODEL

To deal with stress effectively, it is often necessary to change old patterns and substitute new, more productive ones. Though each situation may require a new adaptation, the stress management model presented here should provide a starting point. It won't apply in every situation, particularly if a stressor appears suddenly and permits little time to react. But it should help you to deal with stressors that regularly disturb you and lead to teeth grinding, hand clenching, and similar reactions.

SKILL DEVELOPMENT 7.6

THE STRESS MANAGEMENT MODEL

Stage 1:   *Identify the distress:* What's wrong?

Stage 2:   *Identify your goal or objective:* What would I like to be different?

Stage 3:   *Attempt to alleviate the distress:* What have I done to get rid of the distress?

Stage 4:   *Identify rewards from the status quo:* What do I gain from *not* alleviating the distress?

Stage 5:   *Consider alternative strategies:* What techniques, such as rhetoritherapy, can I *realistically* use to alleviate the distress?

Stage 6:   *Develop an action plan:* What do I do and when do I do it?

Stage 7:   *Perform a follow-up analysis:* Was my plan effective in buffering, controlling, and/or combating the distress?

COMMUNICATION COMPETENCY CHECKUP

The goal of this Communication Competency Checkup is to guide you in putting your skills and knowledge about stress and communication anxiety to use, and to help you summarize the material in this chapter.

Reprinted with special permission of North America Syndicate.

Les, the character in the cartoon, obviously perceives himself as having communication anxiety.

1. Name some common verbal and nonverbal behaviors that Les is likely to display because of the stress he feels.

2. What approaches could Les use to buffer, control, and combat his stress?

3. Define *communication anxiety* as it relates to Les.

4. Besides the negative outcomes he is stating, what are some additional problems caused by being communicatively anxious?

5. Name three specific things Les could do to overcome his communication anxiety.

6. Is Les privately or publicly anxious? Explain your answer.

7. In which context(s) identified in Knowledge Checkup 7.5 is Les most communicatively anxious?

8. List the steps in the Stress Management Model and apply the model to Les's situation.

NOTES

1. For further discussion of burnout, see: Ayala M. Pines, Elliot Aronson, and Ditsa Kafry, *Burnout* (New York: Free Press, 1981).

2. Beele A. Edson, "Communicating Intrapersonally about Stress: The Dynamics of Self," an unpublished paper presented at the Basic Course Conference, Western Speech Communication Association Convention, Tucson, Arizona, February 15, 1986.

3. R. J. Burke and E. R. Greenglass, "Sex Differences in Psychological Burnout in Teachers," *Psychological Reports* 65 (1989): 55–63; E. R. Greenglass and R. J. Burke, "Work and Family Precursors of Burnout in Teachers: Sex Differences," *Sex Roles* 18 (1988): 215–29.

4. Larry A. Samovar and Richard E. Porter, *Communication Between Cultures* (Belmont, CA: Wadsworth Publishing Company, 1991), p. 128.

5. Donald Tubesing, *Kicking Your Stress Habits* (Duluth, MN: Whole Person Associates, 1981).

6. Donald B. Adrell and Mark J. Tager, *Planning for Wellness: A Guidebook for Achieving Optimal Health* (Dubuque, IA: Kendall/Hunt, 1982); Covert Bailey, *Fit or Fat* (Boston: Houghton Mifflin, 1978).

7. For information on the various types of social support available and the benefits, see: Terrance L. Albrecht, Mara B. Adelman, and Associates, *Communicating Social Support* (Newbury Park, CA: Sage, 1987); D. C. Ganster and Bart Victor, "The Impact of Social Support on Mental and Physical Health," *British Journal of Medical Psychology* 61 (1988): 17–36.

8. B. Gottlieb, *Social Support Strategies: Guidelines for Mental Health Practice* (Beverly Hills, CA: Sage, 1983).

9. G. Yukl and D. D. Van Fleet, "Cross-cultural, Multimethod Research on Military Leader Effectiveness," *Organizational Behavior and Human Performance* 30 (1982): 87–108.

10. J. House, *Work Stress and Social Support* (Reading: MA: Addison-Wesley, 1981); S. Jayaratne and W. Chess, "The

Effects of Emotional Support on Perceived Job Stress and Strain," *Journal of Applied Behavioral Science* 20 (1984): 141–53; H. O. F. Veiel, M. Crisand, H. Stroszeck-Somscher, and J. Herrie, "Social Support Networks of Chronically Strained Couples: Similarity and Overlap," *Journal of Social and Personal Relationships* 8 (1991): 279–92.

11. C. Dunkel-Schetter and C. Wrothman, "Dilemmas of Social Support: Parallels Between Victimization and Aging," in S. B. Kiesler, J. N. Morgan, and V. K. Oppenheimer (Eds.), *Aging: Social Change* (New York: Academic Press, 1981), pp. 349–81.

12. Modification of Virginia P. Richmond and James C. McCroskey, *Communication: Apprehension, Avoidance, and Effectiveness, 3d ed.* (Scottsdale, AZ: Gorsuch Scarisbrick Publishers, 1992), pp. 129–31.

13. Philip Zimbardo, *Shyness: What It Is; What to Do About It* (Reading, MA: Addison-Wesley, 1977), pp. 13–14.

14. Richmond and McCroskey, *Communication,* p. 34, plus correspondence with James C. McCroskey.

15. Jules Asher, "Born to Be Shy?" *Psychology Today* (April 1987): 64.

16. Richmond and McCroskey, *Communication.*

17. For a discussion of the research on causes of communication apprehension, see: Gerald M. Phillips, *Help for Shy People* (Englewood Cliffs, NJ: Prentice-Hall, 1981), especially Chapters 3 and 4.

18. John Daly and James McCroskey (Eds.), *Avoiding Communication: Shyness, Reticence, and Communication Apprehension* (Beverly Hills, CA: Sage, 1984), esp.

pp. 125–43. In addition, for an extensive discussion, see: Richmond and McCroskey, *Communication,* and Phillips, *Help for Shy People.*

19. James W. Chesebro et al., "Communication Apprehension and Self-Perceived Communication Competence of At-Risk Students," *Communication Education* 41 (1992): 345–60.

20. For a discussion of the effects of communication apprehension on math, English, reading, and intelligence scores, as well as grades in general, see: John Bourhis and Mike Allen, "Meta-Analysis of the Relationship Between Communication Apprehension and Cognitive Performance," *Communication Education* 41 (1992): 68–76.

21. See Daly and McCroskey, *Avoiding Communication.*

22. Gerald Phillips, "Rhetoritherapy: The Principles of Rhetoric in Training Shy People in Speech Effectiveness," in *Shyness: Perspective on Research and Treatment,* W. H. Jones, J. M. Cheek, and S. R. Briggs (Eds.) (New York: Plenum Press, 1986), pp. 357–74.

23. Susan Glaser, "Oral Communication Apprehension and Avoidance: The Current Status of Treatment Research," *Communication Education* 30 (1981): 323–29; James McCroskey and Virginia Richmond, *The Quiet Ones: Communication Apprehension and Shyness* (Annandale, VA: Speech Communication Association, 1991).

24. Joe Ayres and Theodore S. Hopf, "The Long-Term Effect of Visualization in the Classroom: A Brief Research Report," *Communication Education* 39 (1990): 75–78.

FOR FURTHER INVESTIGATION

Albrecht, K. *Stress and the Manager.* Englewood Cliffs, NJ: Prentice-Hall, 1979.

Ayres, Joe, and Theodore S. Hopf. "Visualization: Is It More Than Extra-Attention?" *Communication Education* 38 (1989): 1–5.

Communication Education 31 (July 1982). (Entire volume is devoted to communication anxiety.)

Daly, John, and James McCroskey (eds.). *Avoiding Communication: Shyness, Reticence, and Communication Apprehension.* Beverly Hills, CA: Sage, 1984.

Dunkel-Schetter, C., and Wortman, C. "Dilemmas of Social Support: Parallels Between Victimization and Aging." In S. B. Kiesler, J. N. Morgan, and V. K. Oppenheimer (eds.), *Aging Social Change.* New York: Academic Press, 1981. (pp. 349–81.)

Ellis, Albert, and William J. Knaus. *Overcoming Procrastination or How to Think and Act Rationally in Spite of Life's Inevitable Hassles.* New York: Signet, 1977.

Emery, Gary, and J. Campbell. *Rapid Relief from Emotional Distress.* New York: Fawcett Columbine, 1986.

Gottlieb, B. "The Development and Application of a Classification Scheme of Informal Helping Behaviors." *Canadian Journal of Behavioral Science* 10 (1978): 105–15.

Gottlieb, B. *Social Support Strategies: Guidelines for Mental Health Practice.* Beverly Hills, CA: Sage, 1983.

Hardley, Robert. *Anxiety and Panic Attacks: Their Cause and Cure.* New York: Rawson Associates, 1985.

House, J. *Work Stress and Social Support.* Reading, MA: Addison-Wesley, 1981.

International Communication Apprehension Newsletter, available from Dr. Arden Watson, The Pennsylvania State University, Delaware County Campus, 25 Yersley Mill Road, Media, PA, 19063.

Jayaratne, S., and Chess, W. "The Effects of Emotional Support on Perceived Job Stress and Strain." *Journal of Applied Behavioral Science* 20 (1984): 141–53.

McQuade, W., and A. Aikman. *Stress: What It Is and What It Can Do to Your Health, How to Fight Back.* New York: E. P. Dutton, 1974.

Morrison, E. *Stress Management for the College Student.* Santa Barbara, CA: Kinko's Copies, 1985.

Mourad, S., and M. Mourad. *Learning to Live with Stress: Building Your Inner Space.* Lorain, OH: W. G. Nord Center, 1984.

Phillips, Gerald. *Help for Shy People.* Englewood Cliffs, NJ: Prentice-Hall, 1981.

Pines, Ayala M., Elliot Aronson, and Ditsa Kafry. *Burnout.* New York: Free Press, 1981.

Richmond, Virginia P., and James C. McCroskey. *Communication: Apprehension, Avoidance, and Effectiveness,* 3d ed. Scottsdale, AZ: Gorsuch Scarisbrick Publishers, 1992.

Sylvester, Sandra. *Living with Stress.* Kansas City, MO: National Catholic Reporter Publishing, Inc., 1985.

Teacher Stress. Columbus, OH: Instruction and Professional Development Division, Ohio Education Association/National Education Association, 1985.

Whitney, E. N., and F. C. Richardson. *Understanding Nutrition.* New York: West Publishing, 1981.

Zimbardo, Phillip. *Shyness: What It Is; What to Do About It.* Reading, MA: Addison-Wesley, 1977.

Zimbardo, Phillip, and Shirley Radl. *The Shyness Workbook.* New York: A & W Visual Library, 1979.

Zorn, Theodore E. "Measuring Motivation to Communicate." *Communication Education* 40 (1991): 385–92.

CHAPTER 8

Dimensions of Interpersonal Process

COMMUNICATION COMPETENCIES

This chapter examines the dimensions of the interpersonal communication process. Specifically, the objective of the chapter is for you to learn to:

- Define the framework for a relationship, including personal and relational goals, the structure of the relationship, and the rules of the relationship.
- Distinguish relationship structures according to dominant/submissive and loving/hostile behaviors.
- Specify the rules for relationships.
- Identify the components of relationship commitment and assess your commitment in an important relationship.
- List the components of intimacy and distinguish an intimate experience from an intimate relationship.
- Identify the resources offered in relationships.
- Understand and adapt to cultural differences in the interpersonal setting.

KEY WORDS

The key words in this chapter are:

relationship	**rules**
complementary relationship	**commitment**
symmetrical relationship	**intimacy**
parallel relationship	**intimate experience**

Write four want ads for people to fill the following relationship vacancies in your life. Specify the characteristics you want in the other individual as well as the personal qualities you have to offer.

1. Advertise for a person with whom you wish to establish a work relationship.
2. Advertise for a person with whom you wish to establish a friendship.
3. Advertise for a person with whom you wish to establish a loving and caring relationship.
4. Select a culture other than your own that you know the most about. Write an advertisement seeking a relationship with a person from that culture.

How do your four advertisements differ from each other?

Do your descriptions relate to each relationship's goal, such as "to have fun," "to get a job done," or "to keep from being bored"? Do they refer to whether you are the superior person in the relationship, "the leader," or the subordinate one, "the follower"? Do some characterizing words focus on the amount of love and affection or hate and hostility you want in the particular relationship? Did you concern yourself with some of the rules that make each relationship unique, such as "to date each other exclusively," or "to have a 50–50 partnership in the business"? Did you use such words as *commitment* or *intimacy?*

What do the variety of types of relationships you have and the myriad ways you describe and distinguish them reveal about yourself?

RELATIONSHIP DIMENSIONS

Relationships come in a variety of forms, from the work-on-a-class-project type to the live-together-forever type. Several sets of dimensions distinguish each relationship from others. One set of dimensions describes the framework for a relationship, such as the rules that guide your behavior. Another set helps you judge the quality of a relationship, such as its levels of intimacy and commitment. At the outset of your investigation of you and your relationships, you should examine your own idea of what a relationship is, because your definition of a relationship predicts its content.

The differences among the advertisements you wrote at the beginning of this chapter reflect the differences in your goals for each relationship.[1] Although the general goal for each—"a work relationship," "a friend relationship," or "a loving relationship"—is prescribed, you meet your specific needs and desires by seeking particular characteristics in a partner in a relationship.

The characteristics you want in a partner reflect how you expect to interact with her or him. For some people, the patterns of interaction in all three relationships might be similar, even if the goals are different. For example, you might want to be the person who controls what happens, whether the goal is to complete a project with a work partner or to see a movie with a friend. For other people, the patterns of interaction may differ for each relationship. For example, you may picture yourself the boss with your work partner, the equal of your friend, and the subservient member of your loving relationship.

You also may believe that different rules of behavior apply to each relationship. For example, "Do your fair share" might guide a work relationship, and the rule "Stick up for the other person" might guide the friend relationship; in the first instance, you want someone who is hardworking; in the second, you seek someone loyal.

Finally, the advertisements you wrote identify what you see as the desirable resources of each relationship, that is, what you want each relationship to provide. Do you picture the work relationship as giving you the chance to get a good grade, earn a promotion, or impress someone? Do you see the friendship as releasing you from boredom? Do you imagine that a loving relationship will supply security, respect, and intimacy? If you analyze your ads carefully, you'll find a lot of useful information about how you personally define your relationships.

On a more formal note, the *Random House Dictionary of the English Language* defines a **relationship** as "a connection, association, or involvement . . . an emotional or other connection between people." Synonyms include *dependence, affinity, concern, alliance, affiliation, association,* and *tie.* Each of these words reveals the complexity of human connectedness.

You consider yourself involved in a relationship if your actions, thoughts, and emotions follow specific patterns.[2] You observe your communication behaviors and notice whether your interaction with the other person seems mutually influential and structured. For example, two people eating in a restaurant share a relationship if they are sitting together, taking each other into account as they talk, and influencing each other at least to the extent that what one says is in response to what the other says.

Relationships are complex. To understand them means breaking them down into their component parts and looking at each part separately, even though you probably rarely sit down and consciously analyze them because relationships often seem to "just happen." For the sake of analysis, however, the components of a relationship are divided into two broad categories: those related to the framework for interaction and those related to the relationship's quality or outcomes.

THE FRAMEWORK FOR INTERACTION

Each of your relationships has goals, structure, and rules that form the context within which you and the other person interact. Your communication both reflects and determines each of the three dimensions for each of your relationships.

GOALS

Relationships form because of some *goal* or outcome that each person wishes to achieve. The goal may be to learn something about yourself, to learn something about the environment, to overcome loneliness, to change another's attitude or behavior, to complete a project, to kill time, to release tension, to be entertained, to help someone, or to become intimate with someone. There may be as many goals as there are individuals, cultures, and relationships.

THE FAR SIDE By GARY LARSON

''And I like honesty in a relationship . . . I'm not into playing games.''

"The Far Side" cartoon by Gary Larson is reprinted by permission of Chronicle Features, San Francisco, CA. All rights reserved.

Skill Development 8.1 will help you look at your relationships with respect to the goals you have for them.

SKILL DEVELOPMENT 8.1

DETERMINING YOUR RELATIONSHIP GOALS

PART I

Reread the ads you wrote at the outset of this chapter. What were your *specific* goals for each type of relationship? List them:

Advertisement 1: _____

Advertisement 2: _____

Advertisement 3: _____

Advertisement 4: _____

PART II

Select three relationships in which you are currently involved that are *not* ideal: (a) one with a coworker/fellow student, (b) a friendship relationship, and, (c) an intimate relationship.

1. What are your goals for each relationship?
   (a) _____
   (b) _____
   (c) _____

2. How do you know these are your goals? _____

_____

You probably found that your advertisements for love, friendship, and work relationships had different goals. On the other hand, you may have found some similarities. Assume, for example, that you seek a person with whom to share a loving relationship who is kind and considerate, a friend who jogs and likes unusual experiences, and a work partner who is responsible and has good research skills. Each set of characteristics reveals different relationship goals: to share a long-term intimate relationship, to provide companionship, and to complete some task efficiently.

Comparing the characteristics you listed in each of your ads with those listed by your classmates should help to clarify your goals for these types of relationships. An advertisement for a work partner that focuses exclusively on intelligence, experience, and a willingness to work hard reveals different goals from one seeking a partner who is easygoing and flexible. Someone advertising for a friend who is a good listener has a different goal from someone who seeks a person with whom to share weekends of mountain climbing. An advertisement for a partner in a loving relationship that lists quiet, warm, and considerate as desired characteristics displays different goals from an ad that seeks someone wild, exciting, and willing to take risks.

As you compare your other-culture advertisement with classmates you probably will be struck by the fact that not all cultures have the same goals for their relationships nor do they apply the same list of traits when seeking partners to fulfill those goals. In Indian and Arabic cultures, for example, the male generally would be interested in a subservient woman. In Scandinavia, on the other hand, many women would be repelled by a male who would want to control them.

Researchers pay more attention to close, personal relationships—"intimate ones"—than to any other relationship because intimacy offers great rewards and exacts great costs. Intimate relationships provide stimulation (an escape from loneliness and boredom) and an opportunity to share experiences (whether a beautiful sunset or a horrible test grade). Intimate relationships frequently present a nonthreatening arena in which to try out new ideas and behaviors, and often increase enjoyment of certain activities (a party with close friends is usually more fun than one with strangers). Intimate relationships also provide the opportunity for self-disclosure, the self-revealing communication that strips away the front you present to others and displays the person you think you really are. Accompanying the rewards, however, are potentially great costs, the greatest of which is rejection by the other person.

Regardless of the particular goals you have for an intimate relationship, you should bear two things in mind. First, people rarely set out to form an intimate relationship in a rational and intellectual way. Their conscious aim often is something other than to begin an intimate relationship. People seldom enter a classroom with a specific plan for leaving with an intimate relationship, although many individuals have met in class and eventually lived together or gotten married.

Second, most relationships are not formed with the primary goal of achieving intimacy. Usually, relationships form as accompaniments to everyday activities. For instance, you like to jog, so you meet people who share the same interest; you may not think about extending the relationship beyond your noontime run. Or a class project may require you to work with another student; your only goal may be to fulfill the assignment.

Nonetheless, your specific goal may be to find someone with whom you can follow a path toward intimacy—a person with whom to share your innermost thoughts and feelings and, eventually, your love. If this is the case, your goal—"to seek out and develop an *intimate* relationship"—is predetermined and conscious, not a by-product of other relationships with different goals. Skill Development 8.2 offers practice in a method for understanding your goals in a particular relationship.

SKILL DEVELOPMENT 8.2

UNDERSTANDING YOUR GOALS

Select an important relationship in which you are now involved (for example, a work relationship or a friendship). Answer these questions regarding that relationship:

1. I am in this relationship in order to . . . .

2. I stay in this relationship with this person because . . . .

3. I want to continue in a relationship with this person until . . . .

4. This relationship will end once . . . .

STRUCTURE

A relationship is like a dance—two people move together in a coordinated display. The partners may glide about smoothly, anticipating each other's movements and responding with grace, or they may appear awkward and out of step. Relationships are distinguished by the *structure* of their communication—how their talk is organized and coordinated—much as dancers are distinguished by their choreography.

Two dimensions characterize the structure of a relationship: dominance/submission and love/hostility.[3] The dimension of dominance/submission describes how much control you and the other person have over each other, while the dimension of love/hostility reflects how much affection or love you give and receive. In Figure 8.1, dominance and submission are the endpoints of the vertical line through the circle, and hostility and love are the endpoints of the horizontal line. The two dimensions are independent of each other, that is, you can be both dominant and loving (stereotypical "parent" behavior), dominant and hostile (stereotypical "exploitive manager" behavior), submissive and loving (stereotypical "good little child" behavior), and submissive and hostile (stereotypical "downtrodden worker" behavior).

The behaviors indicated on the circle represent variations of the behaviors associated with dominance, submission, love, hostility, and their combinations, such as loving and dominant, hostile and submissive. The terms that describe behaviors along the inside edge of the circle (pities, clings, bitter, and exploits) are extreme or exaggerated behaviors, and those toward the center (helps, respects, skeptical, and competes) are moderate or less exaggerated behaviors. For example, the exaggerated form of love is compulsively loving, whereas the moderate form is affectionate.

Your relationships take one of three possible structures: complementary, symmetrical, and parallel.[4]

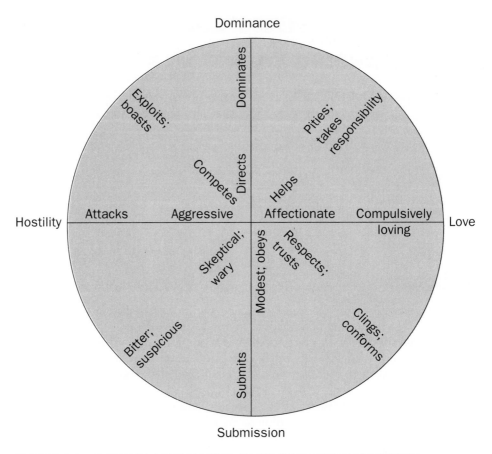

FIGURE 8.1 PRIMARY COMPONENTS OF RELATIONSHIP INTERACTION

In a **complementary relationship**, one partner's behavior complements or completes the other's—the behaviors seem to go together. The relationship is based on differences (for example, one partner may be dominant while the other is submissive) which, when they come together, form a stable relationship. Each partner has particular duties and obligations, whether one "brings home the bacon" while the other "keeps the home fires burning," or one washes the dishes while the other dries. The partners work better in combination than alone.

The relationship between dominant and submissive behaviors is complementary. Dominance tends to provoke its opposite from the other person—subordinance. Submission tends to provoke its opposite—control.

A **symmetrical relationship**, unlike a complementary one, implies balance: the partners contribute equally to their relationship. Whereas the partners in a complementary relationship create a whole from their two separate parts, partners in a symmetrical relationship maintain their individual identities. In the ideal symmetrical relationship (for which there are few examples), power is equally distributed, independence is stressed, and both partners are either submissive or dominant.

Unlike dominant and submissive behaviors, which tend to provoke their op-posites, loving behaviors tend to evoke love and hostile behaviors tend to provoke hostility. For example, when you tell someone "I love you," you probably expect a similar confession. An opposite or neutral response ("I don't love you!" or "Oh") is usually unexpected and unappreciated.

Combining a loving or hostile behavior with a dominant or submissive one tends to provoke the same feeling and the opposite behavior. Loving–dominant be-haviors, such as "pitying the other person," "taking responsibility for the other per-son," or "helping the other person," tend to provoke loving–submissive behaviors from the other person, such as "clinging" and "conforming," or "respecting" and "trusting"; in other words, symmetrical feeling and complementary control behav-ior (see Figure 8.2). For example, a parent's loving–dominant message, "You poor child, here, let me help you with your math homework," is likely to get a loving–submissive message from the child, such as, "Please help me. I'd really appreciate it."

Likewise, loving–submissive behaviors, such as "clings" and "conforms," or "respects" and "trusts," tend to provoke loving–dominant behaviors, such as "pities" and "takes responsibility" or "helps" (see Figure 8.2). For example, the loving–submissive message, "I think it's terrific that you know how to use the new computer in the office," is likely to evoke a loving–dominant message in return: "Let me show you how to use it. It's really not hard once you know what to do."

Hostile–dominant behaviors, such as "exploiting the other person" and "boasting to the other person" or "competing with the other person," tend to provoke hostile–submissive behaviors, such as "bitterness" and "suspicion," or "skepticism" and "wariness" (see Figure 8.3). For example, a manager's hostile–dominant message, "I've been on the job here twice the time you have, so do the job the way I say to do it," is likely to get an employee's hostile–submissive mes-sage in response: "Well, okay, but just because you've been here a long time doesn't make you a genius!"

In turn, hostile–submissive behaviors, such as "bitterness" and "suspicion" or "skepticism" and "wariness," tend to provoke hostile–dominant behaviors, such as "exploitation" and "boastfulness" or "competitiveness." For example, a child's hos-tile–submissive message, "Gee, I never get to do anything I want to do. How

Pities the other person		Clings to other person
Takes resonsibility for the other person		Conforms to the other person's desires
Helps the other person		Respects the other person
		Trusts the other person

FIGURE 8.2   LOVING–HOSTILE BEHAVIOR/LOVING–SUBMISSIVE BEHAVIOR

Exploiting the other person

Boasting to the other person

Competing with the other person

Bitterness toward the other person

Suspicion about the other person

Skepticism toward the other person

Wariness of the other person

FIGURE 8.3   HOSTILE–DOMINANT BEHAVIORS/HOSTILE–SUBMISSIVE BEHAVIORS

come?" is likely to get a parent's hostile–dominant message in return, such as: "I'm the parent and you'll do what I say!"

The third relational structure, **parallel relationship**, is not represented in Figure 8.1. It is a hybrid form in which complementary and symmetrical aspects are combined. One partner may be dominant and the other submissive at times; other times, the partners may reverse roles; and sometimes, both partners may be dominant or both may be submissive. Similarly, the expression of feelings depends on the situation. In general, the parallel structure is the most flexible, allowing contributions to the relationship to vary from time to time. Knowledge Checkup 8.1 will help you analyze the structure of your relationships.

KNOWLEDGE CHECKUP 8.1

RELATIONAL STRUCTURE ANALYSIS

Select two relationships with specific people: one nonfamily, the other, family. Using Figure 8.1 as a guide, indicate the extent to which you and the other person are dominant, submissive, loving, and hostile. Use the ten-point scale to mark your responses.

A. *NONFAMILY RELATIONSHIP*

    1   2   3   4   5   6   7   8   9   10
almost never   almost always

_____ **1.** I am dominant.

_____ **2.** The other person is dominant.

_____ **3.** I am submissive.

_____ **4.** The other person is submissive.

_____ **5.** I am loving.

_____ **6.** The other person is loving.

_____ **7.** I am hostile.

_____ **8.** The other person is hostile.

B. *FAMILY RELATIONSHIP*

1	2	3	4	5	6	7	8	9	10

almost never   almost always

_____ **1.** I am dominant.

_____ **2.** The other person is dominant.

_____ **3.** I am submissive.

_____ **4.** The other person is submissive.

_____ **5.** I am loving.

_____ **6.** The other person is loving.

_____ **7.** I am hostile.

_____ **8.** The other person is hostile.

Using the terms *complementary, symmetrical,* and *parallel,* describe each relationship.

Nonfamily relationship _____ Family relationship _____

Figure 8.4 shows plots for one person's responses to items 1, 3, 5, and 7 for himself, and to items 2, 4, 6, and 8 for his perceptions of his father. (The son's four scores for himself were plotted as follows: The response to item 1 was a 2, so a point was placed on the dominant line at number 2; the response to item 3 was a 7, so a point was placed on the submissive line at number 7; the response to item 5 was a 1, so a point was placed on the loving line at number 1; and the response to item 7 was a 6, so a point was placed on the hostile line at number 6. The four points were joined to form the four-sided figure.)

The son perceives himself as predominantly submissive and hostile (because the four-sided figure formed by his scores falls predominantly into the submissive–hostile quadrant) and his father as predominantly loving and dominant (because most of the four-sided figure formed by the scores for the father falls into the dominant–loving quadrant). Given the son's perception of their relationship as complementary for both control and affection, what predictions could you make for their relationship? (For example, do they fight with each other? If they fight, what do you think the underlying issue is that they fight about?) To determine whether you perceive each of

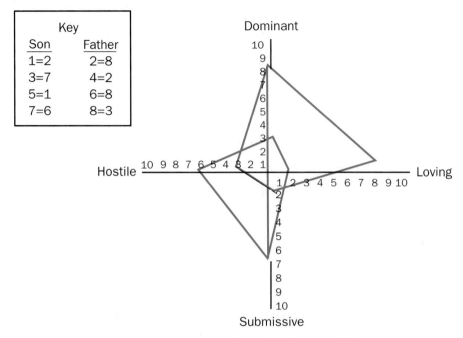

Key	
Son	Father
1=2	2=8
3=7	4=2
5=1	6=8
7=6	8=3

FIGURE 8.4   FATHER–SON RELATIONAL STRUCTURE ANALYSIS

your relationships as predominantly dominant–loving, dominant–hostile, submissive–loving, or submissive–hostile, plot your responses from Knowledge Checkup 8.1 on Figures 8.5 and 8.6.

As you plot your responses to items 1, 3, 5, and 7 (your perceptions of yourself in *each* relationship—nonfamily and family) and to items 2, 4, 6, and 8 (your perceptions of your partner in each relationship—nonfamily and family) on Figures 8.5 and 8.6, consider these questions for your selected nonfamily and family relationships:

1. Does your four-sided figure fall predominantly into any one of the four quadrants? What about your partner's?
2. How do the two figures compare? How do they describe the structure of your relationship?
3. What predictions could you make for your relationship?

Analyzing the structure of your relationships could help you discover why some are more satisfying than others. For example, the father–son relationship in Figure 8.4 is likely to be unsatisfactory from the son's perspective: The two probably fight a lot, the son probably harbors a great deal of quiet resentment, and when they fight the underlying issue is probably who's in control.

Although most people in North America prefer the parallel relationship structure, not every close relationship takes this form.[5] Do you insist on being dominant

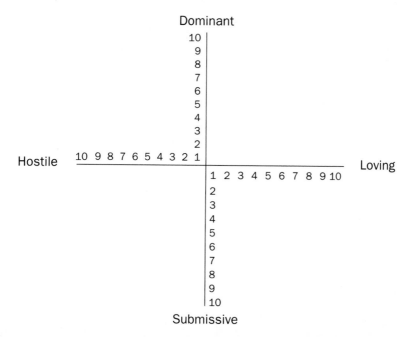

FIGURE 8.5   YOUR NONFAMILY RELATIONAL STRUCTURE ANALYSIS

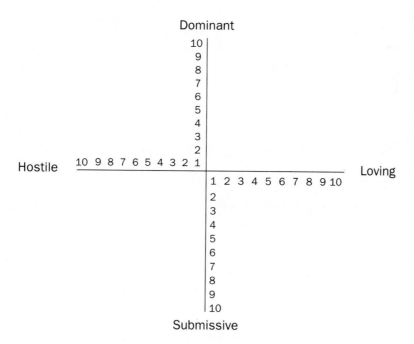

FIGURE 8.6   YOUR FAMILY RELATIONAL STRUCTURE ANALYSIS

or submissive but have a partner who seeks equality? Do you wonder whether your expressions of love will receive loving responses? Questions such as these should help you further analyze the structure of your relationships.

RULES

Rules, the regulations that govern actions in a relationship, are necessary for you to make predictions about another person's behavior. If you don't know the rules governing your interaction, you can't predict whether the person to whom you nod and say hello will in return, ignore you, hit you, or start screaming! But because most people share the same rule for greeting behavior, you can predict a reciprocal response: a nod and hello will get you a nod and hello in return. Rules organize the world for you, add predictability, and reduce uncertainty.

Researchers who have conducted studies in various parts of the world uncovered a small number of rules that help structure relationships.[6] Like all rules, some may be more important than others in particular relationships and in particular societies, and some may even be broken. The five *relational rules* found are:

1. You should respect another's privacy.
2. You should look the other person in the eye during conversations.

3. You should not divulge something that is said in confidence.
4. You should not criticize the other person publicly.
5. You should seek to repay debts, favors, or compliments, no matter how small.

Several specific *structure rules* that help structure particular relationships, such as loving, friendship, and work relationships, also turned up. Specific rules for friendships were:

1. You should stand up for the other person in her or his absence.
2. You should share news of success with her or him.
3. You should show emotional support.
4. You should trust and confide in each other.
5. You should volunteer your help in time of need.
6. You should strive to make the other person happy when you are with her or him.
7. You should not nag the other person.

Knowledge Checkup 8.2 will help you test your understanding of universal and relational rules by looking at them in three of your relationships.

KNOWLEDGE CHECKUP 8.2

ACKNOWLEDGING YOUR RELATIONAL RULES

Select an important opposite-sex relationship, same-sex relationship, and a relationship you have with a member of your family. Using the five relational and seven structural rules in the material presented immediately before this Knowledge Checkup, rate each on a five-point scale as to its importance regarding each of the three relationships. If a rule does not apply, do not place a number in the space.

Use this scale in answering: **1** = very important, **2** = important, **3** = neither important nor unimportant, **4** = not important, and **5** = very unimportant.

OPPOSITE-SEX RELATIONSHIP

Relational rules

1. _____   4. _____

2. _____   5. _____

3. _____

Structural rules

1. _____
2. _____
3. _____
4. _____
5. _____
6. _____
7. _____

SAME-SEX RELATIONSHIP

Relational rules

1. _____
2. _____
3. _____
4. _____
5. _____

Structural rules

1. _____
2. _____
3. _____

4. _____
5. _____
6. _____
7. _____

FAMILY RELATIONSHIP

Relational rules

1. _____
2. _____
3. _____
4. _____
5. _____

Structural rules

1. _____
2. _____
3. _____
4. _____
5. _____
6. _____
7. _____

What differences and similarities do you find relate to the relationships you examined?

How you rate each rule, and the differences and similarities you find among the three relationships, are determined, in part, by your cultural values. It must be kept in mind that the twelve rules are influenced and modified by culture; therefore, others would not necessarily answer the same way. For example, the rule concerning privacy is a perfect illustration of how different cultures can respond differently to the same message. Some cultures don't even have a word or definition for the concept of "trespassing." In relationships in these societies, physical *invasion* of someone's personal territory is simply not a matter of consideration. People touch and get close to others with no thought of doing something that would make the other uncomfortable. Privacy is not valued. In cultures such as those of the Arabs, Greeks, and Mexicans, which have a strong group orientation, seclusion is not part of an individual's set of needs. There is a definite contrast when compared to customs found in the French, English, German, or North American cultures.[7] In the latter, privacy and personal space are valued. Think of what is being said by the proverb "A man's (or woman's) home is his (or her) castle" when compared to the Mexican proverb "Mi casa es su casa" ("My house is your house").

A friendship may evolve into a love relationship. If it does, new rules arise, mostly concerned with self-disclosure and the expression of emotion. Should the love relationship culminate in relationship or a living-together commitment, the number of rules increases dramatically to virtually all forms of interaction, both with the partners and with people outside the relationship. Rules may develop about who can dance with whom at a party (relatives may be OK, but not people one dated in the past), who can have lunch with whom, and even who a person can talk with on the phone. The multitude of rules arises from an attempt to keep the interaction orderly, but the very number of rules points to the high probability of conflict and friction between spouses or relational partners.

Unique rules, as well as universal rules, govern interaction in a work relationship. Less concern is placed on intimacy, but more is placed on task-maintenance rules, such as "Both people should accept a fair share of the workload" and "Workers should cooperate."

Rules also exist for topics that should and should not be discussed.[8] For example, in both platonic and romantic relationships, talking about the current or future state of the relationship may be considered taboo because partners fear that such talk might destroy the relationship. Thus, you might want to talk about making a lifelong commitment, for example, but avoid the topic because you fear scaring away your partner.

To further complicate matters, how rules apply to particular situations may be unclear. For example, knowing that making eye contact with someone you are interested in when talking is important, but being unaware about the rules governing the first kiss. When should it happen? Should it happen? How should you go about it? What should you say, if anything? How can you avoid looking like an idiot or the most desperate person in town?

You may not consciously apply the general rules, but you probably resort to them anyway because they create a structure that makes beginning interaction moderately predictable and not unpleasant. As a relationship grows, however, more rules need to be negotiated. Whether you and your partner sit down face to face and discuss existing rules or ones that need to be created, or whether you proceed in a less formal way, the task cannot be avoided. The more the relationship reflects your own and your partner's individual characteristics, the more specific the rules for your interaction must be.

Analyzing the rules of your relationships can help you make your interactions clearer. Skill Development 8.3 will help you develop a method for analyzing your relationship rules.

SKILL DEVELOPMENT 8.3

ANALYZING YOUR RELATIONSHIP RULES

Select two relationships: an important nonfamily relationship and an important family relationship. Answer each of the following questions.

1. What are three rules that you have for each person?

Nonfamily person _____

_____

Nonfamily person _____

_____

2. What are three of the other person's rules for you?

Nonfamily person _____

_____

Family member _____

_____

3. What are three shared rules that give the relationship excitement?

Nonfamily person _____

_____

Family member _____

_____

4. What are three shared rules that give the relationship stability?

Nonfamily person _____

_____

Family member _____

_____

5. What are three shared rules that give the relationship personal and mutual benefits?

Nonfamily person _____

_____

Family member _____

_____

6. Write two positive and two negative statements about how you feel about the rules. (Are some hard to follow? Are they negotiable?)

Nonfamily person _____

_____

Family member _____

_____

7. How do you ensure that the other person follows the rules?

Nonfamily person _____

_____

Family member _____

_____

8. What does the other person do to make sure you follow the rules?

Nonfamily person _____

_____

Family member _____

_____

QUALITIES AND RESOURCES OF RELATIONSHIPS

Once you understand the goals, structure, and rules that establish the framework for a relationship, you can begin to consider the relationship's quality and the resources it provides. You already have a sense of the characteristics that contribute to a relationship's quality, that is, its "goodness" or "badness." If asked, you could probably rank your relationships along a continuum from good to bad, from high quality to low. Similarly, you could probably also describe your relationships with respect to the resources, or benefits, they provide.

Whereas goals, structure, and rules are "either–or" propositions (your relationship has one goal or another, one type of structure or another, and one set of rules or another), qualities and resources exist in terms of "more or less" (your relationship is more or less intimate, more or less affectionate).

Two qualities that are important for understanding any relationship are commitment and intimacy, and four important resources are affection, esteem, information, and services.

COMMITMENT

Commitment is a popular word to toss into magazine articles and sprinkle into conversations. It appears to imply a great deal about a relationship:

"She's afraid of committing herself to the relationship."

"He considers the expensive birthday present a commitment."

"If you're not committed to completing the project, why did you agree to do it in the first place?"

Before we take a closer look at the notion of commitment, complete the self-analysis in Knowledge Checkup 8.3.

KNOWLEDGE CHECKUP 8.3

COMMITMENT PROBE[9]

Do the following exercise twice. First, think of a person with whom you have a friendship or intimate relationship—whether you are dating, exclusively involved, or married—and with that relationship in mind, mark each statement according to how true it is for you. Then think of a person with whom you have a work / school relationship and, with that relationship in mind, respond to the statements again.

Mark **1** if the statement is definitely false.

Mark **2** if it is mostly false.

Mark **3** if it is neither true nor false.

Mark **4** if it is mostly true.

Mark **5** if it is definitely true.

____ ____ **1.** It is likely that my partner and I will be together six months from now.

____ ____ **2.** I am not attracted to other potential partners.

____ ____ **3.** A potential partner would have to be truly outstanding for me to pursue a new relationship.

____ ____ **4.** It is likely that this relationship will be permanent.

____ ____ **5.** My partner is likely to continue this relationship.

____ ____ **Total**

Total your five responses. This is your commitment score.

A relationship identified as "casual dating" has an average commitment score of 13, one identified as "exclusively involved" has an average score of 17, and a marriage relationship has an average score of 21. Where does your friendship or intimate relationship fit along this continuum?

Although the term *commitment* is often applied to relationships on a path toward intimacy—such as dating relationships—it is equally important in long-term work relationships, particularly partnerships. Scores below 16 indicate a weak or unstable work partnership, one likely to break up if an attractive offer comes along from outside the relationship. The higher the commitment score, the more stable the relationship and the higher the probability that it will continue. Where does your work/school relationship fit along this continuum?

Commitment, a pledge to the continuation of a relationship, has three aspects: your commitment, your perception of the other's commitment, and what it is you are committed to. In general, you link your commitment with the perceived commitment of the other person (consider your response to item 5 in Knowledge Checkup 8.3). If you think your partner is less committed than you, you are likely to decrease commitment; similarly, if you think the other person is more highly committed, you might increase your commitment. A relationship is unstable if the levels of commitment are unequal. For example, if you see your relationship as a long-term involvement to which you're highly committed, a problem may arise if your partner sees it as a casual pastime involving little commitment. An aspect of the commitment to a relationship often centers on shared love. As one couple stated in their commitment ceremony, "The thing that brought us to where we are now is love. The strength we've gained from our love is what pulls us along."[10]

The phrase "commitment to a relationship" is vague, but you usually have a particular object in mind. For example, you may commit yourself to continuing the relationship even if you and your partner are separated by geographical distance, or you may commit yourself to increasing the intimacy of your relationship, or you may commit yourself to working together to increase business sales.

INTIMACY

Intimacy is an umbrella term that includes, among other things, emotional closeness and intellectual sharing.[11] Consider these questions with respect to one of your relationships:

1. How much do you know about each other?
2. To what degree are your life and the other person's life intertwined and interdependent?
3. Do you trust each other?

Each of these questions relates to one aspect of intimacy and underscores the difficulty of defining precisely what intimacy is. Essentially, **intimacy** is a quality of a relationship based on detailed knowledge and deep understanding of the other person. Trying to enumerate specific behaviors ("This relationship is an intimate one because . . .") results in a long list that contains seemingly trivial items.

Intimacy is an expectation you have for a relationship, an anticipation that you and your partner will come to know each other more and more deeply, more and more personally—that you will continue to share intimate experiences.

Intimacy and intimate experiences are not identical. Although any relationship may include an **intimate experience**—a "one-night stand" or a moment of important personal sharing, for example—it is only in intimate relationships that continued intimate experiences can be expected.

The intimacy of a relationship may be determined by examining three factors, each related to the three questions you answered at the beginning of this section. First, what are the breadth and depth of the information you and your partner know about each other? Breadth refers to the number of topics you discuss and depth pertains to how important and personal the information is. As breadth and depth increase, so does intimacy.

Both the breadth and depth of the information we share with our partners reflects our cultural background. In many cultures people are expected to know what someone else is thinking and feeling. Hence, in cultures such as the Japanese, expressions of intimacy are very different from those used in the United States.[12] There is often difficulty when someone from a "revealing" culture, such as North America where *self*-image, *self*-esteem, and *self*-awareness are important and the word "I" appears with great regularity, attempts to get highly personal with someone from a "nonrevealing" culture. The Chinese culture, for example, suspends thought of the self to the degree that there is no specific symbol for selfish. (Actually, the closest symbol for selfishness is two different symbols that mean "I" placed together.) Learning all you can about another person's openness, based on his or her cultural background, helps you decide how much information you should disclose and expect the other person to disclose without making your partner feel uncomfortable.

Second, in what ways are you and the other person's lives interdependent? As you and this person share and learn to depend on each other for services, support, and understanding, you become mutually dependent for the satisfaction of your needs, wants, and desires. Intimacy and interdependence, however, are not related in a simple way—as when one increases the other increases. Rather, the most intimate relationships are characterized by an interdependence that allows each person's maximum satisfaction but also has limits and flexibility so that one person doesn't feel overwhelmed or smothered by the other.

Third, how much do you trust the other person to accept you as you are, to avoid purposely hurting you, to keep your best interests and the best interests of your relationship in mind, to share with you, and to continue the relationship? Your answers determine the degree to which you allow yourself to be vulnerable to your partner. Without trust, the information you share will be mostly superficial. You might fear being exploited, so you keep yourself separate from the other person, perhaps reaching out occasionally to have an intimate experience, but avoiding the belief that intimate experiences characterize your relationship. Skill Development 8.4 provides you with practice in applying a method for analyzing the level of intimacy in a relationship.

SKILL DEVELOPMENT 8.4

ANALYZING INTIMACY IN YOUR RELATIONSHIPS

Think of an important family or nonfamily relationship. Using this scale, rate your intimacy level with this person by evaluating each statement:

5	4	3	2	1
Strongly agree				Strongly disagree

_____ **1.** The other person and I have a great deal of information about each other.

_____ **2.** The other person and I are highly interdependent.

_____ **3.** The other person and I perform a great many services for each other.

_____ **4.** The other person and I support each other.

_____ **5.** The other person and I understand each other.

_____ **6.** The other person and I satisfy each other's needs, wants, and desires.

_____ **7.** The other person and I accept each other as we are.

_____ **8.** The other person and I avoid hurting each other.

_____   *Total score*

Examine each answer. The higher your score, the higher the level of intimacy in the relationship and, therefore, the greater the possibility that the individual item may be an integral part of the relationship.

Examine the total score. Scores of 32 and above indicate a high degree of intimacy, while scores of 20 and below indicate a low degree of intimacy. High scores tend to indicate a relationship that is more fulfilling.

RESOURCES

Relationships, whether intimate or not, serve as sources for tangible benefits, such as money and gifts; intangible benefits, such as affection and emotional support; and service benefits, such as help with your gardening or getting you a book from the library. Important resources in a relationship include affection (expressing and receiving warmth, tenderness, and caring), esteem (obtaining confirmation of who you are in relation to others), services (having things done for you), and information (receiving needed information about yourself and the environment).[13]

Affection and esteem are more important resources in love and friendship relationships than they are in work relationships. By contrast, service and information resources are more important in work relationships than they are in love and friendship relationships. Although some resources may be more important than others in a particular relationship, most relationships have many resources.

A relationship's framework—its goals, structure, and rules—and its qualitative aspects—including commitment, intimacy, and resources—may be joined together within a larger context, that of time. Because relationships are continuously evolving, you can expect that your goals will change; a relationship's structure will change, stabilize, and change even more; some rules will be clarified, others will be abandoned, and new rules will emerge; commitment will vary, as will what you and the other person commit yourselves to; intimacy will increase, stabilize, and continue to change; and new resources will be added, old resources may be discarded, and available resources will vary in importance.

How time affects a relationship depends on the relationship's unique characteristics. Changes are complex because alterations in one aspect of a relationship's framework, such as adding the rule "We date each other exclusively," or in one of its qualitative aspects, such as becoming more intimate, cause modifications in other dimensions of the relationship. For example, adding a rule about exclusivity will most likely cause changes in the relationship's goals (is marriage or a committed relationship a goal now?), structure (should decision making be more evenly shared now?), and what resources are important (are more services expected now?). Relationships are dynamic—continually adapting and developing—as they pass through time. A relationship is not a thing, but a process—an ever-changing process.

COMMUNICATION COMPETENCY CHECKUP

The goal of this Communication Competency Checkup is to guide you in putting your skills and knowledge about interpersonal process to use, and to help you summarize the material in this chapter.

The husband and wife are involved in a conflict. An analysis of their relationship goals, structure, rules, commitment, intimacy, and resources will help clarify some possible sources of their trouble.

1. What are several goals the wife might have for this wife–husband relationship? What are several of the husband's possible goals?

Used with permission of Libby Reid.

2. Describe the probable structure of their relationship in terms of dominance/ submission and love/hostility. Is the relationship complementary, symmetrical, or parallel?

3. List several rules that affect interaction between husbands and wives. What new rules would you recommend for husband–wife relationships and what effects would they have on how husbands and wives relate to each other?

4. How committed do the two people in the picture seem to their wife–husband relationship?

5. Does the relationship between husbands and wives allow for the development of intimacy?

6. What common resources are available to husbands in their marital relationships? What resources are available to wives?

7. In which of these cultures might the female's message and actions be typical? (Mark *T* for typical and *NT* for not typical.) U.S. _____ Japan _____ Iran _____ Sweden _____ Italy _____

Answers: U.S.—*T*, Japan—*NT*, Iran—*NT*, Sweden—*T*, Italy—*NT*)

NOTES

1. Jesse G. Delia, "Some Tentative Thoughts Concerning the Study of Interpersonal Relationships and Their Development," *Western Journal of Speech Communication* 44 (1980): 97–103; Steve Duck, *Understanding Relationships* (New York: Guilford Press, 1991).

2. William W. Wilmot, *Dyadic Communication,* 3d ed. (Reading, MA: Addison-Wesley, 1987).

3. L. S. Benjamin, "Structural Analysis of Social Behavior," *Psychological Review* 81 (1974): 372–425; Rolfe LaForge, "Interpersonal Check List (ICL)," in the *1977 Annual Handbook for Group Facilitators,* John E. Jones and J. William Pfeiffer (Eds.) (La Jolla, CA: University Associates, 1977),pp. 89–96; Timothy Leary, *Interpersonal Diagnosis of Personality* (New York: Ronald Press, 1957).

4. Wilmot, *Dyadic Communication.*

5. Mark Randall Harrington, *The Relationship Between Psychological Sex-Type and Perceptions of Individuals in Complementary, Symmetrical, and Parallel Relationships,* thesis, University of North Carolina at Chapel Hill, 1984.

6. A summary of the series of investigations, including comparisons of the rules for different types of relationships in different parts of the world, is available in Michael Argyle and Monika Henderson, "The Rules of Relationships," in *Understanding Personal Relationships,* Steve Duck and Daniel Perlman (Eds.) (Beverly Hills, CA: Sage, 1985), pp. 63–84.

7. Carol Dolphin Zinner, "Beyond Hall: Variables in the Use of Personal Space," *The Howard Journal of Communications* 1 (Spring 1988): 28–29.

8. A detailed analysis of taboo topics in relationships is available in Leslie A. Baxter and William Wilmot, "Taboo Topics in Close Relationships," *Journal of Social and Personal Relationships* 2 (1985): 253–69.

9. Adapted from Mary Lund, "The Development of Investment and Commitment Scales for Predicting Continuity of Personal Relationships," *Journal of Social and Personal Relationships* 2 (1985): 3–23.

10. Craig Wilson, "Mr. and Mr. Jackson-Paris, Pumping Up Respect," *USA Today,* November 4, 1992, p. 3D. (This article is about Rod and Bob Jackson-Paris, a gay model and a world-famous gay bodybuilder, who were touring the country speaking about relationships and their marriage in a Unitarian ceremony in 1989.)

11. Elaine Hatfield, "The Dangers of Intimacy," in *Communication, Intimacy, and Close Relationships,* Valerian J. Derlega (Ed.) (Orlando: FL: Academic Press, 1984), pp. 207–20.

12. Stella Ting-Toomey, "Intimacy Expressions in Three Cultures: France, Japan, and the United States," *International Journal of Intercultural Relations* 15 (1991): 31–35.

13. J. House, *Work Stress and Social Support* (Reading, MA: Addison-Wesley, 1981); C. Streeter and C. Franklin, "Defining and Measuring Social Support: Guidelines for Social Work Practitioners," *Research on Social Work Practice* 2 (1992): 81–98.

FOR FURTHER INVESTIGATION

Altman, Irwin, and Dalmas Taylor. *Social Penetration: The Development of Interpersonal Relationships.* New York: Holt, Rinehart and Winston, 1973.

Argyle, Michael, and Monika Henderson, "The Rules of Relationships," in Steve Duck and Daniel Perlman, eds., *Understanding Personal Relationships.* Beverly Hills, CA: Sage, 1985. (pp. 63–84).

Baxter, Leslie A., and William Wilmot.

"Taboo Topics in Close Relationships." *Journal of Social and Personal Relationships* 2 (1985): 253–69.

Clark, Don. *Loving Someone Gay* (revised edition). New York: Signet Books, 1991.

Delia, Jesse G. "Some Tentative Thoughts Concerning the Study of Interpersonal Relationships and Their Development." *Western Journal of Speech Communication* 44 (1980): 97–103.

Derlega, Valerian J., (Ed.) *Communication, Intimacy, and Close Relationships.* Orlando, FL: Academic Press, 1984.

Duck, Steve. *Understanding Relationships.* New York: Guilford Press, 1991.

Farrell, Warren. *Why Men Are the Way They Are.* New York: Berkley Books, 1986.

Forward, Susan, and Craig Buck. *Obsessive Love.* New York: Bantam Books, 1991.

Gullo, Stephen, and Connie Church. *Loveshock: How to Recover from a Broken Heart and Love Again.* New York: Simon and Schuster, 1988.

Hendrick, Clyde, and Susan S. Hendrick. *Liking, Loving, and Relating.* Monterey, CA: Brooks/Cole, 1983.

Knapp, Mark L., and Anita Vangelisti. *Interpersonal Communication and Human Relationships,* 2d ed. Boston: Allyn and Bacon, 1992.

Leary, Timothy. *Interpersonal Diagnosis of Personality.* New York: Ronald Press, 1957.

Lund, Mary. "The Development of Investment and Commitment Scales for Predicting Continuity of Personal Relationships." *Journal of Social and Personal Relationships* 2 (1985): 3–23.

Napier, Augustus, and Carl Whitaker. *The Family Crucible.* New York: Bantam Books, 1980.

Pilkington, Constance J., Abraham Tesses, and Deborah Stephens. "Complementarity in Romantic Relationships: A Self-Evaluation Maintenance Respective." *Journal of Social and Personal Relationships* 8 (1991): 481–504.

Powell, John. *Why Am I Afraid to Tell You Who I Am?* Chicago: Argus Communications, 1969.

Ross, Michael. *The Married Homosexual Man.* London: Routledge and Kegan Paul, 1983.

Wilmot, William W. *Dyadic Communication,* 3d ed. Reading, MA: Addison-Wesley, 1987.

CHAPTER 9

Beginning, Maintaining, and Ending Interpersonal Relationships

COMMUNICATION COMPETENCIES

This chapter examines the role of communication in beginning, maintaining, and ending interpersonal relationships. Specifically, the objective of the chapter is for you to learn to:

- Describe the role of attraction in new relationships.
- Recognize several important objectives to be accomplished during the beginning phase of a relationship.
- Apply the five steps of relationship formation to a new relationship.
- Recognize the role of information sharing in the maintenance of a relationship.
- Apply two techniques—developing a supportive and confirming communication climate and self-disclosing—for maintaining and enhancing your relationships.
- Apply several methods for increasing relationship satisfaction.
- Describe the characteristics that distinguish relationship termination processes.
- Recognize the most common communication strategies for relationship termination.
- Recognize cultural variations in interpersonal relationships.

KEY WORDS

The key words in this chapter are:

attractiveness	**self-disclosure**
proximity	**catharsis**
economic model of relationships	**self-clarification**
complementarity	**reciprocity**
similarity	**relational maintenance**
approachability cues	**relationship enhancement**
free information	**impression formation**
supportive and **confirming** behaviors	**manipulation**
attacking and **disconfirming** behaviors	**affinity seeking**

Imagine yourself at a party. A stranger walks toward you. Imagine who this stranger is, including how she or he looks, talks, and acts. What does this stranger believe, value, like, and dislike?

Now, imagine meeting the stranger for the first time. What do you do? What do you say? Are you nervous about this first meeting or is this a person with whom you feel automatically at ease? What happens to the two of you?

You and the stranger find out that you will be working together on an important project. What do you plan to do to ensure that you have a good relationship? Do you presume that a good relationship will "just happen"?

RELATIONAL DEVELOPMENT: BEGINNING, MAINTAINING, AND ENDING RELATIONSHIPS

Establishing a new relationship—one that goes beyond an hour or two of superficial cocktail chatter—is difficult for most of us. Meeting strangers seems to bring out our deepest insecurities and our best-hidden self-perceived flaws.

Although the romantic view of relationships is that they "just happen"—from the magical moment when two lovers swoon at first sight until the tragic end when

From *Do You Hate Your Hips More Than Nuclear War?*, published by Penguin Books, 1988. Used with permission of Libby Reid.

circumstances pull them apart forever—relationships do not drop from the sky fully formed, a gift from some Relationship Fairy. Relational development—whether between lovers, friends, acquaintances, or coworkers—follows a predictable pattern. Relationships have a recognizable beginning, middle, and end, and the communication that takes place during each phase is highly complex.

BEGINNING A RELATIONSHIP

A relationship begins when you are attracted to someone and initiate interaction. Being attracted to someone, however, does not automatically mean that you will initiate interaction. Interaction is usually initiated when you want to learn something about the other person—background, values, interests, and personality—and when you want to create a favorable impression. Regardless of where it may end, the relationship process begins with attraction.

On any given day, you encounter many people with whom you can choose to form a relationship. Not everyone, of course, has an equal probability of being chosen: You are attracted to some people and not to others, just as some are attracted to you and some are not. Each of us carries a mental list of criteria for attraction. Knowledge Checkup 9.1 will help you identify the reasons you may be attracted to someone.

KNOWLEDGE CHECKUP 9.1

CHARACTERISTICS ASSESSMENT

Rank the following characteristics in the order of their importance to you in describing a person with whom you would form a long-term relationship. Rank the most important characteristic 1 and the least important 15.

_____ adaptability

_____ college graduate

_____ creativity

_____ desire for children

_____ exciting personality

_____ good earning capacity

_____ good health

_____ good heredity

_____ good housekeeper

_____ intelligence

_____ kindness and understanding

_____ physical attractiveness

_____ religious orientation

_____ cultural background

_____ similar interests

Attraction

Think of people to whom you are attracted and the traits they share. Do they seem to have similar physical characteristics? Do they live nearby? Do they do things for you without asking for too much in return? Do they have qualities you lack but which seem to fit well with your own? Are they similar to you? Do you have some personal motives for forming a relationship that are more important to you than who or what the other person is? Your answers to these questions correspond to the five bases of attraction: attractiveness, proximity, personal rewards, complementarity, similarity, and personal motives.

Attractiveness   **Attractiveness** is your impression of someone as appealing. The first information you typically receive about a new acquaintance pertains to physical attractiveness. When you call someone attractive, you are usually referring to your perception of the person's physical attributes.

You may have a personal list of desired attributes—what did your stranger at the party look like? But, no universal description of what people find attractive exists. Such a description varies from person to person and from time to time. For example, at one time plumpness was considered attractive; now the preference is for thinness. Tall and slender, brown eyes, and a clear complexion might constitute attractiveness for many people, but not for all and certainly not for all time.

A paradox exists in evaluating attractiveness: Although people may agree that person X is more attractive than person Y, they may strongly disagree on *why* person X is more attractive. However, even in the absence of consensus on a definition of physical attractiveness, attractiveness matters in initial impressions.

The role of culture in both evaluating attractiveness and in forming initial impressions is interesting. Our judgment of beauty, like most aspects of culture, is developed so early in life that we hardly recognize its hidden grip. Yet there are countless studies that tell us that beauty is as much in the eye of the culture as it is in that of the beholder. For example, though certain African tribes stretch their lips to make themselves attractive, extremely big lips are not a North American measurement of attractiveness. And, on several occasions African Americans have protested U.S. beauty pageants because they felt blacks were being judged by white beauty standards. Recent evidence points to the fact that "attractive," within any culture, means

"average."[1] The attractive person has neither a big nose nor a small nose, neither very large eyes nor small eyes, is neither very tall nor very short, and so on.

How high did you rank physical attractiveness in Knowledge Checkup 9.1? A recent survey reveals that men rank the item third and women rank it sixth, which indicates that both groups give high importance to physical beauty.[2]

Often included as an aspect of attractiveness is demeanor, how the other person behaves during an encounter. Someone who follows the rules for interacting, who, for example, maintains eye contact and doesn't criticize, is more likely to be found attractive than someone who is less socially adept. In this instance, "attractive" implies "comfortable." In general, attractive people are assumed to be warmer, more sensitive, kinder, more modest, more sociable, and to make better husbands or wives than their unattractive peers.[3]

It is not surprising that what represents attractive characteristics shifts from culture to culture. For example, in many Asian cultures men would find women who are acquiescent, docile, and quiet far more attractive than women who are spirited, vivacious, and lively.[4]

Proximity Marrying the person next door doesn't happen just in Hollywood musicals, such as *Meet Me in St. Louis* with its love song, "The Boy Next Door." To be attracted to someone takes some interaction, and you are most likely to interact with people whom you encounter frequently. Whether meeting at the mailbox when you both fetch the mail or sitting next to each other in a class, the effect is the same: You get the opportunity to communicate. **Proximity,** how near you are to someone, is an important determinant of attraction.

Familiarity, although it may breed contempt, more often breeds liking. As the other person becomes more predictable, interaction likely increases. Increased interaction, in turn, leads to other bases of attraction. You may go on to discover interests, physical attributes, and personality traits that enhance attraction.

A lack of familiarity is one reason people often fail to develop relationships with others from different cultures. There is a low level of predictability when you are not familiar with the other person. How often are you attracted to someone you don't understand? You would indeed feel uncomfortable if your culture stressed action and activity and you found yourself in the company of someone who believed in a tranquil and calm approach to life. This difference in the pace at which people conduct personal and private matters is often a major barrier to interpersonal understanding.

Personal Rewards   According to an **economic model of relationships,** we are attracted to people with whom a relationship *costs* little yet provides many *rewards.* This calculation may seem self-serving, but it makes sense. Relationships have goals, and achieving goals entails costs. Costs may take many forms: You may have to do something for the other person in return for what he or she does for you; you may be expected to behave in a way that does not fit your self-image; or you may need to expend money, time, or emotional energy. Nevertheless, there is a reward: achieving your relationship's goal. The question is whether the rewards are sufficient to offset the costs.

The reward–cost balance is not assessed simply. The time and effort you invest in a relationship are not tangibly calculable, nor are the rewards you receive. Moreover, you may not even expect your rewards to correspond directly to your investment: Depending on the relationship, you may be satisfied with less, or you may want more. Comparing costs and rewards of relationships is a psychological process, not an accounting procedure that leads to balanced books.[5]

If you think your rewards adequately offset your costs, you will usually perceive a relationship as attractive. If you think your rewards are inadequate, you will probably find the relationship too costly and consider it unattractive. You can ultimately determine the attractiveness of a relationship, however, only after you assess the other relationships open to you. Can you form another relationship? Is the other, new, relationship likely to provide more rewards than the current relationship?

If you are in a relationship that seems, on the whole, unsatisfactory, ask yourself what benefits make the relationship attractive. If you stay in an unattractive relationship, chances are that some reward makes the costs bearable. The reward may be hard to recognize at first, but it's there. Perhaps the reward is not being alone, or not having to change, or not having to seek out and develop another relationship.

Knowledge Checkup 9.2 will help you to carry out a cost–reward analysis.

KNOWLEDGE CHECKUP 9.2

COSTS AND REWARDS

Write the first name of someone important to you. Now, make a list of at least 10 costs and 10 rewards of your relationship with that person. Some examples are:

COSTS

Less time for other friends
Teasing is sometimes hard on my
   self-esteem
Have to spend money

REWARDS

Companionship
Feel fully loved
Have someone to turn to in times
   of stress

PERSON:

MY COSTS

MY REWARDS

Complementarity   **Complementarity** is the attraction of opposites. Although a common saying is that "opposites attract," complementarity in fact is rather limited—not simply to particular people, but to particular people in particular situations. For example, a dominant older sister may enjoy her younger brother's submissive behavior, but she may be annoyed by such behavior in her friends.

Complementarity is at work when you find it enjoyable to talk to someone whose job is completely different from yours or who doesn't agree with you on certain issues.

Taking pleasure in diversity can bring numerous rewards, one of which is discovering that the differences that have kept you away from people might be the very thing that could attract you to them. From learning about new foods to different ways of envisioning God, each culture has something to offer those of us who are willing to be open to new experiences.

But the excitement of exploring differences, although important in some relationships, interestingly enough is not as strong a source of attraction as its opposite, similarity. In general, attitude dissimilarity, especially when discovered during an initial encounter, may immediately spell doom for any possibility of a close relationship.[6]

Similarity   **Similarity** occurs when people have characteristics in common, whether these are looks, attitudes, opinions, values, beliefs, experiences, or ideas.

This principle of attraction gets the most support from published research: Birds of a feather *do* flock together. You are most attracted to those you perceive as similar to yourself. For example, husbands and wives tend to be of similar age (especially in first marriages), education, race, religion, and ethnic background. Partners also tend to hold similar attitudes, opinions, and socioeconomic status. How important similarity is to a relationship depends on several things, including knowing such things as your own attitudes or opinions, knowing the other person's attitudes or opinions, determining how important similarity is for the particular relationship, and determining how important dissimilarity is.[7]

Now more than ever before the notion of similarity takes on new meaning as we approach people who often come from backgrounds that are quite different from our own. What is important to remember is that while cultures might be different in many areas, we can still find similarities among all cultures. A search for similarities will assist you in your efforts to become a competent communicator in interpersonal settings.

Review your ranking of the fifteen items in Knowledge Checkup 9.1 and study them in light of the similarity thesis. You may be surprised to find that you described someone whose characteristics are similar to your own and that you gave the highest rankings to those characteristics you find most important or attractive in yourself. If your ranking didn't follow this pattern, you do not consider similarity important in judging attractiveness. Knowledge Checkup 9.3 provides the opportunity for you to compare your ranking with that of the general population.

KNOWLEDGE CHECKUP 9.3

COMPARING YOUR PREFERENCES WITH GENERAL PREFERENCES[8]

Listed are how the top thirteen characteristics in Knowledge Checkup 9.1 were ranked by the general population. The highest preference in a mate is ranked 1 and the lowest is ranked 13. For example, both males and females ranked "kindness and understanding" as the most important quality in a mate.

Compare your rankings with those of the general population.

1. Are there any significant differences?

2. How might any differences affect your finding a mate?

3. How important is it to know what the other person finds attractive?

4. Are you willing to present a false image or lie to find a mate?

MALES	FEMALES	YOU	
1	1	_____	kindness and understanding
2	2	_____	intelligence
3	6	_____	physical attractiveness
4	3	_____	exciting personality
5	4	_____	good health
6	5	_____	adaptability
7	7	_____	creativity
8	10	_____	desire for children
9	9	_____	college graduate
10	11	_____	good heredity
11	8	_____	good earning capacity
12	12	_____	good housekeeper
13	13	_____	religious orientation

Personal Motives   Other people may attract you because of a variety of personal motives, motives that go beyond how the other person looks, how close she or he is, or perceived similarities and dissimilarities. Sometimes, the who, what, and where of the other person are less important than your personal motives for making initial contact.

There are at least six different personal motives for wanting to initiate conversation with another person.[9] First, you may talk to someone because of the *pleasure* often inherent in such contact—it may be fun, exciting, and stimulating for you. Second, you may initiate contact to *express concern*—to help someone, say thank you, or show encouragement. Third, you may feel the need to talk to someone to *reduce your loneliness,* reduce the burden of some problem, or simply to get reassurance that someone is there to listen to you. Fourth, it is common to "use" others as a *distraction,* to put off doing your work or to take a break from a difficult or boring task. Fifth, talking with someone may help you *relax,* feel less tense. And, sixth, you may initiate a conversation to *entice* someone to do something for you, whether to hold the door while you manage packages or direct you to the nearest restaurant.

Objectives

Once you identify someone with whom you hope to form a relationship, you may pursue several goals: (1) to initiate contact and gather enough information to decide whether to continue the relationship, and (2) to leave the other person with a favorable impression of yourself.

Initiating Contact and Gathering Information Beginning a relationship is often anxiety-provoking. Regardless of your background and education, the odds are you received little or no training in forming relationships. Here are several steps you can take to improve your skills in this area.[10]

Step One: Look for Approachability Cues. The first step in meeting new people is to look for **approachability cues,** indications that the other person is available for conversation. A person may be approachable when she or he smiles at you; is alone, relaxed, not busy, in a place where talking with strangers is okay (such as the student union), or talking with some of your friends; maintains eye contact with you for a moment beyond what is usual (three to ten seconds); has an open body position (arms and legs not crossed); displays a good mood (pleasant facial expression); says or waves hello; or (if you're looking for a prospective mate) has "an empty ring finger."

The approachability cues presented have a strong North American bias. There are, of course, cultural differences in the use of such factors as eye contact, facial expression, gestures, use of space, and vocal variety (e.g., volume and pitch variations). You might, therefore, find yourself using any of the approachability cues with someone who has a different meaning for the message you selected. People from Asian cultures, for example, don't smile frequently or have much eye contact with strangers. A person from one of those societies would, indeed, be put off by your impertinent and brash behavior if you smiled a great deal while talking to him or her, or if you used extensive eye contact.

Step Two: Initiate a Conversation. Once you decide to approach someone, the second step is to initiate a conversation. One technique is to tell the person your reason for approaching. You may ask for information ("I'm new on campus. Can you tell me where the Student Union Building is located?"); introduce yourself ("I'm Bill. I wanted to meet you since we'll be sitting next to each other in this class."); talk about something you have in common ("Did you understand one word of the professor's lecture?"); or offer a sincere compliment ("That's a great picture of Bach on your shirt!").

When initiating a conversation with someone from a different culture, you should keep in mind that in many cultures the members feel uncomfortable talking to strangers. A person from such a society, therefore, might not respond as favorably as one of your North American friends to your attempts at contact. While you may have the best of intentions, he or she may perceive your actions as aggressive and a sign of poor manners.

The "opening line" when initiating contact poses a problem for most people. "What should I say *first?*" is a good question. Knowledge Checkup 9.4 provides a number of examples, as well as the opportunity to recognize your own opening lines.

KNOWLEDGE CHECKUP 9.4

OPENING LINES

Check the following statements you have used to initiate a conversation.

_____ "Nice weather, isn't it?"

_____ "Haven't we met somewhere before?"

_____ "Do you have the time?"

_____ "Do you come here often?"

_____ "I'm new here, can you help me find _____?"

_____ "Seen any good movies lately?"

_____ "What's your major?"

_____ "Got a match?"

_____ "Can I buy you a drink?"

_____ "Do you know how to _____?"

_____ (Your own "favorite") "_____?"

Why would a person use these opening lines? Which three do you consider the most appropriate? When?

_____

Step Three: Find Topics to Talk About. The third step, finding topics to talk about, quickly follows initiating the conversation. Perceived similarities often provide topics of conversation. For example, you may attend the same school or classes, enjoy the same types of food, sports, or movies, or come from the same town. Although perceived differences also may suggest topics of conversation, such talk tends to separate you from the other person rather than bring you closer together.

Recognize that not all cultures are interested in the same topics. What seems like normal conversation in your culture might not be of the least interest in another culture. In the Buddhist tradition, for example, people refrain from all gossip. In North America and England, gossip is a favorite pastime. If you were to employ this conversational technique with a Buddhist, he or she would most likely only respond out of politeness, not interest. Many Asians, after visiting the United States, often express a lack of understanding as to why Americans spend so much time talking about other people and have entire newspapers dedicated to the topic.

Step Four: Talk About a Variety of Topics. The fourth step builds on the third. To gather enough information to decide whether to pursue a relationship, you need information on a variety of topics. Even very limited relationships, such as many between employers and employees, require a range of background knowledge.

You can make transitions to new topics by noting what the other person says and using the information to guide you. Rarely are casual conversations so structured that everything communicated is immediately pertinent. More often, extra or **free information**—elaborations—are provided as well. Use this free information to find new topics of conversation. For example, if you ask someone whether he likes Mexican food and he responds, "Yes. I also like Italian food, French food, and hamburgers and fries. In fact, I like just about every kind of food," you have more information than you requested. You can then use this free information to extend the conversation to talk about food in general, diets, and even travel to foreign places.

Skill Development 9.1 will help you practice probing for information by considering how someone might communicate with you to form a relationship.

SKILL DEVELOPMENT 9.1

PROBING FOR INFORMATION

1. Write a question someone could ask you about something you know (*Example:* "What are your hobbies?").

2. List two follow-up questions the other person could ask you based on your answer. (*Example:* If your hobby is going to the theater, follow-up questions could be, "What plays have you seen lately?" and "Who's your favorite playwright?")

3. Make a list of topics you could discuss when meeting someone for the first time.

You can increase the probability of getting free information by asking questions that require detailed answers instead of ones that can be answered yes or no. A question-probe series, such as the one you developed for Skill Development 9.1, encourages the other person to offer additional pieces of information.

Other techniques for obtaining free information include giving compliments —direct ones, such as "That's a nice dog," or indirect ones, such as "How would you finish this report for the manager?" (which implies the other has knowledge you don't)—and telling something about yourself, which encourages the other person to speak about herself or himself.

Step Five: Share Plans for Future Interaction. The fifth step, sharing your plans for future interaction, completes the first phase of relationship development. If at the end of your first conversation you have enough information to conclude that another meeting is a good idea, communicate this to your partner. You may be indirect ("Are you planning to see the movie the professor recommended this weekend?") or direct ("I'd like you to come with me Saturday night to see the movie the professor recommended"). Being direct is more threatening than being indirect—for both of you; but, it is also more honest and likely to yield the information you need. Indirect statements or questions may be safer, but they are also less useful. Direct communications reveal what people are thinking, feeling, and wanting.

Creating a Favorable Impression   You should convey certain characteristics if you want to continue to interact: *cooperativeness, caring,* and *memorableness.* To be perceived as *cooperative,* you should follow conversational rules and behave according to the norms of the person with whom you're interacting. When you follow the rules, you make it easier for the other person to predict your behavior. You also will seem cooperative, which will further reduce the tension that often accompanies initial interactions.

To be perceived as *caring,* you should solicit information about the other person and listen attentively. Such attention tells the other person, "I care about what you have to say. You're important to me," which increases liking and creates a favorable impression.

As with many interpersonal situations, an awareness of cultural differences is important to keep in mind when attempting to be friendly. People from English, German, and Asian cultures feel uncomfortable when others become too friendly and ask what they perceive to be personal questions. People from these cultures tend to be rather private and believe that only close friends should know about personal matters. In fact, the German saying that, "A friend to everyone is a friend to no one" means that it is better to have a few good friends to talk to than a host of superficial acquaintances.

To be perceived as *memorable,* you should communicate your most dynamic and interesting self-image. You may communicate information that shows you are unique, for example, that you are from a family of ten children; adventurous, that you participate in a dangerous sport; that you are creative, or active, that you write screenplays; that you hold down several jobs.

You need to remember that many cultures do not value individualism as much as they do collectivism. Being memorable to people from a Chinese culture, for example, is not based on what you have done as an individual, but what you have done as a group member.[11] In their thinking, helping your family or your company is far more important than helping yourself. Skill Development 9.2 will help you practice creating a favorable impression by being cooperative, caring, and memorable.

SKILL DEVELOPMENT 9.2

CREATING A FAVORABLE IMPRESSION

To ensure that your relationship partner perceives you as cooperative, caring, and memorable, prepare several alternative means for communicating each impression.

COOPERATIVE

List two conversational rules you can follow to communicate you're cooperative. For example, you can provide the other person with opportunities to speak and you can maintain sustained eye contact with her or him.

1. _____
2. _____

CARING

List two ways you can communicate "I care" to the other person. For example, you can lean forward while listening, nod appropriately, and ask meaningful questions.

1. _____
2. _____

MEMORABLE

List two facts about yourself that are memorable. For example, maybe you have a twin sister or brother, or perhaps you are finally able to return to school and finish the degree you started several years ago.

1. _____
2. _____

The Brass & Fern   by Steve Riehm

Used with permission of Steve Riehm.

MAINTAINING A RELATIONSHIP

When you think you have enough information to decide whether to continue a relationship, the initial phase of relationship development is complete. Deciding to pursue a relationship requires that you examine your goals and quickly assess the probability of attaining them. Will this person be helpful on the term project? Will this person be a good friend? Will this person be the type of spouse you seek? Whatever your needs, if the response is a tentative yes, you move into the second phase of relationship development: maintaining the relationship.

Objectives

Objectives during the maintenance phase of relationship development include developing a framework for the relationship—goals, structure, and rules—and maximizing certain relational qualities—commitment, intimacy, and resources. Tentative explorations of who the other person is give way to a more intense examination. Among the decisions that need to be made are:

- What are your personal goals?
- What are your goals for the relationship?
- What is the best balance between dominance and submission and between love and hostility?
- What rules are important, and what new rules should be developed to meet the unique demands of your particular relationship?
- How committed should you be?
- How important is intimacy?
- What resources are crucial to goal attainment and relational satisfaction?
- How do the answers to all these questions change as the relationship develops?

You can't tackle all these questions in a totally rational way. You can't successfully make lists, check alternatives, assign weights to items, and develop equations. If people behaved this rationally, relationships wouldn't be so interesting or exciting! Rather, you should try to answer these questions spontaneously and unself-consciously.

Achieving Your Objectives

If you aim to answer many or all of the previous questions, you need information—and you will continue to need information throughout the life of your relationship. Information is the basis for relational decision making. Setting the stage for information sharing—making it appropriate to share, as well as encouraging sharing—requires that you use your communication skills to create a confirming, supportive communication climate.

Supportiveness and Confirmation   Your willingness and desire to communicate openly and freely—as well as the degree to which you feel relaxed, comfortable, and cooperative—depend on the extent to which you feel *valued*.[12] **Supportive and confirming behaviors** communicate this message by indicating that you are acknowledged, understood, and accepted. **Attacking** and **disconfirming behaviors** communicate the opposite message and curtail effective communication. In an attacking and disconfirming environment, the aim is to protect yourself, not to share information.

Supportive language has several identifiable characteristics:[13]

1. Because it depends on "I" language, supportive language is descriptive and not evaluative. The emphasis switches from judging the other's behavior (*attacking*)—"You're too quiet"—to describing what you experience (*supportive*)—"When you don't talk I think you're angry."

2. Because it focuses on immediate thoughts and feelings, supportive language is spontaneous and not manipulative. The emphasis switches from following a calculated plan (*attacking*)—"I think it would be best if we considered ending our relationship"—to communicating honestly in the here-and-now (*supportive*)—"I no longer want to be in a commited relationship."

3. Because it focuses on accepting the other person's feelings and putting yourself in the other person's place, supportive language is empathic and not indifferent. The emphasis switches from treating the other person in a neutral

and detached way (*attacking*)—"I don't want to take sides in your fight with your partner"—to communicating your understanding and caring for how the other person feels (*supportive*)—"I can feel how angry you are with your partner."

4. Because it focuses on remaining open to new ideas, perspectives, and the possibility of change, supportive language is provisional and not certain. The emphasis switches from dogmatic declarations (*attacking*)—"We'll handle the problem this way"—to tentative conclusions (*supportive*)—"Let's try the idea and see if it works." People who communicate their certainty also communicate their superiority, their being *right* or *better.*

Just as supportive behavior is best understood by contrasting it with its opposite, attacking behavior, confirming behavior is best understood by contrasting it with its opposite, disconfirming behavior—the "what not to do."[14] How do you feel in each of these situations?

- Someone fails to acknowledge what you say either verbally or nonverbally.

- Someone interrupts you in order to change the topic.

- Someone responds to your comment with an irrelevant or tangential remark.

- When you ask a simple question or make a simple statement, someone responds with an impersonal monologue, such as, "Why, when I was your age, I . . . ."

- Someone's comments are so ambiguous that you can't determine their true meaning.

- Someone's verbal and nonverbal behaviors contradict each other, such as when someone says, "I love you," with a giggle or a yawn.

Communicating that you value the other person entails more than simply avoiding these disconfirming behaviors—although that's an excellent start. You must also acknowledge the other person by communicating that you are physically and mentally available for the interaction. You can do so both nonverbally and verbally.

Nonverbal behaviors that communicate interest and attention include standing no more than a few feet from the other person, maintaining eye contact, making appropriate facial gestures, leaning toward and directly facing the other person, maintaining an open posture, and touching the other person. If you were actually to go out and employ these behaviors, you would probably find the other person speaking more, appearing more animated, and reciprocating your interest and attention.[15]

It is universal for people to want to believe that they are of value and possess some worth, yet the manner in which these feelings are communicated is determined by their culture. Hence, you need to be aware that the advice offered here is based primarily on North American norms. You must realize that prolonged eye contact, touching, being animated, and direct facing are often the messages that make members of some other cultures feel uneasy. If at all possible, know your partner and his or her cultural biases before you decide what is the best way to present yourself.

Verbal behaviors that acknowledge the other person communicate your understanding of what the other is both saying and feeling. Two useful techniques are paraphrasing—putting the other person's thoughts and feelings in your own words —and asking questions. For example:

Statement: "I think it's time to change the work schedule—make some improvements. I'm not sure about who should take vacation time first, but I'm leaning toward my going in early June and your going in late June."

Paraphrase: "You think the old schedule had some problems, right? You sound unsure about what specific changes might help things."

Question: "What are the advantages of changing the schedule?" or "What is the problem you're trying to solve?"

Reflecting thoughts and feelings demonstrates that you're listening and opens the way to continued communication. If your paraphrase is incorrect or your question misses the other person's point, further communication can clarify what was said. If your paraphrase or question is on target, the other person is encouraged to continue talking. Paraphrasing and asking questions compliment the other person, conveying "You are important to me, so I'm listening to what you say and taking note of how you feel." Skill Development 9.3 will help you practice communicating supportively and in a confirming way.

SKILL DEVELOPMENT 9.3

GIVING SUPPORTIVE AND CONFIRMING RESPONSES

The first four items present a nonsupportive, defense-arousing reaction. Give an appropriate supportive response that could substitute for the defensive one.

1. Evaluative: "You're a slob! Your clothes are all over the room!"

Descriptive: _____

_____

2. Manipulative: "Don't you agree that it's a good idea to do your work assignments as soon after receiving them as possible?

Spontaneous: _____

_____

3. Indifferent: "There are always two sides to any argument."

Empathic: _____

_____

4. Certain: "The best thing to do is start working on the assigned paper right now!"

Provisional: _____

_____

5. Provide a confirming answer for the following statement by reflecting both the content and the feelings expressed. Statement: "I'm having a really hard time balancing classes and my work at the department store. I hope I don't mess up both!"

Confirming response: _____

_____

_____

Self-Disclosure **Self-disclosure**—intentionally letting the other person know who you are by honestly communicating self-revealing information—does much to maintain and develop a relationship.[16] It creates a pool of shared knowledge and, therefore, makes it possible to develop joint views, joint goals, and joint decisions. It also helps the partners in a relationship to help each other, keep up with each others' lives, and learn what the other person is thinking, doing, and feeling.[17]

Self-disclosure varies according to the type of relationship. In intimate relationships, there is much self-disclosure that shows a great deal of breadth and depth. (Keisha, for example, reveals to Chris a great many personal thoughts and feelings on a large number of topics.) In contrast, in nonintimate relationships, self-disclosure has little breadth and depth and accounts for only a small percentage of total communication (Keisha reveals little to Chris). Many relationships are characterized by self-disclosure that has little breadth yet great depth. Business partners, for example, may discuss their thoughts and feelings about their work setting in great and personal detail, but avoid discussions of non-work-related matters altogether.

No matter what its depth, breadth, and amount, self-disclosure fulfills several individual and relationship functions.[18] It can be used for:

1. **catharsis,** to help you "get something off your chest";
2. **self-clarification,** to help you learn about your own ideas by talking them out with another person;
3. **reciprocity,** to encourage the other person to disclose (i.e., to reciprocate your disclosure);
4. **relational maintenance,** to inform the other person of changes in your life;
5. **relationship enhancement,** to open up new areas for discussion and increase the depth of messages;

6. **impression formation,** to create a particular impression by disclosing selected information about yourself; and

7. **manipulation,** to get the other person to do what you want.

Knowledge Checkup 9.5 will help you assess your self-disclosing communication behavior.

ASSESSING YOUR SELF-DISCLOSING COMMUNICATION[19]

Imagine yourself in each of the following situations and indicate how open and revealing—self-disclosive—you would be when talking about yourself.

If you would be *completely nondisclosive* (offer no self-revealing information), mark the situation **1.**

If you would be *mostly nondisclosive,* mark the situation **2.**

If you would be *slightly nondisclosive,* mark the situation **3.**

If you would be *disclosive,* mark the situation **4.**

If you would be *mostly disclosive,* mark the situation **5.**

If you would be *completely disclosive* (offer a great deal of self-revealing information), mark the situation **6.**

_____ **1.** You are on a blind date.

_____ **2.** You are in cafeteria with some casual friends.

_____ **3.** You are being introduced to a group of strangers.

_____ **4.** You are in the library with a friend.

_____ **5.** You are sitting next to a stranger on an airplane.

_____ **6.** You are at a party with some friends.

_____ **7.** You are a member of an encounter/sensitivity group.

_____ **8.** It's evening and you are alone with your significant other in his or her home.

_____ **9.** You are eating lunch alone and a stranger asks if she or he may join you.

_____ **10.** You are on a picnic with friends.

_____ **11.** You are in a newly formed discussion group on human sexuality.

_____ **12.** You and a friend are driving to San Francisco.

SCORING:

Add items 1, 5, and 9: _____. This total is your *stranger alone* score. Based on a large sample of college students, scores of 10 through 18 are high and indicate an above average willingness to self-disclose to a stranger alone; scores of 6 and below indicate a below average willingness to disclose; and scores from 7 through 9 indicate an average willingness.

Add items 4, 8, and 12: _____. This total is your *friend alone* score. Scores of 16 through 18 are high and indicate an above average willingness to self-disclose to a friend alone; scores of 11 and below indicate a below average willingness to disclose; and scores from 12 through 15 indicate an average willingness.

Add items 4, 8, and 12: _____. This total is your *friend alone* score. Scores of 16 through 18 are high and indicate an above average willingness to self-disclose to a friend alone; scores of 11 and below indicate a below average willingness to disclose; and scores from 12 through 15 indicate an average willingness.

Add items 2, 6, 10: _____. This total is your *group of friends* score. Scores of 14 through 18 are high and indicate an above average willingness to self-disclose to a group of friends; scores of 9 and below indicate a below average willingness to disclose; and scores from 10 through 13 indicate an average willingness.

Add your four scores together: _____. This is your *total self-disclosure* score. Scores of 52 through 72 are high and indicate an above average willingness to self-disclose; scores of 33 and below indicate a below average willingness to disclose; and scores from 34 through 51 indicate an average willingness.

1. How do your four summative scores compare with each other? Are you more willing to disclose under some circumstances than others?

2. How do your scores compare to the sample of others' scores? Are you more disclosive than others in some circumstances and less disclosive in others?

Your willingness to self-disclose depends on several things,[20] two of which were assessed in Knowledge Checkup 9.5: your relationship with the other person—whether he or she is a friend or stranger—and the situation—whether you are alone or in a group, and whether the setting is more or less intimate. For example, you might be more willing to self-disclose with your friend when alone in her or his house than when in the library. (Other criteria for choosing whether to disclose include the other person's trustworthiness, sincerity, and warmth.)

Reasons for disclosing to a friend differ from those for disclosing to a stranger, regardless of whether the situation is more or less intimate.[21] For example, primary reasons for disclosing to a friend include relationship maintenance, relationship enhancement, and self-clarification, whereas those for disclosing to a stranger are reciprocity and impression formation. The reasons for disclosing to friends and strangers reflect the different goals for each type of relationship. For example, the goal of communicating with a friend is to keep and deepen the relationship while, at the same time, to use the other person to help gain self-understanding, whereas communicating with a stranger has the two-pronged goal of getting the other person to talk (so you can gain information necessary to make decisions about continuing the relationship) while creating a particular—mostly positive—impression of yourself.

When to disclose often is less problematic than *what* to disclose. What you choose to disclose depends on several considerations:

Does the disclosure suit the relationship? For example, highly intimate disclosure in a nonintimate relationship is inappropriate. Also, in early stages of relationship development, positive disclosures are better liked than either negative or boastful disclosures; indeed, boasters are viewed as least socially competent.[22]

Is the disclosure relevant to the relationship? Disclosure about your family to your employer, for example, may not be pertinent to your relationship.

Is the disclosure relevant to the immediate interaction?

How likely is the other person to treat the disclosure with respect?

How constructive is the disclosure likely to be for the relationship?

Can you communicate your disclosure clearly and understandably?

Skill Development 9.4 provides you with a method for increasing the amount of self-disclosure in your communication.

SKILL DEVELOPMENT 9.4

INCREASING YOUR SELF-DISCLOSURE

Examine your responses to the 12 situations presented in Knowledge Checkup 9.5 and consider what aspects of yourself you are unwilling or least willing to share in each.

1. Make a list of some of the information you would keep to yourself—your secrets—in the situations involving friends and in the situations involving strangers.

2. Select your *least* threatening secret and ask yourself what the most horrible consequences would be if you were to reveal it.

3. With your *least* threatening secret and its presumed consequences in mind, tell your secret to the friend or stranger with whom you feel safest.

4. Observe what happens. You will probably learn that your secret is more

threatening to you than it is to others, and that the horrible consequences you imagine rarely come to pass.

5. Continue to think about each secret, its consequences, and telling it to someone. Remember that you do not have to reveal *every* secret or even *everything* about each secret.

Self-disclosure isn't an all-or-nothing proposition; it begins slowly with revealing positive aspects of yourself and progresses—if at all—to greater breadth, depth, and amount. And, in general, openness will wax and wane throughout a conversation as well as an entire relationship.[23] Early disclosures test the situation: Is this person trustworthy? Will this person care about what I say? Each yes bolsters your willingness to self-disclose.

Despite its benefits, self-disclosure is risky. Telling a boss how you feel about the new organizational chart may lead to rebuke, just as telling a friend how you *really* feel about his new shirt may result in hurt feelings. How will the other person feel after the disclosure? What will happen to your relationship if you disclose your real feelings? You may well have to ask the extent to which you should be honest. Total honesty may not always be the "best policy."

The primary fear associated with self-disclosing for both men and women is the fear of rejection.[24] Many men also fear that disclosing will make them look bad and cause them to lose control over other people: "If you know my weaknesses, I will no longer be powerful." Many women, on the other hand, fear the consequences of disclosure for the relationship: "If I disclose, you might use the information against me" or "Disclosing might hurt our relationship." For the majority of men, control is the primary objective; for the majority of women, the relationship itself is the primary objective. These objectives affect how each gender discloses and the reasons each chooses to avoid disclosure.

People who avoid self-disclosing sometimes avoid it because they do not want to receive feedback about themselves. The logic goes like this: "If I don't say anything about myself, you won't either." One way to increase your willingness to self-disclose is to increase your willingness to listen to feedback.

To increase your receptiveness to feedback about yourself consider that you may doubt that others' comments will be relevant, or you may believe that others' comments can hurt you. Once you realize that feedback *may* be relevant (you can decide whether or not it is) and that you *choose* how to feel (you don't have to feel hurt by what someone says, although you can *choose* to—you can also *choose* to feel glad or disappointed), you can begin to open yourself to feedback by not cutting off others' observations and by practicing requests for information. Phrases such as, "Tell me what you think about what I just said" and "How do you feel about my . . .?" encourage the other person to provide feedback. The resulting information will be only as useful as you decide to let it be.

The fears associated with disclosing are great, but the rewards are great as well. As you gain experience in self-disclosing, you should become more skilled at knowing what to reveal and when. Also, your assessment of the potential risks should become more realistic.

Keep in mind that people in some cultures do not feel comfortable revealing personal information. The reasons for this discomfort may not be the same, but the results all mean that you need to be aware of cultural differences. For the Chinese, a preoccupation with talk about the "I" is a sign of selfishness. The Germans, British, and Japanese cultures value privacy and do not like disclosing to very many people.[25]

Affinity Seeking   Using confirming and supporting behaviors, and engaging in positive self-disclosure, are ways to present an appealing image to others. The active process used to get other people to like and feel positive toward you is called **affinity seeking.** People who like you are more willing to give you needed information for relational decision making, as well as participate with you in maintaining a relationship.

You probably have developed a variety of strategies to get others to like you, strategies that have met with some success and, therefore, continue to be used. There are a great many strategies available, although some may fit how you see yourself better than others.[26] When you want someone to like you, do you dress a particular way, cooperate more than usual, behave politely? Knowledge Checkup 9.6 provides you with the opportunity to examine some of the many affinity-seeking strategies available to you.

KNOWLEDGE CHECKUP 9.6

ASSESSING YOUR AFFINITY-SEEKING STRATEGIES[27]

Assume you met someone you find attractive and whom you would like to know better. What would you do to get this person to like and feel positive toward you? Below are 25 strategies. Check those you are *likely* to use.

_____   **1.** Help and assist the other person, for example, run errands

_____   **2.** Present myself as a leader by planning activities

_____   **3.** Present myself as an equal by avoiding showing off

_____   **4.** Act comfortable with the other person (whether I'm comfortable or not)

_____   **5.** Allow the other person to take charge of the conversation and of planning activities

_____   **6.** Follow cultural rules for conversing and socializing

_____   **7.** Present myself as active and enthusiastic

_____ **8.** Encourage the other person to talk by asking questions

_____ **9.** Be entertaining and make the time together enjoyable

_____ **10.** Include the other person in my social activities and in my group of friends

_____ **11.** Lead the other person to believe that the relationship is closer than it actually is

_____ **12.** Pay close attention to the other person and respond to what is said

_____ **13.** Use nonverbal behaviors such as touching and sustained eye contact

_____ **14.** Disclose personal information

_____ **15.** Present myself as cheerful and optimistic

_____ **16.** Present myself as free-thinking and independent

_____ **17.** Try to look well physically

_____ **18.** Highlight past accomplishments and other things to make myself seem interesting to know

_____ **19.** Offer favors or point out what I can do for the other person

_____ **20.** Treat the other person as important and tell others how great the other person is

_____ **21.** Initiate encounters with the other person and make myself available for doing things together

_____ **22.** Show empathy, sensitivity

_____ **23.** Point out similarities I have with the other person

_____ **24.** Be encouraging and supportive, and not be critical of the other person

_____ **25.** Be dependable and sincere—trustworthy

1. What, if anything, do the strategies you checked have in common?

2. Why did you reject those strategies you did not check?

3. What do your affinity-seeking strategies tell you about the kind of relationship you want to have with the other person?

Strategies to get others to like us that appear to be more generally used than others include looking physically attractive, being optimistic, being sensitive, listening attentively, and adhering to conversational rules. Those that appear least used include making yourself available to do things, inviting the person to join your groups, explaining the benefits of the relationship, and lying about how close you really feel.

Women and men go about the business of affinity seeking in different ways. For example, women are more apt to encourage the other person to talk, to be dependable and sincere, to be encouraging and supportive, to disclose personal information, to avoid showing off, and to look physically attractive. Men, on the other hand, are more apt to tell others how wonderful the other person is, present an interesting self, present themselves as leaders, offer favors, highlight past accomplishments, initiate encounters, and stress things in common.

Regardless of which strategies you employ, the goal is the same: to encourage the other person to like you. Whether looking for a work partner, an acquaintance, or a close friend, one or more affinity-seeking strategies are necessary.

ENDING A RELATIONSHIP

Relationships end for a variety of reasons. Goals may be fulfilled and no new goals established. Goals may not be accomplished and there may be little chance of achieving them. The partners may continue to feel lonely despite their relationship. The patterns of interaction may be too fixed, too inflexible, or too boring. The initial attractiveness may fade and nothing new may replace it. New relationships may appear more attractive. Changes in either person may alter the possible rewards: The two may no longer agree on things that were once no problem, and their interests may no longer be compatible. Sexual dysfunction, conflicts with work, financial difficulties, changes in commitment—and endless other possibilities—may plague highly intimate relationships. Relationships are fragile, and the possible threats to their well-being are numerous and powerful.

Reactions to relationship termination may vary from relief to self-recrimination, from happiness to deep depression. Similar to the death of a loved one, the death of a relationship invokes strong responses, strong responses that are often accompanied by heightened defensiveness: denial that the relationship is over, creating logical but untrue explanations for "what went wrong," anger that's generalized to everyone and everything, and the presumption that how you feel is how everyone feels.

Terminating a relationship often involves changes in many of your other relationships. New groups of friends may need to be formed and explanations to friends, relatives, and parents may be required. Your relationship termination affects others' relationships, as well as other relationships of your own.

Several of the most common communication strategies for the disengagement process have been studied.[28] Six critical dimensions describe the variations in relationship disengagements. The first three are:

- Was the onset of relational problems gradual or sudden? Most problems emerge gradually, making it difficult to determine their specific causes and the most clearly related consequences.

▪ Does only one partner want to end the relationship (*unilateral desire*) or do both agree (*bilateral desire*)?

▪ Is a direct or an indirect strategy used to end the relationship?

If you want to end a relationship and the other person does not, you may confront the other person with your desire—a *direct strategy*. You may also arrange to see the other person less—an *indirect strategy*. If both you and the other person wish to end your relationship, a direct strategy would be to talk it out and an indirect strategy would be to decrease the amount of time you spend together.

Strategies vary not only according to whether they're direct or indirect, but also according to whether they're self-oriented or other-oriented. Strategies that seem to have a self-orientation are *fait accompli* ("I've decided this is over!"), *withdrawal* ("I'm going to be busy all next week"), *cost escalation* ("If you want me to go with you, you'll have to give up going out on Fridays with your other friends"), and *attributional conflict* ("It's your fault, jerk!"). Fait accompli takes control away from the other person, inflicting a blow to the other's self-esteem. Withdrawal also limits the other's control. Cost escalation raises the relationship's costs for the other person, and attributional conflict results in hostile communication of disparaging remarks.

In contrast, *state-of-the-relationship talk* ("Where is this relationship going?"), *pseudo-deescalation* ("I think we should see less of each other for a while"—when *no* contact really is desired), *negotiated farewell* ("Let's rationally discuss how to end this without fighting"), and *fading away* (seeing the other person less and disclosing less) are more other-oriented. They allow some face saving for both relationship partners.

Table 9.1 summarizes various methods of ending relationships in four possible situations: unilateral and bilateral desires to exit using a direct strategy, and unilateral and bilateral desires to exit using an indirect strategy. Except for the bilateral-indirect situation, each describes a self-oriented and an other-oriented strategy. The two indirect strategies for terminating a relationship when both people want it to end are other-oriented.

The final three dimensions on which disengagement processes may be distinguished are:

▪ Does it take a long time or a short time to break away? Using an indirect strategy is likely to result in a drawn-out disengagement with several rounds of negotiations. Overreliance on indirectness also is likely to lead both partners to regret that they didn't use a more direct strategy to make the break quicker and less complex.

▪ Are there any attempts to repair the relationship? Partners are more likely to try to repair their relationship if they use an indirect disengagement strategy.

▪ Is the final outcome termination or a restructured relationship? Restructuring may result in a relationship that is successfully repaired and

TABLE 9.1 Strategies for Relationship Disengagement

DESIRE TO EXIT

		Unilateral	Bilateral
S T R A T E G I E S	**Direct**	1. *fait accompli*: declaration that the relationship is over 2. *state-of-the-relationship talk*: discussion of dissatisfaction, relationship problems, and desire to exit	1. *attributional conflict*: hostile argument focused on why termination is necessary 2. *negotiated farewell*: conflict-free discussion to formally end the relationship
	Indirect	1. *withdrawal*: decrease of intimacy and/or contact 2. *pseudo-deescalation*: false declaration of a desire to reduce closeness when the goal is termination 3. *cost escalation*: increase in costs to the other person to maintain the relationship (for example, treat the other disrespectfully)	1. *fading away*: decrease of contact without any discussion of the relationship 2. *pseudo-deescalation*: mutual false declaration of a desire to reduce closeness when the goal is termination

restored to approximately the same state it was in before problems arose, or it may lead to a different relationship with new goals, structure, or rules, or modified commitment, intimacy, or resources. The infrequency with which relationships are successfully restructured demonstrates the difficulty of accomplishing this task to both partners' satisfaction.

The most frequently used disengagement process involves a unilateral desire to exit (one person wants out) coupled with an indirect strategy (the person decreases contact, claims a desire to reduce contact when no contact is really the goal, or makes contact very costly for the other person), with no attempts at repair, which leads to termination without trying to structure a new relationship (the pair say good-bye with no expectation for future contact). For example, Merle wants to break off with Lupe. Merle stops calling Lupe. Lupe calls Merle and asks, "What's wrong?" Merle tells Lupe, "Nothing. I don't want to talk about it. Good-bye." Merle hangs up. (When the goal is a repaired relationship, directness and more involvement in negotiations is a typical pattern.[29])

BUILDING RELATIONAL AWARENESS

Your relationships are what you make them. This is good news because it underscores your active role. You can begin relationships to meet your goals. You can improve relationships that need improvement. And you can end relationships that are best ended.

Here are some thoughts that might help you achieve more effective, satisfying relationships:

1. Be aware that *relationships have goals.* Understanding your goals, the other person's goals, and your mutual goals should provide a firm foundation for obtaining those goals. At the least, understanding all the goals should help you assess the relationship's possibilities.

2. Be aware that *relationships have structure* and that structure can be changed to meet changing needs. Changing patterns of behavior is difficult, but recognizing the patterns that exist and determining which patterns might be better can help the relationship grow in responsible and beneficial ways.

3. Be aware that *relationships have rules.* The rules coordinate interaction and make it more predictable. You have to know the rules to follow them, so talking about rules and reaching mutual understanding can benefit you and your partner. And if you want to change a rule, recognize that doing so is a slow process, one that requires understanding the reasons for the rule in the first place.

4. Be aware that *relationships are always in process.* Like everything else, relationships change with time. Attempting to freeze a relationship at one moment in time is bound to fail. Relationships change as you and the other person change, and as the context for the relationship changes. Although this progression may seem obvious, few people behave as if change is inevitable. The comfort of old habits, old patterns, and old viewpoints can be more powerful than the reality of change. The moment comes when the relationship *as it is* no longer matches what either of the partners *thinks* it is, and the result of their shortsightedness is conflict.

5. Be aware that *relationships require attention.* Creating a supportive and confirming communication climate, appropriately self-disclosing, and using suitable affinity-seeking strategies, are important ways of attending to your relationship. They ensure the exchange of information necessary for meeting your needs and your partner's as well as the needs of the relationship. Talk about your relationship with your partner and deal directly with relational issues.

COMMUNICATION COMPETENCY CHECKUP

The goal of this Communication Competency Checkup is to guide you in putting your skills and knowledge about beginning, maintaining, and ending interpersonal relationships to use, and to help you summarize the material in this chapter.

Male thinks: *We've made eye contact. Now what?*
Female thinks: *We've made eye contact. Now what?*

1. What are the most plausible reasons for any of these pairs of individuals' attraction to each other?

2. Based on the five steps for forming a new relationship, what specific recommendations would you make to each person in response to the question, "Now what?"

3. Assume that your recommendations are good ones and that the two persons begin a relationship. Problems arise, however, because he avoids self-disclosing and she complains that he's too quiet and doesn't seem to care about her. What could each do to help maintain their relationship?

4. The relationship is crumbling. Because you are their friend, they come to you for help. What questions would you ask to gain understanding of their disengagement?

5. You are aware that the two are from different cultures. What recommendations would you make to them based on this awareness?

6. They are so impressed with your insight that they invite you to address their organization. The title for your talk is, "The Relationship Fairy Is Dead—Your Relationships Are Your Choices!" What would you tell the audience about increasing relational satisfaction?

NOTES

1. Judith Langlois and Lori A. Rogg-man, "Attractive Faces Are Only Average," *Psychological Science* 1 (1990): 115–21.

2. A summary of studies concerned with the similarity principle of attraction, what characteristics are perceived as attractive, and the implications of people marrying people with whom they share many similarities, is available in David M. Buss, "Human Mate Selection," *American Scientist* 73 (January–February 1985): 47–51.

3. For a summary of the research on the effects of physical attractiveness, see: Mark L. Knapp, *Interpersonal Communication and Human Relationships* (Boston: Allyn and Bacon, 1984), pp. 141–44; H. T. Reis, J. Nexlek, and L. Wheeler, "Physical Attractiveness in Social Interaction," *Journal of Personality and Social Psychology* 38 (1980): 141–48.

4. Larry A. Samovar and Richard E. Porter, *Communication Between Cultures* (Belmont, CA: Wadsworth Publishing Company, 1991), p. 188.

5. John Thibaut and Harold H. Kelley, *The Social Psychology of Groups* (New York: Wiley, 1959).

6. Michael Sunnafrank, "On Debunking the Attitude Similarity Myth," *Communication Monographs* 59 (1992): 164–79.

7. Elaine Hatfield and Richard L. Rapson, "Similarity and Attraction in Close Relationships," *Communication Monographs* 59 (1992): 209–12; Donn Byrne, "The Transition from Controlled Laboratory Experimentation to Less Controlled Settings: Surprise? Additional Variables Are Operative," *Communication Monographs* 59 (1992): 190–98.

8. Buss, "Human Mate Selection," p. 48.

9. These six motives were identified by Rebecca Rubin, Elizabeth Perse, and Carole A. Barbato, and reported in "Conceptualization and Measurement of Interpersonal Motives," *Human Communication Research* 14 (1988): 602–28.

10. Susan R. Glaser and Anna Eblen, *Toward Communication Competency: Developing Interpersonal Skills,* 2d ed. (New York: Holt, Rinehart and Winston, 1986).

11. Daniel D. Pratt, "Conceptions of Self within China and the United States: Contrasting Foundations for Adult Education," *International Journal of Intercultural Relations* 15 (1991): 287.

12. Ronald D. Gordon, "The Difference Between Feeling Defensive and Feeling Understood," *Journal of Business Communication* 25 (1988): 53–64.

13. Jack R. Gibb, "Defensive Communication," *Journal of Communication* 11 (September 1961): 604–17.

14. Kenneth N. L. Cissna and Evelyn Sieburg, "Patterns of Interactional Confirmation and Disconfirmation," in *Rigor and Imagination: Essays from the Legacy of Gregory Bateson,* C. Wilder-Mott and J. H. Weakland (Eds.) (New York: Praeger, 1981), pp. 253–82.

15. Dale G. Leathers, *Successful Nonverbal Communication: Principles and Applications,* 2d ed. (New York: Macmillan, 1992), pp. 216–18.

16. Valerian J. Derlega, B. Winstead, P. Wong, and M. Greenspan, "Self-Disclosure and Relationship Development: An Attributional Analysis," in *Interpersonal Processes: New Directions in Communication Research,* Michael Roloff and Gerald R. Miller (Eds.) (Beverly Hills, CA: Sage, 1987).

17. Valerian J. Derlega, "Self-Disclosure and Intimate Relationships," in *Communication, Intimacy, and Close Relationships,* Valerian J. Derlega (Ed.) (Orlando, FL: Academic Press, 1984), pp. 1–9; Lawrence B. Rosenfeld and Gary L. Bowen, "Marital Disclosure and Marital Satisfaction: Direct-Effect Versus Interaction-Effect Models," *Western Journal of Speech Communication* 55 (1991): 69–84.

18. Lawrence B. Rosenfeld and W. Leslie Kendrick, "Choosing to Be Open: Subjective Reasons for Self-Disclosing,"

Western Journal of Speech Communication 48 (1984): 326–43.

19. Adapted from Gordon Chelune's *Self-Disclosure Situations Survey.* See Gordon J. Chelune, "The Self-Disclosure Situations Survey. A New Approach to Measuring Self-Disclosure," *JSAS Catalog of Documents in Psychology* 6 (1976): 111–12.

20. Sandra Petronio, "Communication Boundary Management: A Theoretical Model of Managing Disclosure of Private Information Between Married People," *Communication Theory* 1 (1991): 311–35.

21. Rosenfeld and Kendrick, "Choosing to Be Open."

22. Lynn Carol Miller, Linda Lee Cook, Jennifer Tsang, and Faith Morgan, "Should I Brag? Nature and Impact of Positive and Boastful Disclosures for Women and Men," *Human Communication Research* 18 (1992): 364–99.

23. C. Arthur VanLear, "Testing a Cyclical Model of Communicative Openness in Relationship Development: Two Longitudinal Studies," *Communication Monographs* 58 (1991): 337–61.

24. Lawrence B. Rosenfeld, "Self-Disclosure Avoidance: Why I Am Afraid to Tell You Who I Am," *Communication Monographs* 46 (1979): 63–74.

25. William B. Gudykunst and Young Yun Kim, *Communicating with Strangers: An Approach to Intercultural Communication* (New York: McGraw-Hill, 1992), pp. 200–201.

26. F. Scott Christopher and Michael M. Frandsen, "Strategies of Influence in Sex and Dating," *Journal of Social and Personal Relationships* 7 (1990): 89–105.

27. Adapted from Robert A. Bell and John A. Daly, "The Affinity-Seeking Function of Communication," *Communication Monographs* 51 (1984): 91–115; Virginia Richmond, Joan S. Gorham, and Brian J. Furio, "Affinity-Seeking Communication in Collegiate Female-Male Relationships," *Communication Quarterly* 35 (1987): 334–48; Michael G. Garko, "Perspectives on and Conceptualizations of Compliance-Gaining," *Communication Quarterly* 38 (1990): 138–57.

28. The series of studies concerned with relationship disengagement is summarized in Leslie A. Baxter, "Accomplishing Relationship Disengagement," in *Understanding Human Relationships,* Steve Duck and Daniel Perlman (Eds.) (Beverly Hills, CA: Sage, 1985), pp. 243–65. More recent research on these as well as additional strategies used to disengage, include: John A. Courtright, Frank E. Millar, L. Edna Rogers, and Dennis Bagarozzi, "Interaction Dynamics of Relational Negotiation: Reconciliation versus Termination of Distressed Relationships," *Western Journal of Speech Communication* 54 (1990): 429–53; Kathy Kellerman, Rodney Reynoldo, and Josephine Bao-Sun Chen, "Strategies of Conversational Retreat: When Parting Is Not Sweet Sorrow," *Communication Monographs* 58 (1991): 362–83.

29. Courtright, Millar, Rogers, and Bagarozzi, "Interaction Dynamics."

FOR FURTHER INVESTIGATION

Barrett, Martha Barron. *Invisible Lives: The Truth About Millions of Women Loving Women.* New York: Harper and Row, Perennial Library, 1989.

Baxter, Leslie A. "Accomplishing Relationship Disengagement." In Steve Duck and Daniel Perlman, eds. *Understanding Personal Relationships.* Beverly Hills, CA: Sage, 1985 (pp. 243–65).

Bell, Robert A., and John A. Daly. "The Affinity-Seeking Function of Communication." *Communication Monographs* 51 (1984): 91–114.

Bell, Robert A., and Michael E. Roloff.

"Making a Love Connection: Loneliness and Communication Competence in the Dating Marketplace." *Communication Quarterly* 39 (1991): 58–74.

Berzon, Betty. *Permanent Partners: Building Gay and Lesbian Relationships that Last.* New York: Penguin Books, 1989.

Buss, David M. "Human Mate Selection." *American Scientist* 73 (January–February 1985): 47–51.

Chelune, Gordon J., ed. *Self-Disclosure.* San Francisco: Jossey-Bass, 1979.

Courtright, John A., Frank E. Millar, L. Edna Rogers, and Dennis Bagarozzi. "Interactional Dynamics of Relational Negotiation: Reconciliation Versus Termination of Distressed Relationships." *Western Journal of Speech Communication* 54 (1990): 429–53.

Derlega, Valerian J., ed. *Communication, Intimacy, and Close Relationships.* Orlando, FL: Academic Press, 1984.

Douglas, William. "Expectations About Initial Interactions: An Examination of the Effects of Global Uncertainty." *Human Communication Research* 17 (1991): 355–84.

Gibb, Jack R. "Defensive Communication." *Journal of Communication* 11 (September 1961): 141–48.

Glaser, Susan R., and Anna Eblen. *Toward Communication Competency: Developing Interpersonal Skills,* 2d ed. New York: Holt, Rinehart and Winston, 1986.

Hendrix, Harville. *Getting the Love You Want: A Guide for Couples.* New York: Henry Holt, 1988.

Jackson-Paris, Rod, and Bob Jackson-Paris. *Be True to Yourself: A Video Tape,* 21st Century News, 1992.

Johnson, Susan E. *Staying Power: Long Term Lesbian Couples.* Tallahassee, FL: Naiad Press, 1991.

Jourard, Sidney M. *The Transparent Self,* 2d ed. Princeton, NJ: Van Nostrand, 1971.

Knapp, Mark L., and Anita Vangelisti. *Interpersonal Communication and Human Relationships,* 2d ed. Boston: Allyn and Bacon, 1992.

Luft, Joseph. *Of Human Interaction.* Palo Alto, CA: National Press Books, 1969.

Petronio, Sandra, Judith Martin, and Robert Littlefield. "Prerequisite Conditions for Self-Disclosing." *Communication Monographs* 51 (1984): 268–73.

Powell, John. *Why Am I Afraid to Tell You Who I Am?* Chicago: Argus Communications, 1969.

Rosenfeld, Lawrence B. "Communication Climate and Coping Mechanisms in the College Classroom," *Communication Education* 32 (1983): 167–72.

Rosenfeld, Lawrence B. "Self-Disclosure Avoidance: Why I Am Afraid to Tell You Who I Am." *Communication Monographs* 46 (1979): 63–74.

Rosenfeld, Lawrence B., and W. Leslie Kendrick. "Choosing to Be Open: Subjective Reasons for Self-Disclosure." *Western Journal of Speech Communication* 48 (1984): 326–43.

Sieberg, Evelyn. "Confirming and Disconfirming Organizational Communication." In James L. Owen, Paul Page, and Gordon I. Zimmerman, eds., *Communication in Organizations.* New York: West, 1976.

Smalley, Gary, and John Trent. *The Language of Love: A Powerful Way to Maximize Insight, Intimacy, and Understanding.* Pomona, CA: Focus on Family, 1988.

CHAPTER 10

Interpersonal Relationships
in the Family

COMMUNICATION COMPETENCIES

This chapter examines interpersonal relationships in the family. Specifically, the objective of the chapter is for you to learn to:

- Identify family images, themes, boundaries, and biosocial beliefs.
- Identify the communication patterns of families.
- Describe family communication systems and their operation.
- Differentiate between less healthy and more healthy families.
- Describe family conflict and parental authority.
- Identify verbal aggression in family settings.
- Use principles of healthy communication within a family context.

KEY WORDS

The key words in this chapter are:

family	system
live-in couples	presenting problem
couplehood	underlying problem
single-parent family	relational costs
family of origin	relational rewards
images	disengagement
family themes	functional family
boundaries	dysfunctional family
position-oriented family	aggression
person-oriented family	verbal aggression
biosocial attitudes	workshop process of change

A DEFINITION OF FAMILY

If you were to write a Chinese fortune cookie saying for your family, what would it be? If your mother or female guardian were a musical instrument, which one would she be? If you have siblings, and each were an animal, which one would each be? If your father or male guardian were a machine, which one would he be? If you were a flavor of ice cream, which one would you be?

"We are born into a family. We are socialized by a family. We mature from a family. We often create a family, and, if so, use the information and behaviors we learned from a family. And, when we die, we diminish a family. Families affect us greatly . . . they surround us, shape us, and often determine our destiny."[1] A family traditionally has been defined as a group of interconnected people typically with blood or legal ties.[2] "A **family** can be viewed more broadly as a group of people with a past history, a present reality and a future expectation of interconnected mutually influencing relationships."[3] This would include **live-in couples**, heterosexual or homosexual, with or without children, who are unmarried but have a binding relationship; **couple-hoods**, homosexuals who have gone through commitment ceremonies, and **single-parent families,** in which the parent has or has not been married, but lives with a biological or adopted child. Whatever the definition, a family is a complex network of love, jealousy, pride, anxiety, joy, and guilt.

Your **family of origin**, the family in which you grew up, provided you with the foundation for your self-concept and communication competencies. Your

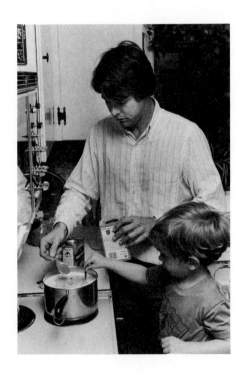

family of origin provided you with your most important lessons in creating, maintaining, and ending interpersonal relationships, and stands as the primary model for how you will create your own family.[4] From our introduction to language to our ways of expressing love, for most of us it is the family of origin that is the first and most important teacher.[5] Just reflect for a moment on some of the most significant attitudes, values, and behaviors that are part of who you are. You will surely discover that most of them can be traced to your family of origin. A family of origin takes us from the womb and begins to teach us self-reliance, how to please and annoy others, responsibility, obedience, dominance, social skills, aggression, loyalty, sex roles, and age roles.

While most of the discussion in this chapter focuses on the family in North America, please remember that families from other cultures offer their children different messages, and hence produce people with specific cultural perceptions and with specialized communication styles. Children born into a family in India often notice women eating after the men have finished, and for these children this is appropriate behavior. This is how they learn about gender roles. In China it is usual for meals to be served from a common bowl, whereas in the United States people usually have their separate plates brought to the table. Each culture teaches its version of sharing. In Mexico grandparents typically live with the family. In the United States grandparents generally live in their own home or in a retirement community. Each culture teaches about aging and the family unit.[6]

The examples are endless. But they all should convey the same message: As cultures differ, so do families—and as families differ, so do individual patterns of communication.

FAMILY IMAGES, THEMES, BOUNDARIES, AND BIOSOCIAL ATTITUDES

Families have unique combinations of images, themes, boundaries, and biosocial attitudes. In some families these traits stay the same for generations, whereas in other families they are in constant flux, paralleling the changes in society. Knowing your family's traits—its images, themes, boundaries, and biosocial attitudes—aids in understanding its communication.

IMAGES

Images are the mental pictures and illusions the family holds of itself and its members. They are the definitions of people that predict how they will behave, including how they will communicate. Think of members of your family. What is your image of each of them—helper, helpless, dynamic, stable? Think back to your answers to the questions at the beginning of this chapter. What kind of musical instrument is your mother or female guardian? What kind of machine is your father or male guardian? Those, and your other answers, are the images you and your family members project, at least from your viewpoint. Knowledge Checkup 10.1 provides the opportunity for you to identify your family's predominant role images.

KNOWLEDGE CHECKUP 10.1

IDENTIFYING YOUR FAMILY'S ROLE IMAGES

Who, if anyone, plays the following roles in your current family or family of origin? (Not all of the roles may be represented in every family.)

1. The martyr—does most of the cooking, serving, and cleaning up. _____
_____

2. The pet—the spoiled one who always gets the last spoonful of stuffing and the biggest slice of cake. _____
_____

3. The victim—two hours late, but it's not her or his fault. It never is! _____
_____

4. The rebel—if everyone's dressed up, he or she wears old jeans, and then sits back and waits for the fireworks. _____
_____

5. The peacemaker—he or she will make sure that everyone stays civil and then be the one to suffer with heartburn. _____
_____

6. The smart one—she or he hasn't seen the movie, but knows it's rotten. You don't even argue. Why invite the fight you know you'll lose? _____
_____

Was it easy to identify the images you hold of your family members? What images are shared by all the members? How do you feel thinking of yourself in one or more of these roles? Do you think each member of your family would complete this checkup similarly?

FAMILY THEMES

Family themes are the patterns of feelings, motives, roles, fantasies, understandings, and rules that family members hold about the family and their relationships with the outside world. Themes are revealed in the special nicknames, roles (who does what), and made-up words families use. They also are revealed by the

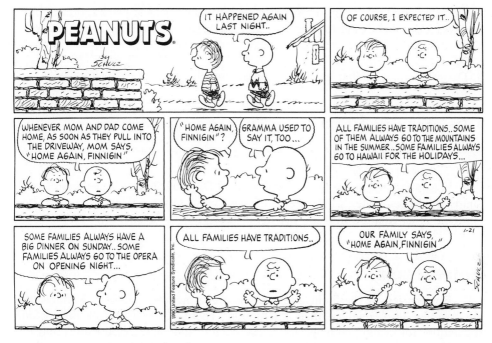

PEANUTS reprinted by permission of UFS, Inc.

rules that guide who talks to whom and who does what and when. For example, if a family rule is, "Children should only speak to their parents when they are spoken to," the theme revealed in this is: "Children should respect their elders and know their place."

Through its themes, a family describes its reality and how it deals with that reality. Some family themes are: "Family business is kept inside the house—we don't show our dirty linen in public," "It is our responsibility to help others less fortunate than ourselves," and "If you're going to do something, do it right."

Knowledge Checkup 10.2 provides the opportunity for you to develop the skill of recognizing and assigning meaning to your family's predominant themes.

KNOWLEDGE CHECKUP 10.2

IDENTIFYING YOUR FAMILY'S THEMES

What are some common themes in your current family or family of origin?

1. Describe one family custom that is important for all members to follow. _____

_____

2. Describe one family story that is repeated over and over at parties, during holidays, and at family get-togethers. _____

_____

3. Describe one wish that all or most family members repeat over and over. _____

_____

4. Describe one family belief that restricts or encourages family thinking. _____

_____

Was it easy to choose themes to describe? Do you think each member of your family would complete this checkup similarly? How do these themes describe your family; that is, what do they tell you about how your family members interact?

BOUNDARIES

Boundaries are the limits a family sets on its members' actions. Families create boundaries to regulate their interaction. These boundaries typically include regulations for dealing with specific ideas, people, and values. Boundaries may encourage or restrict contact with people outside the family's religion or ethnic group. They may allow or forbid intermingling with certain races or social classes. They may encourage or discourage certain liberal or conservative attitudes.

Rules form a large part of family life, whether they are spoken or implied. These rules determine what cannot be talked about (death, alcohol, the way money is spent, sex, or weight), what can be talked about, how certain topics can be expressed ("Mommy is sick" versus "Mommy is drunk"), where certain topics can be talked about (around the kitchen table, only in the house, in the bedroom), and who can talk about certain things with whom (parents only, one parent to a particular child).

Boundaries also create the framework within which family members speak to each other. In a **position-oriented family**, there are sharp boundaries for family roles based on status and social identities related to sex and age. The child in a position-oriented family, for instance, is expected to communicate in defined ways. Such guidelines as "Honor thy mother and father," "Children are to be seen and not heard," and "Act your age" must be respected. Even when older, if the offspring is still seen as the "child," then she or he must fulfill that role.

A **person-oriented family** has flexible boundaries and allows a wide range of communication behaviors related to an individual's needs rather than her or his position in the family. A person-oriented family fosters open communication in which roles are continuously accommodated and the different intents of family members are recognized and dealt with. For example, when a "child" in a person-oriented family grows to adulthood, she or he is treated as an adult and not a child.

Positional families require their children to learn global rules about how to communicate with others, while person-oriented families require children to develop more complex strategies for matching their communication to the intentions of a specific family member. This makes children from position-oriented homes better able to adapt their communication—both to members of the family and those outside the family. Knowledge Checkup 10.3 presents characteristics of position-oriented and person-oriented families for you to identify.

KNOWLEDGE CHECKUP 10.3

CHARACTERISTICS OF POSITION-ORIENTED AND PERSON-ORIENTED FAMILIES

Identify each of the following family characteristics as indicative of a positi? oriented family (a) or a person-oriented family (b).

_____ **1.** Family roles are clearly defined according to status.

_____ **2.** Permissible behavior is broadly defined.

_____ **3.** The family system fosters open communication.

_____ **4.** Family members are assigned clear-cut roles based on sex and age.

ANSWERS: 1—A, 2—B, 3—B, 4—A

BIOSOCIAL ATTITUDES

Biosocial attitudes concern the way the family deals with male and female identity, authority and power, and the rights of family members. Each of us was brought up with notions of what males and females are allowed to do, supposed to do, and are capable of doing. These may have included household roles (boys do the cooking and cleaning, and girls do the car repairs), occupational roles (girls are mechanics, boys are elementary school teachers), areas of responsibility (women are the principal wage earners and men take care of the home), and emotional roles (girls don't cry and boys don't get angry). (If you were taken aback by some of the role identifications given as examples because you thought they were role reversals, you have identified some of the biosocial roles you learned in your family.)

Knowledge Checkup 10.4 will alert you to your biosocial attitudes concerning gender roles.

IDENTIFYING YOUR GENDER ROLE ATTITUDES[7]

Indicate whether primary responsibility for each task should belong to a male (M) or a female (F).

_____ **a.** taking out the garbage

_____ **b.** writing thank-you notes for a family gift

_____ **c.** initiating sexual activity

_____ **d.** changing diapers

_____ **e.** bringing home the major paycheck for household use

_____ **f.** disciplining the children

_____ **g.** cooking

_____ **h.** cleaning the bathroom

_____ **i.** fixing or making arrangements for fixing the car

_____ **j.** taking the children to piano lessons

_____ **k.** taking a child to baseball practice

_____ **l.** fixing the leaky faucet

_____ **m.** changing the bed sheets and pillowcases

_____ **n.** making family investments

_____ **o.** selecting new furniture for the living room

Research indicates North Americans perceive items a, c, e, i, l, and n to be "male activities," and b, d, f, g, h, j, k, m, and o as "female" activities. Give yourself one point for each of your answers that conforms to what was found in the research. A score of 10 or more indicates your biosocial attitudes are parallel to traditional societal thinking from the mid-1970s. How much did your results differ from these? If there were differences, why? How stable do you think biosocial attitudes are considering gender roles?

The task of identifying the self as a boy or a girl is apparently not very difficult, given that by age three most children will identify not only which sex they belong to, but also which jobs are done by men and women, what roles mommies and daddies play, and what kind of behavior is allowed for each sex.[8]

In addition to gender roles, how authority and power are dealt with also describe a family's biosocial attitudes. This can be examined by acknowledging who creates and enforces the rules ("As long as you live in my house, you'll do what I tell you to do," or "Your father makes those decisions"), and the rights of family members regarding such issues as privacy, setting of curfews, and appealing a parent's decision.

Skill Development 10.1 provides the opportunity to observe a family and examine its important themes, boundaries, and biosocial attitudes.

SKILL DEVELOPMENT 10.1

OBSERVING A FAMILY AND MAKING SENSE OF ITS IMAGES, THEMES, BOUNDARIES, AND BIOSOCIAL ATTITUDES

Select a family other than your own with which you are familiar. This could include a family on television or a friend's family.

1. What are some of this family's important images? How do these images affect how the family members communicate?

2. What themes did you have to learn in order to understand the family's interaction?

3. What are some boundaries that guide how members of this family communicate with one another?

4. List several biosocial attitudes found in this family that regulate how the parents and children talk to each other.

5. Based on your analysis, how do the images, themes, boundaries, and biosocial attitudes combine to create the communication pattern unique to this family?

THE FAMILY AS A COMMUNICATION SYSTEM

Family members interact much like characters in a play, movie, or television show. They assume roles, act out events, and share their ideas, thoughts, and beliefs in a coordinated way. Much can be learned about the basic principles of a family's communication by examining the drama they enact, by observing the patterns they follow. Knowledge Checkup 10.5 provides you with the opportunity to create a drama based on your own family.

FANTASIZING A STORY ABOUT YOUR FAMILY

For about three minutes fantasize a story about your family of origin or the family in which you now live. It should be in the form of a play, movie, or television show, with *you* as a main character. *Be sure it has dialogue.* Listen to your own compliments, complaints, and beliefs, and observe yourself as a communicator in the family drama. In addition, note the communication patterns and roles of other family members. (If you find fantasizing difficult, write out your scene like a play script.)

Families, like characters in a play, are organized into systems. A **system** is the pattern of interaction a family uses as its primary or usual mode of operation. This pattern is based on the family's themes, images, boundaries, and biosocial attitudes, as well as rules concerning how messages should travel through the family. For example, in one family, the father may make the decisions and pass the information to the mother, who relays it to the children. In another family, everyone may get together to discuss and agree upon family matters.

How did the characters in your drama communicate? Did everyone have equal access to everyone else? How structured or organized is the pattern of communication? Who talks to whom? How do they talk to each other? Your answers should give you clues to the process and style of your family's communication and, therefore, to your family's communication system.

Regardless of the countless ways in which the infinite number of themes, images, boundaries, and biosocial attitudes may come together to form unique families, in North America several characteristics of family systems seem universal:[9]

1. *Any change in one part of the system causes the entire system to change.* Family members are interdependent. The unit creates a *synergy*—that is, the whole is greater than the sum of parts. Much like the pieces of a mobile, if one part moves or changes, all the other parts move and change. If a family member leaves home to go to college, the system is no longer the same. If a parent loses a job, becomes permanently disabled, or becomes angry with another member, the system is no longer in balance. When that happens, new rules are needed to bring the system back into balance. Healthy families are capable of recreating a balance.

2. *Family systems are complex, adaptive, and information-processing.* A family system is complex because it is constantly in flux. Because a family is made up of people, and because people change as they gain new experiences, age, and mature, the system continuously modifies itself. A family system is adaptive because it develops in response to interaction among its members. The ongoing interaction is bound to lead to strains and tensions, but a well-developed family

system accommodates itself to such difficulties. And systems are information-processing because the basis of a family is the exchange of ideas, attitudes, and beliefs.

3. *People act out what is wrong in their family system.* Arguments, physical conflicts, pouting, and isolation of a family member are all clues that something is wrong. But things are not always as they appear. Often what is dealt with is the **presenting problem**, the problem the family members complain about. However, the presenting problem is usually only a symptom of the **underlying problem**, the real issue. For example, a teenager who complains that she is not permitted to stay overnight at a friend's house may really be crying out for a change in rules that will allow her to make her own decisions and be perceived as mature and independent.

4. *Factors outside the family affect the system.* Laws, economic factors, and societal pressures constantly play on family loyalties and prevent even the most effective systems from operating efficiently and happily. No family can protect itself from wars, job layoffs, natural disasters, and random acts of violence.

5. *A family system creates its children's notions of reality when they are young.* Families make decisions about who each child is and how the child is to interact with others. In other words, your family laid the foundation for your self-concept and who you are today. All of your current relationships are molded by your past experiences, the rules you followed, and the roles you played, unless you have made the difficult effort to overcome those influences.

6. *There are costs and rewards for belonging to a family system.* **Relational costs** are the contributions you make to a relationship—time, money, emotion, loyalty. **Relational rewards** are the benefits you receive for being in the relationship. Members of a family system tend to continue their participation, whether they are physically present or not, as long as they feel that the rewards of the relationships are worth the costs. The payback is not necessarily dollar for dollar, kiss for kiss, and thank you for thank you. Rather, individuals remain satisfied and productive parts of a family as long as their needs are met and they don't feel put upon or taken advantage of. If and when the costs exceed the rewards, **disengagement** takes place and a family member breaks ties, either physically or psychologically. Sometimes, when young people disengage, they may try to punish the rest of the family by running away, getting pregnant, isolating themselves, using drugs or alcohol, or behaving anti-socially. Adults are more likely to break off relationships with all or part of the family, deny access to grandchildren, or refuse to attend family functions.

To operate successfully within a family system, you must examine and understand the connections between yourself and the other elements of the system. Of particular importance is your understanding of the role you play as a family member. In Knowledge Checkup 10.5 you fantasized a drama of your family's actions and communication. What did you discover about yourself? Ask yourself: Who am I in this family? Do I communicate consistently with my role? What are my role identifications? For example, am I the financial provider, the child of a troubled family member who is forcing me to be the parent, the caretaker in a dual-parent working family, the oldest child carrying the burden of success for the entire family, the college student who is an occasional home visitor, or the peacemaker among warring factions? Understanding your role leads you to understand whether you are effectively communicating in your family environment, and enables you to assess what changes you may want to make in your role as a family member.

KNOWLEDGE CHECKUP 10.6

THE FAMILY AS A COMMUNICATION SYSTEM

Which principle of family systems discussed in this section is best displayed by each comment?

1. "My sister doesn't come around much any more. She thinks that all the effort she puts into being a good daughter isn't appreciated." _____

   _____

2. "As my older brother became a teenager, I noticed his relationship with our younger brother became strained and we had to spend a lot of time trying to find out what was happening between them." _____

   _____

3. "With the auto plant closing, my dad is going to be out of work. That's going to put a strain on all of us." _____

   _____

4. "When the last child left for college my parents were totally confused about how to act and what to do without us." _____

   _____

5. "My mother has a violent temper and my sister has been making up all kinds of excuses to stay at her friend's house on weekends." _____

   _____

ANSWERS:

1. There are costs and rewards for belonging to a family system.

2. Family systems are adaptive.

3. Factors outside the family can affect the system.

4. Any change in one part of the system causes the entire system to change.

5. People act out what is wrong in their family system.

LESS HEALTHY VERSUS MORE HEALTHY FAMILIES

"Every family creates its own balance to achieve some sort of stability. As long as family members interact in certain familiar and predictable ways, this balance, or equilibrium, is not upset."[10] In a less healthy family a chaotic system is the way of life and becomes the only thing that family members can depend on. Even battering and incest serve to maintain this precarious family balance. In many instances, the parents in a less healthy family increase the chaos in order to fight the loss of balance and maintain control. Parents least able to promote a more healthy family are those who inflict *ongoing* and *repetitive* trauma, abuse, and/or denigration on their children in a systematic way.

Knowledge Checkup 10.7 will help you analyze whether there were some less healthy elements in your family of origin, and, if so, specifically what some of them were.

CHARACTERISTICS OF LESS HEALTHY FAMILIES[11]

Check the blank if your answer to the questions is yes. When you were a child . . .

_____ 1. Did either or both of your parents tell you you were bad or worthless?

_____ 2. Did either or both call you insulting names?

_____ 3. Did either or both use physical pain to discipline you?

_____ 4. Did you have to take care of either or both of your parents because of their problems?

_____ 5. Were you frightened of either or both much of the time?

_____ 6. Did either or both do anything to you that had to be kept a secret?

_____ 7. Were you afraid to express anger at either or both?

Now that you are an adult . . .

(If either or both of your parents are deceased, base your answers on when they were alive.)

_____ 8. Do either or both still treat you as if you are an inadequate child?

_____ 9. Do you have intense emotional or physical reactions after you spend or anticipate spending time with either or both?

_____ 10. Do either or both control you with threats or guilt?

_____ 11. Do either or both attempt to manipulate you with money?

_____ 12. Do you believe that no matter what you do, it's never good enough for either or both?

_____ 13. Do you believe that someday, somehow, one or both is going to change for the better?

Many people have problematic relationships with their parents. Alone, that doesn't mean you grew up in an abusive or psychologically less healthy environment. However, if you had five or more yes responses to the thirteen items, it is possible that you carry the scars of a less healthy home.

Children of parents in less healthy families tend to blame themselves for their parents' abuse. As a result, they bear the burden of guilt and inadequacy, which makes it extremely difficult for them to develop a positive self-image. The resulting lack of confidence and self-worth can, in turn, color every aspect of their lives,[12] including how they communicate in their relationships.

A less healthy family system is often like a multicar pileup on a freeway in that it causes damage in one person after another, generation after generation. But it is not a system the parents invent. Rather, it stems from the accumulated feelings, rules, interactions, and beliefs that have been handed down from previous generations.[13]

Reasonably mature and caring parents have beliefs that consider the feelings and needs of all family members. They strive to provide a solid basis for their children's development and subsequent independence.[14] But, parents in a less healthy family have beliefs about children that are self-centered and self-serving. The parent believes such things as: "Children should respect their parents no matter what," and "There are only two ways to do things, my way and the wrong way."

"If beliefs are the bones and rules are the flesh of the family system, then 'blind obedience' is the muscle that propels that body. We blindly obey family rules because to disobey is to be a traitor to one's family."[15] In less healthy families the rules are based on family role distortions and rules lead to destructive, self-defeating behavior. The child, for example, is told over and over: "Thou shalt love thy parents." This seemingly entitles the parents to the right to abuse children who are disrespectful. The pressure to obey almost always overshadows the children's conscious needs and desires. Only when the parents can see the destructiveness of the rules clearly can they exercise free choice.

The single most dramatic difference between less healthy and more healthy family systems is the amount of freedom family members have to express themselves as individuals. Healthy families encourage individuality, personal responsibility, and independence. They encourage the development of their children's sense of adequacy and self-respect. Less healthy families discourage individual expression. They react to problems by acting out their fears and frustration with little thought about the consequences for the family members.

FAMILY CONFLICT

There is no one best way for a family to behave or communicate. Nonetheless, communication patterns are the single most important factor in the development of a **functional family**, a family system in which the members have learned to love, conflict with each other, make decisions, handle pain, and assume risk in constructive ways.

Dysfunctional families—families in communication chaos—are like a football team whose players each use a different set of signals. They crash into one another or arrive at the wrong place at the wrong time. Like such football teams, dysfunctional families constantly seem at loose ends. This is usually not the fault of one person, but a lack of communicative teamwork.[16] The most common problems facing dysfunctional families—and the most common sources of their conflict—often center on their unwillingness or inability to communicate about *power struggles in the family* (e.g., how rules are set up, who enforces them, and how biosocial issues are handled), *differences in intimacy needs* (e.g., showing levels of caring, physical and emotional touching, and sexual activity), and *interactional difficulties* (e.g., how to resolve conflicts, make decisions, and interact with each other).

Conflicts invariably arise about the exercise of power—the amount of control the family should be allowed to have over individual members' lives.[17] The ideal balance should enable each person within the family to be most effective in gaining access to what he or she wants. You can measure your family's process by examining the degree of freedom or restraint in each of the member's movements and actions. Is there a hierarchy of power? Do one or two people control all or most of the actions of the others? How are decisions made? Can you make some, any, or all decisions about matters that are important to you?

Family members make varying claims on each other for love, affection, recreational companionship, and understanding. Intimacy plays a role in such matters as feeling loved or unloved; inflicting and submitting to sexual, physical, or verbal abuse; getting praise or being ignored; and being included or left out of family activities.

In addition to conflicts concerning power (who's on the top and who's on the bottom) and intimacy (how emotionally close or how far family members should be from each other), there are conflicts about how to handle conflicts. The next chapter of this book contains information regarding various conflict strategies that apply to all relationships, regardless of whether they are among family or nonfamily members. Specific to families, however, are parent–child conflicts. These conflicts are different from other types of conflicts due to the unique role relationship of the combatants.

How a parent conceives of his or her authority will determine how he or she approaches parent–child conflict. Knowledge Checkup 10.8 focuses on parental authority. If you are a parent, respond to the items based on how you act. If you are not a parent, imagine yourself as a parent and indicate how you would act.

KNOWLEDGE CHECKUP 10.8

USE OF PARENTAL AUTHORITY

Here are some typical things parents do in their relationships with their children. For each statement, mark the column that tells how you as a parent act or would act.

  L = likely to act that way

UL = unlikely to act that way

  ? = uncertain how I would act

L   UL   ?

____ ____ ____   **1.** I would physically remove my child from the piano if he refused to stop banging on it after I had told him it was disturbing me.

____ ____ ____   **2.** I would praise my child for consistently being prompt in coming home to dinner.

____ ____ ____   **3.** I would scold my six-year-old if she demonstrated poor table manners in front of guests.

____ ____ ____   **4.** I would praise my adolescent when I saw him reading literature I approved of.

____ ____ ____   **5.** I would punish my child if she used swear words.

____ ____ ____   **6.** I would reward my child if he showed me a chart indicating that he had not missed brushing his teeth even once in the past month.

____ ____ ____   **7.** I would make my child apologize to another child that she had treated rudely.

_____ _____ _____ **8.** I would praise my child if she remembered to wait at school for me to pick her up.

_____ _____ _____ **9.** I would make my child eat almost everything on his plate before being allowed to leave the table.

_____ _____ _____ **10.** I would require my daughter to take a bath each day and give her a reward for not missing a single day for a month.

_____ _____ _____ **11.** I would punish my child if I caught him telling a lie.

_____ _____ _____ **12.** I would offer my teenage son some kind of reward if he would change his hair style to one I approved of.

_____ _____ _____ **13.** I would punish my child for stealing money from my wallet.

_____ _____ _____ **14.** I would promise my daughter something she wanted badly if she would refrain from using too much makeup.

_____ _____ _____ **15.** I would insist that my child play the piano for relatives or guests.

_____ _____ _____ **16.** I would promise my child something I know he wanted if he would practice his piano lessons for thirty minutes each day.

_____ _____ _____ **17.** I would make my two-year-old remain on the toilet as long as necessary if I knew that she had to go.

_____ _____ _____ **18.** I would set up a system whereby my child could earn a reward if he regularly did his household chores.

_____ _____ _____ **19.** I would punish or threaten to punish my child if she ate between meals after I had told her not to.

_____ _____ _____ **20.** I would promise a reward to encourage my teenager to come home on time after dates.

TALLY:

Count the L's checked before the ODD numbers. _____

Count the L's checked before the EVEN numbers. _____

Add the number of L's. _____

The *odd-numbered* L's indicate the degree to which you do use or would use *punishment* or the *threat of punishment* to control your child or to enforce your solutions to problems.

The *even-numbered* L's indicate the degree to which you do use or would use *rewards* or *incentives* to control your child or to enforce your solutions to problems.

The total number of L's indicates the degree to which you do use or would use both sources of your parental power to control your child. Use the following scale to indicate your power level.

USE OF PUNISHMENT	USE OF REWARD	USE OF BOTH KINDS OF POWER	RATING
0–3	0–3	0–5	Anti-authoritarian
4–5	4–5	6–10	Moderately authoritarian
6–8	6–8	11–15	Considerably authoritarian
9–10	9–10	16–20	Very authoritarian

Through Knowledge Checkup 10.8, you explored one very important aspect of your attitudes toward being a parent—how you use or would use your parental authority. There is no ideal level of authoritarianism. Some situations, such as when physical danger exists (for example, the teenager wants to borrow the family car during an ice storm), may call for a very authoritarian approach; on the other hand, responses to conflicts over issues such as room cleaning, curfews, and taking out the garbage, depend solely on the extent to which these things are important to you. The more important an issue is to you as a parent, the more likely you will behave in an authoritarian manner.

Family conflicts—whether parent–child, spouse–spouse, or among siblings—often revolve around one erroneous thought: "If only you were more like me, or could see that I'm right and you're wrong, I wouldn't have to be upset." Family members, however, are not identical, and no family member has a corner on the truth, and, therefore, conflict erupts.

Family members participate in conflict because they get something out of it. If not, they wouldn't participate in it. Constructive family conflicts provide new information, excitement and stimulation, and the resolution of mutual problems. Destructive family conflicts also have payoffs, such as gaining control over others, placing the blame on someone else in order to get oneself off the hook, and feeling superior to those who are seemingly wrong or inferior. Unfortunately, the benefits of destructive conflict sow the seeds for relational dissatisfaction.

VERBAL AGGRESSION IN FAMILIES

A serious problem with conflict in families is that it may turn into verbal aggression. **Aggression**, sometimes referred to as a type of abuse, is the taking of actions that advance personal goals without concern for the harm they may cause others. **Verbal aggression** includes the use of words to attack another person: nagging, yelling, insulting, attacking character, accusing, rejecting, refusing to talk to, and swearing. Verbal abuse against children and spouses is extremely common in North America. Studies indicate that more than two out of three North American children, and more than three out of four spouses, are victims of verbal aggression. Swearing and attacking character are the two most common specific acts of verbal aggression against spouses and children.[18]

Verbal aggression strongly affects people. For example, the more verbal aggression a child suffers, the greater the probability that the child will be physically aggressive, become delinquent, or have interpersonal problems. In addition, the more verbal aggression a spouse endures, the higher the probability that he or she will experience psychosomatic symptoms, poor health, depression, and suicidal thoughts.

Verbal aggression often leads to physical violence. Contrary to the claim that verbal venting releases pent-up anger and thus avoids physical aggression, it has been found that verbal venting contributes to higher levels of physical attack and violence.[19]

HEALTHY COMMUNICATION WITHIN A FAMILY CONTEXT[20]

Why is it that at some time in every person's life he or she wished to belong to a different family? "In Will's family, they discuss everything before a decision is made." "Alicia's parents would never force her to tell them what happened on a date." The truth is, most families have both healthy and unhealthy communication patterns. The question is one of degree rather than "healthy" or "unhealthy." "To what degree is a family's communication system healthy?" is a better question than, "Is the family's communication system healthy?"

Knowledge Checkup 10.9 provides the opportunity for you to express your beliefs about aspects of family communication found to be most important for families in North American culture.

KNOWLEDGE CHECKUP 10.9

FAMILY COMMUNICATION REACTION INVENTORY[21]

Tell whether you agree or disagree with each statement.

AGREE   **DISAGREE**

_____ _____ 1. Most family members know how to communicate effectively; they just don't take the time to practice what they know.

_____ _____ 2. Family conflict is a symptom of deteriorating family relationships.

_____ _____ **3.** Family conflict should be avoided at all costs.

_____ _____ **4.** Most families function more effectively if there is one central leader.

_____ _____ **5.** Ineffective communication is one of the most important factors leading to family conflict and family tension.

Each of the five items in the knowledge checkup relates to an idea about what makes communication in a family effective or ineffective. For example, with regard to the first item, communication within the family is often difficult because in many families the *members do not know how to communicate effectively.* Most people do not receive effective communication training in their homes or schools, and typically have poor models to follow. Therefore, even if they want to communicate effectively, most people lack the necessary knowledge and skills. This is not to say that they could not improve on their own if they made the effort. It simply means that no matter how diligent they are, if they don't have the skills, they won't be successful. Poor communication is especially common when conflicts arise.

Conflict may be a sign of deteriorating family relationships; however, *conflict is natural.* Conflict becomes destructive when people rather than issues are attacked, when anger is suppressed and allowed to fester, and when problems are solved using authoritarian and divisive means that lead to stress and retaliation.

Family Conflict Should Be Dealt With   Placing conflict on the back burner, attempting to ignore it, smoothing it over, or denying that it exists create tensions. The key to resolution lies in how the conflict is dealt with. General principles of conflict management in the family include:[22]

▪ *It is better to focus on conflicts over small rather than large issues.* Small issues can generally be resolved within a reasonable amount of time and with a reasonable amount of effort. Large issues need planning and, sometimes, outside help for resolution.

▪ *It is better to recognize the differences in power and ability among participants than to ignore or minimize them.* If the family system is based on the dominance of one person, disagreements about his or her use of power may be difficult or impossible to resolve unless that person is willing to give up the control role.

▪ *It is better to avoid solutions that fail to address important concerns of the participants.* A dictated solution, such as, "As long as you live in this house, you will do what I tell you," will not allow all participants to leave the scene with a feeling of satisfaction. Strong feelings that are not resolved in one conflict will resurface later in another.

Many Families Operate Effectively with One Leader   More often than not, if that leader is dictatorial, even if the system is functioning effectively, a power struggle will eventually arise. Members of families are like citizens of countries. As can be seen again and again throughout history, and as exemplified by the overthrow of governments in Eastern Europe during the late 1980s and early 1990s, people can be suppressed only so long. Eventually, they will rise up and fight for their freedom by whatever means they have. A family held together by fear and abuse will eventually self-destruct.

Ineffective Communication Is One of the Most Important Factors that Leads to Family Conflict and Family Tension   If ineffective patterns are clung to, family members will inevitably do something to try to change the system. If change cannot be achieved amicably, the next step is to destroy the system.

A Family System Can Change without Being Destroyed as Long as Family Members Understand that Their Histories Are Usually the Problem, and Not Themselves   Most problems are generations old and have been passed down from person to person. Eventually, they fester into major conflicts.

A Family System Can Develop the Flexibility to Accommodate Bids for Individuality   Some family systems make their members slaves to the will and influences of other family members. Effective communication in a family allows for a person to be part of a unit while still maintaining an individual identity. Knowledge Checkup 10.10 will help you assess the extent to which you have been able to establish an identity separate from your family identity.

KNOWLEDGE CHECKUP 10.10

MY PARENTS, MY FAMILY, AND ME[23]

Check each statement that is true or mostly true for you.

_____ **1.** I am very dependent on my parents for emotional support.

_____ **2.** I have difficulty facing unpleasant truths about my childhood.

_____ **3.** I fail to see the connections between events of my childhood and adult life.

_____ **4.** I have difficulty telling my parents my real *feelings* about our relationship.

_____ **5.** I have difficulty telling my parents my real *thoughts* about our relationship.

_____ **6.** I have difficulty making my needs a priority when dealing with other family members.

_____ **7.** I am unwilling to bar family members from my life even if I feel it is in my best interest.

_____ **8.** I have trouble assessing honestly my relationship with my parents.

_____ **9.** I don't perceive myself as a particularly powerful and confident adult.

_____ **10.** I feel incapable of changing my own behavior without seeking advice of parents and family members.

If you checked 7 or more of the statements you may feel you are too strongly controlled by parental and family influences.

As an individual you have not only the right but the responsibility to reevaluate the way you are treated, what is expected of you, and what you expect of others. To be emotionally and communicatively independent (free to have your own beliefs, feelings, and behaviors), you need not cut yourself off from your parents or anyone else. It is entirely possible to be part of a family while at the same time being a separate individual who determines what is best for him or her.[24]

Many people fail to stand up for themselves because they confuse self-definition with selfishness. You, like most people, were probably brought up with such rules as, "Don't toot your own horn," "Be humble," and "People don't like those who are braggarts." This advice, if taken to heart, may have led you to believe that you shouldn't be an independent person, that you must always put others' interests before your own, and that you should respect people in authority, whether or not they deserve respect.

Understanding Is the Beginning of Change Recognizing the existence of a problem leads to the desire to seek new options. This, in turn, motivates family members to find ways of altering the present mode of operation. The actual change takes place by examining old patterns, discovering what needs to be changed, and learning how to make appropriate changes.

One useful approach to change making is the **workshop process of change.**[25] The family members get together, list the family rules of operation, and test them to see if some are changeable. Once possible changes are identified, a plan of action is developed. The plan may require you to take some difficult or upsetting risks, but these often are necessary to improve the family system. Family members must be honest in dealing with themselves and others so that all, if possible, can start living in and being responsible to the present, rather than retreating into the patterns of the past. This means that all must be willing to see and correct their mistakes, rather than continuing in error. For example, rather than continue the battle over the child's not keeping her bedroom neat, the family must accept that old techniques, such as constant threats, have not worked and that new approaches need to be explored, such as keeping the child's door closed or negotiating a reward system for cleanliness. The hard part is not slipping back into the old and useless patterns while negotiating the change agreement.

A family system built around protecting an alcoholic, a drug user, an abuser, or a tyrant, is unhealthy. Many families continue to operate with such a pattern even though excusing an alcoholic because he or she "can't help it," or is "a wonderful person when he isn't drinking," is destructive to all concerned. In the process, the family becomes dysfunctional and members become slaves to the person they are trying to protect.

SKILL DEVELOPMENT 10.2

APPLYING THE WORKSHOP PROCESS OF CHANGE

Assume you and your family are applying the workshop process of change. Complete steps 1 and 2 as if you were actually participating in the process. Then, picture your family going through the remaining steps:

Step 1:   Each family member lists two family rules that she or he feels enhances family functioning.

Step 2:   Each family member lists two family rules that she or he feels causes her or him personal difficulties.

Step 3:   Each person reads aloud her or his "enhancing rules."

Step 4:   Each person reads aloud her or his "difficulty rules."

Step 5:   A discussion is held in which family members acknowledge the "enhancing rules" and talk about the "difficulty rules" with respect to why the rules exist, whether the rules are appropriate, and what changes could be made, if any.

How successful do you anticipate the workshop process of change to be for your family? What did you learn about your own desire for changing the family rules?

In some instances, families or some members of a family are unable to make needed changes by themselves and require outside help. One-on-one counseling, family counseling, and support groups are often helpful in solving the problems of dysfunctional families. An alcoholic, for example, may turn to Alcoholics Anonymous for assistance, while the other members of the family attend support groups for spouses or children of alcoholics. Similarly, an abuser and the abused may seek individual or joint assistance.

Sometimes family members obtain training and support through such organizations as Marriage Encounters, Parents Anonymous, Family Home Evenings (FHE), Family Anonymous for Parents of Drug Addicts, and Parents and Friends of Gays (P-Flag). All of these groups stress awareness of verbal and nonverbal communication as it affects other people. All emphasize self-disclosure, openness, sharing, risk taking, and trust. All use direction and problem-solving techniques to gain insights into interpersonal communication problems, and highlight the influence of effective intrapersonal communication and a healthy self-concept as the bases for effective communication with others.[26]

Over one-third of a million parents have turned to Parent Effectiveness Training (PET), a system designed to improve direct interpersonal communication in families. Stress is placed on "I" messages, in which personal feelings and observations are expressed, rather than "you" messages, which attack the other person. In addition, a no-lose method of problem solving is taught. As one technique, participants are taught to state how a certain event or activity affects them by expressing their feelings with specific comments, rather than blaming the other person with generalized attacks. For example, an "I" statement such as, "I get upset when I walk into the family room and find empty snack boxes and bags littering the floor," is more effective than saying, "You make me so mad. You're a slob. You are always leaving things around."

The Mormon Church, long known for its recognition of the importance of family solidarity, developed the Family Home Evening (FHE) course in which church members set aside Monday evening of each week for a family group meeting or other activities that underscore that the home is the first and most effective place for children to learn the lessons of life. The program centers on intrapersonal and interpersonal communications.

Both Family Anonymous for Parents of Drug Addicts and Parents and Friends of Gays are specific problem-centered programs to help parents who share a common interest to meet and learn ways to cope with their feelings. Through these programs, parents of drug addicts and gays learn to change negative feelings to positive ones, to replace hostility with understanding, and to live for today without wasting energy on regrets.

COMMUNICATION COMPETENCY CHECKUP

The goal of this Communication Competency Checkup is to guide you in putting your skills and knowledge about interpersonal relationships in the family to use, and to help you summarize the material in this chapter.

The husband and wife in this cartoon display many of the family communication principles discussed in this chapter.

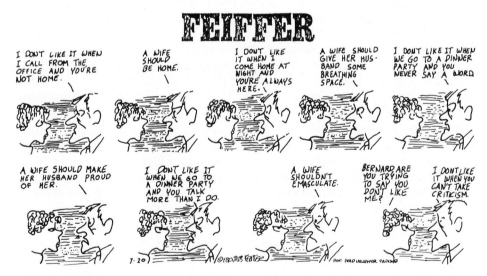

1. What is Bernard's image of his wife?

2. Identify two family themes that are displayed in this interaction.

3. What rules does Bernard have concerning how his wife should behave? What do these rules "tell you" about Bernard's boundaries?

4. Name at least one biosocial attitude that is displayed by Bernard.

5. Is Bernard displaying the attitudes of a person in a position-oriented or a person-oriented family?

6. Bernard mentions several presenting problems. Are these the true issues in this interchange? If not, what might be the underlying problem?

7. If Bernard and his wife have children, what do you assume is Bernard's view of his authority? What about his wife's view of her authority?

8. If you were a marriage counselor working with this couple, what three specific recommendations would you make to improve their communication?

NOTES

1. Judy Goldberg, "Family Communication," unpublished syllabus, Arapahoe Community College, with materials drawn principally from David Kantor and W. Lehr, *Inside the Family: Toward a Theory of Family Process* (San Francisco: Jossey-Bass, 1975).

2. For a discussion of definitional issues and the family, see Kathleen M. Glavin and Bernard J. Brommel. *Family Communication: Cohesion and Change,* 3d ed. (New York: HarperCollins, 1991), pp. 2–11.

3. Ibid., p. 193.

4. C. Arthur VanLear, "Marital Communication Across the Generations: Learning and Rebellion, Continuity and Change," *Journal of Social and Personal Relationships* 9 (1992): 103–23.

5. Virginia Satir, *The New Peoplemaking* (Mountain View, CA: Science and Behavior Books, 1988), Chapter 2.

6. Larry A. Samovar, Richard E. Porter, and Nemi C. Jain, *Understanding Intercultural Communication* (Belmont, CA: Wadsworth Publishing Company, 1981), pp. 99–101.

7. Based on questions from an activity developed by Thomas Gordon, in *Parent Ef-*
fectiveness Training (New York: New American Library, 1975).

8. Deborah Tannen, *You Just Don't Understand: Men and Women in Conversation* (New York: William Morrow, 1990), p. 44.

9. Janet Yerby, Nancy Buerkel-Rothfuss, and Arthur P. Bochner, *Understanding Family Communication* (Scottsdale, AZ: Gorsuch Scarisbrick Publishers, 1990), pp. 67–81; Galvin and Brommel, *Family Communication,* pp. 33–70; S. R. Marks, "Toward a Systems Theory of Marital Quality," *Journal of Marriage and the Family* 51.1 (1989): 15–26.

10. Susan Forward, *Toxic Parents* (New York: Bantam Press, 1989), jacket copy.

11. Ibid., p. 7.

12. Ibid., pp. 6–7.

13. Ibid., p. 136.

14. Ibid.

15. Ibid.

16. Morton Hunt, "When Everyday Stress Turns Serious," *Family Circle* (August 5, 1989), p. 53.

17. Gail G. Whitchurch, "Linkages in Conjugal Violence and Communication: A Review and Critical Appraisal," paper

presented at the third national Family Violence Conference for Researchers, Durham, NH, July 1987.

18. Murray A. Straus, Stephen Sweet, and Yvonne M. Vissing, "Verbal Aggression Against Spouses and Children in a Nationally Representative Sample of American Families," paper presented at the annual meeting of the Speech Communication Association, San Francisco, November 18, 1989. This research is part of the Family Violence Research program of the Family Research Laboratory, University of New Hampshire, Durham, NH 03824, funded by the National Institute of Mental Health.

19. Teresa Chandler, "Perceptions of Verbal and Physical Aggression in Interpersonal Violence," paper presented at the meeting of the Eastern Communication Association, Baltimore, April 1988.

20. For a discussion of characteristics of successful families, together with a test of "family competence," see: W. Robert Beavers and Robert B. Hampson, *Successful Families: Assessment and Intervention* (New York: W. W. Norton, 1990).

21. Based on Steven Beebe and Marilyn Swinton, "Teaching the College Course: Resources and Methods for Teaching the Family Communcation Course," paper presented

at the meeting of the Speech Communication Association, Boston, November 1987.

22. Judy Goldberg, based on the writing of Robert O. Bloom.

23. Based on Susan Forward, *Toxic Parents,* p. 234.

24. F. G. Lopez, V. L. Campbell, and C. E. Watkins, "Effects of Marital and Family Coalition Patterns on College Students' Adjustment," *Journal of College Students,* 30 (1989): 46–50.

25. This approach was developed by psychologist Michael Popkin in a video, "Active Parenting." For a summary of this approach, see: Barbara Burtoff, "Family Pow-Wows," *Chronicle-Telegram* [Elyria, Ohio] (October 1985), p. B1.

26. There are many local and national organizations that offer families help. Calling a local social service agency, a mental health facility, city mental health departments, or consulting the yellow pages of a telephone book can lead to discovering resources. College campus student counseling centers, as well as hotlines, are additional resources. For an extended discussion of the procedures such help sources provide, see: Galvin and Brommel, *Family Communication,* Chapter 14.

FOR FURTHER INVESTIGATION

Ambert, Anne-Marie. *The Effects of Children on Parents.* Bingham, NY: The Haworth Press, 1992.

Barret, Robert L., and Bryan E. Robinson. *Gay Fathers.* Lexington, MA: Lexington Books, 1990.

Beatty, Michael. *Romantic Dialogue: Communication in Dating and Marriage.* Englewood, CO: Morton Publishing Company, 1986).

Bevers, W. Robert. *Psychotherapy and Growth: A Family Systems Perspective.* New York: Brunner/Mazel, 1977.

Bevers, W. Robert, and Robert B. Hampson,

Successful Families: Assessment and Intervention. New York: W. W. Norton, 1990.

Borisoff, Deborah, and Lisa Merrill. *The Power to Communicate: Gender Differences as Barriers.* Chicago, IL: Waveland Press, Inc., 1985.

Brandt, Anthony. "Avoiding Couple Karate." *Psychology Today* (October 1982): 38–43.

Butler, Becky, ed. *Ceremonies of the Heart: Celebrating Lesbian Unions.* Seattle: Seal Press, 1990.

Galvin, Kathleen, and Bernard J. Brommel.

Family Communication: Cohesion and Change, 3d ed. New York: HarperCollins, 1991.

Forward, Susan. *Men Who Hate Women and the Women Who Love Them Back.* New York: Bantam, 1986.

Forward, Susan. *Toxic Parents.* New York: Bantam Books, 1989.

Gullo, Stephen, and Connie Church. *Loveshock: How to Recover from a Broken Heart and Love Again.* New York: Simon and Shuster, 1988.

Island, David, and Patrick Letellier. *Men Who Beat the Men Who Love Them.* New York: Harrington Park Press, 1991.

Leman, Kevin. *Growing Up Firstborn.* New York: Delcorte Press, 1989.

Marks, S. R. "Toward a Systems Theory of Marital Quality." *Journal of Marriage and the Family* 51.1 (1989): 15–26.

Markus, Hazel. "Sibling Personalities: The Luck of the Draw." *Psychology Today* (June 1981): 35.

Nussbaum, Jon F., Teresa Thompson, and James D. Robinson. *Communication and Aging.* New York: Harper and Row, 1989.

Pearson, Judy. *Communication in the Family,* 2d ed. New York: Harper and Row, 1992.

Steier, Frederick, M. Duncan Stanton, and Thomas C. Todd, "Patterns of Turn-Taking and Alliance Formation in Family Communication." *Journal of Communication* 32.3 (1982): 148–60.

Stewart, Lea P., Pamela J. Cooper, and Sheryl A. Friedly. *Communication Between the Sexes: Sex Differences and Sex-Role Stereotypes.* Scottsdale, AZ: Gorsuch Scarisbrick Publishers, 1986.

Tseng, Wen-Shin, and Jing Hsu. *Culture and Family.* Bingham, NY: The Haworth Press, 1992.

Yerby, Janet, Nancy Buerkel-Rothfuss, and Arthur P. Bochner. *Understanding Family Communication.* Scottsdale, AZ: Gorsuch Scarisbrick Publishers, 1990.

Wilmot, William *Dyadic Communication,* 3d ed. New York: Random House, 1987.

Warren, Clay, and Michael Neer. "Family Sex Communication Orientation." *Journal of Applied Communication Research* (Fall 1986): 86–104.

CHAPTER 11

Managing Relational Discord

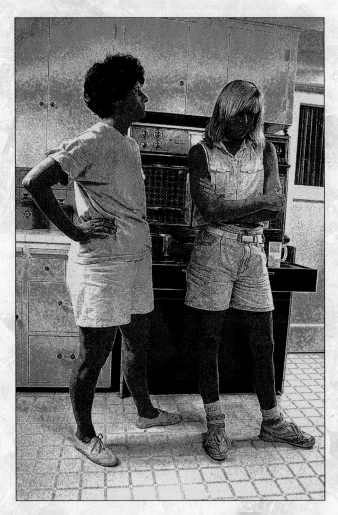

COMMUNICATION COMPETENCIES

This chapter examines the process of managing relational discord. Specifically, the objective of the chapter is for you to learn to:

- Describe the three distinguishing features of conflict situations and use them to analyze your own conflicts.
- Recognize the sources of your personal view of conflict.
- Analyze the constructive and destructive consequences of your conflicts.
- Describe your conflict strategies and style, and assess their advantages and disadvantages.
- Respond assertively in conflict situations.
- Describe the advantages and disadvantages of win-lose, lose-lose, and win-win approaches to conflict.
- Apply a win-win conflict management technique.
- Describe types of difficult people and how to deal with them.
- Assess the process and outcomes of a conflict.
- Recognize cultural differences in interpersonal conflict.

KEY WORDS

The key words in this chapter are:

conflict	integration
interpersonal conflict	conflict style
intrapersonal conflict	nonassertive behavior
interdependent	indirect aggression
sexual harassment	direct aggression
bristle statements	assertion
avoidance	A*S*S*E*R*T formula
smoothing over	win–lose conflict management
dominance	lose–lose conflict management
compromise	win–win conflict management

Kevin and Serena, who are in their early twenties, have been married for nine months. Serena's parents were against the marriage, as they felt Kevin was immature. Kevin is aware of their feelings.

KEVIN: Let's go out Friday night.

SERENA: Where do you want to go?

KEVIN: How about going to a movie?

SERENA: OK, but I don't want to see one of your usual choices—a flick with lots of killing.

KEVIN: What's the matter with action movies?

SERENA: You're just trying to act macho by going to that kind of film.

KEVIN: You think I have to act at being macho?

SERENA: I didn't say that.

KEVIN: I'm not man enough for you? You never complained before. I'm more a man than your wimpy father.

SERENA: Of all the . . . why are you making nasty cracks about my dad?

KEVIN: And your mother is no better, she's always nagging. I guess that's where you get it from!

SERENA: You can just go out by yourself Friday night, and maybe forever, you jerk!

CONFLICT AND CONFLICT SITUATIONS

When you think of the word *conflict,* what metaphors do you think of? If you are typical, you probably conjure up: "Conflict is war," "Conflict is explosive," or "Conflict is a game in which no one wins."

Your own experiences probably confirm that a conflict-free relationship between normal human beings is unlikely. Interpersonal problems are inevitable whenever two individuals participate in an ongoing relationship. The inevitability of conflict, however, shouldn't disturb you. In fact, conflict can play a positive role in healthy and growing relationships. And though conflict may be impossible to eliminate, it can be managed successfully with appropriate communication skills.

What do you do when you're involved in a conflict? Do you scream, cry, call names, throw things, hit walls or people? Do you stop talking, withdraw, glare at the other person, mutter hostile remarks under your breath? Do you try to reason things out, discuss the problem, seek solutions that satisfy both your needs and the needs of the other person? Do you behave differently in different conflicts?

Although types of conflicts and responses to conflict vary, they all share, at least in North American culture, some common characteristics.[1]

A DEFINITION OF CONFLICT

A **conflict** is any situation in which you perceive that another person, with whom you're interdependent, is frustrating or might frustrate, the satisfaction of some concern, need, want, or desire of yours. The source of the conflict could be your perception of a limited resource (such as money), or an individual difference between you and the other person (such as differences in gender or differences in how you and the other person define your relationship).

You may believe that even better than a conflict that ends happily is no conflict at all. You may wish for, hope for, and even work for peace between nations, between groups within a nation, between individuals, and in your own relationships. How successful are you? Is peace—*real* peace, not merely a cease-fire—possible?

Knowledge Checkup 11.1 will help you grasp the basic outline of all conflict situations.

KNOWLEDGE CHECKUP 11.1

ANALYSIS OF RELATIONSHIP DISCORD

Reread the Serena and Kevin scenario presented at the beginning of this chapter. Assuming you are Kevin, complete the following, using the information presented in that interchange.

1. I (Kevin) *want* (Kevin's concern, need, want) _____ *but* (the

other person) Serena *wants* (Serena's concern, need, want) _____.

2. Describe how Serena and Kevin are interdependent in ways that affect the conflict.

3. Describe the possible sources of their conflict.

Complete the "I want . . . but . . . wants" for one of your important relational conflicts.

4. I *want* _____, *but* _____ *wants*

_____

5. Describe the possible sources of the conflict you just related: _____

_____

Frustration

Conflict is a process that begins when you perceive that someone else has either frustrated some concern of yours, such as obtaining a goal, or is going to frustrate some concern of yours. For example:

I want *to switch jobs with a coworker,*
but *the supervisor*
wants *people to stay in the jobs they were hired to do.*

I want *to go to a comedy club Friday night,*
but *my companion*
wants *to go to a concert.*

I want *to borrow money,*
but *my friend* doesn't
want to *lend it to me.*

If you communicate your concern to the other person, you have an **interpersonal conflict**, a conflict between people: *you request* the job swap *from* your *supervisor; you tell* your *companion you want* to go to the comedy club; *you tell* your *friend* that you *want* to borrow money.

If you decide to resolve the conflict on your own, you have an **intrapersonal conflict**, a conflict within a person. You may decide that the supervisor is too inflexible and that it wouldn't pay to ask about switching jobs. You may decide to keep your frustration about not being able to go where you want to go on Friday night because you fear you'll harm your current relationship if you say something. Without talking to your friend, you may decide that your friend wouldn't lend you the money even if you asked for it. However, you are likely to communicate your frustration by being curt with your supervisor, withdrawn from your companion, or sarcastic with your friend. Recognizing interdependence, and resolving conflicts interpersonally, may well be less taxing in the long run.

Not all cultures perceive conflict in the same manner or employ the same methods for dealing with it. In most of the Middle Eastern and Mediterranean cultures conflict is accepted as an important part of life. These cultures take great delight and pleasure in haggling and arguing. These arguments are often very heated and, if they don't take place, one or the other person may feel cheated. Haggling, for example, is expected when purchasing goods in many South American and Arabic cultures. North American tourists while traveling to these areas have found that this haggling is so imbued in the interpersonal communication process that attempting to purchase something from a shopkeeper without negotiating may well lead to the person not selling them the desired item. In fact, "French and Arab men (not women) find argument stimulating."[2]

On the other hand, there is a Chinese proverb that states, "The first person to raise his voice loses the argument." People from conflict avoidance societies believe that the best way to deal with conflict is to handle it on their own without confronting the other person. They embrace the philosophy that face-to-face confrontations are to be avoided.[3] So strong is the notion of self-restraint in dealing with conflict that the Japanese have a word in their language ("wa") that reminds their members that interpersonal harmony is essential. The Japanese believe that each of us comes to an encounter with this feeling of "wa" (harmony) already inside of us, and that communication between people should foster this harmony, *not* disrupt it. This concept invades nearly every aspect of Japanese life. People often wear surgical masks in public to keep from giving their colds to others. The words, "I am very sorry" ("soo-mee-mah-sehn") are heard with great regularity. This aversion to conflict is even manifested in the Japanese legal system. In general, Japanese feel such distaste for using the court because of its combative nature, that they try to resolve disputes without lawyers. In fact, it is estimated that the Japanese only have one lawyer for every 10,000 people, while in the United States, a culture that values assertive behavior, there is one lawyer for every 50 people.

Interdependence

You and the other person in your "I want . . . but . . . wants. . ." example are **interdependent**; that is, you depend on each other and need each other in some way. Parents and children, workers and supervisors, and partners in a relationship all depend on each other for something, whether it's care, affection, goods, or services. Without interdependence, there is no interpersonal conflict.

You and your supervisor need each other to solve the problem of how you can swap jobs with a coworker. If you both saw the job change in the same way, there would be no conflict.

You and your companion need each other to solve the problem of how to satisfy your desire to have some influence over where you go. If you both were to define your relationship the same way—as casual and nonexclusive or as serious and exclusive—there would be no conflict.

As a person who needs money, and has a friend who has money, together you need to resolve the problem of scarce resources. If you were not friends, or both of you had the money you needed—if you were not interdependent—there would be no conflict.

How are you and the other person in Knowledge Checkup 11.1 interdependent? (See questions 4 and 5.)

Sources of Conflict

The frustration that triggers your conflict has a source. Four common sources of conflict are limited resources, individual differences, differences in defining your relationship, and competition.[4]

Limited Resources   Limited resources are a widespread source of conflict. You may feel that any problem could be solved if there were more money, more time,

more space, more equipment, or more people to help. For example, if you and your parent had only one car to share, the limited resource—the car—may have been a source of conflict.

Individual Differences   Individual differences are probably the most common and least often acknowledged source of conflict. Each person's perceptions of the world are uniquely her or his own, based on her or his past experiences, background, and history, and interpretations and responses to events. No two people view the same object or event in exactly the same way; these perceptual differences may trigger conflicts.

Among the typical sources of frustration are individual differences in gender, attitudes, beliefs, values, experiences, upbringing, and education. For example, your supervisor may believe that not rocking the boat is an important goal and has little experience with training methods that differ from how he or she was trained ("You get a job and stay in it"). You might enjoy taking risks and have training in a variety of positions in the organization. The differences may not matter under most circumstances, but when you request to swap positions with a coworker, the stage is set for conflict.

Differences in Defining Your Relationship   The third general source of conflict stems from your view of your relationship: You and the other person may define your roles in the relationship differently, or you may define the relationship itself differently. For example, you may want to socialize with other people because you see your current relationship as unable to fulfill your needs; you view yourselves as steady but not serious long-term partners. The other person may define the relationship as serious, and define your roles as intimate friends and prospective spouses. Under these circumstances, your desire to see other people triggers a conflict, one born of your different definitions of the relationship.

Competition

> Competition is an inescapable fact of life. From the nursery to the nursing home, from the bedroom to the boardroom, in politics and business and school and sports and everyday conversation, human beings are in constant competition with each other. We compete for jobs, grades, social position, sex, friendship, money, power, even love. So pervasive is the competitive urge that it frequently governs our behavior even when we are unaware of its influence. From the time we are very small, it is a fundamental aspect of the process by which we develop our self-esteem, our social assurance, our very identity.[5]

Not all cultures perceive conflict arising out of the same situations. An examination of "competition" is a vivid illustration of how culture and perception are linked. In cultures that do not value competition with the same intensity as North Americans do, there is less likely to be conflict when competition does arise. In the Native American and Mexican cultures, for example, people seldom compete with the same aggressive attitude as do members of the predominantly North American culture. People from these cultures are apt to withdraw rather than stand toe-to-toe and "slug it out." In fact, "assertive speech and behavior are a sign of discourtesy, restlessness, self-centeredness, and a lack of discipline."[6] Historically, this is one of the factors that caused the Native Americans, unlike their image as portrayed in old Hollywood cavalry movies, to be taken advantage of. The same is true of the Indian tribes in Mexico, especially the kind and trusting Mayans, as they met and dealt with their European invaders. This does not mean to imply that these cultures avoid conflict, but rather it underscores the notion that conflict and competition are defined differently by different cultures.

Skill Development 11.1 will help you practice identifying the sources of a conflict—a skill useful as a first step toward conflict resolution.

SKILL DEVELOPMENT 11.1

IDENTIFYING THE SOURCES OF CONFLICT

In Knowledge Checkup 11.1 you investigated the Kevin and Serena interaction described at the beginning of the chapter in which their conflict about going out on a Friday night ended when Serena told Kevin to go by himself. Review that interaction and your answers to questions 1, 2, and 3 of Knowledge Checkup 11.1. What are the sources of this conflict? Why did you select the answers you chose?

Examine your important relational conflict described in questions 4 and 5 of Knowledge Checkup 11.1. What are the sources of this conflict? Why did you select these causes?

SEXUAL HARASSMENT

Sexual harassment is the "unwelcome sexual advances, requests for sexual favors, and other verbal and physical conduct of a sexual nature."[7] Sexual harassment can be *real,* and not just a matter of two people perceiving the same behavior differently. However, differences in perception are often a part of the problem of sexual harassment. For example, testimony given during the William Kennedy Smith trial, in which he was charged with date rape of Patricia Bowman, highlights differences in perception of the "same" event. Ms. Bowman reported that she "bumped into" Mr. Smith, and that this event led to their talking and, eventually, the development of a relationship in which she needed to use direct strategies to avoid a sexual encounter (she told him to "stop" and that "she did not want to have intercourse"). Mr. Smith reported the initial encounter—ostensibly the same event—with different words, and these words reflected his different perception. He reported she "brushed up against him" and "stood very close" to him. Along with other behaviors, Mr. Smith reported that he "thought we were going to have sex." Her "bump" was his "brush," and their encounter was off on the road to conflict.[8] Similar misunderstandings seem to have been present in the interactions between Clarence Thomas and Anita Hill, who accused the now Supreme Court Justice of sexual harassment in the work environment.

What was the basis for these differences in the "opinion" of what happened? Basically, although there are many similarities in the ways North American women and men initiate sexual contact and talk about sexuality, there are also a great many differences—and these differences can serve as an important source of conflict and misunderstanding. First, many men and women view casual social interaction differently: Typically men, more than women, consider that these interactions have the potential to develop into sexual encounters. Women, by contrast, tend to regard interactions as the bases for friendship and possibly a relationship. Secondly, men view flirtatious behavior as somewhat sexual, whereas women are more likely to distinguish between "friendly" and "sexual" flirtatious behavior. Finally, traditionally a cultural norm seems to exist that suggests men are supposed to initiate sexual encounters and women are supposed to avoid them—a norm that ensures miscommunication and conflict as men and women try to determine what the other person "really" means.[9]

Sexual harassment does not always target the woman as victim. Though not as commonly reported, men may also be the victims of sexual harassment by women as well as by other men. In addition, there are cultural differences regarding sexual harassment. Because of the variances in some cultures regarding the roles and the expectations of females, sexual harassment, as understood in Northern American culture, is an alien concept because of what is expected of each gender.

PERCEPTIONS OF CONFLICT

Can you think of a situation in which limited resources, individual differences, or differences in definitions of the relationship do *not* exist? Such a situation would require individuals who were identical in their concerns, wants, needs, desires, attitudes, beliefs, values, goals, and perceptions of the other person and the relationship. Even identical twins raised in the same household are not *that* similar.

Given that no two people are identical, it follows that conflict is natural and inevitable. A comic strip expressed the normality of conflict this way: Cathy (in the syndicated cartoon of the same name), talking to several of her coworkers, says, "I want just one normal week. Is that so much to ask? Just one normal week where I have normal non-hysterical work days, and come home to normal non-crisis-point relationships." One of her coworkers tells her, "I've *never* had a week like that," and another says, "Me neither." She responds, "Me neither" and, addressing the reader, adds: "Why does the one experience no one has ever had keep seeming like the normal one?"[10]

The answer to Cathy's question requires a look at three main socializing agents: the family, educational institutions, and television.

FAMILY

Perceptions of conflict are based on your early experiences with your family. How was conflict between your parents treated? Was it something to do openly, in front of you and your siblings, or was it something to be hidden behind closed doors late at night? Was it handled in productive ways so that the outcomes were positive, or were most conflicts screaming bouts followed by periods of cool silence? "Don't fight in front of the children" may be a norm in many families, but the message it communicates is that conflict is wrong, unfit for children.

As conflicts rage around you (whether conducted quietly or not), you're taught: "Don't fight with your brother!" "If you don't have something nice to say, don't say anything at all!" "Don't talk back!" "*Real* friends don't fight!" The intended point of these messages is the same: Conflict is unnatural, something that good people who like each other don't do. But these messages are pitted against reality: People who love each other *do* fight, just as siblings and spouses who really care for each other do.

"And they lived happily ever after" is a phrase common to fairy tales, not *real* relationships between *real* people. Adopting the fairy tale version of life can create frustration for yourself and your partner. Yet people are inclined to ask, "What's wrong with us that we fight?" rather than reject the unrealistic and unattainable fairy tale ending.

EDUCATIONAL INSTITUTIONS

The message about conflict that you learn in educational institutions probably is similar to the one you learned at home: Conflict is bad. In elementary grades, a fight with a classmate means being sent to the principal and possibly having your parents called in for a conference. Instead of teaching youngsters how to deal constructively with their conflicts—how to define their problems and communicate their feelings and needs to each other to find mutually satisfactory resolutions—schools typically punish children for perfectly understandable and predictable behavior.

Because open conflicts between teachers and students are forbidden, more subtle expressions of discord prevail. Instructors and students and bosses and workers often exchange **bristle statements**, comments that each knows probably will trigger the other's anger. For example, an instructor may tell a student, "It's in the book—try reading it," or "No one forced you to take this course," while a student may ask, "Are we doing anything important in class today?" or "Do spelling and grammar count?" A boss may tell a worker, "You've been working here long enough to know that," or "We don't do it that way here," while a worker may say, "My last boss gave me a lot of useful feedback," or "If I had the right equipment I could do the job right." Each attacks the other in ways that sidestep the issue. Educational institutions teach students to fight dirty when conflicts are perceived as dirty.

TELEVISION

You may have spent more hours watching television than you have spent in school, and you have probably learned more about day-to-day life from the tube than from your teachers. What are conflicts like in the programs you watch? In half-hour programs, you see complex problems being solved in twenty-four minutes plus commercials. In one-hour programs, even more complex problems get resolved in about fifty minutes plus commercials. But real life is *not* made up of half-hour and one-hour segments. Nor is real-life made up of what happens in movies, comic books, and Saturday morning cartoons.

Your own life is not realistically portrayed on television, so when your conflicts fail to conform to television-style conflicts and resolutions, you probably assume that something is wrong with *you.* "What's wrong with *me,* and what's wrong with *us,* that our conflicts last for a long time, rarely end neatly, and aren't as glamorous or as gloriously dramatic as the conflicts on TV?" Television may embody the modern fairy tale where, in the end, everybody but the villain lives happily ever after, but is this reality?

CONSEQUENCES OF CONFLICT

Your early experiences no doubt introduced you to many of the negative consequences of conflict, and they may have persuaded you that conflict is something to be avoided. But conflict also may have positive consequences that benefit your work, your relationships, and you personally.

EFFECTS ON WORK

Conflict is dysfunctional when it keeps you from doing your work. It takes time and energy to engage in or avoid a conflict. Also, an unresolved conflict requires a great deal of thought about who said what, when, and how, as well as what caused the conflict and what can be done about it. When you have a conflict on your mind, reading one page of a textbook may take an hour, concentrating on a lecture may be difficult, and dealing with a customer may be almost impossible.

Conflict also may be dysfunctional when it forces conformity. If you fear that open conflict may lead to public ridicule, blame, or harsh punishment, you are likely to accept whatever happens and keep your frustrations to yourself in order to avoid the harassment.

In contrast, conflict is functional when it increases your motivation to interact with the person causing your frustration, to discuss the areas of conflict, and to arrive at new and better solutions to the problem. Conflict often yields results when heightened excitement and interaction get channeled into direct confrontations that focus on resolution.

Knowledge Checkup 11.2 will help you recognize the consequences of a conflict with which you are familiar.

KNOWLEDGE CHECKUP 11.2

CONFLICT CONSEQUENCES

Choose a novel you've read or a movie you've seen that focuses on personal or family relationships (for example, films like *Boyz in the Hood, Used People, The Great Santini, Raise the Red Lantern, The Prince of Tides, Like Water for Chocolate,* and *Ordinary People*).

1. Describe one of the major conflicts portrayed.

2. Describe the negative consequences of the conflict.

3. Describe the positive consequences.

4. Based on your observations, agree or disagree with these statements:

    a. Conflicts threaten the integrity of relationships.

    b. Conflicts strengthen relationships.

    c. Relationship growth is a consequence of conflict.

EFFECTS ON RELATIONSHIPS

Conflicts are dysfunctional when they threaten the integrity of a relationship. Given that half the marriages in the United States end in divorce, conflicts obviously threaten and destroy relationships.[11] If two persons perceive that an important problem cannot be resolved within the confines of their relationship, they may terminate the relationship. Indeed, even if a relationship is not terminated, research has found that wives and husbands who believe that conflicts and disagreements are healthy report greater marital satisfaction than those who view them as unhealthy.[12]

Conflicts are functional when they promote relationship growth, which can happen in two ways. First, *conflicts require negotiation about how to negotiate.* How will you and your partner communicate your thoughts and feelings? How will you agree on a solution? As you answer these questions you develop new strategies for interacting with each other.

Second, *conflicts require the exchange of new information about the subject of the dispute.* Information about each person's needs, wants, desires, and goals is necessary to generate and select a mutually satisfactory solution to the problem. Acquiring and using new strategies for interacting, plus gaining and using new information, equal relational growth.

PERSONAL EFFECTS

A conflict is dysfunctional when it leaves you feeling foolish, inadequate, or cruel. Insults such as "You're stupid," whether you say them or someone says them to you, are personally destructive. If you say them, they testify to your cruelty; if someone says them to you, they prompt self-doubt and feelings of inadequacy, or possibly fury.

In contrast, functional conflicts increase your self-understanding and feelings of self-worth. You learn about yourself, how you view certain issues, and how strongly you feel about them. You also increase your ability to see life through someone else's eyes, to understand how others think and feel about issues that are important to them.

Knowledge Checkup 11.3 will help you assess whether your conflicts are primarily functional or dysfunctional by focusing on your verbal shooting gallery.

KNOWLEDGE CHECKUP 11.3

INVENTORY OF YOUR VERBAL SHOOTING GALLERY

Think about conflicts you have had with your parents, siblings, companions, and friends. Which of these phrases (or similar ones) did you use? Circle all those which are part of or like your verbal shooting gallery.

"You're stupid!"

"I hate you!"

"You're just like your father/mother/sister/brother!"

"I wish you were dead!"

"If you loved me you wouldn't . . ."

"You think that's a problem? That's nothing!"

"If you'd do it my way . . ."

"I told you so!"

"Your problem is easy to trace: poor toilet training!"

"Why do you always . . . ?"

"Can't you ever do anything right?"

"For an idiot, that's a good answer!"

"That's ridiculous!"

"You're ridiculous!"

How do you feel when someone says to *you* the phrases you circled?

APPROACHES TO CONFLICT

You learned early in life how to manage conflicts. The particular conflict strategies you use are developed from your interactions with your parents and siblings, teachers and classmates, friends and enemies—and from familiar television programs. Your responses to conflict are probably automatic, which poses a problem: Automatic responses are difficult to recognize, yet you must recognize them before change is possible.

CONFLICT STRATEGIES

When your needs seem incompatible with other people's needs, how do you react? What strategies do you use to resolve your conflicts? Knowledge Checkup 11.4 will help you increase your awareness of the conflict strategies you use.

KNOWLEDGE CHECKUP 11.4

YOUR CONFLICT MODE[13]

Consider situations in which you find your wishes differing from those of another person. How do you usually respond to such situations? In each pair below, circle the **A** or **B** statement which is *most characteristic* of your behavior. In some case, neither answer may be very typical of your behavior. In that case, select the response which you would be *more likely* to use.

1. A. There are times when I let others take responsibility for solving the problem.
   B. Rather than negotiate the things on which we disagree, I try to stress those things upon which we both agree.

2. A. I try to find a compromise solution.
   B. I attempt to deal with all of the other person's and my concerns.

3. A. I am usually firm in pursuing my goals.
   B. I might try to soothe the other's feelings and preserve our relationship.

4. A. I try to find a compromise solution.
   B. I sometimes sacrifice my own wishes for the wishes of the other person.

5. A. I consistently seek the other's help in working out a solution.
   B. I try to do what is necessary to avoid useless tensions.

6. A. I try to avoid creating unpleasantness for myself.
   B. I try to win my position.

7. A. I try to postpone the issue until I have had some time to think it over.
   B. I give up some points in exchange for others.

8. A. I am usually firm in pursuing my goals.
   B. I attempt to get all concerns and issues immediately out in the open.

9. A. I feel that differences are not always worth worrying about.
   B. I make some effort to get my way.

10. A. I am firm in pursuing my goals.
    B. I try to find a compromise solution.

11. A. I attempt to get all concerns and issues immediately out in the open.
    B. I might try to soothe the other's feelings and preserve our relationship.

12. A. I sometimes avoid taking positions which would create controversy.
    B. I will let the other person have some of his/her positions if the person lets me have some of mine.

13. A. I propose a middle ground.
    B. I press to get my points made.

14. A. I tell the other person my ideas and ask for his/hers.
    B. I try to show the other person the logic and benefits of my position.

15. A. I might try to soothe the other's feelings and preserve our relationship.
    B. I try to do what is necessary to avoid tensions.

SCORING:

For question 1, circle the **A** or **B** according to your answer; for question 2, circle the **A** or **B** according to your answer. Repeat the process for all fifteen questions.

	D	I	C	A	S
1.				A	B
2.		B	A		
3.	A				B
4.			A		B
5.		A		B	
6.	B			A	
7.			B	A	
8.	A	B			
9.	B			A	
10.	A		B		
11.		A			B
12.			B	A	
13.	B		A		
14.	B	A			
15.				B	A

Number of **A**s and **B**s circled in column D (Dominance) _____

Number of **A**s and **B**s circled in column I (Integration) _____

Number of **A**s and **B**s circled in column C (Compromise) _____

Number of **A**s and **B**s circled in column A (Avoidance) _____

Number of **A**s and **B**s circled in column S (Smoothing Over) _____

On which of the five strategies did you score highest and on which did you score lowest? You may use different strategies in different situations, but the odds are that you have a favorite strategy that you use whether or not it is most appropriate for the situation. In order to understand and evaluate your conflict strategies, you need to know your typical responses to conflict so that you can examine their appropriateness and make decisions about their use. If you understand which strategy is best for a given conflict, you can increase the range of your responses and, therefore, react more effectively.

Each of the five conflict strategies balances differing amounts of self-satisfaction and concern for the other person. Being too concerned with the other person's welfare may leave your own needs unsatisfied, while concern only for yourself may seem self-aggrandizing, even if you do get what you want. Each strategy has advantages and disadvantages that must be weighed against the demands of the situation: No one strategy suits every situation.[14]

Your strategies for dealing with conflict echo both your individual personality and your cultural background, as well as characteristics of your relationship, such as its intimacy.[15] These strategies are reflected in the manner in which you communicate. For instance, in Asian cultures, where people seek to avoid direct face-to-face conflict, communication strategies usually include cautious and indirect speech, taking time to sense another's mood before venturing an opinion, and avoiding disagreement in the presence of other people.

Avoidance

Also called denial or withdrawal, **avoidance** strategy posits that a conflict will just go away if it is ignored. Only rarely, however, does a conflict permanently go away, so people who use this strategy must worry that their conflict will recur.

The biggest problem with avoidance strategy is that neither your needs nor the other person's needs are satisfied. Though you may be able to persuade yourself that your needs are unimportant, you will likely find out differently in time. You can intellectually reject the issue as trivial, but your body may respond with stress-related disorders, such as headaches and ulcers.

Of course, avoidance sometimes is an appropriate response to a conflict. *If* neither the issue nor your relationship with the other person is very important to you, withdrawal may be a reasonable strategy. But don't fool yourself about the true importance of these two variables.

What was your avoidance score on Knowledge Checkup 11.4? Was it your highest or lowest score of the five conflict strategy scores? A high score, in comparison to the others, indicates that this is your typical strategy, and a low score indicates that this is your atypical strategy.

Smoothing Over

Also called an obliging or suppression strategy, a **smoothing-over** strategy shows concern for the other person but not for yourself. This strategy aims to satisfy the other person's concerns to the neglect of your own. It grows out of the notions that "nice people don't fight" and "if you don't have something nice to say, then don't say anything."

Smoothing over is often used as a delaying tactic, to keep things peaceful until the conflict goes away. However, because your needs have been subverted, the conflict does not go away. Just like people who avoid open conflict, people who smooth things over must always worry that the problem will recur.

A smoothing strategy does suit some conflicts. *If* your concern is really unimportant to you and *if* maintaining your relationship with the other person is very important, smoothing over may be effective. But once again, an honest assessment of the importance of these two factors is crucial.

What was your smoothing-over score on Knowledge Checkup 11.4? A high score, in comparison to the others, indicates that this is your typical strategy, and a low score indicates that this is your atypical strategy.

Dominance

Also called power or forcing, **dominance** is the reverse of smoothing over: It focuses on your own needs at the expense of the other person's. Your ability to dominate the other person may come from your position (you may be the supervisor, the parent, or the person with the needed information), your physical size or strength, or your control of rewards and punishments. "Do what I want or else!" is a common threat from those who try to use dominance to solve their problems.

The primary problem with this strategy is that, while your own needs may be satisfied, those of the other person remain unsatisfied, which will likely breed resentment, hostility, and a desire for revenge. For example, a mother who refuses to give her teenage son the car when he needs it may satisfy her need to use the car herself or her need to confirm that she's in charge, but her son is likely to retaliate by refusing to cooperate in some future situation.

There are times when a dominating strategy is appropriate. For example, an emergency situation may call for quick and decisive action, and discussion may make matters worse. When a small child runs into a busy street, you must return her to the sidewalk quickly. You and the child may have incompatible goals and both feel frustrated, but the circumstance requires a dominating strategy to avoid disaster.

On the whole, however, a dominating strategy is rarely the best one. It should be used only *if* your goal is very important to you and *if* your relationship with the other person is of little or no importance. Remember that once you create a situation with you as the winner and the other person as the loser, you probably also create an enemy.

What was your dominance score on Knowledge Checkup 11.4? A high score, in comparison to the others, indicates that this is your typical strategy, and a low score indicates that this is your atypical strategy.

Compromise

Also called bargaining or negotiating, **compromise** is a sharing strategy designed to satisfy everyone's concerns to some extent. The aim is to give up something to gain something.

Although compromise seems ideal in theory, in reality it rarely resolves conflicts. Getting your own way at another's expense (dominating), or letting another have her or his way at your expense (smoothing over), may be forestalled by compromise, but compromise usually does not permanently resolve conflicts.

Compromise may be a popular conflict strategy because people generally believe that something is better than nothing. If the odds of getting your needs fully satisfied are slight, or if the end result may be no satisfaction at all, a little satisfaction may seem a worthy goal. The problem with compromise, however, is that people rarely negotiate in good faith. Because they assume that they'll have to give in a little, they inflate their demands. And because they assume that something is better than nothing, they are willing to compromise on matters that are truly important to them and thus should not be conceded. If both persons operate on the assumption that honesty may *not* be the best policy, they try to deceive each other by arguing for irrelevant issues that they can later relinquish as bargaining chips. For example, union negotiators often include extraneous items in their list of demands so that they can seem to be giving something up when they withdraw those items from negotiation.

Finally, working out a fair compromise requires communication skills that may be too advanced for many people. For example, you need to communicate exactly what your concerns are and what you are and are not willing to give up. You also need to listen actively to determine how the other person's concerns do and do not conflict with your own.

If your goal and your relationship are both moderately important to you, compromise may be an appropriate conflict strategy, but the importance of these two variables and the level of both individuals' communication skills are crucial determinants.

What was your compromise score on Knowledge Checkup 11.4? A high score, in comparison to the others, indicates that this is your typical strategy, and a low score indicates that this is your atypical strategy.

Integration

Also referred to as collaboration and problem solving, **integration** has as its goal the full satisfaction of your own and the other person's concerns. By definition alone, this strategy may seem to be the best one, but it has limited usefulness. *If* the goal and the relationship are both very important, integration may be the most appropriate strategy to employ. However, in most cases, either the concern or the relationship is not very important or both are of only moderate importance.

Besides taking the most time, an integrating strategy requires the widest range of well-developed communication skills. For example, you must be able to self-disclose openly and honestly about your own needs and to listen actively to the disclosures of the other person. You must be able to see the problem from the other person's perspective and integrate that perspective with your own. You must integrate your needs with the other person's needs to be able to generate creative and mutually satisfying solutions. You must also realize that the issues at stake in the conflict are more important than the contestants' egos.

What was your integration score on Knowledge Checkup 11.4? A high score, in comparison to the others, indicates that this is your typical strategy, and a low score indicates that this is your atypical strategy.

SKILL DEVELOPMENT 11.2

SELECTING A CONFLICT STRATEGY[16]

José and Valaya are, for the most part, a very happily married couple living in a small town in Virginia. José has a job at a computer company, and seems to be "moving up fast." Valaya has a job working for the mayor. Both have graduate degrees, and were lucky enough to find jobs in the same small town.

One day José arrives home and is very excited. He has just been offered a very prestigious promotion, accompanied by a substantial raise. If he takes it, he will be a vice president of the company. However, the new position does entail a move to Chicago. He thinks Valaya will be excited about the promotion, too. He tells her about it with great enthusiasm. She responds with dejection:

JOSÉ: Valaya, I know this means moving, and that you like your job, but I'm sure you can find something in Chicago.

VALAYA: But José, I *hate* big cities, most of all Chicago, and I'm just now feeling *settled* in my job, and I love it. I don't want to move!

JOSÉ: But Valaya, don't be ridiculous. Chicago is a wonderful place, and I'm sure there would be more opportunities for you to advance your career there than in this small-time town.

VALAYA: I just don't want to move, and that's that.

JOSÉ: You're making $21,000, and I'm making $39,000. If I take the promotion, I'll be making $65,000, with no end in sight. Don't you think you're being selfish?

VALAYA: Don't you think *you're* being selfish?

JOSÉ: I don't believe this! I thought you'd be happy for me! See you later, I'm going out with the guys. They at least appreciate me.

SITUATION 1:

1. Describe the conflict between José and Valaya.

2. Identify each person's conflict strategy.

3. Based on the conflict strategies, how important did the conflict issue seem to be to each person? What specific behaviors did Valaya and José display that support your conclusion?

4. Based on the conflict, how important did the relationship seem to be for each person? What specific behaviors did each display that support your conclusion?

SITUATION 2

1. Describe a conflict involving you and one other person.

2. Identify your conflict strategy. What behaviors support your identification?

3. Given the importance of the conflict issue and the relationship, was your strategy appropriate? Why was it appropriate or inappropriate? If it wasn't appropriate, which strategy would have been?

4. Identify the other person's conflict strategy. What behaviors support your identification?

5. Based on the other person's conflict strategy, what is your assessment of the importance of the conflict issue and the relationship for the other person?

CONFLICT STYLES

Although your conflict strategy may vary from situation to situation, your **conflict style**, the characteristic way you express yourself in a conflict, remains fairly stable. The questionnaire in Knowledge Checkup 11.5 should help you determine your personal conflict style.

KNOWLEDGE CHECKUP 11.5

CONFLICT BEHAVIOR SCALE[17]

Indicate, on a scale of 1 to 7, the degree to which each of the statements describes your conflict behavior. Use the following scale: **1** = never, **2** = very seldom, **3** = seldom, **4** = sometimes, **5** = often, **6** = very often, and **7** = always.

_____ **1.** I blend ideas with others to create new solutions to conflict.

_____ **2.** I shy away from topics that are sources of disputes.

_____ **3.** I steadfastly insist on my position being accepted during a conflict.

_____ **4.** I try to find solutions that combine a variety of viewpoints.

_____ **5.** I steer clear of disagreeable situations.

_____ **6.** I do not give in to other people's ideas.

_____ **7.** I look for middle-of-the-road solutions that satisfy both my needs and the needs of the other person.

_____ **8.** I avoid a person I suspect of wanting to discuss a disagreement.

_____ **9.** I minimize the significance of a conflict.

_____ **10.** I build an integrated solution from the issues raised in a dispute.

_____ **11.** I stress a point I am making by hitting my fist on the table when I insist the other person is wrong.

_____ **12.** I threaten people to reach a settlement that helps me satisfy my needs.

_____ **13.** I shout when trying to get others to accept my position.

_____ **14.** I look for mutually satisfying creative solutions to conflicts.

_____ **15.** I keep quiet about my views in order to avoid disagreements.

SCORING:

Add your scores for questionnaire items 2, 5, 8, 9, 15: _____ This is your score for *nonassertiveness*. A high numerical score (29 or above) means you perceive yourself to have a tendency to use this style often. A low numerical score (11 or below) means you perceive that you use this style rarely.

Add your scores for items 1, 4, 7, 10, 14: _____ This is your *assertion* score. A high numerical score (29 or above) means you perceive yourself to have a tendency to use this style often. A low numerical score (11 or below) means you perceive that you use this style rarely.

Add your scores for items 3, 6, 11, 12, 13: _____ This is your *aggression* score. A high numerical score (29 or above) means you perceive yourself to have a tendency to use this style often. A low numerical score (11 or below) means you perceive that you use this style rarely.

Compare the scores on the three dimensions to see which style you perceive yourself to be using most.

To manage your conflicts successfully requires that the other person be aware of your concerns. Of the conflict styles, nonassertion fails to communicate directly that there is a problem, and direct aggression communicates your concerns in a way that is almost guaranteed to raise more problems.[18]

Nonassertion

Reluctance to communicate your feelings and thoughts characterizes **nonassertive behavior** (also called passive behavior). Linked with avoidance strategies, nonassertive behavior virtually ensures that your concerns go unsatisfied, unless you are lucky or the other person takes pity on you. A nonassertive person will fail to take action or will take action with someone completely uninvolved in the conflict. For example, you would be nonassertive if you received an incorrect bill from the gas company but, instead of demanding a correction, you paid the bill and said nothing or complained to a friend about the unfairness of big business. Neither course of action informs the gas company that there is a problem.

Nonassertive communicators often defend their behavior by saying, "It wasn't the best time [or place] to talk," or "I didn't think the other person was ready to hear what I wanted to say," or "They won't like me if I say what's on my mind." Such excuses normally have nothing to do with the actual situation; they merely justify avoiding an unpleasant exchange or a possible confrontation.

Several nonverbal cues accompany nonassertiveness, including rapid eye blinking, avoiding eye contact, squinting, repeated swallowing, throat clearing, tightening or pursing the lips, tensing and wrinkling the forehead, covering the mouth while speaking, shifting weight from foot to foot, nervous giggling, and preening behaviors, such as hair smoothing, beard stroking, and fingernail cleaning. Notice whether you employ these behaviors. If you do, assess whether you want to change your conflict style.

Some theorists divide nonassertiveness into two categories: nonconfrontation and indirect aggression. In this approach, nonconfrontation is the same as what has been described as nonassertion, while **indirect aggression** is the expression of concerns in a disguised way. Rather than stating the real issue, you attack in various ways. These include:

- *Attacking the other person directly but avoiding the real issue* (you receive a grade of *D* on a paper and, bursting into the professor's office, tell her, "I think you're a lousy teacher!");

- *Attacking the person indirectly* ("What was your curve for the grades on the last set of papers?");

- *Lying about your real feelings* ("I've thought about the *D* you gave me, and I really think I deserved it.");

- *Manipulating the situation* ("I know you don't believe in extra credit assignments, but if I do another paper on the same topic, will you read it and give me your comments?");

- *Embarrassing the person* ("My lack of ability to write reflects your lack of ability to teach!");

- *Hinting about the problem* ("Do you think I can still get an *A* in your course?");

- *Withholding something from the other person*—some service, compliance with a request, or courtesy ("I forgot to pick up the papers that you wanted to give out in class today");

- *Inviting the person to feel guilty* ("No, no, it's okay if you give me a *D* and I lose my scholarship"[19]); and

- *Using sarcasm* ("You want me to write better papers? Great advice coming from a teacher with ten typos on a five-page exam!").

Indirect aggression is risky for several reasons. First, because you communicate your concerns indirectly, the other person may miss the point. Second, even if the other person understands your message, she or he may decide to ignore it because your indirectness offers a ready excuse: "I didn't know what you wanted!" Third, indirect aggression is risky because people who feel manipulated often respond angrily. Even if the other person does what you want, the relationship may be damaged and future conflicts may be more difficult to resolve.

Be aware that there are many cultures that employ nonassertive behaviors as their primary means of defusing conflict. While it might seem like a trivial example, reflect for a moment on the subtle differences toward conflict in how two cultures deal with the posting of signs that carry potentially antagonistic messages. In the United States a sign would read NO DOGS ALLOWED. In England, a reserved culture that does not relish outward displays of conflict, the same sign would read WE REGRET THAT IN THE INTEREST OF HYGIENE DOGS ARE NOT ALLOWED ON THESE PREMISES.

Signs, of course, are not the only way the English seek to avoid harsh disagreements. Disputes often begin with phrases such as, "I may be wrong, but . . . ," or "There is just a very minor point in what you are saying that worries me a little."

The British are not the only ones who employ indirect methods to deal with conflict. Cultures such as the Chinese and Japanese have a strong faith in intuition and highly value collectivism in the indirect approach, and even believe at times that the other person will sense feelings of anger or conflict without a single word having to be spoken.[20]

Direct Aggression

Direct aggression, unlike nonassertiveness and indirect aggression, is easy to recognize. **Direct aggression** is the open expression of feelings, needs, wants, desires, and ideas *at the expense of others.* People who use direct aggression try to dominate and possibly humiliate the other person by acting self-righteously, as if they're superior, certain of themselves, and know what's best for everyone. For example, in response to the request to use the family car, the teenager's mother may say: "No, I want to use it, and I don't care that you need it to go see your friends. I have to go to the store and that's more important!" In this way, the mother clearly declares that her needs will be satisfied at the expense of the teen's.

Direct aggression may get you what you want, but the costs are high. Initial hurt and humiliation may fade, but a loser is often left feeling angry, resentful, and vengeful, and is apt to retaliate in kind. Direct aggression begets further direct aggression, ensuring continued lack of cooperation and hostility.

Skill Development 11.3 provides you with the opportunity to practice nonassertive, indirect aggression, and direct aggression responses. This should help you recognize when you respond in one of these ways.

SKILL DEVELOPMENT 11.3

RESPONDING TO RELATIONSHIP DISCORD

Respond to the situation with a statement or action that represents each conflict style noted below.

Your instructor explains that she is going to a convention at the end of the semester and will have to give the final exam two days early. You already have two tests that day.

1. Nonassertion: _____

_____

_____

2. Indirect aggression: _____

_____

_____

3. Direct aggression: _____

_____

_____

Assertion

Assertion is the direct statement of needs and wants. Because it is direct, assertion is more closely related to direct aggression than to either indirect aggression or nonassertiveness. Assertive communication lacks an important element of direct aggression, however; it *expresses thoughts and feelings directly and clearly without judging or dictating to others.* It is honest and has as its goal the resolution of conflict. Unlike direct aggression, assertiveness does not mean

winning at the other person's expense—it attacks the problem, not the person.[21]

An assertive style has several advantages over other conflict styles. It increases the probability that your concerns will be satisfied and that you'll feel good about yourself. In addition, others are more likely to understand your needs and, possibly, work with you in managing the conflict. Relationships are often improved when assertiveness is used because the participants know exactly what they are in conflict about.

Assertive communication is useful in both simple and complex situations. The way you assert yourself will depend on who you are in conflict with and how involved the problem is.

Assertive Skills for Simple Situations   A conflict situation is simple when the problem is narrow and well-defined and you are not emotionally close to the other person. Such conflicts can be handled by stating your perception of the facts. For example, if you receive a bill from your school charging you for a class you did not sign up to take, you could assert yourself in three different ways. You could call the business office and say:

1. "Hello, this is _____. I received my tuition bill today and I'm being charged for a class I'm not taking."
2. "Hello, this is _____. I know you're probably not the person who's responsible, but I received my tuition bill today and I'm being charged for a class I'm not taking."
3. "Hello, this is _____. I received my tuition bill today and I'm being charged for a class I'm not taking. I would like the overcharge removed."

All three assertive comments are variations on the same theme—stating your perception of the facts. In the first instance, you simply present the facts with the assumption that once the other person knows them, he or she will resolve the problem. The advantage of this assertion is that it does not accuse the other person of anything, states exactly what's frustrating you, and does not back the other person into a corner.

The second assertion takes into account the role of the other person in the conflict situation. This recognizes his or her needs and softens the impact of the message.

The third assertion goes one step further. You not only state the facts, but you also specify what needs to be done to satisfy your concerns.

In none of these three assertions do you tell the person *how* to do what you feel needs to be done, which forestalls a defensive response. Defensiveness is common when you command someone to do something, when you overstate your case, when you don't clearly state what's wrong, or when you implicitly communicate, "I know more about your job than you do."

Skill Development 11.4 will help you practice assertive communication in simple, straightforward problem situations.

STATING SIMPLE ASSERTIONS

George and you are from the same hometown. George has a car and the agreement you made at the beginning of the semester was that if you did his laundry, George would drive you home for Thanksgiving vacation. It's the Monday before vacation and George tells you that his Wednesday class has been canceled and the new plan is to go home Tuesday. You have an exam on Wednesday. Your instructor has stated that there will be no makeup exams given, no matter the excuse.

Write three statements, each reflecting a different type of assertion that may be used in this conflict situation:

1. _____

2. _____

3. _____

Assertive Skills for Complex Situations   A conflict situation is complex if it has one or more of the following characteristics: It is a long-term dispute, it involves people to whom you're emotionally close, there is a strong possibility of physical or verbal violence, and there are differences in power. Such cases require more detailed assertive responses.

A complex assertive message can be expressed by using the **A*S*S*E*R*T formula**:

A: Describe the *action* that prompted the need for the assertive message. Your description should be behavioral; that is, it should focus on *who* is involved, the *circumstances* that are relevant, and the *specific behaviors* that are the source of your frustration and that trigger the assertive message. The expression of a descriptive message is clear and objective—for example, "When we discuss a serious matter, you joke around."

S: Express your *subjective interpretation* of the action. Using "I" language, offer your interpretation of the behavior you describe. Separate this subjective interpretation from the objective description. For example, "When you joke around, I think you want to avoid talking about the serious issue under discussion."

S: Express your *sensations* related to the action. Say how you feel about the behavior as precisely as possible even if you are somewhat confused. Try to include the intensity of your feelings. Does the joking make you thoughtful, sad, or grief-stricken? Are you distracted, surprised, or amazed? Are you apprehensive, fearful, or filled with terror? Are you annoyed, angry, or enraged?

ZiGGY®

ZIGGY copyright 1991 ZIGGY AND FRIENDS, INC. Dist. by UNIVERSAL
PRESS SYNDICATE. Reprinted with permission. All rights reserved.

For example, "I feel angry when you don't stop kidding around. I also feel
frustrated because I don't know what to do to get you to take what we're talking
about seriously."

E: Indicate the *effects* of the action. Effects can focus on *you* ("I want to
avoid discussing serious matters with you because you joke around"), on the
other person ("I think you're missing out on some good discussions that might
improve our relationship"), or on *others* ("I think people misinterpret the
importance of our relationship when they see you joke around about serious
matters").

R: Make your *request.* Indicate what specific behaviors you want. For
example, "When we discuss a serious matter, I would like you to stop telling
jokes and kidding around." (Note that the request ends with a period, not an
exclamation point—it is a statement, not a command.)

T: *Tell* your intentions: "If we can't resolve this problem, I'll avoid
discussing serious issues with you."

Skill Development 11.5 will help you practice using the A*S*S*E*R*T
method.

A*S*S*E*R*T YOURSELF

Early in the semester a friend asked you if she could copy your accounting homework. Throughout the semester she has continued to ask, each time apologizing and saying she won't ask again. She has all sorts of excuses why she can't do the homework, including "no time," "doesn't understand," "forgot to write down the assignment." Last night you told her you won't give her your homework again. Today she again asks for it, pleading this is the last time, and, "anyway, that's what friends are for." You've had it! Use the A*S*S*E*R*T formula to present your view of the situation to your friend.

A: _____

_____

_____

S: _____

_____

_____

S: _____

_____

_____

E: _____

_____

_____

R: _____

_____

_____

T: _____

_____

_____

Be aware that many cultures feel uncomfortable with assertive behavior and, therefore, offer their members a communication style that is almost opposite to the one found in the United States. For example, in the Filipino culture few things are as important as smooth interpersonal relationships. The aversion to assertive behavior is strong there because they value people who appear to be timid, submissive, humble, and modest. Hence, your attempts to be assertive to a Filipino, or a person of other cultures with a similar orientation, may not yield the results you had in mind. Patience and understanding are what is needed to resolve conflicts with people of cultures other than your own. If possible, fit the style of the culture of the person with whom you are dealing.

Now that you know the differences among nonassertion, indirect aggression, direct aggression, and assertion styles—as they apply to North American society— if appropriate, put what you know into action!

GENDER DIFFERENCES AND CONFLICT

"No close relationship, no matter how ideal for both partners, maintains uniformly high satisfaction; no close relationship is without its ups and downs."[22] Of the many factors that potentially affect the process and outcome of relational conflict, gender is especially important. Gender appears linked to what comprises discontent, how dissatisfaction is expressed, managed, and resolved, and how both processes and outcomes are regarded by the relationship partners.

As shown in Table 11.1, females and males differ in their responses to conflict. Males tend to want to retain their independence and distance in a relationship, while females want interdependence, cooperative sharing, intimacy, and caring.[23] Because of these differences in wants, men and women tend to communicate, express, and deal with conflict in different manners. Women are inclined to recognize conflicts and make active efforts to identify, discuss, and work toward resolution. Men, on the other hand, tend to deny, avoid, or run away from conflict, or deal with the problem by stating what they think should be done and assuming that the matter is taken care of.[24] Women tend to respond to crises by attending to the processes of communication and encouraging mutual involvement, whereas men respond by protecting their self-interests.[25]

MANAGING RELATIONSHIP DISCORD

The successful management of relationship discord depends on several prerequisites: You must be able to analyze the conflict situation, understand your thoughts and feelings about conflict in general, and recognize your usual conflict strategies and styles. You must then determine your goal, choose the most effective approach, and implement the appropriate procedures. There are three general approaches to managing conflict: win–lose, lose–lose, and win–win.

TABLE 11.1 Female and male differences in responses to conflict

FEMALE	MALE
orientation: equity and caring; connections with and responsibility to other	*orientation*: equality of rights and fairness; adherence to abstract principles, rules
interact to achieve closeness and interdependence	interact for instrumental purposes; seek autonomy and distance
attend to interpersonal dynamics to assess relationship's health	less aware of interpersonal dynamics
encourage mutual involvement	protect self-interest
crisis is defined as caused by problems in the relationship	crisis is defined as caused by problems external to the relationship
concern with the impact of the relationship on personal identity	neither self- nor relationship-centered
response to conflict focuses mainly on the relationship	response to conflict focuses on rules and being evasive until a unilateral decision is reached

WIN–LOSE CONFLICT MANAGEMENT

In the **win–lose** approach to conflict, one person wins and the other loses. If your goal is to win and have the other person lose (the goal of a dominance strategy), or to lose and have the other person win (the goal of a smoothing-over strategy)—regardless of the situation—you are likely to take a win–lose approach.

People often use the win–lose approach to conflict management, even when it isn't necessary. Most of the conflicts you observed or participated in while growing up were probably treated as win–lose. For example, television programs stress the hero–villain conflict, with the hero almost always winning. Sports stress the bottom line: The team that scores the most points wins. Promotions at work may be limited to a select few: Some get ahead, some don't. At home, conflicts with siblings and spouses are often win–lose: You get to watch the television program you want and your brother doesn't, you turn down your radio so that your roommate can study, though you don't want to, and the cookie you want goes to your guest. Even our political system, majority rule, is a win–lose approach to conflict management. One candidate wins, the other loses; one party comes into power, the other waits in the wings until it wins.

The unequal power that distinguishes win–lose conflicts tends to damage relationships. Power may take the form of physical force, control over rewards and punishments, or cunning. For example, if you want to study but your friend wants to watch television, you might threaten physical violence: "Shut that off or you're dead meat"; threaten the loss of a reward: "You're not going to get any help from me when you're short of time on your project"; threaten a nonphysical punishment: "Shut it off or I'll watch television the next time *you* want to study"; or use cunning to get your way: "It's okay if you watch television while I study—it doesn't distract me *too* much [sigh]."

In some cases—when resources are limited and only one person or group can succeed, for instance—a win–lose approach to managing conflict is appropriate. For these situations, the interaction is competitive, not cooperative. For example, only one person can get the newly purchased computer.

A win–lose approach is also appropriate when the person with whom you're in conflict chooses it. Sometimes another person ignores your repeated invitations to approach a conflict cooperatively and instead insists on being competitive. You must then decide whether to accept the win–lose approach and attempt to win, be the loser, or change the situation so that your needs will be met in another way. For example, when you pull into a gas station, if someone pulls in alongside you and takes the pump you planned on using, you can argue over your right to use the pump because you pulled in first, you can brood while you wait for the latecomer to finish using the pump, or you can use another pump.

Finally, a win–lose approach is appropriate when the other person is clearly behaving improperly. Few would disagree that drunk drivers, people trying to carry weapons aboard planes, and child abusers should all be restrained.

LOSE–LOSE CONFLICT MANAGEMENT

In the **lose–lose** approach to conflict, neither your goals nor the other person's goals are fully satisfied. There may be some gain, but something important is also lost. It may seem ridiculous to purposely manage a conflict so that the outcomes are unsatisfactory to everyone, but one of the most popular conflict strategies, compromise, is actually a lose–lose approach. The lose–lose nature of compromise is evident in its outcomes. No sooner is a labor management compromise reached than one side or the other complains about what they had to give up and threatens to drive a harder bargain the next time. A couple arguing about whether to dine at a Mexican restaurant or a Chinese one may compromise and eat Italian food, although neither really was in the mood for it. Two nations may compromise by dividing up a disputed territory, but the resulting hard feelings and lost lives are likely to fuel further conflicts.

A lose–lose approach to managing conflict may be appropriate when the odds of fully satisfying your concerns are low or the chances of getting nothing at all are high. In addition, a lose–lose approach can usefully reduce tension in a conflict long enough for a different, more productive and long-lasting approach to be found.

USUAL OUTCOMES OF WIN–LOSE AND LOSE–LOSE CONFLICTS

Win–lose and lose–lose approaches to managing relationship discord are more common than an approach in which everyone wins. As a result, the outcomes of most conflicts are dysfunctional and negative.

In a typical conflict, *people rarely give in since their egos are at stake.* Rather than admit that the other person may be right, they try to reconceptualize the problem or the issues. By saying, "Oh, *that's* what you mean. Well, that's *different,*" people can save face by claiming that there really was no conflict in the first place. In the absence of such face-saving devices, the conflict may rage on indefinitely.

In a typical conflict, *biases are obvious and selfishness predominates.* You see yourself as "good" and the other as "bad," yourself as "trustworthy" and the other as "deceitful," yourself as "open" and the other as "sneaky." Even if one person tries to be cooperative (and in almost every conflict, each person makes bids for cooperation), the other person ignores the attempt. Cooperative behavior from a "bad, sneaky, deceitful" person is not deemed credible.

In a typical conflict, *tactics become more coercive* as the discord persists. Because you see the other person as bad, your trust decreases and your suspicion increases. You tell yourself, "The only way to deal with this untrustworthy sneak is to force him to do what I want."

In a typical conflict, *the original issue gets lost and the conflict spreads to other issues.* Although the source of the problem gets lost in the struggle, new issues, such as hurt feelings and resentment, arise; the conflict spreads to new eas: "If I can't trust you to file the papers when I ask you to [the original i how can I trust you to organize the files [a seemingly related issue] or ty necessary letters [an unrelated issue]?"

In a typical conflict, *you and other person grow apart as human beings,* lo the ability to communicate with each other as individuals, and see each other only as roles or symbols. A police officer who stops you after you go through a red light may change from "Officer Long", a unique individual (based on a past incident when he came to your house to investigate a break-in), to "officer," a role; to "cop," a negative term for the role; and, finally, to "pig," an animal symbolizing disrespect for law enforcement officials. Of course, you can't reason with a "pig," so productive communication ceases.

At the end of a typical lose–lose or win–lose conflict, *neither you nor the other person gets exactly what you want* (even though it may seem so in the short run), the possibility for a continuing relationship is damaged, and neither of you has positive self-feelings. A more productive way to management relationship discord is the win–win approach.

WIN–WIN CONFLICT MANAGEMENT

The purpose of **win–win conflict management** is to satisfy everyone's needs. This approach recognizes the importance of both the issue and the participants; neither person gives up something crucial and neither one feels that the relationship was damaged by the conflict management process or its outcomes. Success hinges on dedication to the win–win process and to the other person, mutual respect, and strong communication skills. Although true win–win conflict management is sometimes difficult to carry out, the results justify the effort.

The steps in win–win conflict management are:

STEP 1: *Define the conflict for yourself before approaching the other person.* This requires some self-analysis: What is your concern? Who or what is frustrating you? What is the source of conflict?

Once you understand the conflict from your perspective, approach the other person and agree on a time to talk. Don't spring the conflict on the other person without warning or bring it up when there isn't enough time to deal with it. If the other person feels attacked, he or she may become defensive, which will make it difficult for you to establish a supportive climate. Also agree on an appropriate place for your discussion. Certain locations may inhibit open and honest interaction. Attempting to deal with conflict in a public place, such as a restaurant, virtually assures failure.

STEP 2: *Communicate your understanding of the problem assertively to the other person.* This approach includes describing the other person's behaviors, as they affect you, in a direct, clear, nonjudgmental way. You must also communicate your interpretation of the situation and your feelings.

Once your own concerns are clear, invite the other person to express her or his concerns. Listen carefully to the content of the message and try to perceive the feelings that accompany it. Share your perceptions of the other person's point of view without labels ("That's stupid!") or insults ("You're crazy!"). Be sure you can state your partner's perspective to her or his satisfaction. Then reverse the process and encourage your partner to reiterate your point of view to your satisfaction.

When you complete this step, both you and your partner will have defined the problem specifically, described your feelings, and recounted the actions that led to the conflict and perpetuated it.

STEP 3:   *Based on your understanding of your own and the other's perspective, arrive at a mutual, shared definition of the problem and a mutual, shared goal.* Consider your areas of agreement and disagreement; figure out how you're dependent on one another. Discuss the consequences of the conflict for each of you.

STEP 4:   *Communicate your cooperative intentions.* Let your partner know that your aim is to satisfy the needs of both of you and to achieve your shared goals, and that you do not want to win by being competitive or combative. If you can (and it may be difficult under stressful conditions), communicate your intention in a calm, firm voice and invite your partner to join you in being cooperative.

Successful conflict resolution is impossible unless both you and your partner are motivated to behave cooperatively. If your partner is reluctant to cooperate, you may want to discuss what each of you gets out of continuing the conflict. Perhaps the conflict gives you something to complain about or an excuse to end the relationship. Or perhaps you feel threatened because a solution to your shared problem will require changes in your behavior. Whatever the reasons, they must be recognized and overcome before you can proceed.

STEP 5:   *Generate solutions to your shared problem.* Avoid discussing or evaluating each solution as it is generated; instead, generate as many ideas as you can. If you and your partner agree to defer evaluation, the number of possible solutions should be high. Be spontaneous and creative and build on each other's suggestions. Remember that even a foolish-sounding solution may contain a shred of useful information.[26]

STEP 6:   *After you've suggested all the solutions you can think of, evaluate them and select the best one.* How might each solution satisfy the shared goal? How easy or difficult would each be to implement?

STEP 7:   *Implement the solution.* First, be sure that you and your partner truly agree on which solution to implement. Make sure that you both agree fully and that you're not agreeing because you're tired, because you want to please your partner, or for some other reason that will later undermine the solution.

Second, agree on who does what, when, and how. If you don't specify the particulars, the groundwork may well be laid for the next conflict.

Third, do what needs to be done.

STEP 8: *Plan to check on how the solution is working.* You may have to adjust your plan or scrap the solution and generate a new one. The need for modification is a predictable consequence of changes brought on by time and an inability to foresee all possible outcomes during the initial problem-solving stage.

Although this eight-step procedure takes a lot of work, it pays off: in the end, both you and your partner will get what you want, strengthen your relationship, and feel good about yourselves. Furthermore, in the long run, the win–win approach takes less effort than do the other two approaches. Most importantly, the win–win approach lets you productively confront the problem—you don't have to let it fester unresolved. Win–lose and lose–lose approaches require repeated attempts to resolve the problems they themselves create, while the win–win approach usually gets at the problem and eliminates it.

Knowledge Checkup 11.6 will help you practice recognizing the three different negotiating styles. Recognizing each style is an important step in using each one when appropriate.

KNOWLEDGE CHECKUP 11.6

IDENTIFY THE NEGOTIATING STYLE

Identify the negotiating style being used in each of the situations, which is based on the conflict of your friend wanting to go to the movie while you want to study.

1. You discuss it and both happily agree that you both will study until a half-hour before the film starts, go to the movie, and then come right back to finish studying. Style _____

2. Your friend tells you that for the past three weeks she or he has done what you wanted to do. You give in and go to the movie, but are upset the rest of the evening. Style _____

3. Your friend refuses to study and you refuse to go to the movie. You both get so angry that she or he doesn't go to the movie, you don't study, and you both spend the evening pouting, slamming doors, and being obnoxious toward each other. Style _____

4. Your friend goes to the movie and you study. Style _____

ANSWERS: 1—WIN–WIN; 2—WIN-LOSE; 3—LOSE-LOSE; 4—WIN–WIN

OPTIONS FOR RESOLVING CONFLICT

In resolving conflict, at least tree options for change seem available: change the other person, try to alter the conflict conditions, or try to change your own behavior.

Trying to change the other person is nearly impossible.

People don't change unless they want to do so. Most people have found a system of operation that seems to work for them, or at least they have tried one on and feel comfortable using it, for whatever reasons. To lecture or point out the frailties or negatives of the style being used is often an exercise in futility. This does not mean that no change is possible, but you have to have the other person agree if there is going to be any lasting alterations in behavior.

Altering conflict conditions is a more hopeful solution.

By increasing the resources available, altering the interdependency, or changing the perceptions of the people or the goals, there may be some hope of altering the conflict. For example, sufficient resources are not available—such as money, or time, or other people to help out—and supplying these needed resources may be the way of dealing with the problem. Hiring help to clean the house or take care of the children may be the solution to giving a married couple the time they need to relax together. This could relieve the pressures of all work and no play that resulted in the stress they experienced.

One way to alter a conflict situation is to prescribe particular behaviors to enact when particular circumstances arise. The prescription takes one of two forms:

If _____ happens, then _____ *must/should* be done.

or

If _____ happens, then _____ *must not/ should not* be done.

Examples of ways to change the conflict situation are:

Situation 1: Frankie is the one-year-old child of Maria and Tom. Frankie has gotten into the habit of screaming and crying when he doesn't get his way. The physician has indicated that as long as Maria continues to pick up the child he will become more and more manipulative. Tom and Maria have been arguing over this matter for weeks.

Prescribed behavior: *When* Frankie throws a tantrum, then Maria *must not* pick him up.

Situation 2: Dennis has a pattern of withdrawing and pouting when he perceives someone is "picking on him." This is a source of major conflict between Dennis and his friend Chris.

Prescribed behavior: *When* Dennis withdraws because his feelings are hurt, Chris *must* let Dennis know how this is making Chris feel and let Dennis know that Chris will leave the apartment for a cooling-off period.

The prescribed behavior approach is an excellent method to use when the problem can be isolated and the participants are willing to work toward changing past patterns. Skill Development 11.6 will help you practice using the prescribed behavior approach.

PUTTING THE PRESCRIBED BEHAVIOR APPROACH INTO ACTION

Situation: Lois, Diane, and Tia have been friends since junior high school. Recently, Tia feels overwhelmed because Lois and Diane make plans to do things without asking her and then expect her to go along with them. If Tia refuses, they get angry and accuse her of trying to break up the friendship by being selfish. The three of them agree that they don't want to break up the longstanding friendship, but need some guidelines by which to operate.

Write two prescribed behavior resolutions.

When _____

must _____.

When _____

must not _____.

Changing your own behavior can be positive if you really want to make a change and you have the experience or abilities to do what is necessary.

Some people really want to change the way they deal with conflict but lack the skills. The materials in this chapter have been and are intended to reenforce those skills you already have and give you a new repertoire of competencies to use.

DEALING WITH DIFFICULT PEOPLE[27]

Sometimes conflicts occur when we encounter difficult people. These people tend to fall into prescribed categories: the complainer, the know-it-all, the hostile-aggressor, the clam, the wet blanket, and the agreeable person.

The *complainer* gripes constantly, but does nothing to improve the situation except complain. The *know-it-all* has all the right answers and, therefore, never has to listen to anyone else. The *hostile-aggressive* person bullies his or her way through life and, when that doesn't work, throws a tantrum, while the *clam* never participates so you have no way of knowing how she or he feels or thinks. The *wet blanket* believes that nothing which is not completely in her or his control will work and that others don't care about her or his feelings. The *agreeable person* wants to please so much that he or she will agree to take on tasks that can't possibly be handled.

How can these people be dealt with in a constructive conflict resolution style?

Since *complainers* feel powerless to determine their own fate, complaining seems their only choice of behavior. So, listen with attention to the complaints, even if you feel impatient or annoyed, and allow the person to blow off steam. Acknowledge that you've heard the complaint by paraphrasing it. Make the person take responsibility for doing something about the complaint so it is more than just whining words. Get the complainer to try to come up with a specific solution to the problem that is realistic and, if possible, encourage him or her to take on the task of carrying out the solution.

Know-it-alls are often difficult to deal with since they believe they are right. They act the way they do—arrogant and assertive—because the world is seen as a chaotic place in which facts and knowledge give power, and since these people derive power from knowledge, they think other people's observations are irrelevant. Normally, know-it-alls are excellent debaters. In dealing with this person, make sure you've done your homework and are prepared: Ask questions rather than make statements, and try to direct the conversation from concepts and theories to more concrete points. Acknowledge the input and try to get specific action. For example, "Yes, I agree that's how things should be done. Now, how do we go about it?" It does no good to get as arrogant as the know-it-alls.

One of the most difficult things to do when confronting a *hostile–aggressive person* is to avoid shouting back. Since the hostile-aggressive person tends to have a strong sense of the way things should be done and an incredible capacity for feeling hurt or wronged, he or she is often an insecure person whose bluster is an effective but thin defense. When hostile-aggressives shout, let them vent. Let them wind down. Ask them to sit down (most people are less aggressive when seated) and then present your point of view, always maintaining direct eye contact. For example, in dealing with a teenager angry at her mother, look her directly in the eye as you say, "I can see that you feel your mother is wrong, but she is doing what she feels is in your best interest." If the person continues to rant, calmly repeat the same phrase over and over. You aren't telling her she is wrong, but you've acknowledged the viewpoint.

The *clam* uses silence. She or he hides fears or strongly felt emotions by withdrawing and not communicating. If you want to get along with a clam, first give up trying to understand what the silence means. Instead, work toward opening the person up by asking open-ended questions, questions requiring more than one- word answers. Ask, "What do you think about that?" or "What can we do to solve the problem?" You will have to be patient. Wait for the response. If, after a reasonable period the person doesn't answer, ask the question again.

Wet blankets can sap your strength since they believe that they must be involved in every step of any action or it won't work. They also believe that those in power are incapable or don't care. Be careful not to get dragged down into their despair. Make optimistic but realistic comments about the situation or past similar situations; don't try to talk wet blankets out of their negativism—it just won't work. Don't offer solutions until the problem has been fully discussed. When a solution is discussed, raise the question of the negative events that might occur.

The *agreeable people* of the world have a strong desire to be liked. To do this they often make commitments they can't fulfill. They volunteer for impossible tasks, take on more than they can handle, accept deadlines they can't meet. Keep agreeable people from making unrealistic commitments. Encourage them to be realistic and remove the fear that they have that you won't like them if they don't do everything.

Skill Development 11.7 will help you practice communicating with difficult people.

| SKILL DEVELOPMENT 11.7 |

DEALING WITH DIFFICULT PEOPLE

Identify the "difficult people type" and specifically indicate how you would communicate to each:

Situation: The University Social Committee is meeting.

1. Miguelle always comes up with the first suggestion and then goes on to prove adamantly he is right.
   Miguelle: "There is only one theme for the party. We should have a toga blast. According to the report from last year's social committee, it was the most popular event held. Besides, before I transferred here I was in charge of a toga party on the other campus, and it was great."
   Type:
   An appropriate action:

2. Bill, who is nearly failing school because he is taking a full academic load, holding a part-time job, serving on three university committees, and acting as treasurer of his fraternity, immediately agrees with Miguelle and says, "I'll volunteer to get the togas, order the food, and decorate."
   Type:
   An appropriate action:

3. Regina: "That's a lousy idea. Nothing we ever do around here is any fun. This is going to be another flop. Why can't we ever do something that isn't dumb?"

Type:

An appropriate action:

4. Ariel: (Jumps out of his chair and screams) "This is totally stupid! Everyone is always giving in to Miguelle just because he transferred here from a Big Ten school. What a bunch of wimps! You always get led around by your noses! You never listen to my ideas or anyone else's, only Miguelle's!"

Type:

An appropriate action:

5. Mika just sits there, saying nothing, as usual.

Type:

An appropriate action:

Types: Miguelle—Know-It-All; Bill—Agreeable person; Regina—Complainer; Ariel—Hostile-Aggressive; Mika—The Clam

ASSESSING CONFLICT PROCESSES AND OUTCOMES

Assessing the process and outcomes of a conflict can help you understand its constructive and destructive consequences.[28] Are your communication skills effective for managing relationship discord? What can you do to improve your conflict management strategies?

Skill Development 11.8 will help you analyze the process of a conflict by building a process profile.

SKILL DEVELOPMENT 11.8

BUILDING A CONFLICT PROCESS PROFILE

Think of a recently resolved conflict in which you and another person were involved and write a brief summary of the situation. Using the answers below each question, circle the word that best describes the process of the conflict.

1. To what extent did each person agree that there was a problem?

strongly agreed   agreed   disagreed   strongly disagreed

2. To what extent did each person agree on what the problem was?

strongly agreed   agreed   disagreed   strongly disagreed

3. How did each person appear to enter into the discussion?

cooperatively   somewhat cooperatively   somewhat competitively   competitively

4. How were possible solutions generated?

cooperatively   somewhat cooperatively   somewhat competitively   competitively

5. How were the possible solutions evaluated?

cooperatively   somewhat cooperatively   somewhat competitively   competitively

6. How committed was each person to the selected solution?

very committed   committed   somewhat committed   uncommitted

7. To what extent did each person agree on how to implement the solution?

strongly agreed   agreed   disagreed   strongly disagreed

8. How were feelings and ideas expressed?

openly   somewhat openly   guardedly   not at all

9. To what extent did each person perceive the problem from the other's perspective?

totally   moderately   somewhat   hardly at all

After you have answered the nine questions, join your circled answers with a line going from the first one to the last. This line graphically represents your Conflict Process Profile. If the line stays mainly to the left, your conflict process was constructive, but if it stays mainly to the right, your conflict process was probably dysfunctional. If your circled answers form a jagged line, you can pinpoint your weak areas by looking at the items for which your responses fell to the right side.

1. What were the constructive aspects of your conflict process?

2. What were the dysfunctional aspects of your conflict process?

3. What did you learn about yourself as a participant in this conflict that you can apply to future conflicts?

The analysis of a conflict has two parts. You have already completed the first part, an assessment of the conflict process. The second part focuses on outcomes.

Skill Development 11.9 will help you analyze the outcomes of a conflict by developing an outcomes profile.

SKILL DEVELOPMENT 11.9

DEVELOPING A CONFLICT OUTCOMES PROFILE

Based on the same situation that you used to complete Skill Development 11.8, circle the word below each question that best describes the process of your conflict.

1. How effective was the solution in dealing with the problem?

effective   somewhat effective   somewhat ineffective   ineffective

2. How did you feel about yourself and your behavior while you were working toward conflict resolution?

positive   somewhat positive   somewhat negative   negative

3. How did you feel about the other person and her or his behavior while you were working toward conflict resolution?

positive   somewhat positive   somewhat negative   negative

4. How did you feel about your and the other person's relationship before the conflict?

positive   somewhat positive   somewhat negative   negative

5. How did you feel about the relationship after the conflict was resolved?

positive   somewhat positive   somewhat negative   negative

Join your circled answers with a line going from the first response (1) to the last (5). This line graphically represents your Conflict Outcomes Profile. A line that stays predominantly to the left represents a constructive conflict, while a line that stays predominantly to the right suggests a dysfunctional conflict. Questions for which your circled responses fall to the right indicate your trouble spots.

1. What were the constructive aspects of your conflict outcomes?

2. What were the dysfunctional aspects of your conflict outcomes?

3. What did you learn about yourself as a participant in this conflict that you can apply to future conflicts?

Every conflict has the potential to be constructive—to help you, the other person, and your relationship. Your understanding of conflict and how to manage it can increase your ability to communicate effectively and, therefore, increase the probability of your having constructive conflicts.

COMMUNICATION COMPETENCY CHECKUP

The goal of this Communication Competency Checkup is to guide you in putting your skills and knowledge about managing relational discord to use, and to help you summarize the material in this chapter.

"Harrison, we never fight.
I've heard that people who really love each other fight."

Drawing by Weber; © 1979 The New Yorker Magazine, Inc.

1. Is the woman correct in her assessment of conflict being a normal part of relationships? Assume this interchange followed the statement made in the cartoon:

   HE: You're always looking for trouble, leave well enough alone.

   SHE: Why do you always change the subject and not want to talk about things that bother either of us?

HE: You sound just like your mother. She always wanted to talk things to death. She would start fights so she could be the winner. That woman had a nasty mouth.

SHE: That is the stupidest thing I ever heard of. That's ridiculous. Why are you always saying nasty things about my mother?

HE: There you go again, calling me stupid and ridiculous. You asked whether people who love each other fight? Well, I usually just keep quiet, but if you want to fight, I'll give you a good one!

SHE: All I did was tell you what I heard.

2. Describe the conflict between him and her with respect to their interdependence and the sources of their conflict.

3. Describe the relational discord using the want-but-wants formula.

4. What are the possible consequences of this conflict?

5. What are the possible effects on the relationship of this conflict?

6. What tools of the verbal shooting gallery is she using?

7. Which conflict strategy did she describe that he used?

8. Which conflict strategy does he describe her mother using?

9. Give an example of direct aggression used in this conflict.

10. What simple assertion could he have made, rather than his opening statement, in order to avoid the confrontation?

11. Assume that she has "bated" him before about the same issue. Write an A*S*S*E*R*T script that he could have used rather than the approach he took.

12. What conflict management style does he attribute to her mother?

13. "How can I assess what the results of the conflict are?" he asks you. Describe a procedure he can use to assess whether conflict process was functional or not.

14. If these people were Asian or English, would this type of conflict probably take place? Why or why not? Write a statement to put under the cartoon that would represent either of those cultures.

NOTES

1. Joyce Hocker and William W. Wilmot, *Interpersonal Conflict,* 3d ed. (Dubuque, IA: Wm. C. Brown, 1991).

2. Lennie Copeland and Lewis Griggs, *Going International* (New York: Random House, 1985), p. 109.

3. Diana Rowland, *Japanese Business Etiquette* (New York: Warner Books, 1985), p. 5.

4. Hocker and Wilmot, *Interpersonal Conflict.*

5. Harvey L. Ruben, *Competing, Understanding, and Winning the Strategic Games We All Play* (New York: Lippincott & Crowell, 1980), as quoted in John W. (Sam) Keltner, *Mediation—Toward a Civilized System of Dispute* (Annandale, VA, Speech Communication Association, 1987), p. 5.

6. Larry A. Samovar and Richard E. Porter, *Communication Between Cultures* (Belmont, CA: Wadsworth Publishing Company, 1991), p. 108.

7. G. L. Mastalli, "Appendix: The Legal Context," *Harvard Business Review* 59.2 (1981): 94–95.

8. Ann L. Darling, "Talking About Sex in the Classroom: What Can We Learn from the William Kennedy Smith Trial?" paper presented at the meeting of the Speech Communication Association, Chicago, November 1992.

9. C. L. Muehlenhard and L. C. Hollabaugh, "Do Women Sometimes Say No When They Mean Yes? The Prevalence and Correlates of Women's Token Resistance to Sex," *Journal of Personality and Social Psychology* 54 (1988): 872–79.

10. Cathy Guisewite, *Cathy,* Universal Press Syndicate, April 18, 1985.

11. Kathleen M. Galvin and Bernard J. Brommel, *Family Communication: Cohesion and Change,* 3d ed. (New York: HarperCollins, 1991), pp. 7–11.

12. Susan E. Crohan, "Marital Happiness and Spousal Consensus on Beliefs About Marital Conflict: A Longitudinal Investigation," *Journal of Social and Personal Relationships* 9 (1992): 89–102.

13. *Thomas-Kilmann Conflict Mode Instrument,* a handout; Joyce L. Hocker and William W. Wilmot, "Teaching a College Course on Conflict and Communication," Western Communication Association, Tucson, Arizona, February 1986.

14. Daniel Canary and William R. Cupach, "Relational and Episodic Characteristics Associated with Conflict Tactics," *Journal of Social and Personal Relationships* 5 (1988): 305–25; Hocker and Wilmot, *Interpersonal Conflict;* David W. Miguelleson, *Human Relations and Your Career,* 2d ed. (Englewood Cliffs, NJ: Prentice-Hall, 1987), chapters 9 and 10.

15. Karen J. Prager, "Intimacy Status and Couple Conflict Resolution," *Journal of Social and Personal Relationships* 8 (1991): 505–26.

16. Based on the handout, Hocker and Wilmot, "Teaching a College Course."

17. Ibid., original source Putnam/Wilson Conflict Styles Instrument.

18. Alex F. Osborn, *Applied Imagination,* rev. ed. (New York: Scribners, 1957).

19. Anita Vangelisti, John A. Daly, and Janine Rae Rudnick, "Making People Feel Guilty in Conversation: Techniques and Correlates," *Human Communication Research* 18 (1991): 3–39.

20. William B. Gudykunst and Stella Ting-Toomey, *Culture and Interpersonal Communication* (Newbury Park, CA: Sage Publications, 1988), p. 158.

21. Dominick Infante and C. J. Wigley III, "Verbal Aggressiveness: An Interpersonal Model and Measure," *Communication Monographs* 53 (1986): 61–69.

22. C. E. Rusbult, "Responses to Dissatisfaction in Close Relationships: The Exit-Voice-Loyalty-Neglect Model," in *Intimate Relationships: Development, Dynamics and Deterioration,* Daniel Perlman and Steve Duck (Eds.) (London: Sage, 1987), p. 209.

23. For a discussion of male-female differences, see: M. F. Belenky, B. M. Clinchy, N. R. Goldberger, and J. M. Tarule, *Women's Ways of Knowing: The Development of Self, Voice and Mind* (New York: Basic Books, 1986); N. Chodorow, *The Reproduction of Motherhood* (Berkeley: University of California Press, 1978); Carol Gilligan, *In a Different Voice: Psychological Theory and Women's Development* (Cambridge, MA: Harvard University Press, 1982); Deborah Tannen, *You Just Don't Understand: Women and Men in Conversation* (New York: Morrow, 1990).

24. C. E. Rusbult and J. Iwaniszek, "Problem-solving in Male and Female Homosexual and Heterosexual Relationships," unpublished manuscript, University of Kentucky, Lexington, 1986.

25. Julia T. Wood and Lawrence B. Rosenfeld, "Gender, Sexual Preference and Definitions and Responses to Relationship Crises," unpublished manuscript, Department of Speech Communication, University of North Carolina at Chapel Hill, 1991.

26. Osborn, *Applied Imagination.*

27. Based on materials from Robert Bramson, *Coping with Difficult People in Business and in Life* (New York: Dell, 1988); G. Corey, *I Never Knew I Had A Choice* (Pacific Grove, CA: Brooks-Cole, 1990); Michael Doyle and David Straus, *How to Make Meetings Work* (New York: Jove Publishing, 1986).

28. Ronald B. Adler, *Confidence in Communication: A Guide to Assertive and Social Skills* (New York: Holt, Rinehart and Winston, 1977).

FOR FURTHER INVESTIGATION

Bach, George R., and Peter Wyden. *The Intimate Enemy.* New York: Avon, 1968.

Barnland, Dean. *Communicative Styles of Japanese and Americans: Images and Realities.* Belmont, CA: Wadsworth Publishing Company, 1989.

Bower, Sharon, and Gordon H. Bower. *Asserting Yourself: A Practical Guide for Positive Change.* Reading, MA: Addison-Wesley, 1976.

Ellis, Donald G., and B. Aubrey Fisher, "Phases of Conflict in Small Group Development." *Human Communication Research* 1 (1975): 195–212.

Fisher, Roger, and W. Ury. *Getting to Yes: Negotiating Agreement Without Giving In.* Boston: Houghton-Mifflin, 1981.

Forward, Susan. *Men Who Hate Women and the Women Who Love Them.* New York: Bantam, 1986.

Halpern, Howard. *How to Break Your Addiction to a Person.* New York: Bantam, 1983.

Handly, Robert. *Anxiety and Panic Attacks: Their Cause and Cure.* New York: Rawson and Associates, 1985.

Hocker, Joyce L., and William W. Wilmot. *Interpersonal Conflict,* 3d ed. Dubuque, IA: Wm. C. Brown, 1991.

Johnson, David W., and Frank P. Johnson. *Joining Together,* 4th ed. Englewood Cliffs, NJ: Prentice-Hall, 1992.

Keltner, John W. (Sam). *Mediation—Toward a Civilized System of Dispute Resolution.* Annandale, VA: Speech Communication Association, 1987.

Kincaid, D. L., ed. *Communication Theory: Eastern and Western Perspectives.* San Diego: Academic Press, 1987.

Kline, Nathan. *From Sad to Glad.* New York: Ballantine, 1974.

Pearson, Judy C. *Gender and Communica-*

tion, 3d ed. Dubuque, IA: Wm. C. Brown, 1991.

Rosenfeld, Lawrence B., and Mary W. Jarrard. "Student Coping Mechanisms in Sexist and Nonsexist Professors' Classes." *Communication Education* 35 (1986): 157–62.

Thomas, Kenneth. "Conflict and Conflict Management." In Marvin D. Dunnette, ed., *Handbook of Industrial and Organizational Psychology.* Chicago: Rand McNally, 1976.

CHAPTER 12

Creativity, Power, and Interpersonal Satisfaction

COMMUNICATION COMPETENCIES

This chapter examines the relationship of creativity and power to interpersonal satisfaction. Specifically, the objective of the chapter is for you to learn to:

- Recognize the differences between creative and more usual thinking.
- Specify the relational benefits of being creative.
- Recognize cultural and personal obstacles to creativity.
- Develop your creativity by learning how to form new associations, apply the technique of analytic breakdown, and manipulate the details of objects.
- Recognize the consequences of feeling both powerful and powerless.
- Determine your sources of power in particular relationships.
- Develop strategies for enhancing your power.
- Choose the most appropriate sources of power in particular circumstances.
- Increase the extent to which your language reflects feelings of powerfulness.

KEY WORDS

The key words in this chapter are:

creative thinking	legitimate power
usual thinking	commitment
power	compliance
powerless	powerful language
formal power bases	powerless language
informal power bases	hedges
expert power	qualifiers
referent power	hesitations
associative power	tag question
reward power	disclaimers
coercive power	

What happens when you and a partner in a relationship have a problem? What do you do to resolve your differences? Circle the number of those responses that best describe how you go about solving problems in your relationships.

1. I look for a method and a plan for solving the problem.
2. I think a lot about how I'm approaching the problem while trying to resolve it.
3. I discard alternatives quickly and try to identify the best solution.
4. I conduct an orderly search for additional information.
5. I redefine the problem as I proceed.
6. I rely on my hunches.
7. I consider a number of alternatives and options simultaneously.
8. I jump from one step to another and back again as I analyze the situation.

The first four statements describe people's *usual thinking* about problem solving, whereas the second four define a less typical, more *creative approach*. If you circled more in the second group than the first, you may be a creative problem solver.

CREATIVITY

Creativity is one of the buzz words of the late twentieth century: In modern North American thinking, to be creative is to be valued—even if the creative person may sometimes be labeled as an eccentric, a nonconformist, or a troublemaker. We value creativity because it affords us the ability to create things that are new and different and to think in unusual ways—and the new and the unusual are what make life exciting! Ironically, we may label creative people negatively because they force us to think in different modes, approach typical problem-solving techniques from new perspectives, and, in general, decrease our feeling secure.

Creative thinking, also called lateral or divergent thinking, parallels the mind's process of scanning laterally, looking for alternatives and ideas and expanding and diverging as it continues (see Figure 12.1). **Usual thinking**, also called vertical or convergent thinking, is more linear, concerning itself with one alternative or idea at a time and building one thought on the other, vertically, in a process that converges as it proceeds, narrowing in on fewer and fewer ideas and alternatives.

Are you more comfortable with creative or usual thinking? Usual thinkers are more comfortable with creating a well-developed plan for solving a problem, understanding how to approach a problem, and conducting an orderly search for information. They often ignore hunches, refrain from redefining a problem, and avoid considering several alternatives simultaneously.

In contrast, creative thinking requires a "looseness" that includes relying on hunches, avoiding overpreparedness, allowing a problem to be redefined as new

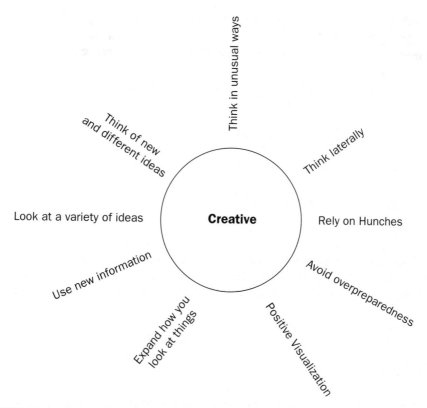

FIGURE 12.1   CHARACTERISTICS OF CREATIVITY

information arises, and simultaneously looking at a variety of ideas and alternatives. Creativity calls for faith in yourself—faith that you can do what needs to be done by *expanding* how you look at things instead of *narrowing* your focus.

Creativity offers many benefits, all of which can contribute to the quality of relationships:

▪ Creativity is essential if you hope to solve difficult mutual problems that conventional approaches usually can't settle.

▪ Creativity can keep you out of ruts. When you can predict the contents of a ten-minute dialogue that you and another person will have, you are in a well-worn rut, one that could increase feelings of dissatisfaction and boredom. It is common for couples, after knowing each other for a long time, to avoid certain topics altogether because each knows what both will say and how each will react. The end result can be a stifled, though safe, relationship.

▪ Creativity is important if you hope to discover alternatives that are potentially easier and more satisfying ways of doing things—whether dividing up household chores, deciding where to go on a night out, or completing a group assignment.

- Creativity is important if you want to discover new ways for your relationships to develop.

- Creativity is useful if you are to adapt effectively to the many and diverse cultures that you will be facing.

The potential benefits of being creative have a common goal: more satisfying, exciting, developing relationships.

OBSTACLES TO CREATIVITY

Small children are naturally creative, probably because no one has yet told them to "think logically" or to "stay in the lines when you color." They think of unique methods of reaching the cookie jar on top of the refrigerator, novel ways of putting unconnected thoughts together (a child we know was told to "look at the car being towed," which he converted to "look at the Carbine Toad," a two-gun-carrying, ten-gallon hat-wearing frog), and poetic ways to use language (referring to "smashed" rather than "mashed" potatoes, a "rubbish" rather than "rummage" sale, and the sink "overfloating"). Guess the age of the author who, upon seeing a sunset, declared: "I'd love to go for a ride on the rays and go to bed in sheets made of clouds."[1]

A four-year-old made that unique and creative statement. Before the age of four, a child spends as much as half the time dreaming, having hundreds of unconnected thoughts; from about three to five years of age, he or she spends half the time engaged in poetic thinking, intuitively making associations and using metaphors and similes; and from about age four to age six, half the time is spent inventing, putting the poetic similes to practical use, such as by turning a stool, a drawer, and a counter top into "steps" to climb to some desired cookies.[2]

You may have trouble remembering your own creative acts as a child because of the obstacles that parents and teachers raised in your path—obstacles that said, "Don't be creative." Most of us heard do's and don'ts that included, "Don't make a fool of yourself," "Follow the rules," and "That's not the right way to do this."

Creative people are often difficult to understand, cope with, and be around,. While people speak of creativity with respect, they often prefer that it belong to someone else's offspring. (Few parents would wish their child to write poetry like Emily Dickinson if it also meant that the child be a social isolate, as she was.)

Obstacles to creativity may be classified as either cultural or personal barriers.

Cultural Obstacles

Cultural obstacles stem from the values and attitudes that our society considers important. For example, where on the one hand, the high value that North American society places on individuality and competition should encourage the

risk taking required for creative problem solving, the high value it also places on logic and practicality may inhibit solutions requiring feelings and imagination. Adults learn that to be other than serious and humorless—except during specified times—is to risk being perceived as frivolous. For example, although teachers may say they like students who are creative, challenging, and assertive, they really seem to prefer students who are pleasant, compliant, and obedient.[3]

Personal Obstacles

There are three *personal obstacles* to creativity: habitual ways of doing things, beliefs about how things are, and fear of failure. Examining these three obstacles can make you aware of their negative effects.

Habitual Ways of Doing Things   People tend to act swiftly, guided only by their habits. Habits curb the natural urge to be creative. As a brief experiment, try the following: Fold your arms across your chest. Note which arm is on top. Now, put your arms at your side and, once again, fold them across your chest—only this time change which arm is on top. How does this feel?

Most people feel uncomfortable changing their customary way of doing things, and some find it difficult to do at all. When crossing their arms in an unaccustomed way, some people, for example, wind up holding an elbow without realizing it; others must give the task some strong concentration; and still others keep rotating their arms, unable to decide when to stop.

What habits determine your interaction when you meet someone for the first time? Do you always say the same things in the same order, such as, "Hi, my name is _____," followed by, "How are you?," followed by, "Hardly anyone in this area was born here, so where are you from?" What happens when the answer to your first question is, "I just got out of the hospital"? Do you automatically ask where the person is from, even though a different question would be more appropriate? How ingrained is your meeting-new-people habit?

Not all habits are harmful, of course. Most habits, in themselves, are helpful, such as when a task is easily performed or done very often. These tasks do not require reflection or the development of "new and improved ways" of doing them. However, not all tasks can or should be accomplished while on "automatic pilot." When you fail to question the "why" of these habits, you hinder your effectiveness in solving new problems and interacting with people.

Most habitual ways of *behaving* are easy to recognize once they're pointed out. Habitual ways of *looking at things* are more difficult to recognize and they inhibit creative thinking. People often believe that solutions and ideas can be found in comfortable, usual ways of looking at things, and often they fall into the habit of presuming that a problem has only one solution—especially after they have found the solution.

Look at the droodle (a drawing that appears meaningless until it is given a title) in Figure 12.2. One possible title for this illustration is "Two Corpuscles Who Loved in Vein." Can you think of other titles?

Because the problem of what the drawing means is solved by the title, you may find it difficult to come up with other titles. Similarly, if you yourself had generated a title, instead of being given one, coming up with other titles also might be troublesome. Once you know one title, you may accept it as the *only* solution and have difficulty devising other choices.

The first step to overcoming such a limited viewpoint is to recognize your habits, and the second step is to break away from them. To be creative and develop new ideas, you must stop your customary ways of behaving and looking at things.

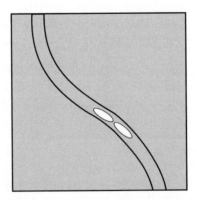

FIGURE 12.2   DROODLE

And to change your typical responses, you must reject the comfortable answers that habits automatically provide. Knowledge Checkup 12.1 provides you with the opportunity to examine a habit many people share: saying no before imaginatively thinking of what the answer actually is.

KNOWLEDGE CHECKUP 12.1

EXAMINING THE HABIT OF SAYING NO

Do you think you could recognize at least twenty-five varieties of dogs? If you're a dog enthusiast, you probably would answer yes. You may have answered yes even if you were not. But most people answer no, even though they probably know most, if not all, of these thirty-three breeds:

Boxer	Dalmatian	St. Bernard
Bloodhound	Great Dane	Beagle
German Shepherd	English Setter	Pointer
Labrador Retriever	Scottish Terrier	Fox Terrier
Pekingese	Dachshund	Collie
Boston (Bull) Terrier	Pomeranian	Mixed
English Springer Spaniel	Doberman Pincher	Dingo
Irish Setter	English Bulldog	Spitz
Golden Retriever	Chow	French Poodle
Afghan	Greyhound	Samoan
Sheep Dog	Chihuahua	Siberian Husky

You probably know more about almost anything than you give yourself credit for. The mental habit of saying no to a question rather than making the effort to figure out the answer curtails thinking and stifles creativity. You are probably more creative than you realize! In fact, you could probably generate another long list of breeds of dogs to add to the one in the knowledge checkup—or did you automatically say, "No, I can't"?

Beliefs   A second obstacle to your creativity is your beliefs about the world, about how things "are." Although reality is based only on perception, people usually create beliefs about the world around them and then fail to think any further. *The* *belief becomes the reality.* The six blind men of Hindustan, to whom you were introduced in Chapter 5 on language, each examined a different part of an elephant and described the whole elephant based on that part. They missed the reality of the elephant by accepting the belief that "What I perceive is all there is to perceive."

Do you believe that married couples should live happily ever after, that men should work outside the home and "bring home the bacon," and that women should stay home and take care of the children? If you mistake your beliefs for reality, how do you begin to respond to marital arguments (your own or others) or other people's differing definitions of their roles in relationships?

Creativity requires open-mindedness, the willingness to receive new information, perspectives, assumptions, beliefs, and opinions. Recognize that your beliefs are merely beliefs—not reality—and you can begin to stimulate your creativity, to think in new and exciting ways. Skill Development 12.1 provides you with the opportunity to overcome some old beliefs.

SKILL DEVELOPMENT 12.1

OVERCOMING BELIEFS

Connect the nine dots by using *no more than four straight lines* without lifting your pen or pencil from the paper. Create at least two solutions.

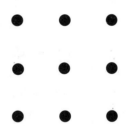

There are a variety of ways to connect the nine dots, and each requires overcoming a belief. Look at the examples on page 411.

To complete the exercise any of those ways, you needed to overcome the belief that it's important to stay within the lines of the imaginary box. For instance, in Example 1, you needed to go outside the box.

Look at example 2. This solution requires that you overcome the belief that lines are thin and that "no more than four" does not mean "four."

Look at example 3. This solution requires that you overcome the belief that you can't alter the drawing of the dots, or that "connect" means "go through the center."

A fourth approach folds the page accordion style so that the three rows of dots are touching each other. You can then connect them all with one thin line—as long as you can overcome the belief that the page needs to remain flat.

Did you create any other solutions?

Fear of Failure When people have creative thoughts, they often hesitate to share them. Knowledge Checkup 12.2 will help you to identify some of your own reasons for keeping new ideas to yourself.

KNOWLEDGE CHECKUP 12.2

IDENTIFYING REASONS FOR NOT SHARING CREATIVE THOUGHTS

Check each reason you might have for not sharing one of your creative, imaginative, unique, or novel ideas.

_____ I was afraid.

_____ It sounded stupid.

_____ It seemed impractical.

_____ It was too odd.

_____ It was too abstract.

_____ People would think I was crazy.

_____ It was too personal.

_____ It was hard to express.

_____ It wasn't like other people's ideas.

_____ People would make fun of me.

_____ I was taught to be seen and not heard.

_____ I wanted to agree with what others had to say.

_____ It was foolish.

_____ Other _____

At the root of all these reasons for avoiding sharing creative thoughts is the fear of failing at something, whether it is failing at being a "strong person" (who is fearless and sane), an "intelligent person" (who is smart and practical), a "good communicator" (who is agreeable and able to put complex ideas into understandable words), or some other type of person.[4]

Like most people, you might be anxious about expressing your ideas. This often prevents you from offering or even considering all the ideas you think up. You may have learned—and believe—that new ideas are ridiculed, that your ideas don't count for much, that you need to be perfect, or that people want agreement, not creativity.

DEVELOPING YOUR CREATIVITY

Regardless of the many obstacles to creativity, the situation is not hopeless: no one is doomed to be unimaginative, dull, and boring. There are simple ways to exercise your mind back into shape—mental aerobics—that include forming new associations, using analytic breakdown, and manipulating details. As a result, you will be capable of handling relationships and confronting daily problems with energy and, importantly, creativity.

Forming New Associations

Many of the associations people make stem from fixed ways of looking at things that they learned as children and never bothered to change. For example, consider your automatic responses to these word combinations:

bread and _____

ham and _____

hot and _____

short and _____

If you said "butter," "eggs" or "cheese," "cold," and "tall" or "fat," you made habitual responses. Such associations are made almost by reflex. Skill Development 12.2 provides you with several opportunities for breaking old habits and *forming new associations.*

SKILL DEVELOPMENT 12.2

FORMING NEW ASSOCIATIONS[5]

PART I

Pick two words at random from the following list. Combine them to invent a new product or something that improves on either of the two original items. (For example, an "apple suitcase" can be a suitcase in the shape of an apple, a suitcase made especially to transport apples or an Apple computer, or maybe a suitcase made of apple skins.) Do this for two pairs of words.

apple	suitcase	glass	basket
bottle	hook	shoe	pen
hand	star	phone	wax
chair	magazine	band	comb
tar	disk	clip	typewriter

Association 1: _____

Association 2: _____

PART II

Write two rhyming words that apply to each of the following definitions. For example, "boob tube" is a pair of rhyming words that together define "television."

1. A feline rug
2. A useless musical percussion instrument
3. An ill person brought up in the "back woods"
4. An angry young male
5. A person who murders for the fun of it

PART III

Find one word that ties together each group of three words. For example, the words "base," "meat," and "bearing" all have the word "ball" in common (as in a baseball, a meatball, and a ball bearing).

1. night, bulb, and sky
2. ever, bean, and light
3. down, over, and through

Activities such as these help you develop skills that expand how you perceive things. If you have the opportunity, share your responses with your classmates. Sharing perceptions expands your perceptual frame and enriches your way of looking at things. What word combinations struck you as unique and imaginative? How did your rhymes compare with those created by others? Did you all agree that a feline rug is a *cat mat,* a broken percussion instrument a *bum drum,* an ill person from the "back woods" a *sick hick,* an angry young male a *mad lad,* and a person who murders for the fun of it a *thriller killer?* And did you think of "light," "green," and "run" as possible tie-ins?

The only way to form new associations is through conscious effort. The more you set aside habitual associations and practice making new connections, the higher the probability that you will be creative in other aspects of your life, including your relationships.

Analytic Breakdown

A second technique for increasing your creativity is *analytical breakdown* in which a complex problem is broken into its individual components, listing as many alternatives as possible for each component, and then combining the alternatives to create new variations. Assume, for example, that you wanted to improve staff meetings in an office. This is a complex problem that can be broken down into several key issues. For example, one issue is *when* to have a meeting, a second is *where* to have it, a third is *who* should attend, and a fourth is *what* to discuss. As you consider the situation, you note that *when* includes (at least) before opening, morning, lunchtime, afternoon, and after closing; *where* includes (at least) your office, someone else's office, the coffee room, a restaurant, someone's house, and a

---

TABLE 12.1 ANALYTIC BREAKDOWN: HOW TO IMPROVE STAFF MEETINGS

WHEN	WHERE	WHO	WHAT
before opening	my office	everyone	office procedures
morning	another office	managers	interface: public
lunchtime	coffee room	staff	salary
afternoon	house	managers/staff	new personnel
after closing	restaurant	one dept.	scheduling
	park	two+ depts.	new products
			productivity

nearby park; *who* includes (at least) everyone, managers only, staff only, managers and staff, personnel from one office, and personnel from two or more departments; and *what* includes (at least) discussion of office procedures, dealing with the public, salary concerns, new personnel issues, scheduling, new product possibilities, and improving productivity.

By placing one key issue at the top of a column and generating a list of alternatives for each heading, you can begin to see possibilities that you may not have thought of before (Table 12.1). When the information is laid out in columns, you can visualize the various combinations that will lead to a variety of potential meeting formats.

Skill Development 12.3 will help you practice using the technique of analytic breakdown when planning weekend activities.

SKILL DEVELOPMENT 12.3

DOING AN ANALYTIC BREAKDOWN

Problem: Jointly planning activities with a close friend for the upcoming weekend to ensure the greatest amount of fun.

1. Divide the problem into its component parts. (For example, one component might be *who* could join you and your friend over the weekend, a second might be *where* you could go, a third might be *when* you could plan to do something, and a fourth might be *what* you could do.)

2. Divide a sheet of paper into as many columns as you have components and head each column with the name of a different component (you may use the four components suggested here and add to them).

3. Generate as many alternatives as possible under each heading.

4. Select the combination of choices from each column that solves the problem in the most satisfactory way. To find the best solution, you may want to develop several combinations and compare and contrast them.

Manipulating Details

A third method for increasing creativity is *manipulating the details* that you notice about an object. For example, you can change something by enlarging it, making it smaller, dividing it, rotating it, stretching it, hardening it, softening it, flattening it, flipping it, squeezing it, freezing it, heating it, rearranging it, shortening it, changing it, fluffing it up, and patting it down.

Consider that dollhouses, midget racers, and the many items made for travel, such as hair dryers, resulted from applying the verb *minify*. Large-print books resulted from applying the verb *enlarge*. Frozen food and other forms of packaging all came from attempts to manipulate the details of an object. In Skill Development 12.4, you will manipulate details to find a creative solution to a problem.

SKILL DEVELOPMENT 12.4

CREATING NEW GIFT IDEAS: MANIPULATING THE DETAILS OF A FORK

Create ten unique gifts for friends by manipulating the details of a fork. (Assume you can create anything that you think of.) For example, you may *enlarge*—and give one friend a ten-foot sculpture of a fork to put in front of her restaurant, or you might wish to *extend*—and give a very busy friend a fork with a one-foot handle so he can eat while standing. Be creative!

As you gain experience with forming new associations, doing analytic breakdowns, and manipulating the details of objects, you will stretch your mind and increase your capacity for creativity. The benefit to be gained—more satisfying relationships—is well worth the effort.

Just as being more creative increases the satisfaction and enjoyment you can experience in all your relationships, so does being more powerful. And there are a variety of creative ways for increasing your power—your influence and your feeling of being in control—in your relationships.

POWER

Consider the following four questions: Is your answer to each a *definite yes* (Y), a *possible yes* (PY), a *tentative no* (TN), or an *unequivocal no* (N)?

_____ 1. Do you have confidence in yourself, trust your feelings, and maintain a sense of personal worth regardless of the reactions of others?

_____ 2. Do you like yourself, including your perceived faults?

_____ 3. Do you remain optimistic even when someone finds fault with something you've done?

_____ 4. Do you feel self-confident enough to encourage the people around you to develop their abilities even though they may surpass your own?

The extent to which you responded positively to each question reflects your feelings of being powerful, of being in control of your options. People with power are more likely to be happy with themselves and their relationships, to enjoy physical and emotional health, to savor their work and play, and to feel the most self-satisfaction. People without power are likely to feel less happy with themselves and their relationships, less likely to enjoy physical and emotional health, less satisfied with their work and play, and less self-satisfaction. The powerless are more likely to be depressed and suffer from a range of mental illnesses.

A DEFINITION OF POWER

Power is the ability to control what happens—to create things you want to happen and to block things you don't want to happen.[6] To put it simply, *power* is the ability to choose. Roget's Thesaurus lists the following synonyms for powerful: *potent, capable, strong, competent, energetic, influential,* and *productive.* In contrast, the synonyms for *powerless* are *impotent, incapable, weak,* and *incompetent.*

Defining power as the ability to control what happens and to choose, clarifies several preconceptions. First, the power to choose is not bad, but rather something that is exercised in every human transaction. The view of power as bad may stem from its abuse (often in the form of winning at someone else's expense), from its contradiction of the belief that all humans should be equal, or from its waste (as when there's really no opportunity to gain anything and large amounts of resources are thrown away in the process, such as spending time and money on a former romantic partner who does not intend to begin a new relationship with you). In fact, power, the ability to make choices, is desirable, not bad.

Based on the definition, it is also simplistic to say that one person is "more powerful" than another or that someone is "powerless." Every person may be more or less powerful or powerless, depending on the situation, its dimensions, and its participants. Thus, you have power and you are powerful—maybe not with everyone, at all times, and in every circumstance, but certainly with some people, at some times, and in particular settings.

While powerful people may be corrupt, it is not their power itself that corrupts, but their need or desire to win at others' expense. It is not power that is a problem, but the feeling of powerlessness. People who feel they are **powerless**—who feel they cannot control events in their lives or affect others—often make life miserable for themselves and those around them.

People who feel powerless often lack the ability to make choices about their relationships, such as which to maintain and which to terminate. They may feel that they don't have the ability to make choices and, therefore, settle for unsatisfying relationships. The result is individuals who have no aspirations—people who accept unsatisfying relationships when they could continue seeking better ones. Their behavior is not as energetic as it could be if they felt powerful.

People who feel powerless tend to take out their hostilities and frustrations on others, usually those they perceive as even less powerful. For example, a parent having problems with his or her boss at work—and who feels powerless to do anything about it—may be unusually harsh with his or her children.

People who feel powerless tend to form "failure-support groups." They get together with others who feel powerless and collectively blame their problems on other people. Blaming their problems on others ensures that they will continue to feel powerless. For example, students who get together to complain about their low grades on an examination and blame the instructor for not developing a good test are not likely to seek help. After all, they convince each other, they are powerless to change the system.

People who feel powerless tend to withdraw from people and situations that increase their feelings of powerlessness. This only increases their feelings of powerlessness because loners are rarely influential.

Powerlessness, not power, often destroys relationships. People who are empowered are aware of their resources, their strengths, their weaknesses, and their uniqueness as individuals. They also are clear about what they want to accomplish and, most importantly, optimistic about their ability to achieve their goals. The powerless feel less well equipped and less qualified to make choices that affect their relationships.

People in North American culture generally are raised to believe that they have great power over their lives and even the lives of others, that they are "masters of their own fate," "captains of their ships," and that they "pull themselves up by their bootstraps." Not only do they want power, and think they deserve it, they do not want other people to have power over them. They often leave home at an early age so their parents will not have power over them, and make teachers, police, and bosses the brunt of jokes because they do not like the power these people have or are given. They hear cries of black power, gray power, and gay power. Women and minority groups ask for power so that they can have freedom from internal and external restraints. In short, they are taught in North America not to be powerless. This, of course, is not the case with all cultures. Most of the world, in fact, believes that an outside source or fate, be it "God," "the gods," "reincarnation," or "nature," controls their lives. Power, for these cultures, is a basic fact of society. It is not something they feel they want or need. Muslims use the phrase "it is Allah's will" and Hindus believe that it is their karma being acted out. In both instances, people who do not feel powerless, per se, but instead believe in a philosophy of "what will be, will be." It is not their mission to seek power, nor in most instances do they rebel against the fact that they do not have power. In most instances, they hold the view that the legitimacy of power is irrelevant.[7]

Knowledge Checkup 12.3 will help you assess your own feelings of empowerment.

KNOWLEDGE CHECKUP 12.3

HOW POWERFUL DO YOU FEEL?[8]

Think of one of your important relationships and keep it in mind as you respond to the questionnaire. Each item has two alternatives. Your task is to divide 10 points between the two alternatives according to how well each describes you. You may give all 10 points to one alternative and none to the other, split the points evenly, 5 and 5, or assign any other combination of 10 points that seems appropriate.

1. When the other person says something with which I disagree, I
_____ a. assume my position is correct.
_____ b. assume what the other person says is correct.

2. When I get angry at the other person, I
_____ a. ask the other person to stop the behavior that offends me.
_____ b. say little, not knowing quite what to do.

3. When something goes wrong in the relationship, I
_____ a. try to solve the problem.
_____ b. try to find out who's at fault.

4. When I participate in the relationship, it is important that I
_____ a. live up to my own expectations.
_____ b. live up to the expectations of the other person.

5. In general, I try to surround myself with people
_____ a. whom I respect.
_____ b. who respect me.

SCORING

Add all of your *a* responses.   *a* = _____
Add all of your *b* responses.   *b* = _____

The two totals, *a* and *b,* indicate how powerful you feel in the relationship you chose. The total number of points is 50, so one score could be 50 and the other zero, although that is unlikely.

If your *b* score is greater than your *a* score by 10 or more points, you probably feel somewhat powerless in your relationship because you see the other person's choices as more important than your own.

If your two scores are within 10 points of each other, you are probably unsure of your own power and your potential to influence others.

If your *a* score is greater than your *b* score by 10 or more points, you most likely feel quite powerful and in control of the choices you make in the relationship.

Once you understand your own feelings of empowerment and the importance of feeling empowered, you can take two further steps to increase your feelings of power: (1) determine your power bases, or sources of power; and (2) develop strategies for enhancing your power.

DETERMINING YOUR POWER BASES

Knowledge Checkup 12.4 is designed to help you assess the sources of your power.

ASSESSING YOUR SOURCES OF POWER[9]

With two relationships in mind—one with a close friend and one with a work partner who is not a close friend—indicate the extent to which each statement is true of you. Use the following scale:

5 = the statement is true
4 = the statement is sometimes true
3 = the statement is neither true nor false
2 = the statement is sometimes false
1 = the statement is false

CLOSE FRIEND	WORK PARTNER	
_____	_____	**1.** I try to set a good example for the other person.
_____	_____	**2.** The other person considers me an expert.
_____	_____	**3.** Because of the nature of our relationship, I carry a great deal of authority with the other person.
_____	_____	**4.** I can help the other person achieve his or her goals.
_____	_____	**5.** The other person is impressed by people I know.
_____	_____	**6.** I can keep the other person from achieving his or her goals or satisfying his or her wants.
_____	_____	**7.** The other person sees me as having a lot in common with her or him.
_____	_____	**8.** The other person knows I have no trouble handling my responsibilities in the relationship.
_____	_____	**9.** The other person respects my authority.
_____	_____	**10.** I have something the other person wants or values, and I can make it available to her or him.

_____ _____ **11.** I can find someone else to influence the other person if I so wish.

_____ _____ **12.** I can hurt the other person.

SCORING

Add your responses to items 4 and 10. This is your *reward power* score:
  Close Friend: _____ Work Partner: _____

Add your responses to items 6 and 12. This is your *coercive power* score.
  Close Friend: _____ Work Partner: _____

Add your responses to items 3 and 9. This is your *legitimate power* score.
  Close Friend: _____ Work Partner: _____

Add your responses to items 2 and 8. This is your *expert power* score.
  Close Friend: _____ Work Partner: _____

Add your responses to items 1 and 7. This is your *referent power* score.
  Close Friend: _____ Work Partner: _____

Add your responses to items 5 and 11. This is your *associative power* score.
  Close Friend: _____ Work Partner: _____

Scores of 8 to 10 for a category are high; you perceive that this is a very important source of power for the relationship. Scores of 5 to 7 for a category are moderate; you perceive that this is a potentially important source of power for the relationship, but is not particularly significant right now. Scores of 2 to 4 for a category are low; you perceive that this is an unimportant source of power for the relationship.

The six sources of power measured in Knowledge Checkup 12.4, and outlined in Table 12.2, fall into two broad categories, formal and informal. **Formal power bases** reflect your role (boss versus coworker) or the nature of the relationship (friend versus acquaintance), while **informal power bases** relate to perceptions of your abilities, qualities, and traits.

The three informal bases of power are *expert power,* your perceived skill and knowledge; *referent power,* how well you are liked; and *associative power,* which is based on who you know. The three formal bases of power are *reward power,* your perceived ability to reward others; *coercive power,* your perceived ability to punish; and *legitimate power,* your perceived right to make requests because of your relationship with the other person.

Is your formal power a stronger base than your informal one? Or is the opposite true? Do you have one or two particular sources of power with your close friend? What sources of power do you have with your coworker? Do both persons perceive you as having the same sources of power? And which sources of power do you lack, if any?

ENHANCING YOUR SOURCES OF POWER

If you perceive yourself as having little power, or very limited sources of power, you can remedy the situation. Each of the six sources of power can be developed through the use of particular strategies.[10]

Expert Power

Expert power is your capacity to influence another person because of the knowledge and skills you are presumed to have. Note that *being* an expert and being *perceived* as an expert are two different things and that to use your expertise, you must be perceived as an expert. To build expert power, you need to communicate your expertise to the other person. You can do this by mentioning your background and training, demonstrating that you are well informed on topics that are important to the other person, and accomplishing tasks competently and *noticeably*. In other words, you need to call attention to yourself. For example, telling your friend that you had experience cooking when you worked for a local restaurant should help gain you expert power in the kitchen.

People telling others about their power is not a universal trait. You will be in contact with people who, because of their cultural background, will not *tell you* about their expert power. There are two reasons for this. First, there are cultures, such as the Asian, in which people do not talk about themselves. Too much self-focus is considered a form of bragging or boasting. Individuality is "systematically repressed."[11] Second, cultures that have a nonverbal rather than a verbal tradition believe that people possess an intuitive *feeling* about each other and, as such, do not have to state what is "known" by both parties. If they have power, you will just know it. In these cultures there is a belief that, "It is the heart always that sees, before the head can see."

Referent Power

Referent power is probably the most important source of power because it's based on personal loyalty, friendship, affection, and admiration. The key to securing this power base is to demonstrate your friendliness and trustworthiness. For example, emphasize the similarities between yourself and the other person, such as background, goals, attitudes, and values. The more similarities the better. It also helps to communicate your support for the other person, give her or him the benefit of the doubt, and create symbols that bind you together, such as in-jokes and a special language. If you smile frequently, encourage and support the other person, and share secret handshakes and expressions, you will increase your chances of having referent power.

As you would suspect, it is very difficult to use referent power in an intercultural setting. This technique is based on your stressing any similarities that exist between you and your communication partner. When the other person's culture is different from your own, it might be hard to locate key similarities. There are, of course, similarities between all people and all cultures, such as wanting relational satisfaction, having as a goal a good life, and seeking the meaning of life. But, the task of locating these similarities is compounded when past experiences are quite different and you are each unfamiliar with the other person's customs.

Associative Power

Associative power is based on your acquaintance with people the other person holds in high esteem. Referring to acquaintances is often risky because the name you mention may be irrelevant or unfamiliar to the other person, or because you may be perceived as a snob or a name-dropper. Nonetheless, if you pick an appropriate name, you have a good chance of increasing your influence. To benefit from associative power, make sure the name you choose is known by the person you want to impress, and avoid name-dropping too often.

Reward Power

Expert and referent power are based on your perceived abilities and traits. Associative power stems from whom you know. By contrast, reward, coercive, and legitimate power are related to your relationship with the other person. **Reward power** requires that you be perceived as the best or only source of desired rewards. To possess reward power, you must (1) know what the other person wants, (2) amass the objects of desire, (3) communicate that you have the desired objects, and (4) specify what the other person must do to get them. For example, you know that your friend wants a place to hold an end-of-term party and you have access to a private cabin. You communicate that the cabin is yours to give and then you spell out what the other person needs to do to get it.

Be careful! If the object is seen as a bribe, or if you dangle rewards too often, you're likely to meet resistance or seem manipulative.

Coercive Power

In contrast to reward power, which is based on positive outcomes, **coercive power** is based on negative outcomes that are used as weapons. To exercise coercive power, you need to (1) know what weapons the other person fears most, (2) acquire them, (3) communicate that you have them, and (4) persuade the other person that you're willing to use them. For example, when you originally split a project, even though your coworker's typing skills are poor and yours are well-developed, you agreed that your partner would do the final typing. You can make it clear that if he or she does not comply with your requests, you will refuse to work with her or him on another project.

Because people tend to resist coercive power, whether by punching the power broker in the nose or by slowly withdrawing from contact, it is best to avoid its use. There are times, however, when you have no option but to act coercively. During these times, be as calm and reasonable as possible, and act only if you are certain that it's the most effective power base at your disposal. The goal is to be perceived as fair—even if you're using a source of power that's disliked.

Legitimate Power

Legitimate power stems from one person perceiving that another person has the right to make requests because of the position that the other person occupies or because of the nature of the relationship. For example, in a parent–child relationship, children perceive that parents have the right to make requests of them; in a military relationship, lieutenants perceive that generals have the right to make requests of them; in a work relationship, workers perceive that the boss has the right to make requests of them; and in a committed relationship, spouses often feel that their partners have the right to ask them favors. To increase your legitimate power, you must either move into a new position or role that has more authority (for example, become the boss), change the nature of the relationship (from acquaintance to friend), or persuade the other person that you have more authority by changing the expectations of your position. Call yourself an "administrative assistant" instead of a "secretary," and others' views of your power may change!

TABLE 12.2 INFORMAL AND FORMAL POWER BASES

INFORMAL POWER BASES	SOURCE OF POWER
Expert Power	Person is perceived as having knowledge and skills relevant to the particular task or activity
Referent Power	Person is perceived as loyal, friendly, and trustworthy
Associative Power	Person is perceived as knowing others who are influential

FORMAL POWER BASES	SOURCE OF POWER
Reward Power	Person is perceived as the best or only source of an object of desire
Coercive Power	Person is perceived as capable of producing a negative outcome
Legitimate Power	Persons' role or relationship is perceived as granting certain rights and privileges

CHOOSING YOUR POWER BASE

Which power base should you use?[12] The answer depends in part on the kind of influence you desire—whether you want **commitment** or **compliance** from the other person. When people are committed to a request, they feel enthusiastic about it, agree that it is a good idea, and believe that it's the right thing to do. When they merely comply with a request, they obey reluctantly, without believing in the goodness of the idea.

The choice of a power base also depends on how much time you have: Some sources of power are likely to get quicker action. If you want to get things done quickly, with little or no discussion, and if others need not feel committed to your request, you may find that reward and coercive power work best. But both sources of power have drawbacks.

If you plan to use coercive power, you must expect to be disliked. In addition, the more you use coercive power the less effective it tends to become, so your threats must escalate. For example, to get children to eat their vegetables, parents may first threaten them with no dessert, then with no television, and ultimately with grounding for longer and longer periods of time. Finally, because coercive power causes so much resentment, you'll need to develop a strategy for ensuring that your request is obeyed and watch the outcomes. (A child can devise a hundred ways to make it *seem* as if the vegetables have been eaten, and can retaliate in a variety of stressful ways, including crying, tantrums, poor grades, and embarrassing conduct in public.)

Reward power raises some of the same problems. For example, a reward often needs to be increased regularly to maintain the same effect. Bringing home flowers once a week ceases to be a reward as soon as it is *expected* that you'll bring them home. And if you skip a week, it may be perceived as punishment. Also, when you use reward power routinely, you're likely to get results only if you keep an eye on the other person to make sure what you request is done.

Using legitimate power in combination with small doses of reward and coercive power can be effective; however, the best you can usually hope for is compliance without enthusiastic support.

If your request is very important and if you want commitment, expert and referent power are the most productive. An expert who communicates a request without arrogance or insult is more likely to get commitment than compliance, as long as others truly perceive her or him as an expert.

Because it has the highest probability of obtaining commitment on the widest range of requests, referent power is perhaps the most useful source of power. Unlike expert power, which inspires commitment to the *request,* referent power inspires commitment to *you.* An expert can only make requests that relate to her or his perceived area of expertise, but someone with referent power can make requests in any area.

The primary drawback of referent power is that it takes a great deal of time to develop. Relationships need to move from the stranger stage through the acquaintance stage before a low level of friendship is established and referent power can begin to gain strength.

In North American culture most sources of power are enhanced through communication. Communicating to others that you are knowledgeable and skillful enhances your expert power. Communicating to others that you are their friend enhances your referent power. Communicating to others that you know people they hold in high esteem enhances your associative power. Communicating to others that you are the best or only source of their rewards enhances your reward power. Communicating to others that you have and will use weapons they fear enhances your coercive power. As you communicate both verbally and nonverbally, you signal your feelings of power and powerlessness.

Powerful and Powerless Language

Powerful language creates an impression of strength, capability, and control. **Powerless language** creates a perception of being incompetent and passive. Several language habits contribute to perceptions of powerlessness. For example, **hedges**—words that limit your responsibility for what you say—and **qualifiers**—words that modify what you say—detract from the certainty of a statement. For instance, "kind of," "I think," and "I guess" indicate that you are unsure of yourself. Consider the degree of assertiveness in "I guess I'll leave work today at 5:00" versus "I'll leave at 5:00." Hedges, more than other forms of powerless language, decrease perceptions of authoritativeness; on the other hand, hesitations decrease perceptions of both authoritativeness and sociability.[13]

While North Americans often equate hedging with a lack of power, other cultures take a somewhat different view of language. Because they do not wish to offend, the Japanese intentionally use language that is characterized by hedge words, qualifiers, and ambiguity. Being too blunt in the Japanese culture can cause others discomfort; hence, language is used to moderate instead of assert. In fact, in most Japanese sentences the verb comes at the end of the sentence so the "action" part of the statement can be postponed. The Mexican culture, with its strong emphasis on cooperation, also uses hedging to smooth over interpersonal relationships. By not taking a firm stand with their speech language, Mexicans believe they will not make others feel ill at ease.

Hesitations, like hedges and qualifiers, also suggest uncertainty. Whether you add "um," "er," or "well" to your speech, you create the perception that you are unsure about what you are saying. Compare "I . . . well . . . er . . . want you to know that . . . well . . . I'll be leaving today at . . . uh . . . 5:00" to "I want you to know I'll be leaving at 5:00."

Tag questions, unnecessary questions added to statements, signal that you lack confidence in what you're saying or are unwilling to take a stand. For example, "right?" or "OK?" at the end of a statement requests approval or agreement. Note the difference between "I'm leaving today at 5:00, right?" and "I'm leaving today at 5:00."

Disclaimers, expressions that excuse what you're saying or ask another person to bear with you while you make a point, indicate uncertainty and communicate subservience. For instance, compare "I probably shouldn't say this, but I'm leaving at 5:00" or "If you'll just let me tell you one more thing, I want to say I'm leaving at 5:00" to "I'm leaving at 5:00."

If your language is powerless, and you are interacting with people from North America, you probably will be perceived as incompetent and passive, as opposed to competent and dynamic. You will not be considered as attractive as someone who uses powerful language. And because you will be perceived as less competent, dynamic, and attractive, you will not be as influential as someone who uses powerful speech.

Remember, you will be in contact with people from cultures that do not apply the same yardsticks for the measurement of competence and attractiveness as you do. These cultures also have a different definition for the so-called *dynamic* person. They find the person who is still, modest, reserved, thoughtful, and careful with words to be the most powerful, credible, and attractive. In the Japanese, Indonesian, and Chinese cultures, for example, people who speak too well are often perceived as having low credibility. In addition, "a person who is quiet and spends more time listening than speaking is more credible."[14] Think of the advice contained in the Japanese proverb, "He who speaks has not knowledge and he who has knowledge does not speak," or the Indonesian proverb that tells people that "Empty cans clatter the loudest." In short, be careful of your own ethnocentrism when you use powerful language with people of other cultures. Those messages might be construed in quite a different way than would be the case if you were speaking to someone from your culture.

With this in mind, to be perceived as powerful in North American society, eliminate—as much as possible—the use of hedges, qualifiers, hesitations, tag questions, and disclaimers. Skill Development 12.5 will help you eliminate powerless language from your messages.

SKILL DEVELOPMENT 12.5

ELIMINATING POWERLESS LANGUAGE

Rewrite the following paragraph by substituting powerful language for powerless language.

> I was like, uh, hoping that, uh, if you'd like we could go out this weekend, you know? Gee, I'd understand if you're busy—sometimes I am, too, but, well, uh, I thought that, well, if you're not busy or doing anything you'd like maybe to go out with me. Yes? I'm having a hard time expressing myself.

The most powerful way this could be rewritten is as follows:

> I would like you to go out with me this weekend.

This straightforward statement eliminates the hedges ("I was hoping" and "I thought"), qualifiers ("maybe"), hesitations ("uh" and "well"), tag questions ("you know?" and "yes?"), and the disclaimer ("I'm having a hard time expressing myself"). Also, it increases perceptions of power by changing the question, "I was like, uh, hoping that, uh, if you'd like we could go out this weekend, you know?" to a statement.

COMMUNICATION COMPETENCY CHECKUP

The goal of this Communication Competency Checkup is to guide you in putting your skills and knowledge about creativity, power, and interpersonal satisfaction to use, and to help you summarize the material in this chapter.

After reading the cartoon on the next page, put yourself in the role of the listener. Your friend just told you she is tired of playing the game of "Herb's right" even when Herb is wrong. (The capital of Kansas is Topeka.) Help her to understand how she can use creativity and power to improve her relationship with Herb.

SINGLE SLICES

I let Herb win arguments occasionally to feed his ego. Although conceding things like Wichita being the capitol of Kansas does get hard to take.

Copyright, 1989, *Los Angeles Times Syndicate*. Reprinted with permission.

1. What relational benefits might she obtain from creatively solving her problem with Herb?

2. What cultural and personal obstacles to creatively solving her problem might she encounter?

3. She tells you, "I'm tired of pretending that Herb is right when he says something wrong. I wish I could think of a way to change the situation." Explain three techniques she can use to develop her capacity for creative problem solving.

4. "I want more influence with him, especially when it comes to discussing things about the United States," she tells you. What questions could you ask to help her assess the power bases she has in her relationship with Herb?

5. What techniques could she employ to increase her power in Herb's and her relationship?

6. How could she determine which sources of power might be best to use in her relationship with Herb?

7. How could she reduce the extent to which her language makes her appear powerless and increase the extent to which it makes her appear powerful?

NOTES

1. Stephen Lehane, *The Creative Child* (Englewood Cliffs, NJ: Prentice-Hall, 1979).

2. Lehane describes the stages of creative growth children go through and provides strategies for helping children develop and maintain their creativity.

3. Sarah Trenholm and Toby Rose, "The Compliant Communicator: Teacher

Perceptions of Appropriate Classroom Behavior, *Western Journal of Speech Communication* 45 (1981): 13–26.

4. John Powell, *Why Am I Afraid to Tell You Who I Am?* (Miles, IL: Argus Publishing Company, 1968); Lawrence Rosenfeld, "Self-Disclosure Avoidance: Why I Am Afraid to Tell You Who I Am," *Communication Monographs* 46 (1979): 63–74.

5. These exercises are adapted from those developed by Noller, Parnes, and Biondi. For more information and other exercises designed to develop creativity, see: Ruth B. Noller, Sidney J. Parnes, and Angelo M. Biondi, *Creative Actionbook* (New York: Scribner's, 1976).

6. Robert A. Barraclough and Robert A. Stewart, "Power and Control: Social Science Perspectives," in *Power in the Classroom,* Virginia P. Richmond and James C. McCroskey (Eds.) (Hillsdale, NJ: Lawrence Erlbaum, 1992), pp. 1–4.

7. George A. Borden, *Cultural Orientation: An Approach to Understanding Intercultural Communication* (Englewood Cliffs, NJ: Prentice-Hall, 1991), p. 116.

8. Adapted from Pamela Cuming, "Empowerment Profile," *The Power Handbook* (Boston: CBI, 1981), pp. 2–5.

9. Adapted from Pamela Cuming, "Determining Your Power Bases," *The Power Handbook* (Boston: CBI: 1981), pp. 57–59; D. L. Dieterly and B. Schneider, "The Effect of Organizational Environment on Perceived Climate and Power," *Organizational Behavior and Human Performance* 11 (1974): 334–35. Also see, Robert A. Barraclough and Robert A. Stewart, "Power and Control: Social Science Perspectives," in *Power in the Classroom,* pp. 1–18.

10. John A. Daly and Pamelo Kreiser, "Affinity in the Classroom," in *Power in the Classroom,* pp. 121–44; Timothy G. Plax and Patricia Kearney, "Teacher Power in the Classroom: Defining and Advancing a Program of Research," in *Power in the Classroom,* pp. 67–84.

11. Jan Servaes, "Cultural Identity in East and West," *The Howard Journal of Communication* 1 (Summer 1988), p. 64.

12. Gary A. Yukl, *Leadership in Organizations,* 2d ed. (Englewood Cliffs, NJ: Prentice-Hall, 1989), pp. 43–49.

13. In addition to the findings for hesitations and hedges, Hosman found that extensive use of any one of the powerless language forms was enough to be perceived negatively; that is, it did not require the use of several in combination. Lawrence A. Hosman, "The Evaluative Consequences of Hedges, Hesitations, and Intensifiers: Powerful and Powerless Speech Styles," *Human Communication Research* 15 (1989): 383–406.

14. Larry A. Samovar and Richard E. Porter, *Communication Between Cultures* (Belmont, CA: Wadsworth Publishing Company, 1991), p. 106.

FOR FURTHER INVESTIGATION

Bradac, James J., and Anthony Mulac. "A Molecular View of Powerful and Powerless Speech Styles: Attributional Consequences of Specific Language Features and Communicator Intentions." *Communication Monographs* 51 (1984): 307–19.

Conrad, Charles. "Communication, Power and Politics in Organizations." In *Strategic Organizational Communication,* 2d ed. New York: Holt, Rinehart and Winston, 1990, pp. 212–240.

Cuming, Pamela. *The Power Handbook.* Boston: CBI: 1981.

DeBono, Edward. *Lateral Thinking: Creativity Step by Step.* New York: Harper and Row, 1970.

Dieterly, D. L., and B. Schneider. "The Effect of Organizational Environment on Perceived Climate and Power." *Organizational Behavior and Human Performance* 11 (1974): 334–35.

French, John R. P., Jr., and Bertram Raven. "The Bases of Social Power." In Dorwin

Cartwright, (Ed.), *Studies in Social Power*. Ann Arbor, MI: Institute for Social Research, 1959.

Hare, A. Paul. "Creativity." In *Creativity in Small Groups*. Beverly Hills, CA: Sage, 1982, pp. 155–80.

Hosman, Lawrence A. "The Evaluative Consequences of Hedges, Hesitations, and Intensifiers: Powerful and Powerless Speech Styles." *Human Communication Research* 15 (1989): 383–406.

Johnson, Craig E. "An Introduction to Powerful and Powerless Talk in the Classroom." *Communication Education* 36 (1987): 167–72.

Parnes, Sidney J., Ruth B. Noller, and Angelo M. Biondi. *Guide to Creative Action*. New York: Scribner's, 1977.

These are possible solutions to the nine-dot exercise on page 390.

EXAMPLE 1

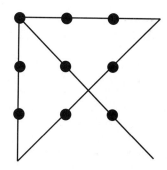

Note that this configuration can be rotated to produce four "different" solutions.

EXAMPLE 2

This solution is comprised of one thick line that passes through all nine dots.

EXAMPLE 3

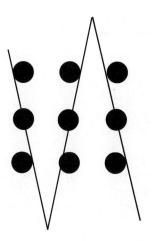

This solution requires enlarging the nine dots, which will allow three straight lines to touch the left, center, and right side respectively of the three dots in each vertical row.

INDEX

NOTES